FEDERAL ABORTION POLITICS

A Documentary History

Series Editor

NEAL DEVINS
with Wendy L. Watson

T0347322

SERIES CONTENTS

VOLUME

3

JUDICIAL NOMINATIONS

Edited by

NEAL DEVINS
with Wendy L. Watson

Routledge
Taylor & Francis Group

LONDON AND NEW YORK

First published 1995 by Garland Publishing, Inc.

2 Park Square, Milton Park, Abingdon, Oxfordshire OX14 4RN
52 Vanderbilt Avenue, New York, NY 10017

Routledge is an imprint of the Taylor & Francis Group, an informa business

First issued in paperback 2019

Library of Congress Cataloging-in-Publication Data
(Revised for volume 3)

Federal abortion politics.

    Includes bibliographical references.
    Contents: v. 1. Congressional action — v. 2. Executive initiatives — v. 3. Judicial nominations.
    1. Abortion—Law and legislation—United States—History. I. Devins, Neal E. II. Watson, Wendy L.
KF3771.F43 1995   344.73'04192   94-49562
ISBN 0-8153-1906-1   347.3044192
ISBN 0-8153-1907-X
ISBN 0-8153-1908-8

ISBN 13: 978-0-8153-1908-5 (hbk)
ISBN 13: 978-1-138-87470-1 (pbk)

CONTENTS

VOLUME III: JUDICIAL NOMINATIONS

PREFACE

On January 22, 1973, the Supreme Court issued its decision in *Roe v. Wade*. Holding that a woman's substantive due process right to terminate her pregnancy in the early months outweighed state interests in maternal health and fetal protection, the Court struck down a Texas law permitting abortions only to save the life of the mother. The Court concluded both that the state's interest in potential human life is not compelling until the third trimester of pregnancy (once the fetus becomes viable) and that the state's interest in promulgating *reasonable* maternal health regulations is not compelling until after the first trimester of pregnancy. Consequently, during the first trimester, the abortion decision is left to the woman (in consultation with her physician).

By valuing a woman's right to privacy over potential human life and by imposing a trimester standard that reads like a legislative abortion code, *Roe* spurred elected government into action. It functioned as a political catalyst rather than the last word on abortion. For much of the past two decades, abortion has shaped a broad spectrum of domestic and foreign policies. For example, the abortion dispute has dramatically altered the enactment of Medicaid and other appropriations and, perhaps more dramatically, the process of selecting and confirming judges and executive branch officials.

The abortion dispute vividly illustrates the pervasiveness of interchanges between the courts and elected government. Because the 1992 Supreme Court decision in *Planned Parenthood v. Casey*, which moderated *Roe*, has quieted the abortion dispute, it seems especially appropriate to examine the ways in which the courts and elected government have shaped each other. This series will facilitate that examination. By providing a comprehensive survey of federal abortion politics, this series offers readers a better overall understanding of the dynamic of our federal political system.

This series offers a representative sampling of primary documents which reflect the arguments, positions, and passions of the key players in this long drama. In so doing, this series provides a thorough understanding of many of the controversies, issues, and events which have shaped current federal abortion policy and which have set the stage for abortion's prominent position in the political history of the last two decades. The documentary nature of this history offers readers a window on the dramatic events as they unfolded, providing a clear view of the nuances of the debate without editorial interpretation.

This series is divided into three volumes, with each part containing multiple case studies. Volume One (two books) considers legislative initiatives; Volume Two (two books) reviews executive initiatives; and Volume Three (one book) examines judicial nominations. Abortion funding, clinic access legislation, freedom of choice and human life legislative proposals, and proposed constitutional amendments are considered in Part One. Presidential positions, federal family planning regulation (domestic and international), fetal tissue research, and governmental briefs and arguments in abortion-related Supreme Court litigation are the subject of Part Two. The effect that the abortion dispute has had on the process of nominating and confirming Supreme Court Justices is canvassed in Part Three. While each of the three parts principally addresses the role of a particular branch, all of the case studies consider the participation of and offer documents from each of the three branches, giving the reader a sense of the way in which the branches interact in the policy-making process.

Each case study is prefaced by a brief textual overview of the relevant controversy. These histories provide a general context of the issues, lending perspective to the documentary section. Following the textual background sections are itemized lists of the documents in each chapter.

The majority of the pages in each case study are primary documents chronicling the involvement of elected and appointed government officials in the development of policy. Some of the documents were selected from readily available sources such as the Congressional Record; the Federal Register; hearings before and reports by Committees and Subcommittees of both houses of Congress; executive orders and presidential statements from the Weekly Compilation of Presidential Papers and the Public Papers of the Presidents; and briefs of federal amici and parties before the Supreme Court. Many of the documents, however, were obtained from less accessible sources; these include letters and agency documents requested under the Freedom of Information Act as well as internal White House documents collected from the Nixon, Ford, and Carter presidential libraries.

The editors sorted through tens of thousands of pages of primary documents to find those documents and portions of documents which best conveyed the flavor of the debate and those which highlighted the positions of the people most central to the debate. While these volumes contain only a fraction of the primary documents which the abortion issue has generated, this history contains the most critical documents and provides a representative sampling of other documents illustrating the federal abortion debate.

To the extent practicable, documents have been reproduced in their original form. In some instances, concerns of length and readability have necessitated the typesetting of document excerpts obtained from the Congressional Record, the Federal Register, the Code of Federal Regulations, and the Weekly Compilation of Presidential Papers.

The identification, reproduction, typesetting, and formatting of the documents and other materials contained in this series has been facilitated through the hard work and good nature of numerous individuals both at Garland and the College of William and Mary. At Garland, special thanks are owed to Alan Shomsky, Jennifer Sorenson and especially Leo Balk and Claudia Hirsch (whose gentle prodding and enthusiasm played an instrumental role in the completion of this project). At William and Mary, several law and public policy students assisted both in document identification and production, including Donna Buddenhagen, Paula Hannaford, Matt Ide, Megan Kelly, Christine Moseley, Phil Runkel, Susan Seiger, Ann Shepherd, Brad Wagshull, and especially Jeanne Locascio. The Faculty Support Center at William and Mary played a critical role in document preparation, especially Della W. Harris, Sherry L. Thomas and Melanie E. McElrath. Finally, the Marshall-Wythe School of Law and Thomas Jefferson Program in Public Policy provided the necessary financial and support staff resources to make this project a reality.

ACKNOWLEDGMENTS

We would like to thank the authors and copyright holders of the following works, who permitted their inclusion in this book:

Robert Bork, Neutral Principles and Some First Amendment Problems, 47 Indiana Law Journal 1 (1971). Reprinted by permission of the Indiana Law Journal and Fred B. Rothman and Company.

Ruth Bader Ginsburg, Some thoughts on Autonomy and Equality in Relation to Roe v. Wade. 63 North Carolina Law Review 35 (1984). Reprinted by permission of the North Carolina Law Review Association

Ruth Bader Ginsburg, Speaking in Judicial Voice. 67 New York University Law Review 1185 (1992). Reprinted by permission.

Stephen J. Markman, Judicial Selection: Merit, Ideology and Politics - The Reagan Years at 33-35, 37 (1990). Published by the National Legal Center For The Public Interest.

Ronald Reagan, Abortion and the Conscience of the Nation (1984). Reprinted by permission.

White House Report: Information on Judge Bork's Qualifications, Judicial Record and Related Subjects. This article originally appeared in 9 Cardozo Law Review 187 (1987).

White House Analysis of Judge Bork's Record: Statement of Committee Consultants. This article originally appeared in 9 Cardozo Law Review 219 (1987).

INTRODUCTION*

Roe v. Wade was designed to help put an end to the abortion dispute. Justice Harry Blackmun put forth a trimester test governing state authority over the abortion decision both to make clear what the Court intended and to foreclose future governmental efforts to sidestep the Court's decision. Over objections by Justice Potter Stewart that his draft opinion was "inflexibly 'legislative,'" Blackmun nonetheless persisted in his efforts to clarify the reaches and limits of governmental authority in this area.[1]

Twenty-two years later, the abortion dispute—while beginning to cool down—persists, and Blackmun's belief that *Roe* might settle the issue seems to have been—to put it mildly—hopelessly naive. What Blackmun did not take into account was the inevitable backlash from elected government at both the state and federal level. "Judges," as Ruth Bader Ginsburg has written, "play an *interdependent* role in our democracy. They do not alone shape legal doctrine but . . . they participate in a dialogue with other organs of government, and the people as well."[2] Indeed, Ginsburg went so far as to suggest in March 1993 that *Roe* "prolonged divisiveness and deferred stable settlement of the [abortion] issue" by short-circuiting early, 1970's legislative reform efforts.[3] Although Justice Ginsburg overstates her claim,[4]

---

* This Introduction is an adaptation of Neal Devins, Through the Looking Glass: What Abortion Teaches Us About American Politics, 94 Columbia Law Review 293 (1994).

[1] Bob Woodward, The Abortion Papers, Washington Post, D-1, Jan. 22, 1989.

[2] Ruth Bader Ginsburg, Speaking in a Judicial Voice, 67 New York University Law Review 1185, 1198 (1993).

[3] *Id.* at 1208.

[4] *See* David Garrow, History Lesson for the Judge, Washington Post, C-3, June 20, 1993.

there is no doubt that *Roe* is a point of departure, not a point of termination, in studying the constitutionality of abortion.

A simple comparison of elected branch interest in abortion before and after *Roe* makes clear that the abortion dispute is not controlled by nine individuals working in isolation. Prior to *Roe*, abortion was a matter of some state and limited national attention. In the decade preceding *Roe*, after nearly a century of political dormancy, four states repealed and fifteen states—while still limiting abortion rights— liberalized their abortion laws.[5] Congress, and the White House, for the most part, were content to leave the abortion issue in the hands of state government. Congressional action was limited and designed to preserve the anti-abortion status quo ante.[6] Executive branch action was equally limited and typically reaffirmed state authority.[7]

Elected government action since *Roe* makes clear that the Supreme Court's nationalization of abortion rights was anything but the last word on the subject. Over the past twenty years, the abortion dispute has spread throughout the American political system. *Roe v. Wade* and *Pennsylvania v. Casey* notwithstanding,[8] abortion is hardly the sole province of the judiciary. While abortion politics and court decisionmaking are closely linked—especially through the nomination and confirmation of federal judges—the sweep of abortion-related policy is far too broad for any one branch of government to dominate.

---

[5]   *See* Austin Sarat, Abortion and the Courts: Uncertain Boundaries of Law and Politics 125-127 in Allan Sindler ed., American Politics and Public Policy (1982); Eva P. Rubin, Abortion, Politics, and the Courts, 11-29 (2nd ed., 1987).

[6]   By including abortion restrictions in a handful of family planning and health-related bills, Congress simply honored 46 states' abortion legislation.

[7]   In 1971, for example, the Nixon administration restricted the performance of abortion in military hospitals to bases located in states with legalized abortion. This episode is discussed in Lee Epstein & Joseph F. Kobylka, The Supreme Court and Legal Change 154 (1992).

[8]   Roe v. Wade, 410 U.S. 113 (1973); Pennsylvania v. Casey, 112 S.Ct. 2791 (1992).

The abortion drama, if nothing else, demonstrates that the elected branches can influence the shaping of constitutional values in many ways. The executive branch has been extremely active in its attempts to regulate abortion. Presidential appointments to courts and government agencies, the use of the powers to recommend as well as veto legislation, and the exercise of symbolic leadership through bully pulpit speeches all figure prominently in the abortion dispute. Furthermore, federal departments and agencies involved in health and family planning, civil rights, foreign policy, and the budget have all found themselves in the midst of the abortion controversy.[9] Congress and its committees too have been vigorous players in the abortion dispute. Through its roles both as lawmaker and overseer of governmental agencies and departments, Congress is continuously involved in shaping and limiting abortion rights.

Abortion, finally, is not simply about federal decisionmaking. A vigorous dialogue has emerged between state legislatures and the federal courts. The legislatures constantly enact, review, and modify laws governing such areas as pre-abortion counselling, waiting periods, and juvenile and spousal rights. In conjunction with Congress, the White House, and the states, interest groups are also actively involved in this political dynamic. Pro-life forces, for example, played a prominent role in the election of Ronald Reagan and have been active participants in the crafting of anti-abortion legislation and regulation. Pro-choice forces have also come to understand the pivotal role played by political action, with the American Civil Liberties Union and National Abortion Rights Action League both calling Congress "our Court of last resort."[10]

---

[9] These departments and agencies include Department of Justice, Surgeon General, National Institute for Health, Food and Drug Administration, Equal Employment Opportunity Commission, Civil Rights Commission, Department of State, U.S. Agency for International Development, Department of Defense, Civil Service Commission and Office of Management and Budget. The United States' delegation to the United Nations is also involved in the abortion controversy.

[10] *quoted in* Louis Fisher and Neal Devins, Political Dynamics of Constitutional Law 7 (1992).

The volume of post-*Roe* elected branch initiatives is truly remarkable. Irrespective of one's views of elected government's efforts here, the abortion dispute clearly provides a revealing glimpse into the workings of American political institutions. Although elected branch interpretation figures prominently in all areas of constitutional decisionmaking, abortion is the indisputable perfect candidate for a full length examination of the role played by nonjudicial forces in the shaping of constitutional values. This three-part collection is such an undertaking, at least with respect to 1973-94 federal abortion politics. Through case studies on Congress's and the White House's role on numerous legislative, regulatory, and judicial initiatives, this collection calls attention to the pivotal role played by elected government in establishing constitutional norms.

I. The Role of Elected Government in Shaping Constitutional Values

Each and every feature of the abortion dispute is dominated by elected government action. Before a case comes to court, Congress or the states must enact a law or the executive must promulgate a regulation. Once a case is in court, the states, the Justice Department, and Congressional coalitions—sometimes as parties and sometimes as amici—inform the judiciary of their views. Through the appointments-confirmation process, moreover, the President and Senate control the composition of the federal bench. After a case is adjudicated, elected government may seek to expand or limit the holding through a number of techniques ranging from the interpretation of the judicial ruling to the nullification of the ruling through constitutional amendment.

Nothing about the above inventory of elected branch influences is unique to the abortion debate. Issues such as school desegregation, women in the military, flag burning, war powers, search and seizure, and the legislative veto follow a similar pattern. What makes governmental conduct in the abortion dispute unique is the intensity of elected branch interest and, with it, the evolution of an extraordinary portfolio of legislative-executive-judicial dialogues. Through this portfolio of constitutional dialogues, the abortion dispute serves as a lens through which to view the political dynamics of constitutional law.

Congress. Congress has repeatedly shied away from taking an absolutist position on abortion. It has rejected human life legislation, as well as a proposed constitutional amendment defining the beginning of life as conception and specifying that fetuses are persons for Fourteenth Amendment purposes.[11] These proposals would have done more than overturn *Roe* and return the abortion issue to the states. The specification of fetuses as legal persons was designed to prevent states from permitting abortions unless the mother's life was in jeopardy. Congress also rejected a more modest "federalism amendment" that would have allowed states to regulate abortion as they saw fit. Another example of this unwillingness to endorse extremist positions is Congress's repudiation of proposals to strip federal courts, including the U.S. Supreme Court, of jurisdiction in abortion cases. These proposals would leave state courts free to follow, limit, or abandon *Roe.* Of all these measures, only the federalism amendment made it out of committee where it was soundly defeated on the Senate Floor.

Congress is far more inclined to pass legislation limiting abortion funding than to restrict access to abortion by more direct means. Starting in 1976, Congress, through the Hyde Amendment, has barred the use of Medicaid funds for most abortions.[12] Congress has also used its appropriations powers to set abortion-related restrictions on programs involving family planning, foreign aid, legal services, military hospitals, the Bureau of Prisons, and the Peace Corps. Congress has also limited the use of federal and local funds for abortions in the District of Columbia.[13]

---

[11] *See* Volume I, Chapter 4: Anti-Abortion Legislation and Proposed Constitutional Amendments.

[12] *See* Volume I, Chapter 1: Abortion Funding Issues. The precise terms of the Hyde Amendment change from year to year—sometimes allowing for abortions where the mother's life is in jeopardy, other times providing funds for the victims of rape and incest, and one year also authorizing the funding of abortions when there is a risk of "severe and long-lasting physical health damage."

[13] *See* Volume I, Chapter 1: Abortion Funding Issues. Despite its apparent receptiveness to funding prohibitions, Congress has flatly and repeatedly declined to enact a permanent Hyde Amendment.

Congressional action extends beyond the adoption of funding restrictions and rejection of efforts to overrule *Roe*. Congress has approved a handful of measures that affect abortion rights outside the context of federal funding prohibitions. The Pregnancy Discrimination Act, both by defining discrimination on the basis of pregnancy as sex discrimination and providing that employers may exempt abortions from health insurance benefits, lowers the relative costs for a woman to carry her pregnancy to term.[14] Congress also undertook to encourage alternatives to abortion in its Adolescent Family Life Act.[15] This legislation, better known as the "chastity act," enabled religious organizations to seek federal funds, among other things, to promote sexual abstinence as a method of birth control among teenagers. Organizations, religious and otherwise, could not participate in the program if they engaged in abortion counselling.

Congressional action, moreover, is not always hostile to abortion rights. Following the Supreme Court's 1991 approval, in *Rust v. Sullivan*, of regulations prohibiting federally funded family planning programs from mentioning abortion, Congress sought to nullify the regulations (only to be thwarted by a presidential veto).[16] Furthermore, Congress's willingness to protect abortion rights with legislation appears on the rise. Shortly after Clinton took over the White House, Congress enacted the National Institutes of Health Revitalization Act of 1993, reversing a Reagan Bush-era moratorium on federally funded research that uses aborted fetal tissue.[17] Congress also enacted the Freedom of Access to Clinic Entrances Act of 1994 which nullified the Supreme Court's 1993 decision, in *Bray v. Alexandria Women's Health Clinic*, that existing federal civil rights legislation is not applicable to blockades of abortion clinics by

---

[14]   *See* Volume I, Chapter 2: The Pregnancy Discrimination Act.

[15]   *See* Volume I, Chapter 3: The Adolescent Family Life Act.

[16]   Characterizing the regulations denial of "quality health care" to "low income pregnant women" as "bizarre and cruel," Congress approved a rider prohibiting federal funding of the regulations. *See* Volume II, Chapter 3: Title X and the Gag Rule.

[17]   *See* Volume II, Chapter 7: Fetal Tissue Research.

Operation Rescue and other pro-life groups.[18] Specifically, Freedom of Access legislation prohibits the use or threat of force to a woman seeking an abortion or any individual who assists that woman.

Congress also participates in the abortion dispute through the use of its powers outside of lawmaking. The Senate Judiciary Committee, since the 1981 nomination of Sandra Day O'Connor, has made a nominee's views on abortion the sine qua non of the confirmation process.[19] This singlemindedness figured largely in the defeat of Robert Bork. More significant, the fixation of both the Judiciary Committee and interest groups in the abortion dispute may have contributed to Justices O'Connor, Kennedy and Souter affirming the "central holding of *Roe*" in *Casey*.[20]

The confirmation process, of course, extends to executive branch officials as well as Article III judges. Starting with the Carter administration, presidential appointees for such positions as Secretary of Health and Human Services, Surgeon General, Attorney General, Solicitor General, and Director of the Office of Personnel Management have come to the Senate with a track record on the abortion issue. The Senate grants the president great leeway here. Although the Senate will explore the nominee's personal views on abortion and how those views will affect her management of government resources, abortion is not a litmus test issue. Charles Fried, who had filed a brief calling for *Roe*'s reversal prior to Reagan's nominating him Solicitor General, spoke of being "surprised by how pleasant and interesting the [courtesy call] meetings with the most liberal Democratic Senators—Kennedy, Metzenbaum, Simon—turned out to be."[21] Nonetheless, the Senate uses these hearings to make nominees well aware of the high stakes nature of abortion politics. Joseph Califano, Secretary of Health, Education, and Welfare under Carter, put it this

---

[18]   113 S.Ct. 753 (1993). *See* Volume I, Chapter 6: *Bray* and Operation Rescue.

[19]   *See* Volume III.

[20]   See Stephen J. Wermeil, Confirming the Constitution, 56 Law & Contemporary Problems 121 (Autumn 1993).

[21]   Charles Fried, Order and Law, 36 (1991).

way: "[Following a round of questioning about abortion,] [t]he tension in the room eased a little as other senators asked questions on Social Security, balancing the budget, eliminating paperwork, busing, race discrimination, [etc.]."[22]

Congress, moreover, seeks to shape constitutional doctrine through its participation in litigation. When the Supreme Court upheld the constitutionality of the Hyde Amendment in *Harris v. McRae*, for example, a bipartisan coalition of over 200 Congressional amici argued that "[t]o tamper with [the inviolable and exclusive power of the purse] is to tamper with the very essence of constitutional, representative government."[23] In recent years, pro-choice and pro-life legislators have lined up on opposite sides of state regulation cases. These filings, although principally symbolic, are nonetheless instructive in measuring legislative attitudes. In *Thornburgh v. American College of Obstetricians*, eighty-one pro-choice legislators publicly scolded Solicitor General Charles Fried for having "taken an extraordinary and unprecedented step" in calling for *Roe*'s reversal.[24]

Congress, finally, participates in the abortion dispute through its oversight of governmental programs. When the U.S. Civil Rights Commission published a report advocating abortion rights in 1975, Congress expressed its displeasure with the agency by forbidding future studies on this issue.[25] Congress likewise enacted legislation in 1985 to express its dissatisfaction with the Office of Personnel

---

[22]   Joseph Califano, Governing America, 59 (1981).

[23]   Brief of Rep. Jim Wright [and other Members of Congress], 14, Harris v. McRae, 448 U.S. 297 (1980).

[24]   Thornburgh v. American College of Obstetricians and Gynecologists, 476 U.S. 747 (1986); Brief of Sen. Robert Packwood et al, 3, Thornburgh v. American College of Obstetricians and Gynecologists, 476 U.S. 747 (1986). Cite this volume.

[25]   *See* Frederick S. Jaffee et al, *Abortion Politics: Private Morality and Public Policy* 57 (1981). Rather than criticize the substance of the Commission's arguments, Congress thought the Commission strayed too far from its statutory mandate in studying abortion rights.

Management's (OPM) treatment of Combined Federal Campaign contributions to Planned Parenthood. OPM, then headed by pro-life activist Donald Devine, excluded Planned Parenthood from the list of approved charities that federal employees could donate to through a payroll deduction. Following a series of court decisions, including a Supreme Court decision, suggesting that the Planned Parenthood exclusion might well be an impermissible attempt to snuff out a particular point of view, Congress enacted legislation in 1985 blocking the exclusion of advocacy groups from the Combined Federal Campaign.[26]

In addition to the enactment of punitive legislation, Congressional oversight also, and more typically, takes the form of legislative jawboning. When the Reagan administration announced its proposed regulations on family planning programs, congressional supporters, including 106 cosigners of a letter of support to HHS Secretary Otis Brown, encouraged the administration to stick to its guns and promulgate the regulations in final form.[27] Opponents, in contrast, pleaded with the administration to suspend the regulations; accusing the administration of "succumb[ing] to political pressure" and describing the proposal as "not in the best interest of the 5,000,000 low income people that depend upon the program each year for family planning services."[28]

The President. The preeminence of the abortion issue in presidential politics is tellingly revealed by the remarkable speed and vigor with which the Clinton administration put its pro-choice policies into effect. Having made campaign pledges to work for the enactment of the Freedom of Choice Act and to appoint federal judges "who believe . . . [in] the constitutional right to privacy and the right to

---

[26]   *See* Planned Parenthood Fed'n of America v. Devine, No. 83-2118 (D.D.C. Sept. 14, 1983); Michelle McKeegan, Abortion Politics: Mutiny in the Ranks of the Right, 48-52 (1992).

[27]   *See* Volume II, Chapter 3: Title X and the Gag Rule.

[28]   Letter from Sen. Edward Kennedy to Secretary of Health and Human Services Otis Bowen, Oct. 30, 1987.

choose,"[29] Clinton wasted little time in waving the pro-choice banner. On January 22, 1993, two days after his inauguration, Clinton dismantled the pro-life regulatory initiatives of the Reagan and Bush administrations. Speaking of our national "[goal] to protect individual freedom" and his vision "of an America where abortion is safe and legal, but rare," Clinton directed his Secretaries of Health and Human Services and Defense as well as the Administrators of the Food and Drug Administration and U.S. Agency for International Development (AID) to rescind existing anti-abortion regulations.[30] As a result, the ban on fetal tissue research was lifted, limits on the ability of family planning of programs to mention abortion were suspended, privately funded abortions at military hospitals were permitted, the moratorium on the importation of the abortifacient RU-486 was suspended, and limitations on the use of private funds by pro-choice organizations that also receive AID funds was suspended. In the first six months of his administration, moreover, Clinton advanced his pro-choice agenda through legislative initiatives, court filings, and judicial appointments. During this time, Clinton supported abortion coverage in his national health care package and proposed a budget that did not include the Hyde Amendment and other abortion funding prohibitions.[31] Clinton, in addition to supporting the Freedom of Choice Act, also stood behind legislative efforts to guarantee access to abortion clinics and fetal tissue research. On the judicial front, Clinton told reporters that he settled on Ruth Bader Ginsburg as his Supreme Court nominee "after he became convinced that she was 'clearly pro-choice'"[32]

---

[29]   Reuter Transcript Report, ABC's Prime Time Live, Oct. 29, 1992.

[30]   Remarks on Signing Memorandums on Medical Research and Reproductive Health, 29 Weekly Compilation of Presidential Documents 85 (Jan. 22, 1993). Cite this volume.

[31]   *See* Stephen Barr, Abortion Coverage Proposed, Washington Post, A-1, Apr. 6, 1993. Clinton also proposed to allow federal employee health insurance plans to cover abortions. *Id.*

[32]   *quoted in* Michael Kranish & Joel P. Engardio, Clinton Defends Methods, Boston Globe, 1, June 16, 1993. Cite this volume.

Finally, before the Supreme Court, Clinton's Solicitor General argued that federal racketeering laws apply to the activities of Operation Rescue.[33]

The range and ferocity of Clinton administration action makes clear that the White House can be an active and somewhat one-sided participant in all phases of the abortion dispute. Before the election of Ronald Reagan, however, abortion was an important but not front burner issue for the executive. Prior to *Roe*, the White House saw abortion as a states rights issue and left it alone. In the 1972 election, for example, Richard Nixon spoke of "abortion as an unacceptable form of population control" but proposed no federal action while George McGovern made clear that he had "never advocated federal action to repeal [abortion] laws" and that, if elected, he "would take no such action."[34] After *Roe*, abortion was too much on the national political agenda to be dismissed by the White House. The Ford administration, for example, could not help but confront questions regarding the eligibility of abortion under federal health care programs. In the 1976 election, moreover, Ford and Carter both sought out the Catholic electorate by opposing public funding of abortion.[35] When Carter was elected, he justified the disproportionate burden that poor women suffer under the Hyde Amendment by observing that "there are many things in life that are not fair, that wealthy people can afford and poor people can't."[36] Neither Carter nor Ford played an activist role in the abortion dispute, however. Abortion did not figure prominently in their judicial appointments; neither asked the courts to either affirm or disavow *Roe*; legislation and constitutional amendments were not proposed; and regulatory initiatives were modest in scope and sweep.

---

[33] *See* Brief for the United States as Amicus Curiae in NOW v. Scheidler, 114 S.Ct. 798 (1994) (No. 92-780). *See also* Volume I, Chapter 6: *Bray* and Operation Rescue.

[34] *quoted in* Barbara H. Craig & David M. O'Brien, Abortion and American Politics 158-59 (1993).

[35] *See* Volume II, Chapter 1: Presidential Positions on Abortion.

[36] Pub. Papers, 1977 (II), at 1237.

The 1980 election of Ronald Reagan changed all that. Indeed, to understand the range of options available to the executive one cannot help but focus on the Reagan administration. Reagan campaigned on a platform that "support[ed] a constitutional amendment to restore protection of the right to life for unborn children" and "support[ed] the congressional efforts to restrict the use of taxpayers' dollars for abortions."[37] Once in office, as Reagan Solicitor General Charles Fried put it, "[t]he Reagan administration made *Roe v. Wade* the symbol of everything that had gone wrong in law, particularly constitutional law."[38] In Reagan's view, *Roe v. Wade* was as divisive and as wrong as *Dred Scott.*

Reagan was generally ineffective in his efforts to push through a pro-life legislative agenda. With or without White House cheerleading, Congress was unwilling to approve a constitutional amendment, to enact a permanent Hyde amendment, to legislatively prohibit family planning recipients from referring pregnant women for abortions, and to statutorily define a fetus as a legal person. In contrast to the president's limited power to push through a legislative agenda on a reluctant Congress, Reagan's influence was profound on matters squarely within the executive's domain—judicial and administrative appointments, court filings, regulation, and the power to veto or to approve legislation enacted by the Congress.

Court filings and judicial appointments are the most direct ways in which the executive seeks to shape constitutional law. Reagan and his appointees spoke of judicial restraint and vigorously opposed court "create[d]" privacy rights.[39] In advancing this judicial philosophy, the administration clearly heeded pro-life Senators and interest group

---

[37]   1980 Republican Party Platform, *reprinted in* 36 Cong. Q. Almanac 58-B, 62-B (1980).

[38]   Fried *supra* note 21 at 72.

[39]   According to his Assistant Attorney General in charge of judicial selections, Stephen Markman, "would have been derelict of his constitutional duty if he were to have appointed judges who were willing to create new constitutional 'rights' out of thin air." Stephen Markman, Judicial Selection: The Reagan Years *reprinted in* Judicial Selection: Merit, Ideology, and Politics 33 (1990).

concerns and, arguably, gave these groups a veto over prospective nominees. This strategy, more importantly, worked: Reagan appointees were "much more resistant to abortion rights than were the appointees of his predecessors."[40] The Reagan administration also advanced its judicial philosophy through briefs and oral arguments before the lower federal courts and the Supreme Court. In many instances, the administration defended its regulatory agenda in court. In some instances (typically before the Supreme Court), the administration appeared as an amicus to inform the Court of its views on state authority to regulate abortion. His first term Solicitor General Rex Lee, although falling short of asking the Court to overturn *Roe*, suggested that the Justices replace the trimester test with a more lenient undue burden standard.[41] Reagan's second term Solicitor General Charles Fried took the plunge and argued that *Roe* was "so far flawed and . . . a source of such instability" that it should be overturned.[42]

The Reagan administration also reshaped abortion rights through its management of the administrative state. The most controversial of these regulatory initiatives is the so-called "gag rule" that the Supreme Court ultimately upheld in *Rust v. Sullivan*.[43] The story begins in 1970 when Congress added to Title X, a comprehensive family planning statute, an explicit prohibition against appropriating funds "where abortion is a method of family planning."[44] The Carter administration interpreted the funding ban narrowly, mandating that Title X recipients provide "non-directive counseling" on "pregnancy

---

[40]   Steve Alumbaugh and C. K. Rowland, The Links between Platform-based Appointment Criteria and Trial Judges' Abortion Judgements, 74 Judicature 153 (1990).

[41]   *See* Volume II, Chapter 2: Executive and Congressional Participation in Court.

[42]   *See Id.*

[43]   *See* Volume II, Chapter 3: Title X and the Gag Rule.

[44]   84 Stat. 1504, 1508 (1970).

termination."[45] The Reagan administration vehemently opposed these regulations and ultimately elected to override the Carter scheme through its own regulatory initiatives.[46]

The Supreme Court approved the Reagan scheme because "substantial deference is accorded" to the executive in its interpretation of statutes.[47] This holding, as the varying approaches of the Carter and Reagan administrations reveal, accords the executive broad latitude in filling the gaps of statutory language. Moreover, as Congress's failed attempt to statutorily overrule the gag order suggests, it may well take a two-thirds supermajority for Congress to trump the regulatory initiatives of the executive. The Reagan—and later the Bush—administration made good use of this regulatory authority to advance its pro-life agenda. Policies on fetal tissue research,[48] U.S. AID grant recipients,[49] the importation of RU-486,[50] and military hospitals were all promulgated pursuant to the executive's authority to implement the laws.

The effective exercise of his rulemaking authority requires the President to appoint like-minded individuals to administer abortion-related programs. Witness Reagan's regulatory appointees. According to political scientists George Eads and Mike Fix, these individuals were "selected for their symbolic value rather than their administrative skills" and "there was no appreciable fear of the damage controversial

---

[45] Program Guidelines for Project Grants for Family Planning Services, Part II, 8.6 at 13 (1981).

[46] The Reagan administration had earlier (and unsuccessfully) proposed legislation to prohibit Title X recipients from discussing abortion as a family planning alternative.

[47] Rust v. Sullivan, 11! S.Ct. 1759, 1767 (1991).

[48] *See* Volume II, Chapter 7: Fetal Tissue Research.

[49] *See* Volume II, Chapter 4: Foreign Aid and the Mexico City Policy.

[50] *See* Volume II, Chapter 5: RU486: The Abortion Pill.

appointees could generate."[51] On abortion-related issues, not surprisingly, a number of Reagan appointees came from the right to life movement:[52] OPM head Donald Devine had run the Life Amendment PAC; Centers for Disease Control director James Mason had opposed abortion rights as head of Utah's state health department; Health and Human Services secretary Richard Sweiker had, as a U.S. Senator, sponsored a constitutional amendment to overturn *Roe*; Title X family planning program head Marjorie Mecklenburg was a founder of the National Right to Life Committee and her eventual successor Jo Ann Gasper had been editor of the *Right Woman*; and Surgeon General C. Everett Koop had written and lectured against abortion. The Reagan administration also made opposition to abortion a litmus test for key government posts. Charles Fried's nomination for Solicitor General, for example, hinged on his willingness, as Acting Solicitor General, to ask the Supreme Court to overturn *Roe*.[53] This policy cohesiveness stands in sharp contrast to the Carter administration where top Health, Education, and Welfare (HEW) appointees participated in a meeting organized by White House advisor Midge Costanza to protest against Carter and his HEW Secretary Joseph Califano's opposition to federal funding of abortion.[54] Reagan administration policy cohesiveness also helps explain the effectiveness of Reagan's regulatory campaign against abortion.

Another significant presidential weapon is the veto power. The veto power, as the experiences of the Bush administration demonstrate, can be used in two ways. First, the president can block

---

[51]   George C. Eads & Michael Fix, Relief or Reform 143 (1984).

[52]   These examples are taken from Michelle McKeegan's book *Abortion Politics*.   McKeegan *supra* note 26 at 48 (Devine), 53 (Mason), 66 (Sweicker), 67 (Mecklenberg), 114 (Gasper), 121 (Koop). Although her biographical background on these Reagan appointees is accurate, it should be noted that McKeegan's book is the work of an advocate hostile to Reagan's "New Right" anti-abortion agenda.

[53]   *See* Stephen Wermeil, Reagan Names Fried to Become Solicitor General, Wall Street Journal, 64, Sept. 26, 1985.

[54]   *See* Califano *supra* note 22 at 65.

congressionally supported programs that he disfavors. Bush's veto of legislative efforts to reinstate fetal tissue research and suspend the gag rule fit this category.[55] Second, the veto power can sometimes be used to force Congress to adopt a presidentially supported program. This is precisely what occurred when Congress refused to reenact a 1989 provision of the D.C. spending bill prohibiting the expenditure of both federal and city funds to pay for abortions.[56] Bush vetoed the bill and demanded that Congress reinsert the city funding prohibition. Recognizing the necessity of getting a spending bill passed and failing to override the Bush veto, Congress ultimately capitulated and reinserted the prohibition of both federal and city abortion expenditures.

The States. The states, although not a part of this documentary history, are as prominent as the federal government in shaping the abortion dispute. Prior to *Roe*, abortion battles were the near exclusive province of the states. Since *Roe*, the states have been afforded and have taken advantage of "multiple opportunities for thwarting compliance with, or implementation of [*Roe*]."[57] With recent decisions like *Webster v. Reproductive Health Services* and *Planned Parenthood v. Casey* acknowledging broad state authority to regulate (if not prohibit) abortion,[58] the scope of abortion rights seems to hinge on state politics.

Roe v. Wade, although setting in motion the contemporary abortion dispute, did not appear in a political vacuum. Actions in the 1960s by the American Law Institute, American Medical Association, and various religious organizations spurred nineteen states to liberalize their criminal statutes governing abortion. Of equal significance, only three states (Louisiana, New Hampshire, Pennsylvania) prohibited all

---

[55]   *See* 137 Cong. Rec. H 10,491, Nov. 19, 1991 (daily ed.) (gag rule); Public Papers 1992-93(I) 1005 (fetal tissue).

[56]   *See* Volume I, Chapter 1: Abortion Funding Issues.

[57]   Craig & O'Brien, *supra* note 34 at 77.

[58]   *See* Volume II, Chapter 2: Executive and Congressional Participation in Court.

abortions. In the early 1970s, although thirty-four states had rejected reform initiatives,[59] more dramatic change seemed possible. The National Conference on Commissioners on Uniform State Laws drafted a Uniform Abortion Act, which would have placed no limitations on abortion during the first twenty weeks of pregnancy.

The Court in *Roe* sought to ride the crest of these reform efforts. State responses to *Roe*, however, reveal that the nation was not prepared to accept the Court's decision. Indeed, in the year following *Roe*, 260 bills aimed at restricting abortion rights were introduced and thirty-nine enacted. Moreover, by turning abortion rights advocates' principal objective into a constitutional mandate, reform efforts were now the province of groups seeking to chip away at, if not destroy, *Roe*.

Anti-abortion interests had huge success. From 1973 to 1989, 306 abortion measures were passed by forty-eight states. The principal weapons of *Roe*'s opponents were attempts to make abortion less attractive through so-called "burden creation" strategies. These strategies included increasing the risks of undergoing an abortion (statutes forbidding a safe abortion method—saline amniocentesis— while permitting more dangerous abortion techniques); reducing accessibility to medical facilities that perform abortions (statutes demanding that all abortion be performed in a hospital and zoning laws restricting the number of abortion clinics); increasing the cost of abortions (statutes requiring physician or pathologist involvement in abortion procedures); and establishing detailed pre-abortion procedures (statutes requiring women to be informed of the "medical risks" of abortion and to wait at least twenty-four hours after consenting to the abortion procedure).[60]

Just as *Roe* transformed state abortion politics in 1973, the Court's 1989 *Webster* decision signaled a new era in abortion politics. On the brink of overturning *Roe*, the Court declared "the rigid *Roe*

---

[59]   *See* Lynn D. Wardle and Mary Ann Q. Wood, A Lawyer Looks at Abortion 43 (1982).

[60]   *See* Albert M. Pearson & Paul M. Kurtz, The Abortion Controversy: A Study in Law and Politics, 8 Harvard Journal of Law and Public Policy 427 (1985). For an alternative typology, *see* Rubin *supra* note 5 at 127-30.

framework" unworkable and opened the door to anti-abortion legislation by approving, among other things, second trimester fetal viability tests.[61] In the days following *Webster*, pro-choice and pro-life interest groups predicted an avalanche of anti-abortion legislation.[62]

Webster did not live up to its interest group billing. From 1989-1992, only fourteen statutes were enacted; nine pro-choice and five pro-life. This paucity of enacted bills prompted the Alan Gutmacher Institute to conclude that "[t]he wholesale changes in abortion law that had been widely predicted by activists, political pundits and the media [are yet to occur. Instead,] . . . law makers stayed in the 'safe', familiar, middle ground."[63] From this mixed (in result) and modest (in volume) legislative output, it is readily apparent that there are now "two powerful, determined, and politically active forces—one on each side of the abortion issue—and caught in the middle [are] the state politicians."[64]

This conclusion is hardly pathbreaking but it goes a long way towards explaining the events of the past few years. It explains, for example, that legislative inertia can be a measure of a decision's impact. It also suggests that pro-choice interests are politically dominant in states that protect abortion rights and, correspondingly, that pro-life interests are dominant in states that enact anti-abortion measures. Otherwise, pro-choice interests would have enough clout to kill off pro-life initiatives and vice versa.

---

[61]   492 U.S. 490 (1989).

[62]   Representative Chris Smith, chair of the Congressional Pro-Life Caucus, beamed that *Webster* will "lead to the enactment of state laws" and the "saving of many children." Press Conference, Federal News Service, July 3, 1989; Kate Michelman, Executive Director of NARAL, warned of "[w]omen's lives hang[ing] by a thread, and [that] the Justices this morning handed the state politicians a pair of scissors." Press Conference, Federal News Service, July 3, 1989.

[63]   State Reproductive Health Monitor, i December 1990.

[64]   Craig & O'Brien, *supra* note 34 at 299.

State abortion politics is also the story of the often pivotal role played by state court judges. Before *Roe*, several state courts struck down anti-abortion laws.[65] After the Supreme Court concluded in *Harris v. McRae* that a congressional prohibition on the use of Medicaid funds for abortions did not violate the equal protection clause,[66] courts in California, Connecticut, Massachusetts, Michigan, New Jersey, and Oregon interpreted their own constitutions to protect the right of indigent women to a state-funded abortion. The New Jersey Supreme Court pointed out that "state Constitutions are separate sources of individual freedoms and restrictions on the exercise of power by the Legislature. . . . Although the state Constitution may encompass a smaller universe than the federal Constitution, our constellation of rights may be more complete."[67]

Ten states' constitutions contain explicit privacy provisions and several others contain clauses that have been interpreted to protect the right to privacy. Some state courts have applied these provisions to protect abortion rights. For example, the California Supreme Court ruled that "the federal right of privacy . . . is more limited than the corresponding right in the California Constitution" and that restrictions on abortion funding for indigent women therefore violated California's explicit privacy right.[68]

Victories in state court, moreover, do not end the political struggle. Instead, the state legislature and voters engage state courts in a dialogue over the meaning of the state constitution. Take the case of California. In 1981 the California Supreme Court declared that the legislature cannot restrict state funding for abortions for indigent

---

[65]   Survey of Abortion Law, 1980 Arizona State Law Journal 67, 106-11 (1980). Rubin, *supra* note 5 at 31-57.

[66]   448 U.S. 297 (1980).

[67]   Right to Choose v. Byrne, 450 A.2d 925, 931 (N.J. 1982).

[68]   Committee to Defend Reproductive Rights v. Myers, 625 P.2d 779, 796 (Cal. 1981). Following *Webster*, pro-choice groups scored impressive court victories in California and Florida.   American Academy of Pediatrics v. Van de Kemp, 263 Cal. Rptr. 45 (1989); *In re T.W.*, 551 So. 2d 1186 (Fla. 1989).

women. For the next decade, the legislature nonetheless passed laws restricting the funding. Each of those years the courts struck the laws down and reinstated the funding.[69] Conservatives attempted to make use of the ballot box to remove liberal judges. California Chief Justice Rose Elizabeth Bird and two other justices were ousted in 1986 when conservatives targeted them for electoral defeat. A five-two conservative majority now dominates the court, but it continues to issue an expansive interpretation of California's privacy right.

Webster and *Casey*, by substituting an "undue burden" test for *Roe*'s trimester standard, have made state politics the fulcrum of the abortion dispute. Prior to *Webster*, *Roe* and its progeny left little room for significant state regulation. That state legislators were activists during this *Roe* to *Webster* period yet are extraordinarily cautious today says a good deal about state attitudes both towards abortions and towards the Supreme Court.

II. On Constitutional Dialogues and the Abortion Dispute

The abortion dispute reveals that the shaping of constitutional values is a dynamic process in which the courts, the executive, and the legislature engage in a dialogue with each other at both the federal and state level. The Supreme Court has moderated *Roe*'s stringent trimester standard thanks to presidentially nominated and Senate confirmed judicial appointments, amicus filings by the Solicitor General and Congressional interests, and state legislators whose willingness to legislatively challenge *Roe* created repeated opportunities for the Court to fine tune its abortion doctrine. With *Webster* and *Casey*, the Court recognizes that state legislatures and courts will likely play the pivotal role in defining the reaches and limits of abortion rights.

Congress and the White House have also shaped abortion rights and participated in a dialogue with the courts and each other through legislative enactments and administrative rulemaking. Congress puts into law a vision of constitutional meaning whenever it enacts abortion-related legislation; the executive likewise participates in these

---

[69] Philip Hager, Court Again Rejects Curbs on Abortions, L.A. Times, Nov. 17, 1989, at A3.

matters through the president's signing of this legislation and the Justice Department's defense of these measures; the courts, finally, adjudicate constitutional challenges to these enactments. Administrative rulemaking follows a similar interactive course—agency heads engage in constitutional interpretation when promulgating regulations; the executive, moreover, defends these regulations in court and fends off Congressional attacks through testimony, and if need be, the veto power; Congress also participates in rulemaking through its confirmation of agency heads, oversight of government programs, amici filings in court, and occasionally through legislation to moderate disfavored initiatives; the courts, finally, have entered the fray through decisions concerning the scope of executive power to interpret vague statutory language.

This dynamic is pervasive. It clearly shows the judiciary to be one part of a constitutional dialogue that involves all of government. Take the case of the Reagan-Bush federal family planning rules. Congress's 1991 efforts to statutorily override these family planning regulations were intended to express dissatisfaction with the executive for promulgating the order and the Supreme Court for upholding it.

The Supreme Court seems quite comfortable with and is, in part, responsible for the current state of affairs. Court doctrine has both shaped and been shaped by elected branch decisionmaking. *Roe* nationalized abortion rights at a time when state reform efforts, while on the rise, could not guarantee success. Twenty-two years later, as reflected in the failure of statutory and constitutional amendment repeal efforts as well as *Casey*'s utilization of stare decisis to reaffirm *Roe*, the durability of the "central holding of *Roe*" seems assured. The Court, however, has given way to elected branch counter-initiatives. Abortion funding restrictions have been upheld, some parental rights have been recognized, and the Court has left the development of administrative regulations to the political process. Furthermore, while rejecting Reagan and Bush administration efforts to overturn *Roe*, the "undue burden" test advocated by Reagan Solicitor General Rex Lee in *Akron* seems the governing standard in state regulation cases.

Our system is one, as Justice Ginsburg rightly observed at her confirmation hearing, where "courts do not guard constitutional rights alone. Courts share that profound responsibility with Congress, the president, the states, and the people."[70] The abortion dispute makes clear that this dynamic is never-ending. This state of perpetual change, rather than being problematic, is the greatest strength of this dynamic process. Changing circumstances demand that constitutional meaning not be too inflexible. Just as the judiciary leaves its mark on society, so does society drive the agenda and decisions of the courts. "[The] great tides and currents which engulf the rest of men," as Justice Cardozo put it, "do not turn aside in their course and pass the judges by."[71] Elected government action, by treating the Constitution as part and parcel of everyday politics, ensures that constitutional doctrine and decisionmakers operate within the confines of contemporary mores.

---

[70]   Joan Biskupic, Ginsburg's Graduation, Washington Post, A-1, A-6, July 21, 1993.

[71]   Benjamin Cardozo, The Nature of the Judicial Process, 168 (1921).

Judicial Nominations

1

JUSTICE SANDRA DAY O'CONNOR

President Reagan's choice of Sandra Day O'Connor to be his first Supreme Court nominee presented the Senate with an interesting conundrum. On the one hand, O'Connor had the patronage of Reagan, an avowed pro-life president who had made no secret of his willingness to use the appointment power to change the face of the Court, and O'Connor was known to be personally opposed to abortion. On the other hand, however, Reagan's promise to appoint the first woman to the Court may well have dominated the selection process, overshadowing ideological concerns. Indeed, O'Connor had a record of voting against pro-life legislation during her tenure with the Arizona state legislature.

As a result, the confirmation hearings of Sandra Day O'Connor dealt heavily with the issue of abortion, and she drew intense scrutiny from both sides of the issue. Although O'Connor attempted to defer some of the more pointed questions (specifically those questions which addressed the propriety of *Roe* itself), she spoke at length about her personal views on abortion. Nevertheless, while answering the Senator's questions with apparent candor she managed to leave them with little clue about how she would vote on future abortion cases.

Throughout the hearings, O'Connor stated repeatedly that she was personally opposed to abortion as a method of birth control. Yet she qualified her response by noting that as a member of the Supreme Court she would put aside her personal views when deciding cases. Furthermore, when questioned on how she would advise Congress to deal with the subject of abortion, she stated that judges should not be in the business of creating public policy. O'Connor thus succeeded in creating the impression that her views on abortion were moderate and that she was capable of divorcing her moral beliefs from her judicial philosophy.

O'Connor addressed her seemingly pro-choice voting record head-on. There were four bills at issue. The first would have repealed an Arizona law which made abortion a felony, except in cases where the mother's life was endangered; O'Connor stated that she supported the measure only in the absence of a less sweeping alternative and noted that she was ultimately instrumental in the bill's quiet death. The second bill would have established a state policy of providing contraceptive information to the public; O'Connor noted that prophylactic measures reduced the need for abortions. The third measure, which O'Connor failed to support, would have asked Congress to pass a pro-life constitutional amendment; O'Connor claimed that the measure had not received the level of consideration due such an important request. The final bill was a stadium construction bill which contained a nongermane rider which would have prohibited abortions in any facility under the Arizona Board of Regents; O'Connor claimed she voted against the measure because of a dislike for the use of substantive appropriations riders.

O'Connor's confirmation hearings were, ultimately, a two-fronted attack on the issue of abortion. Remarkably, O'Connor managed to answer the questions of Senators on both sides of the issue with considerable candor without tipping her hand about her future voting. The result was the appeasement of an initially wary Judiciary Committee and the unanimous confirmation of Sandra Day O'Connor. Furthermore, O'Connor's confirmation, as the first woman ever nominated to the Supreme Court, was never in jeopardy. As a result, some commentators have speculated that the Senators did not grill O'Connor as much as they might have and that her answers really didn't matter all that much. *See, e.g.* Wermiel, Confirming the Constitution: The Role of the Senate Judiciary Committee, 56 L. and Contemporary Problems 122, 129 (1993).

Ironically, in the long run O'Connor proved both pro-choice and pro-life skeptics right -- or wrong, depending on how you choose to look at it. O'Connor's plurality opinion in *Planned Parenthood v. Casey* cut a line down the middle of the abortion issue with the creation of the "undue burden" standard for abortion regulation. 112 S.Ct. 2791 (1992). The *Casey* decision, which has redefined abortion jurisprudence, reaffirmed *Roe* while simultaneously giving state governments considerable leeway to regulate the abortion procedure. If the Senate was unable to define O'Connor as either a pro-choice or a pro-life nominee during her confirmation hearings, it may have been because she was a genuine moderate on the issue of abortion.

Justice Sandra Day O'Connor
Documents

NOMINATION OF SANDRA DAY O'CONNOR

HEARINGS

BEFORE THE

COMMITTEE ON THE JUDICIARY
UNITED STATES SENATE

NINETY-SEVENTH CONGRESS

FIRST SESSION

ON

THE NOMINATION OF JUDGE SANDRA DAY O'CONNOR OF
ARIZONA TO SERVE AS AN ASSOCIATE JUSTICE OF THE
SUPREME COURT OF THE UNITED STATES

SEPTEMBER 9, 10, AND 11, 1981

Serial No. J–97–51

Printed for the use of the Committee on the Judiciary

U.S. GOVERNMENT PRINTING OFFICE

87-101 O   WASHINGTON : 1982

PERSONAL AND JUDICIAL PHILOSOPHY ON ABORTION

The CHAIRMAN. Judge O'Connor, there has been much discussion regarding your views on the subject of abortion. Would you discuss your philosophy on abortion, both personal and judicial, and explain your actions as a State senator in Arizona on certain specific matters: First, your 1970 committee vote in favor of House bill No. 20, which would have repealed Arizona's felony statutes on abortion. Then I have three other instances I will inquire about.

Judge O'CONNOR. Very well. May I preface my response by saying that the personal views and philosophies, in my view, of a Supreme Court Justice and indeed any judge should be set aside insofar as it is possible to do that in resolving matters that come before the Court.

Issues that come before the Court should be resolved based on the facts of that particular case or matter and on the law applicable to those facts, and any constitutional principles applicable to those facts. They should not be based on the personal views and ideology of the judge with regard to that particular matter or issue.

Now, having explained that, I would like to say that my own view in the area of abortion is that I am opposed to it as a matter of birth control or otherwise. The subject of abortion is a valid one, in my view, for legislative action subject to any constitutional restraints or limitations.

I think a great deal has been written about my vote in a Senate Judiciary Committee in 1970 on a bill called House bill No. 20, which would have repealed Arizona's abortion statutes. Now in reviewing that, I would like to state first of all that that vote occurred some 11 years ago, to be exact, and was one which was not easily recalled by me, Mr. Chairman. In fact, the committee records when I looked them up did not reflect my vote nor that of other members, with one exception.

It was necessary for me, then, to eventually take time to look at news media accounts and determine from a contemporary article a reflection of the vote on that particular occasion. The bill did not go to the floor of the Senate for a vote; it was held in the Senate Caucus and the committee vote was a vote which would have taken it out of that committee with a recommendation to the full Senate.

The bill is one which concerned a repeal of Arizona's then statutes which made it a felony, punishable by from 2 to 5 years in prison, for anyone providing any substance or means to procure a miscarriage unless it was necessary to save the life of the mother. It would have, for example, subjected anyone who assisted a young woman who, for instance, was a rape victim in securing a D. & C. procedure within hours or even days of that rape.

At that time I believed that some change in Arizona statutes was appropriate, and had a bill been presented to me that was less sweeping than House bill No. 20, I would have supported that. It was not, and the news accounts reflect that I supported the committee action in putting the bill out of committee, where it then died in the caucus.

I would say that my own knowledge and awareness of the issues and concerns that many people have about the question of abortion has increased since those days. It was not the subject of a great deal of public attention or concern at the time it came before the committee in 1970. I would not have voted, I think, Mr. Chairman, for a simple repealer thereafter.

The CHAIRMAN. Now the second instance was your cosponsorship in 1973 of Senate bill No. 1190, which would have provided family planning services, including surgical procedures, even for minors without parental consent.

Judge O'CONNOR. Senate bill No. 1190 in 1973 was a bill in which the prime sponsor was from the city of Tucson, and it had nine other cosigners on the bill. I was one of those cosigners.

I viewed the bill as a bill which did not deal with abortion but which would have established as a State policy in Arizona, a policy of encouraging the availability of contraceptive information to people generally. The bill at the time, I think, was rather loosely drafted, and I can understand why some might read it and say, "What does this mean?"

That did not particularly concern me at the time because I knew that the bill would go through the committee process and be amended substantially before we would see it again. That was a rather typical practice, at least in the Arizona legislature. Indeed, the bill was assigned to a public health and welfare committee where it was amended in a number of respects.

It did not provide for any surgical procedure for an abortion, as has been reported inaccurately by some. The only reference in the bill to a surgical procedure was the following. It was one that said:

A physician may perform appropriate surgical procedures for the prevention of conception upon any adult who requests such procedure in writing.

That particular provision, I believe, was subsequently amended out in committee but, be that as it may, it was in the bill on introduction.

Mr. Chairman, I supported the availability of contraceptive information to the public generally. Arizona had a statute or statutes on the books at that time, in 1973, which did restrict rather dramatically the availability of information about contraception to the public generally. It seemed to me that perhaps the best way to avoid having people who were seeking abortions was to enable people not to become pregnant unwittingly or without the intention of doing so.

The CHAIRMAN. The third instance, your 1974 vote against House Concurrent Memorial No. 2002, which urged Congress to pass a constitutional amendment against abortion.

Judge O'CONNOR. Mr. Chairman, as you perhaps recall, the *Rowe v. Wade* decision was handed down in 1973. I would like to mention that in that year following that decision, when concerns began to be expressed, I requested the preparation in 1973 of Senate bill No. 1333 which gave hospitals and physicians and employees the right not to participate in or contribute to any abortion proceeding if they chose not to do so and objected, notwithstanding their employment. That bill did pass the State Senate and became law.

The following year, in 1974, less than a year following the *Rowe v. Wade* decision, a House Memorial was introduced in the Arizona House of Representatives. It would have urged Congress to amend the Constitution to provide that the word person in the 5th and 14th amendments applies to the unborn at every stage of development, except in an emergency when there is a reasonable medical certainty that continuation of the pregnancy would cause the death of the mother. The amendment was further amended in the Senate Judiciary Committee.

I did not support the memorial at that time, either in committee or in the caucus.

The CHAIRMAN. Excuse me. My time is up, but you are right in the midst of your question. We will finish abortion, one more instance, and we will give the other members the same additional time, if you will proceed.

Judge O'CONNOR. I voted against it, Mr. Chairman, because I was not sure at that time that we had given the proper amount of reflection or consideration to what action, if any, was appropriate by way of a constitutional amendment in connection with the *Rowe v. Wade* decision.

It seems to me, at least, that amendments to the Constitution are very serious matters and should be undertaken after a great deal of study and thought, and not hastily. I think a tremendous amount of work needs to go into the text and the concept being expressed in any proposed amendment. I did not feel at that time that that kind of consideration had been given to the measure. I understand that the Congress is still wrestling with that issue after some years from that date, which was in 1974.

Thank you, Mr. Chairman.

The CHAIRMAN. Now the last instance is concerning a vote in 1974 against a successful amendment to a stadium construction bill which limited the availability of abortions.

Judge O'CONNOR. Also in 1974, which was an active year in the Arizona Legislature with regard to the issue of abortion, the Senate had originated a bill that allowed the University of Arizona to issue bonds to expand its football stadium. That bill passed the State Senate and went to the House of Representatives.

In the House it was amended to add a nongermane rider which would have prohibited the performance of abortions in any facility under the jurisdiction of the Arizona Board of Regents. When the measure returned to the Senate, at that time I was the Senate majority leader and I was very concerned because the whole subject had become one that was controversial within our own membership.

I was concerned as majority leader that we not encourage a practice of the addition of nongermane riders to Senate bills which we had passed without that kind of a provision. Indeed, Arizona's constitution has a provision which prohibits the putting together of bills or measures or riders dealing with more than one subject. I did oppose the addition by the House of the nongermane rider when it came back.

It might be of interest, though, to know, Mr. Chairman, that also in 1974 there was another Senate bill which would have provided for a medical assistance program for the medically needy. That was Senate bill No. 1165. It contained a provision that no benefits would be provided for abortions except when deemed medically necessary to save the life of the mother, or where the pregnancy had resulted from rape, incest, or criminal action. I supported that bill together with that provision and the measure did pass and become law.

The CHAIRMAN. Thank you. My time is up. We will now call upon Senator Biden.

Senator BIDEN. Thank you, Mr. Chairman.

September 11, 1981

The Honorable Strom Thurmond
Chairman
Committee on the Judiciary
United States Senate
Washington, D.C. 20510

Dear Mr. Chairman:

In his letter of September 9, 1981, Senator Humphrey
sets forth the following questions:

1. Do you believe that all human beings should be
    regarded as persons for the purposes of the
    right to life protected by the Fifth and Four-
    teenth Amendments?

2. In your opinion, is the unborn child a human being?

3. What is your opinion of the decision of the Supreme
    Court in the 1973 abortion cases, Roe v. Wade and Doe
    v. Bolton?

4. Do you believe the Constitution should be interpreted
    to permit the states to prohibit abortion? If your
    answer is yes, are there any types of abortions where
    you think the Constitution should be interpreted so
    as not to allow such prohibition?

5. Do you think the Constitution should be interpreted
    to permit the states to require the consent of parents
    before their unmarried, unemancipated minor child
    has an abortion performed on her?

6. Do you think the Constitution should be interpreted
    to permit the states to require the consent of parents
    before their unmarried, unemancipated minor child is
    sterilized?

7. Do you think the Constitution should be interpreted to
    permit the states to require the consent of parents
    before their unmarried, unemancipated minor child is
    given contraceptives by a third party?

The first and second questions concern the definition of human
life and the legal consequences which attach to that definition.
Congress is currently considering proposals directly addressed to
these issues. Questions concerning the validity and effect of
these proposals, if any are passed, might well be presented to
the Supreme Court for decision.

A nominee to the Court must refrain from expressing any
view on an issue which may be presented to the Court. A federal
judge is required by law to "disqualify himself in any proceeding
in which his impartiality might reasonably be questioned." 28
U.S.C. § 455; see Code of Judicial Conduct, Canon 3C. If a nominee
to the Supreme Court were to state how he or she would rule in a
particular case, it would suggest that, as a Justice, the nominee
would not impartially consider the arguments presented by each
litigant. If a nominee were to commit to a prospective ruling

in response to a question from a Senator, there is an even more serious appearance of impropriety, because it may seem that the nominee has pledged to take a particular view of the law in return for the Senator's vote. In either circumstance, the nominee may be disqualified when the case or issue comes before the Court. As Justice Frankfurter stated in Offutt v. United States, 348 U.S. 11 (1954), a core component of justice is the appearance of justice. It would clearly tarnish the appearance of justice for me to state in advance how I would decide a particular case or issue.

Other nominees to the Supreme Court have scrupulously refrained from commenting on the merits of recent Court decisions or specific matters which may come before the Court. Justice Stewart, for example, declined at his confirmation hearings to answer questions concerning Brown v. Board of Education, noting that pending and future cases raised issues affected by that decision and that "a serious problem of simple judicial ethics" would arise if he were to commit himself as a nominee. Hearings at 62-63. The late Justice Harlan declined to respond to questions about the then-recent Steel Seizure cases, Hearings at 167, 174, and stated that if he were to comment upon cases which might come before him it would raise "the gravest kind of question as to whether I was qualified to sit on that Court." Hearings at 138. More recently, the Chief Justice declined to comment on a Supreme Court redistricting decision which was criticized by a Senator, noting, "I should certainly observe the proprieties by not undertaking to comment on anything which might come either before the court on which I now sit or on any other court on which I may sit." Hearings at 18.

Questions three and four directly raise the issue of the correctness of particular Supreme Court decisions. In Roe v. Wade and Doe v. Bolton the Supreme Court held that states may not prohibit abortions during the first trimester of pregnancy. Questions related to the issues reached in these decisions may come before the Court, and the Court may also be asked to reconsider the decisions themselves. For the reasons I have stated in this letter as well as in my testimony before the Senate Committee on the Judiciary, it would therefore be inappropriate for me to answer questions three and four.

The fifth question concerns the constitutional validity of a law requiring parental consent prior to the performance of an abortion on an unmarried, unemancipated minor child. Several state statutes dealing with this subject have come before the Court and have resulted in sharply divided decisions. In Planned Parenthood v. Danforth, 428 U.S. 52 (1976), the Court ruled unconstitutional a statute requiring parental consent before an unmarried person under 18 could obtain an abortion. The Court specifically noted, however, that it was not ruling that every minor was capable of giving effective consent, simply that giving an absolute veto to the parents in all cases was invalid. In Bellotti v. Baird, 443 U.S. 622 (1979), the Court struck down a statute which required parental or judicial consent prior to the performance of an abortion on an unmarried minor. The Court failed to agree on a majority rationale. Just last Term, however, in H.L. v. Matheson, 101 S.Ct. 1154 (1981), the Court upheld a Utah statute requiring notification of parents prior to an abortion, at least as the statute was applied to an unmarried, unemancipated minor who had not made any claim as to her own maturity. These decisions indicate that the area is a particularly troublesome one for the Court, and also one in which future cases can be expected to arise.

The Supreme Court has recognized that "the parents' claim to authority in their own household is basic in the structure of our society." <u>Ginsberg</u> v. <u>New York</u>, 390 U.S. 629, 639 (1958) (plurality). My sense of family values is such that I would hope that any minor considering an abortion would seek the guidance and counseling of her parents.

The sixth question concerns the constitutional validity of a law requiring parental consent before an unmarried, unemancipated minor child is sterilized. Once again I would hope that any minor considering such a drastic and usually irreversible step would seek the guidance of his or her parents and family. It would be inappropriate for me, however, to express any view in response to a specific question concerning the legality of a parental consent law, because the whole area of the constitutionality of statutes requiring parental consent is in a stage of development and because such statutes are likely to be presented to the Court for review. My hesitation is also based on the fact that I have not had the benefit of a specific factual case, briefs, or arguments.

The final question concerns the constitutional validity of a law requiring the consent of parents before an unmarried, unemancipated minor child is given contraceptives by a third party. In <u>Carey</u> v. <u>Population Services International</u>, 431 U.S. 678 (1977), the Court struck down a law making it a crime for anyone to sell or distribute nonprescription contraceptives to anyone under 16. The case, however, did not involve a parental consent requirement; indeed, Justice Powell found the law offensive precisely because it applied to parents and interfered with their rights to raise their children. <u>Id</u>. at 708 (concurring opinion). A three-judge district court found a state law prohibiting family planning assistance to minors in the absence of parental consent unconstitutional as interfering with the minor's rights, <u>T.H.</u> v. <u>Jones</u>, 425 F.Supp. 873, 881 (Utah 1975), but when the case reached the Supreme Court it was affirmed on other grounds, 425 U.S. 986 (1976). The constitutional question is therefore still open, and I must respectfully decline any further comments for the reasons set forth previously.

Mr. Chairman, I appreciate the opportunity to set forth my views on these matters in response to Senator Humphrey's letter.

Sincerely,

Sandra Day O'Connor

NOMINATION OF SANDRA DAY O'CONNOR

U.S. SENATE,
COMMITTEE ON THE JUDICIARY,
Washington, D.C.

The committee met, pursuant to notice, at 10:05 a.m., in room 1202, Dirksen Senate Office Building, Senator Strom Thurmond (chairman of the committee) presiding.

Also present: Senators Laxalt, Dole, East, Grassley, Denton, Specter, Biden, Byrd, Metzenbaum, DeConcini, Leahy, and Baucus.

Staff present: Vinton D. Lide, chief counsel; Quentin Crommelin, Jr., staff director; Duke Short, chief investigator; and Candie Bruse, chief clerk.

The CHAIRMAN. The Judiciary Committee will come to order.

The questioning of Judge Sandra O'Connor will resume. Judge O'Connor, I would remind you that you are still under oath.

Judge O'CONNOR. Thank you.

The CHAIRMAN. I shall now call upon the last Senator, I believe, on the second round, the distinguished Senator from Alabama, Mr. Denton.

TESTIMONY OF HON. SANDRA DAY O'CONNOR, NOMINATED TO BE ASSOCIATE JUSTICE, U.S. SUPREME COURT—Resumed

Senator DENTON. Thank you, Mr. Chairman.

Good morning, Judge O'Connor.

Judge O'CONNOR. Good morning.

Senator DENTON. At the outset, let me clear up what amounted to a misunderstanding on my part yesterday. I had questioned you on your personal views on abortion, and you stated during that exchange, "It remains offensive at all levels," and stated that you think it is a problem at any level.

Then I thought I heard you say that you would not be in favor of abortion even to save the life of the mother. After several others had thought the same thing, and then having been questioned by some news people, I did look at the transcript and so forth and find out that that is not what you said.

You actually said: "Would I personally object to drawing the line to saving the life of the mother? No, I would not." You went on to say: "Are there other areas?" Then you said: "Possibly."

Therefore, I would have to withdraw my statement since it was based on error in understanding you. I misunderstood you. I would have to say that it appears that indeed you are not more conservative than I on that issue, and I would remind you that legislatively the Congress has done what it could to outlaw or forbid pay-

(237)

ments for Government funding of abortion except to save the life of the mother.

That is where Congress drew the line but we could not go any further than just stop Goverment funding for it. We could not get into the legislation of abortion with respect to the public because we were preempted by a Supreme Court manifestation of judicial activism in the *Roe* v. *Wade* decision. Therefore, there is a real problem of that judicial activism, and I am sure that not all of my colleagues would agree that it is the wrong kind but, nevertheless, there was that example.

Therefore, I have learned that you are less conservative than I, and as I go into the Kenneth Starr memorandum I would refer to a previous statement of yours which said that you felt that your personal feelings should not constitute the basis of decisions made on this matter or any other matter in the Supreme Court, before the Supreme Court, but rather that if there is a constitutional principle which applies, it should be the determining factor.

I submit that in the Declaration we do have the statement, "all men created equal," et cetera, "endowed by their Creator with certain inalienable rights. Among these are life * * *." Then in the Constitution, in the Bill of Rights, article 5, "No person can be deprived of life without due process of law."

Senator East, as you know, has been conducting hearings to determine whether or not a fetus is a person. I agree that that is a very difficult question. I do not agree that it is difficult to determine that it is human life. I believe that that is irrefutable.

I believe that, as I said before, our democracy is predicated on respect, infinite respect, for human life. Socrates, whom we may be proving right these days, has said that a democracy cannot work because sooner or later the people will perceive that they can get their hands in the till; elected officials will cater to that trend, and bankruptcy will result. I think we are on the way to proving that, were on the way to proving that true. We are trying to turn that around.

He also indicated that the majority would crunch the minority in every case in a democracy. By our system we have been proving him wrong so far—and I am justifying why I am going into the Kenneth Starr memorandum and the abortion issue further.

The Judeo-Christian ethic brought compassion into the picture. The ethic did not exist as a religious principle in Socrates' day. He tried to talk about a "one god" thing and they poisoned him because he did not believe in all of the gods being the way to go. Therefore, we do have a substantial portion of the world believing in that God, and among those nations the United States has been one of the more notable.

That ethic of compassion applied to the dog-eat-dog majority rule in the political sense, and the otherwise dog-eat-dog, free-enterprise system, is in my opinion what has gotten us to the point where we have proved Socrates wrong, have made a success out of democracy. To me, compassion is the key to civil rights, to human rights, to caring for the needy, to the survival of a democracy. If you break down compassion, you will find the prefix "com"—with—and the word "passion"—passion for what? Humanity, infinite, godlike humanity.

The human life in the womb is the most needy, most dependent, most helpless minority, for which—for whom, depending on how you want to look at it—we must have compassion. Our real political, economic, military, and psychological problems from my point of view—and I thought of this a great deal in prison and after coming home—all stem from our growing preoccupation—which has been repeated over and over in history—as a nation becomes more preoccupied with luxury than necessity, we have become "me-istic." We have stopped thinking about the other guy as much, our wife or our husband, our brother, our fellow of another color, our colleague of another color.

I believe that abortion is the opposite of compassion for that being which needs it the most. I believe that history will prove that once a nation goes that way, from an ethic like ours, as Nazi Germany did, you immediately get involved with infanticide, euthanasia, genocide, and the whole idea of selective murder. This brings into play the question of the convenience of the existence of that person which is based on human judgment. That is why I feel so strongly about what might be called fetal rights, the right to survival on the part of that human life.

I do not believe, with you, that learning more about fetuses will ever change the fact that there is life there, God-given life which we do not understand, and we do not even know what makes grass grow. How can we get into the process of deciding, for convenience or for money—because that kid is going to cost money if it is born—or embarrassment that we want to spare the 13- or 14-year-old girl—and you have said that you are opposed to it for birth control purposes.

However, I want to know what you meant yesterday when you said, "Are there other areas?"—besides saving the life of the mother—and then you said, "Possibly." I would have to say that that is less conservative than that which Congress has indicated as its collective will, and it leaves me befuddled as to where you are. I feel I have gotten nowhere, in that you have said possibly there are other areas. We could go on for perhaps a month, and if that is all the specific you are going to be, I would not know at all where you are coming from philosophically on that issue.

Judge O'CONNOR. Senator Denton, I believe that I recounted previously for the committee my vote in the legislature on funding in connection with the bill for providing medical care to indigents, where I did support a measure that provided for certain exclusions in addition to what was necessary to save the life of the mother. In that instance it included instances of rape and incest, criminal actions, and I supported that.

Senator DENTON. However, the criminal action—a little baby to be—is not involved in.

Judge O'CONNOR. I simply was trying to indicate, Senator Denton, where I had had occasion to vote as a legislator on the issue. These are very difficult questions for the legislator because, of course, people—many people—share your very eloquent views and your very perceptive views on this most pressing problem.

There are others who, perhaps out of different concerns, might draw the line in some slightly different fashion or indeed in some substantially different fashion, and these are the troubling issues that come before a legislator when asked to specifically draw the line. I appreciate that problem. I think I can simply indicate to you how I voted at that time on that issue.

Senator DENTON. OK. Well, with respect to some of those votes, then, I would like to go into the document which has become known as the Starr memorandum. I would preface that by a question. You feel abortion is personally abhorrent and repugnant. Would it follow that you believe the unborn ought to be legally protected? If so, how and at what stage of their development?

Judge O'CONNOR. Senator Denton, excuse me. Is that your question?

Senator DENTON. Yes. You have stated that you feel it is personally abhorrent and repugnant, and that it is a legislative matter to deal with it. Do you mean by that that we should legally protect the unborn? If so, how, considering the *Roe* v. *Wade* activism from the judicial branch?

Judge O'CONNOR. Well, Senator Denton, a legislative body at the State level today would be limited in that effort by the limitations placed in the *Roe* v. *Wade* decision. I recognize that. If a State legislature today were to try to draw the lines, it would have to reckon with that decision, which of course places substantial limitations on the freedom of State legislative bodies presently.

Senator DENTON. Until that decision is changed or if something comes up to render it subject to change, it makes your appointment extremely important and your philosophy on that matter extremely important. Therefore, I hope you can appreciate the interest of those tens of millions—and there are tens of millions on the other side—who are interested in your position on that. I am not clear that we have drawn much out. Let me get on this——

Judge O'CONNOR. Senator Denton, I do appreciate the concerns and the strongly held views of so many people on this issue.

Senator DENTON. I understand that.

On July 7, 1981, you had two telephone conversations with Kenneth W. Starr, counselor to the Attorney General of the United States.

Judge O'CONNOR. Excuse me. On what date, please?

Senator DENTON. July 7, 1981, is my information.

Did you state in one or both of those conversations that you "know well the Arizona leader of the right-to-life movement, a prominent female physician in Phoenix, and have never had any disputes or controversies with her"?

Judge O'CONNOR. Senator Denton, I am sure that I indicated that I knew Dr. Gerster. Indeed, she lives in the same community in which I live, the Scottsdale-Paradise Valley area.

Senator DENTON. Yes, and you are acquaintances.

Judge O'CONNOR. We have children who have attended the same school, and I have seen her on any number of occasions.

I had occasion, of course, to see her in 1974 in my capacity as a legislator as well. She at that time was interested in the house memorial 2002, dealing with the question of whether the Arizona Legislature should recommend to the Congress an amendment of the U.S. Constitution as a means of addressing the *Roe* v. *Wade* decision. Dr. Gerster——

Senator DENTON. Excuse me. I do not mean to be impolite but in the interest of trying to stay within the time, the only part of the question that I am—the question deals with whether or not you said that you had never had any disputes or controversies with that leader, Dr. Gerster. Did you say that, because the Starr memorandum is quoted as having had you saying that?

Judge O'CONNOR. Senator Denton, I am sure that I did indicate that and I would like to explain precisely why I said that.

As a legislator, I had many instances in which people would come before the legislature and espouse a particular position with regard to a particular bill. I as a legislator was obligated to listen to those views along with the views of others, and then ultimately cast a vote. My receiving of information of that sort and ultimately casting a vote, even if it were cast in a manner other than that being espoused by the speaker, did not cast me in my view in the role of being an adversary.

I did not feel that in my position as a legislator, that every time I voted against a measure that someone in the public sector was supporting publicly in front of me, that I became an adversary. I was not a leader in connection with the passage or defeat of house memorial 2002. I was a legislator——

Senator DENTON. I understand. I really do understand the thrust of your answer. It does appear, however, that the thrust that one would take from that answer which was quoted is that you and the right-to-life movement leader there really had no disputes on probably that issue. That I think might have been gleaned from that statement. I leave that to speculation. It certainly would have been my inference from it.

Judge O'CONNOR. Well, Senator Denton, I think that it is important to recognize that what I am trying to reflect is that because I may have voted differently than Dr. Gerster would have, had she been a legislator, does not mean that we are adversaries.

Senator DENTON. Yes, I understand. However, there has been much opposition to your nomination and public statements by Dr. Gerster, which probably we will hear some of later, concerning her opposition to many of your past legislative decisions. Therefore, there was an inconsistency, not in what your attitude was or what your statement was but I think with respect to the thrust of what that inclusion in Mr. Starr's report might have been intepreted as meaning.

Did you tell Mr. Starr that you did not remember how you voted on a bill to legalize abortion in Arizona, or that there is no record of how you voted on legislation to legalize abortion in Arizona? I believe we heard you say that you had some difficulty remembering one, and you had to get it out of a newspaper because it was not in the legislative records. Somebody in Arizona has said that that was the equivalent of not remembering how one would have voted on the Panama Canal issue.

Judge O'CONNOR. Senator Denton, as I explained I think in the first day of these hearings, with respect to house bill 20 I frankly had no recollection of the vote. We voted on literally thousands of measures and that bill never went to the floor for a vote. I tended to remember with more clarity those measures which required a vote on the merits on the floor. Committee votes are something else: Technically speaking, you are not voting on the merits in a committee vote. You are voting to put it out of committee with a certain recommendation.

In the year 1970, as reflected in the newspaper articles which I eventually unearthed, house bill 20 was not a major issue at that time in terms of having much public attention, in terms of having many people at a committee hearing, in any other way. It was simply not a measure that attracted that much attention.

In addition, house bill 20 was destined never to go to the floor in the State senate. I think it was widely known and believed even when it was in committee that it would never emerge from the Republican caucus. The votes were never there. It was a dead bill.

Senator DENTON. Yes. Then it might be relevant to follow up: You stated that some change in Arizona statutes was appropriate, and "had a bill been presented to me that was less sweeping than H.B. 20, I would have supported that. It was not." You broke off, but you meant it was not introduced. Is that correct?

Judge O'CONNOR. That is correct.

Senator DENTON. Can you then remember why you did not support S.B. 216, which was a more conservative bill regarding abortion which was pending in the Senate Judiciary Committee after March 23, 1970, roughly a month before the committee's vote on H.B. 20?

Judge O'CONNOR. Senator Denton, was that Senator McNulty's bill, if you know?

Senator DENTON. The bill provided for therapeutic abortions in cases involving rape, incest, or the life of the mother.

I have just been informed that my time is up.

It was Senator McNulty's bill, yes.

May she finish the answer to this question, Mr. Chairman?

The CHAIRMAN. She may finish the answer to your question.

Judge O'CONNOR. Senator Denton, as I recall that bill it provided for an elaborate mechanism of counseling services and other mechanisms for dealing with the question, and I was not satisfied that the complicated mechanism and structure of that bill was a workable one.

Senator DENTON. OK. Thank you, Judge O'Connor.

With my time up, Mr. Chairman, I would ask unanimous consent that a speech I made on August 26, 1981 delivered in Birmingham, Ala., on the subject of adolescent pregnancy be made a part of the record on this because it deals with the subject.

Sir, I must respectfully submit that, considering the importance of the matters being questioned into, although I am a freshman Senator, relatively inexperienced, I feel quite frustrated that these matters have not been developed in my opinion to the degree required for such an important appointment as a lifetime appointment to the Supreme Court. I just would like to mention that to you at this time as my feeling.

The CHAIRMAN. All Senators had 15 minutes on the first round and 15 minutes on the second round, except Senator Simpson who is not here today for his second round and so waives it, and Senator Heflin who has stated he did not care for a second round, and Senator Robert Byrd, the distinguished minority leader, who has not had either round on account of his duties.

19

Senator, out of my great respect for you, I will call on Senator Byrd and then come back to you for an extra 15 minutes which will give you three 15-minute rounds, if that is agreeable.

Senator DENTON. It will certainly offer more opportunity, sir.

The CHAIRMAN. Senator Byrd of West Virginia.

Senator BYRD. Mr. Chairman, thank you.

I will be very glad to wait and let the Senator complete his line of questions. I have found that it is very important that a Senator be able to finish his line of questions without interruption. I thank you for allowing me to speak at this time but if the Senator would like to complete his questions, I can wait another 15 minutes. I have very little to say and I can say it in 2 minutes but I would be very happy to wait.

The CHAIRMAN. All right. Senator Denton, we will call on you now and give you an extra 15 minutes.

Senator DENTON. All right, sir. Thank you.

The complicated mechanisms to which you refer, Judge O'Connor, I would not think would be ruled out in view of the complexity of the issue and so forth. I would have thought that you would allow that those complicated mechanisms should be considered—in continuance of your remarks, as we were broken off.

Judge O'CONNOR. Senator Denton, again I would ask you to reflect on the fact that we are talking about the year 1970. That was a time when at least my perception as a State legislator in Arizona indicated that this subject was not the subject of the public attention and concern that it is today.

I did not perceive very much in the way of public support at that time for the invocation of expensive counseling machinery in connection with this area. It is simply something that was basically a new approach being suggested in the legislature and I was not satisfied at that time that that was an appropriate approach.

STARR MEMORANDUM

Senator DENTON. OK. You keep referring to the social awareness, and so forth, and yet I keep remembering your statement about constitutional principle. I believe that upon further reflection on your part you might see a connection, and I believe you may have already begun to see a connection between the constitutional provision for protection of life and due process maybe, and this issue, and certainly the statement in the Declaration of Independence, and so forth.

The Starr memorandum makes no mention at all of your April 23, 1974 vote against a House-opposed right-to-life memorial which called on the U.S. Congress to constitutionally protect the life of the unborn. Was that discussed with Mr. Starr? If not, why not?

Judge O'CONNOR. Senator Denton, I certainly believe that it was. That memorial was the subject of a good deal of concern. Of course, I have not seen the so-called Starr memorandum. I have seen references in the newspaper to it but I did not see it. If I am correct in your date, that is something that occurred after the nomination had been announced, or the selection, rather, had been announced by the President.

Senator DENTON. Well, since this memorandum is such an important issue with so many people and such an important issue bearing on the subject we are discussing, I would ask permission from the chairman to deliver this memorandum—a copy of it, it is relatively brief—to Judge O'Connor, sir, so that she can address——

The CHAIRMAN. The staff will deliver a copy of the memorandum to Judge O'Connor.

Senator DENTON. Mr. Chairman, I would respectfully request that a copy of the memorandum be placed in the record.

The CHAIRMAN. Without objection, it will be placed in the record.

[Material to be supplied follows:]

OFFICE OF THE ATTORNEY GENERAL,
Washington, D.C., July 7, 1981.

Memorandum for the Attorney General.
From: Kenneth W. Starr, Counselor to the Attorney General.

On Monday, July 6, 1981, I spoke by phone on two occasions with Judge O'Connor. She provided the following information with respect to her public record on family-related issues:

As a trial and appellate judge, she has not had occasion to rule on any issue relating to abortion.

Contrary to media reports, she has never attended or spoken at a women's rights conference on abortion.

She was involved in the following legislative initiatives as a State Senator in Arizona:

In 1973, she requested the preparation of a bill, which was subsequently enacted, which gave the right to hospitals, physicians and medical personnel not to participate in abortions if the institution or individual chose not to do so. The measure, Senate Bill 1133, was passed in 1973.

In 1973, she was a co-sponsor (along with 10 other Senators) of a bill that would permit state agencies to participate in "family planning" activities and to disseminate information with respect to family planning. The bill made no express mention of abortion and was not viewed by then Senator O'Connor as an abortion measure. The bill died in Committee. She recalls no controversy with respect to the bill and is unaware of any hearings on the proposed measure.

In 1974, Senate Bill 1245 was passed by the Senate. Supported by Senator O'Connor, the bill as passed would have permitted the University of Arizona to issue bonds to expand existing sports facilities. In the House, and amendment was added providing that no abortions could be performed at any educational facility under the jurisdiction of the Arizona Board of Regents. Upon the measure's return from the House, Senator O'Connor voted against the bill as amended, on the ground that the Arizona Constitution forbade enactment of legislation treating unrelated subject matters. In her view, the anti-abortion rider was unrelated to the primary purpose of the bill, namely empowering the University to issue bonds to expand sports facilities. Her reasons for so voting are nowhere stated on the record.

In 1970, House Bill 20 was considered by the Senate Committee on which Senator O'Connor then served. As passed by the House, the bill would have repealed Arizona's then extant criminal prohibitions against abortion. The Committee majority voted in favor of this pre-*Roe* v. *Wade* measure; a minority on the Committee voted against it. There is no record of how Senator O'Connor voted, and she indicated that she has no recollection of how she voted. (One Senator voting against the measure did have his vote recorded.)

Judge O'Connor further indicated, in response to my questions, that she had never been a leader or outspoken advocate on behalf of either pro-life or abortion-rights organizations. She knows well the Arizona leader of the right-to-life movement, a prominent female physician in Phoenix, and has never had any disputes or controversies with her.

Senator DENTON. If I may, Mrs. O'Connor, I would ask you to read it because I am going to ask if you think that the memorandum could be characterized as a fair representation of your record on the abortion issue.

The CHAIRMAN. Now as I understand, this memorandum was made by Mr. Starr of the Justice Department——

Senator DENTON. Sir, I have no other——

The CHAIRMAN [continuing]. To the Attorney General. It was not made by the witness, Judge O'Connor. I just wanted to get the record straight on that.

Senator DENTON. It appears, sir, the dateline, the heading is "Office of the Attorney General, Washington, D.C., Memorandum for the Attorney General from Kenneth W. Starr, Counselor to the Attorney General." I have no——

The CHAIRMAN. Of course, Judge O'Connor is not responsible for what some member of the Justice Department wrote to the Attorney General.

Senator DENTON. Yes, sir, I totally agree.

The CHAIRMAN. However, we admit the memorandum for such consideration as it deserves.

Senator METZENBAUM. I wonder if the Senator from Alabama could make a copy of that memorandum available to other members of the committee, please.

Senator DOLE. Yes, sir. I have one other here so we could make a copy of it, Mr. Chairman.

The CHAIRMAN. Staff informs me that copies of the memorandum are being made available and will be handed around.

Senator Denton, you may proceed.

Senator DENTON. All right.

Judge O'Connor, as a lawyer, would you say that this memorandum could be characterized as being a fair representation of your record on the abortion issue?

Judge O'CONNOR. Senator Denton, it is somewhat incomplete. It does not reflect my vote in 1974 on the funding of medical care for the indigent, and so forth. I think it is not totally complete on that issue.

Senator DENTON. It has been represented or perceived by many that that memorandum, which many understand to have been the principal input to the President regarding your record, you might say is a bit optimistic from the standpoint of those who are prolife in its characterization of your record. That is why I brought it forward.

Judge O'CONNOR. Senator Denton, I can only comment——

The CHAIRMAN. If you will pardon me just a minute, now, Senator, if you are going to the process by which the President made his selection, that is one thing. The question we are considering here is her fitness for this position. I have no objection if you wish to ask the question but I want to emphasize this: that we, the members of this committee, will determine her fitness for this position and not the method by which the President went about making his selection. That was his business and not ours.

You may proceed.

Senator DENTON. Yes, sir, I totally accept that admonition.

Her statements in the memorandum are relevant to the issue of deciding where she stands or figuring out where she stands on this issue.

The CHAIRMAN. I think you can ask any question as to where she stands on the issues but as to what the President had in mind when he selected her, that is another question. I do not think that would be appropriate, for her to try to interpret or imagine what the President had in mind when he made this selection.

NOMINATION OF SANDRA DAY O'CONNOR

SEPTEMBER 18 (legislative day, SEPTEMBER 9), 1981.—Ordered to be printed

Mr. THURMOND, from the Committee on the Judiciary, submitted the following

REPORT

together with

ADDITIONAL, SUPPLEMENTAL, AND SEPARATE VIEWS

[To accompany the nomination of Sandra Day O'Connor]

The Committee on the Judiciary, to which was referred the nomination of Sandra Day O'Connor, of Arizona, to be an Associate Justice of the Supreme Court of the United States, having considered the same, by a vote of 17 yeas and 1 vote of "present," reports favorably thereon, with the recommendation that the nomination be confirmed by the U.S. Senate.

The committee has concluded that Judge O'Connor is extraordinarily well-qualified for the position to which she has been nominated.

ADDITIONAL VIEWS OF SENATORS EAST, GRASSLEY AND DENTON

It is the solemn duty of this committee to assist the Senate in its obligation to determine whether to consent to judicial nominations put forward by the President. Never is this duty more solemn than when the nomination is to a seat on the Supreme Court, for the decisions of that Court are among the most binding and far-reaching of all the decisions made by the Federal Government.

If this Committee is to perform its duty to assist the Senate in passing its judgment upon a nomination to the Supreme Court, it must be fully informed on the question of whether or not the nominee would prove to be a good Justice. The committee must know the judicial philosophy of the nominee. It must know the nominee's stand on important constitutional issues, including how the nominee would interpret specific provisions of the Constitution. It must know the nominee's fundamental social and economic philosophy insofar as that philosophy would guide the nominee in interpreting the Constitution. For this knowledge to be valuable, it must extend beyond general assurances and vague discussions.

Last week, the Committee on the Judiciary held 3 days of hearings on the nomination of Sandra Day O'Connor to serve as Associate Justice of the Supreme Court. The Chairman is to be commended for his masterful leadership during those hearings, and for their extent and breadth. But while the hearings granted the committee every opportunity to inquire about Judge O'Connor's judicial philosophy, Judge O'Connor's vague and general answers to the questions posed prevented the Senators from learning much about her judicial philosophy. Many of the questions asked the nominee to provide the same degree of illumination on her constitutional views as has been available on the constitutional views of previous nominees who have had more experience with these issues. These questions would not have impaired the nominee's ability to decide future cases, but Judge O'Connor nevertheless refused to provide responses to many of the questions.

Judge O'Connor's judicial record and published work on constitutional questions is limited. The Senate has no guidance on how she will interpret the Constitution other than the guidance she offered during the 3 days she appeared before the committee. Unfortunately, however, she failed to answer those questions which are most valuable in determining how she will perform as an Associate Justice of the Supreme Court. This failure makes it extremely difficult for this Committee to discharge its duty faithfully with respect to her nomination.

Perhaps more important, this failure may set a dangerous precedent for future nominations to the Supreme Court. It is necessary, therefore, that the record show the dissatisfaction of some members of this Committee with the nature of the statements offered by Judge O'Connor in response to questioning by members of this Committee. The Senate cannot well perform its advice and consent function under such circumstances.

JOHN P. EAST.
CHARLES E. GRASSLEY.
JEREMIAH DENTON.

(2)

SUPPLEMENTAL VIEWS OF SENATOR CHARLES E. GRASSLEY REGARDING THE NOMINATION OF SANDRA DAY O'CONNOR TO BE AN ASSOCIATE JUSTICE OF THE U.S. SUPREME COURT

One of the most important roles a Senator plays is in the advice and consent process which accompanies the executive branch nominations to the Federal judiciary. As a member of the Senate Judiciary Committee, I take this role very seriously. It is in this committee where the record is established regarding the qualification, competence and judicial philosophy of nominees who will perhaps serve for the rest of their lives on the Federal bench. Whether or not a nominee is confirmed will most often depend on what is in the committee record; given that premise it is essential that the record be as complete as possible. It is only because I feel that the record could have been more exhaustive that I file these supplemental views.

I stated at the time of the announcement of Judge O'Connor's nomination that I would keep an open mind until after the hearing process was completed and the record was established. I reviewed all of the testimony and weighed it very carefully before casting my vote in favor of Judge O'Connor's nomination.

I shared the concerns voiced by many of my constituents, that Judge O'Connor might be in favor of abortion on demand. However, during the course of the hearings she answered many questions directed by myself and other committee members to the issue of abortion and those answers along with strong supportive testimony given by active pro-life Arizona State legislators convinced me to vote in favor of her confirmation. My only reservation is that she refused to comment specifically on the *Roe* v. *Wade* decision stating that she was fearful that she may be committing herself to decide a certain way in similar cases which may come before the Supreme Court.

I do not agree with Judge O'Connor that commenting on past Supreme Court decisions is a commitment to hold a certain way on future cases and I feel that in order that we, as Senators, fulfill our duty it is incumbent upon us to discover a nominee's judicial philosophy. An integral part of that philosophy is most likely indicative of the nominee's perception of constitutional law, including specific decisions.

In that we had a very limited number of judicial opinions rendered by Judge O'Connor on constitutional questions it was my hope, by asking specific questions regarding past Supreme Court decisions, that the committee might obtain a clearer understanding of her philosophy. It was never my intent to obtain a commitment from Judge O'Connor that she would hold either to affirm or reverse certain cases in the future. My purpose was to satisfy my questions regarding Judge O'Connor's record in that I felt it was less complete than many other Supreme Court nominees who have had extensive experience either on the Federal bench or in leadership positions in the profession of law.

Public statements and judicial opinions by those past nominees resulted in an abundance of material to draw from in attempting to discover their views on constitutional issues, material which was lacking with regard to Judge O'Connor.

It is with only that reservation that I cast my vote enthusiastically for Judge O'Connor's confirmation. She demonstrated to me that she is and will continue to be a thoroughly competent judge who renders well reasoned, thoughtful opinions and who will be a contributing factor in providing the Supreme Court with new direction, one which will be a reflection of the Reagan administration's philosophy of interpretation of the Constitution not a redrafting thereof.

CHARLES E. GRASSLEY.

SEPARATE VIEWS OF SENATOR JEREMIAH DENTON ON THE NOMINATION OF SANDRA DAY O'CONNOR TO THE U.S. SUPREME COURT

The Senate Judiciary Committee has, without dissent, recommended the confirmation of Mrs. Sandra Day O'Connor as an Associate Justice of the U.S. Supreme Court. Although I am new to the Senate, I am quite uncomfortable with the point of view so prevalent in the O'Connor hearings regarding the proper role of the committee in the confirmation process.

Primarily, I am troubled by the contention that a nominee need not discuss, endorse or criticize specific Supreme Court decisions. The basis for this contention is that such discussion would lead to later disqualification when cases arise that are similar to those that led to the establishment of a particular doctrine.

In my view, acceptance of this argument by the committee has created a particularly unfortunate situation in light of this nominee's past actions with regard to legislation on abortion and the limited number of judicial decisions upon which to determine her views on this and other issues. I had regarded as relatively unimportant the nominee's previous voting record on the abortion issue because Judge O'Connor had indicated that she had had a personal change of heart on the subject of abortion. Thus I had hoped to make a decision about her fitness for office on the basis of answers given to questions posed in the committee hearing. However, the nominee repeatedly declined to answer questions about her view of the legal issues presented in the case of *Roe* v. *Wade*. Relying upon the argument advanced earlier, she stated that, in her opinion, any criticism of that decision would prejudice her with regard to the abortions question.

Others have reasoned that neither this nor any other "single issue" should stand in the way of the confirmation of the nominee. I respectfully disagree with the notion that the rights of unborn human beings represent a single divisive issue that should not overshadow the otherwise excellent credentials of Judge O'Connor. Abortion—the wrongful taking of a human life—is not simply a political issue; the question of when life begins and of how it should be protected at all stages is essentially a civil rights question, and one which I believe is of immense importance.

The denigration of human life by increasingly relying on subjective measures of its "quality" or "meaningfulness" rather than on the principle that all life is God-given is frighteningly reminiscent of Hitlerian ideology. If government by judicial fiat removes the protection of the right to life from a class of individuals—in this case the unborn human being—then, the protection guaranteed others—the handicapped, the aged and the terminally ill—might also be lost in the years to come. Moreover, biomedical research is quickly producing a whole series of new ethical questions about the nature and meaning of

(5)

28

life. The Supreme Court's decision in *Roe* v. *Wade* indicated a judicial willingness to alter fundamental historic protections by defining the concept of "person" so as to permit the elimination of the fetus, even as science was widening the concept of life.

This Nation is currently involved in a dialogue that must not cease until it resolves this fundamental question of human rights. The terrible reality of the debate over abortion is that it has divided households, it has divided friends and it has divided this body. We cannot dismiss the abortion issue when considering judicial nominees simply because the Nation has not reached a consensus. Every public official, and indeed, most citizens should exercise their right to speak out on this issue. It seems that once in every century a nation faces such a pivotal question, and I and millions of others cannot divorce the concept of the right to life from the concept of equal justice under the law.

The Supreme Court in its holding in *Roe* v. *Wade* asserted final authority over the rights of the unborn fetus. Many argue that the Congress and the States have, in the course of a decade, reached a point at which further legislative remedy of abortion excesses is impossible without the approval of the Court. Prospective Justices cannot argue convincingly that the widespread controversy surrounding this issue makes their public pronouncements any more subject to criticism than the statements of the elected officials who must give advice and consent concerning judicial appointments. Prospective Justices might find that their criticism of a particular doctrine could make confirmation a more difficult process, but it does not mean that they will or should find themselves in violation of the statutes, ethical canons and other judicial renderings governing disqualification of Supreme Court Justices.

However, I recognize that others for whom I have enormous respect, including the Chairman of this Committee, agree with Judge O'Connor in her caution in replying to questions that attempt to elicit her views as to the correctness of prior decisions of the Court. Many of those same people are highly respected opponents of the abortion procedure. All the same, I do not believe that this Committee can properly fulfill its duty to the rest of the Senate regarding any judicial nomination when it lacks an accurate estimate of the nominee's position respecting an issue of overriding importance to the general welfare of the United States.

In this context, I personally view the committee's role as a separate and distinct function from the decision which must now be made by the Senate as a whole. I respectfully contend that the committee should serve as an investigatorial body with respect to these nominations—eliciting as thorough and precise responses to specific questions as it possibly can—in order that the rest of the Senate can make a fully informed decision on the nomination. The role of the full Senate I would liken to that of judge—assessing the committee proceedings and judging the nominee on qualifications, experience, integrity and opinions on basic legal questions.

This investigatorial responsibility of the Committee is even more awesome when considered in light of the fact that this appointment is one of life tenure. This is not a four-year, assistant secretary appointment. If confirmed, the nominee will have continuous potential for influencing a critically important issue for an indefinite period.

Given my own position on this most basic question of human life, and given the reluctance of Judge O'Connor to address the legal question of abortion in a forthright manner, I could not, in my perceived role as investigator, assent on hope nor dissent on uncertainty, with respect to my vote in the Committee.

My vote on the floor of the Senate may well be different because of the way I view my role as Committee member specifically and Senator generally—and for some other reasons. As a Senator on the floor, I do not feel obliged to restrict my judgment on the nominee to what was revealed within the Committee hearings.

But in the final analysis, I believe the Committee on the Judiciary may have abrogated, in large measure, part of the responsibility of the Senate's constitutional role with respect to this most important nomination.

JEREMIAH DENTON,
U.S. Senator.

2

JUSTICE ANTONIN SCALIA AND CHIEF JUSTICE WILLIAM REHNQUIST

With the retirement of Chief Justice Warren Burger, President Ronald Reagan simultaneously nominated then-Associate Justice William Rehnquist to the position of Chief Justice and Antonin Scalia to the position Associate Justice. Despite abortion playing a pivotal role in the confirmation of Reagan's first Supreme Court appointee--Sandra Day O'Connor--the Senate's confirmation of Rehnquist and Scalia glossed over abortion in favor of other topics of debate.

Although William Rehnquist was already on the Court, and so his confirmation would not change the Court's ideological composition, the American public viewed the ascension of Rehnquist to the most powerful position on the Court as, at the very least, a gesture symbolic of the Reagan administration's conservative agenda. Indeed, Rehnquist's change in title had the potential to be truly significant; the Chief Justice's authority to assign opinions to particular Justices and the subtle leadership role of the Chief Justice give the Chief Justice slightly more ability to direct the Court than the Associate Justices. The Senators did ask Rehnquist innocuous questions about the leadership role of the Chief Justice, yet none of them inquired about the direction in which Rehnquist--if given an opportunity--would steer the Court on the privacy issue.

Some members of the Senate did take the opportunity offered by the confirmation hearings to revisit some of the issues raised in Rehnquist's original confirmation to the Court and some of the controversy surrounding his tenure as Associate Justice. Specifically, Senators Biden and Kennedy made repeated reference to allegations that Rehnquist harassed voters at an Arizona polling place during the elections held in 1960; restrictive covenants on homes that he had purchased in Vermont and Arizona; his failure to recuse himself from a case with which he had been involved while he was an Assistant Attorney General in the Nixon Justice Department; and his reputation as the "lone dissenter" on the Court. Remarkably, despite their open disapproval of Rehnquist's constitutional jurisprudence, Rehnquist's critics failed to question him closely on even theoretical issues of precedent, *stare decisis*, or privacy, much less *Roe v. Wade* itself.

Antonin Scalia's confirmation was far less complicated than Rehnquist's. In fact, the Judiciary Committee limited its report to a short, favorable paragraph; similarly, Senate "debate" on the confirmation was limited to praise for Scalia's past performance and hopes for his success. Overall, the remarks on the Senate floor show less concern over Scalia's ideology or judicial philosophy than over his ethnic background (Scalia became the first Italian-American to sit on the Supreme Court).

While it might be expected that Scalia's devout Catholicism and his strong ties to the Federalist Society and other conservative interests would naturally tend to focus Senate questioning and testimony on the abortion issue, this was not the case. During the confirmation hearings, Scalia was asked whether he would have to recuse himself from a case involving abortion because of his strong religious beliefs. Scalia responded in the negative, arguing that recusal was appropriate only if the judge or Justice was so closely tied to an issue that he or she could not apply the Constitution in an impartial manner. The Senators chose not to pursue the issue further. Moreover, the witnesses at the hearings--including women's groups who opposed Scalia--touched only briefly, if at all, on the abortion issue. The concern of women's groups, instead, was Scalia's conservative approach to sex discrimination.

Similarly, Scalia neatly avoided any hard questioning on the issue of *stare decisis*. He confined his remarks on the issue to the rather vague statement that some precedents should be given more weight than others. He declined to elaborate, explaining that his answer had bearing on a case he was currently hearing. The Senate accepted this response and left the issue alone.

The content and style of these "twin" confirmation hearings were decidedly different. For Rehnquist, the Senators appeared to shift all attention away from the usual list of questions and topics, focusing instead--with single-minded ferocity--on Rehnquist's property holdings and his decisions while on the Court. For Scalia, on the other hand, the Senators brought up hard and controversial issues, but failed to pursue definitive answers with any real vigor. While the formulas were different, the bottom lines were identical: the confirmations of William Rehnquist and Antonin Scalia lacked the expected abortion-related vitriol.

Justice Antonin Scalia and
Chief Justice William Rehnquist
Documents

22 Weekly Comp. Pres. Doc. 1065
Aug. 9, 1986

United States Supreme Court Nominations

My fellow Americans:

Shakespeare's reminder that "the world is full of ornament" and the "outward shows" are "least themselves" has always had a special relevance for the political world, but it was especially so last week here in Washington.

The United States Senate began hearings on the nominations of William Rehnquist and Antonin Scalia, men I've named to the position of Chief Justice of the Supreme Court and Associate Justice of the Court. These hearings are a healthy process, mandated by the Constitution. Even though they produce a lot of outward show and ornament, they provide the American people with an opportunity to evaluate for themselves the quality of a President's appointments.

To be sure, there were many serious allegations by political opponents of Justice Rehnquist and Judge Scalia. One Democratic Senator announced he would vote against Justice Rehnquist even before the hearings started. There were dark hints about what might be found in documents Judge Rehnquist wrote while a Justice Department official many years ago. To deal with these unfounded charges, I took the unusual step of permitting the Senate committee to see the documents themselves. Of course, there was nothing there but legal analyses and other routine communications. The hysterical charges of coverup and stonewalling were revealed for what they were: political posturing. I was sorry to have to release these documents, but Supreme Court nominations are so important that I did not want my nominees to enter upon their responsibilities under any cloud. And so, I was delighted that when all was said and done our nominees emerged unscathed from last week's hearings.

Justice Rehnquist, recognized even during his early years as a brilliant mind, graduated first in his class from Stanford Law School. He clerked for the Supreme Court, an early mark of distinction in any legal career. He then returned to Arizona to practice law, coming back to Washington some years later to serve as an Assistant Attorney General in the Department of Justice. Most important, for the past 15 years he has served as a Justice of the Supreme Court with extraordinary diligence and craftsmanship. His opinions are renowned for their clarity of reasoning and precision of expression. And when his colleagues on the Supreme Court learned that I would nominate Justice Rehnquist to preside as Chief Justice, they were unanimous in expressing pleasure and approval. It's hard to imagine higher praise for anyone in the legal profession than that.

Turning to Judge Antonin Scalia, he's regarded in the legal profession as a superb jurist, a first-class intellect, and a warm and persuasive person. He has served in the Department of Justice, taught law at the University of Chicago and the University of Virginia, and served since 1982 as a judge on the U.S. Court of Appeals here in the District of Columbia. The American Bar Association gave Judge Scalia, as they gave Justice Rehnquist, their highest rating. I might add that as the father of nine children Judge Scalia holds family values in high esteem. And I was especially delighted with his nomination, because Judge Scalia is the first Italian-American in history to be named to the Supreme Court.

Beyond their undoubted legal qualifications, Justice Rehnquist and Judge Scalia embody a certain approach to the law, an approach that as your President I consider it my duty to endorse, indeed to insist upon.

The background here is important. You see, during the last few election campaigns, one of the principal points I made to the American people was the need for a real change in the makeup of the Federal judiciary. I pointed out that too many judges were taking upon themselves the prerogatives of elected officials. Instead of interpreting the law according to the intent of the Constitution and the Congress, they were simply using the courts to strike down laws that displeased them politically or philosophically. I argued the need for judges who would interpret law, not make it. The people, through their elected representatives, make our laws; and the people deserve to have these laws enforced as they were written.

Of course this upsets those who disagree with me politically, and I have a lurking suspicion that politics had more than a little to do with some of the tactics used against Justice Rehnquist. But I'm confident that, mindful of their superb legal qualifications, the Senate will confirm Justice Rehnquist and Judge Scalia. And I can assure you: We will appoint more judges like them to the Federal bench. If I may quote Shakespeare again now that the political commotion of the confirmation hearings is over: "All's well that ends well."

S. Hrg. 99-1064

NOMINATION OF JUDGE ANTONIN SCALIA

HEARINGS

BEFORE THE

COMMITTEE ON THE JUDICIARY
UNITED STATES SENATE

NINETY-NINTH CONGRESS

SECOND SESSION

ON THE

NOMINATION OF JUDGE ANTONIN SCALIA, TO BE ASSOCIATE JUSTICE
OF THE SUPREME COURT OF THE UNITED STATES

AUGUST 5 AND 6, 1986

Serial No. J-99-119

Printed for the use of the Committee on the Judiciary

U.S. GOVERNMENT PRINTING OFFICE

66-852 O   WASHINGTON : 1987

For sale by the Superintendent of Documents, Congressional Sales Office
U.S. Government Printing Office, Washington, DC 20402

The CHAIRMAN. The distinguished Senator from Massachusetts.

Senator KENNEDY. Thank you, Mr. Chairman.

Our ranking Member, Senator Biden, is currently on the floor with the introduction of legislation dealing with drug regulation, and he will be over here very shortly. But I will proceed, if I might.

Judge Scalia, if you were confirmed, do you expect to overrule the *Roe* v. *Wade?*

Judge SCALIA. Excuse me?

Senator KENNEDY. Do you expect to overrule the *Roe* v. *Wade* Supreme Court decision if you are confirmed?

Judge SCALIA. Senator, I do not think it would be proper for me to answer that question.

The CHAIRMAN. I agree with you. I do not think it is proper to ask any question that he has to act on or may have to act on.

Judge SCALIA. I mean, if I can say why. Let us assume that I have people arguing before me to do it or not to do it. I think it is quite a thing to be arguing to somebody who you know has made a representation in the course of his confirmation hearings, and that is, by way of condition to his being confirmed, that he will do this or do that. I think I would be in a very bad position to adjudicate the case without being accused of having a less than impartial view of the matter.

Senator KENNEDY. There have been at least some reports that that was one of the considerations in your nomination. There are a lot of other, clearly, strengths which you bring to your own qualifications. But I am interested in what precedence you put on that decision being on the lawbooks. I am interested in your own concept in stare decisis. Do you believe in it? What is it going to take to overrule an existing Supreme Court decision?

Judge SCALIA. As you know, Senator, they are sometimes overruled.

Senator KENNEDY. I am interested in your view.

Judge SCALIA. My view is that they are sometimes overruled. And I think that——

Senator KENNEDY. But what weight do you give them?

Judge SCALIA [continuing]. I will not say that I will never overrule prior Supreme Court precedent.

Senator KENNEDY. Well, what weight do you give the precedents of the Supreme Court? Are they given any weight? Are they given some weight? Are they given a lot of weight? Or does it depend on your view——

Judge SCALIA. It does not depend on my view. It depends on the nature of the precedent, the nature of the issue.

Let us assume that somebody runs in from Princeton University, and on the basis of the latest historical research, he or she has discovered a lost document which shows that it was never intended that the Supreme Court should have the authority to declare a statute unconstitutional. I would not necessarily reverse *Marbury* v. *Madison* on the basis of something like that.

To some extent, Government even at the Supreme Court level is a practical exercise. There are some things that are done, and when they are done, they are done and you move on. Now, which of those you think are so woven in the fabric of law that mistakes made are too late to correct, and which are not, that is a difficult question to answer. It can only be answered in the context of a particular case, and I do not think that I should answer anything in the context of a particular case.

Senator KENNEDY. Well, do I understand that your answer with regard to Supreme Court decisions is that some of them are more powerful, more significant, than others in terms of how you would view in overruling them or overturning them?

Judge SCALIA. Yes, I think so, Senator. May I supplement——

Senator KENNEDY. And you are not prepared on this issue to say where that decision comes out, as I understand it?

Judge SCALIA. That is right, Senator. And maybe I can be a little more forthcoming in response to your first question.

As you followed it up, you said that some thought that that is why I was going onto the Court.

I assure you, I have no agenda. I am not going onto the Court with a list of things that I want to do. My only agenda is to be a good judge. I decide the cases brought before me. And I try to decide them according to the law as best as I can figure it out. But it is not a programmatic matter, as far as I am concerned.

Senator KENNEDY. Well, that is part of this whole process, giving you an opportunity to speak to those questions. But it is also part of this process to find out what kind of relevancy you give to previous Court decisions, and how significant they are in terms of your own legal experience, and when they might be overturned and when they might not be.

And as I gather from your answer, that is kind of a variable, that some have stronger standing than others, and that that is your view. But in terms of that particular view, you are not prepared to indicate, at least in that case, in the *Roe* v. *Wade* case, where you come out, as to whether you feel that that is a strong precedent or a weak precedent.

But evidently you believe that some precedents are weaker and some are stronger in the doctrine of stare decisis.

Judge SCALIA. That is right, sir. And nobody arguing that case before me should think that he is arguing to somebody who has his mind made up either way.

Senator KENNEDY. Well, then, what is the relevance of the previous decision? Does that have any weight in your mind?

Judge SCALIA. Of course.

Senator KENNEDY. Well, could you tell us how much?

Judge SCALIA. That is the question you asked earlier, Senator. And that is precisely the question——

Senator KENNEDY. I know it.

The CHAIRMAN. Thank you.

The distinguished Senator from Maryland.

Senator MATHIAS. Thank you, Mr. Chairman.

Judge Scalia, as you well know, one of the special qualities a judge must have is the ability to put aside very deeply held personal beliefs in order to apply the law and the Constitution fairly and equitably to every litigant who stands before him.

Your exchange with Senator Kennedy on the subject of *Roe* v. *Wade* suggests an area where you have written—and I am not trying now to lead you down the pathways of the future. We will look back to the road of the past.

You have written on the subject of *Roe* v. *Wade,* and while I do not pretend to be an expert on every word you have written, I believe you have expressed doubts about that decision, both on moral as well as jurisprudential grounds.

Judge SCALIA. I am not sure the latter is true, Senator. I think I may have criticized the decision, but I do not recall passing moral judgment on the issue.

But I agree with your opening statement, that one of the primary qualifications for a judge is to set aside personal views.

Senator MATHIAS. However it may be with your article on *Roe* v. *Wade,* the problem remains. What does a judge do about a very deeply held personal position, a personal moral conviction, which may be pertinent to a matter before the Court?

Judge SCALIA. Well, Senator, one of the moral obligations that a judge has is the obligation to live in a democratic society and to be bound by the determinations of that democratic society. If he feels that he cannot be, then he should not be sitting as a judge.

There are doubtless laws on the books apart from abortion that I might not agree with, that I might think are misguided, perhaps some that I might even think in the largest sense are immoral in the results that they produce. In no way would I let that influence my determination of how they apply. And if indeed I felt that I could not separate my repugnance for the law from my impartial judgment of what the Constitution permits the society to do, I would recuse myself from the case.

Senator MATHIAS. I had a similar conversation with Judge Noonan of the ninth circuit at the time his nomination was before this committee. He has very strong feeling on the abortion question. But he came out at about the position that you have just expressed, that it would be necessary, if not desirable, for him to recuse himself on cases that touched so closely on that issue in which he had been an advocate, a strong spokesman working in that field.

Judge SCALIA. That is not quite what I said, Senator. I did not say that I would recuse myself in the——

Senator MATHIAS. Well, that is where I wanted to press you. How would you deal with the problem?

Judge SCALIA. I do not know what Judge Noonan told you. Judge Noonan had indeed written considerably in the field and had been one of the leading advocates.

Senator MATHIAS. He was a strong activist and was affiliated with a number of activist organizations.

Judge SCALIA. I do not think I fall into that category.

Senator MATHIAS. Under what circumstances would you think a judge who had not had that kind of a background should recuse himself?

Judge SCALIA. Only where he himself is personally convinced that he cannot decide the question impartially because he feels so strongly about the morality of the issue. And it is not at all unusual for Justices to have to confront such cases. *United States* v. *Reynolds,* for example, which held that it was constitutional for a State to prohibit bigamy. Now, that was certainly a moral issue. The issue of monogamy for the Justices sitting on that case. They obviously—at least many of them must have had religious views about the matter and they did not feel it necessary, those who had those views, to disqualify themselves. And I do not think that any judge has to unless he or she is personally convinced that the issue has so beclouded his or her judgment that the Constitution would not be applied impartially.

I do not intend to disqualify myself except where that is the case, as far as the type of question you ask about is concerned.

Senator MATHIAS. When you were with us in 1982, you said:

I would disqualify myself in any case in which I believe my connection with one of the litigants, or any other circumstances, would cause my judgment to be distorted in favor of one of the parties. I would further disqualify myself if the situation arose in which even though my judgment would not be distorted, a reasonable person would believe that my judgment would be distorted. That does not mean anyone in the world but a reasonable person.

Judge SCALIA. That is right.

Senator MATHIAS. Is that the position that you will carry with you from the court of appeals to the Supreme Court?

Judge SCALIA. Yes, it is, Senator. And what I am further saying is that I do not think that reasonable people think that the moral views that judges may hold on one piece of legislation or one decision or another so automatically beclouds their judgment that they must disqualify themselves.

I do not think that the records of the Supreme Court could possibly be read to establish that as the basis of disqualification on bigamy, on capital punishment, on an enormous number of things that men and women on the Court have had strong moral views doubtless and have sat nonetheless.

Senator MATHIAS. Now, you very carefully, and I think properly, limited this problem by saying that does not mean anybody in the world but a reasonable person.

But if a reasonable litigant actually believed that your judgment would be distorted because of some strong personal bias or belief, would that dissuade you from sitting on a case?

Judge SCALIA. I think the statute reads that way, Senator. I have the statute somewhere. I am quite sure that the way you put it is about the way the statute reads, requiring disqualification. If I may, title 28, United States Code, section 455: "Any justice, judge or magistrate of the United States shall disqualify himself in any proceeding in which his impartiality might reasonably be questioned."

National Organization for Women, Inc.

1401 New York Avenue, N.W., Suite 800 • Washington, D.C. 20005-2102 • (202) 347-2279

Testimony of
Eleanor Cutri Smeal
President, of the National Organization for Women

On Behalf of the National Organization for Women
and the National Women's Political Caucus

Before the Senate Committee on the Judiciary
on the Nomination of Antonin Scalia for Associate Justice
August 5, 1986

III. Philosophical Opposition to Constitutional Rights of
Individuals

While Judge Scalia's record in these cases is of grave
concern to NOW, we are equally appalled by his philosophical
opposition to constitutionally guaranteed rights for individuals.

His notion that the rights of individuals are only those
which the majority confers, and not guaranteed by the
Constitution regardless of majority views, would, if it became
the dominant view, serve to undermine the Constitution and in
particular the Bill of Rights which he is sworn to protect and
defend.

During a public discussion sponsored by the American
Enterprise Institute, Judge Scalia, at that time a visiting
scholar for the Institute, made crystal clear his view not only
on abortion rights but individual Constitutional rights in
general:

> In the abortion situation, for example, what right
> exists - the right of the woman who wants an abortion to
> have one, or the right of the unborn child not to be
> aborted? In the past that was considered to be a
> societal decision that would be made through the
> democratic process. But now the courts have shown
> themselves willing to make that decision for us ...
> The courts' expansion stems, in part, from their
> function of deciding what are constitutional rights.
> Much of their activity is in that area, and I think they
> have gone too far. They have found rights where society
> never believed they existed.
> The courts have enforced other rights, so-called, on
> which there is no societal agreement, from the abortion
> cases, at one extreme, to school dress codes and things
> of that sort. There is no national consensus about
> those things and there never has been. The courts have
> no business being there. That is one of the problems;
> they are calling rights things which we do not all agree
> on.

Mr. Chairperson, members of the Committee, I cannot convey adequately the alarm with which the National Organization for Women greeted these words by Judge Scalia.

The very notion that rights are determined by consensus has to rank among the most appalling concepts we have ever encountered.

To begin with, consensus means agreement by almost everyone, if not everyone. Given the definition, I am sure we can all agree that there are few things in our national life in which we have consensus, in light of the broad diversity and make-up of American society.

Just how large a majority must Judge Scalia have to confront in order to deem that there is a consensus on a given question? Will a simple majority suffice? Is a 74 percent majority, enormous by most standards, large enough to convince him?

As we have submitted earlier to this Committee, the latest public opinion poll on the question of abortion shows that 74 percent of Americans support the Supreme Court's 1973 ruling on legalized abortion.

We doubt, however, that this is the real issue for Judge Scalia, anymore than it is the real issue for the National Organization for Women.

NOW believes that women have the right to abortion, as a matter of privacy and of individual rights, regardless of what public opinion polls show.

And we believe Judge Scalia holds the view that no such right exists, regardless of what public opinion polls show. In fact the Reagan Administration has made it abundantly clear that hostility to the Roe v. Wade decision is part of the screening process for nomination to the federal judiciary at all levels.

We would submit that unless the Reagan Administration was totally confident of Judge Scalia's views on abortion rights, his name would not be before this Committee. Period.

But in addition to the abortion issue, which is of crucial importance to our organization, we would ask this Committee to examine closely Judge Scalia's concern that the courts "are calling rights things which we do not all agree on."

Is this simply another way of stating Justice Rehnquist's appalling claim that "in the long run it is the majority who will determine what the constitutional rights of the minority are."

Again, I would refer the Committee to Judge Scalia's standards of general societal agreement and national consensus. As we mentioned earlier the latest public opinion poll on the question of judicial response to racial and sex discrimination shows that 63 percent of Americans believe our judges should be committed to equal rights for women and minorities. Again, is this, a larger majority than elected Ronald Reagan President, large enough to satisfy Judge Scalia's standards?

I believe we know the answer to that, and I believe this Committee does also.

Judge Scalia does not believe the rights of women and minorities are determined by majority opinion any more than we do. Either the Constitution and the laws of our nation confer these rights or they do not, regardless of shifting political majorities.

The fact that the majority now supports these rights is simply a credit to the people of this nation that at long last we have come to recognize, as a people, that in order to remain true to our ideals, we must in fact constantly pursue "liberty and justice for all."

The people of this nation have come to the realization that these rights exist.

We believe it is evidence of Judge Scalia's extremist viewpoint on Constitutional rights that he refuses to concede their existence.

This is not testimony to his independence and intelligence as a jurist. It is testimony to his unfitness to preside as one of a nine-member panel whose job it is to defend Constitutional rights.

In line with Judge Scalia's pronouncements on "national consensus," "societal agreement," and abortion in the AEI panel discussion, he also said that in drawing the line in the area of constitutional rights, "it would fall short of making fundamental, social determinations that ought to be made through the democratic process, but that the society has not yet made. I think the Court has done that in a number of recent cases. In the busing cases ... there was no need for the courts to say that the inevitable remedy for unlawful segregation is busing. Many other remedies might have been applied. It was not necessary for the courts to step in and say what must be done, especially in the teeth of an apparent societal determination that the costs are too high in terms of other values of the society."

Now, Judge Scalia didn't offer in that discussion any suggestions as to what those "many other remedies" might be, only that he was sure they existed.

What he was really saying, we know from both experience and from other of his writings, is that the Court is only there to rule, not to provide remedies for injustice, and that if the executive and legislative branches choose not to enforce a ruling, then so be it -- regardless of how abominable the injustice.

Does anyone, including Judge Scalia, seriously believe that Southern school systems, not to mention school systems elsewhere, as well as public accommodations in the South, would really have integrated on their own if the Court had not forced enforcement of its ruling?

Does anyone, including Judge Scalia, seriously believe that the majority in this instance would not have continued to deny the black minority in this nation its rights if that majority thought it could get away with it?

Now, in that same discussion which, incidentally, was titled, "An Imperial Judiciary: Fact or Myth?", Judge Scalia went on to say that the Court doesn't always have to "go along with the consensus of the day. The Court may find that the traditional consensus of the society is against the current consensus. If that is the case, then the Court overrides the present beliefs of society on the basis of its historical beliefs. I can understand that."

"But when neither history nor current social perception demands that something be called unlawful, I cannot understand how the Court can find it to be so."

You should know that when confronted with the suggestion that both the traditional consensus and the contemporary consensus were against school desegregation in 1954, Judge Scalia replied that he didn't "believe that is true. Most of the country did not consider separate black schools proper in 1954."

Considering the history of the decade that followed the Brown v. Board of Education, I think we can say with confidence that Martin Luther King, Jr. would have been surprised to learn this from Judge Scalia.

While it is somewhat comforting to know that Judge Scalia ended the discussion of Brown v. Board of Education with the comment that, "In any event, the results of that decision have been very good," we are still left more than a little confused. The results of that decision, after all, also included the remedy of busing, and Judge Scalia doesn't believe the Court should order remedies.

We also find a great deal of danger in Judge Scalia's belief that it is proper for the Court to override the present beliefs of society on the basis of its historical beliefs.

It is staggering to contemplate the list of contemporary beliefs that would be at risk in the hands of a Justice Scalia, certainly sex and racial discrimination being just two areas of belief.

Just as frightening is the fact that Judge Scalia made no provision for the reverse: that it is proper for the Court to override historical beliefs on the basis of the present beliefs of society.

These are just a few instances in which Judge Scalia's logic falls apart upon analysis.

We would ask the Committee also to consider the following commentary from an article written by Judge Scalia in 1980, titled "The Judges are Coming", and reprinted in the Congressional Record of July 21, 1980, at the request of former Congressman Daniel Crane of Illinois:

> Thus, the Congress passes a law requiring the Department of Health, Education and Welfare to assure the elimination of "sex discrimination" in federally assisted educational programs. Everyone applauds. Who, after all, can be in favor of sex discrimination? It soon develops, however (as Congress knew when it passed the law), that "elimination of sex discrimination" is only a slogan. To some, it means little more than equal job opportunity and equal pay for equal work. To others, it includes also the expenditure of equal funds on men's and women's sports; or even the prohibition of all-male or all-female team sports; and to still others (quite seriously) the elimination of father-son dinners, unisex dorms or even unisex toilets. Who is to tell us, then, what the Congress meant - when in point of fact it did not know what it meant, and quite obviously did not want to know for fear of antagonizing one or the other side of the sexual revolution? The answer, of course, is the courts. In lawsuits challenging HEW's actions, they will ultimately develop for us a whole body of law concerning sex discrimination on the basis of virtually no guidance from our elected representatives in Congress.

In this case, Judge Scalia conveniently overlooks the fact that federal regulations were written and enforced by the Department of Health, Education and Welfare to enforce the provisions of Title IX of the Civil Rights Act. These regulations were based upon the public hearings and input and the legislative history of the Act.

He chooses to ignore that these regulations were enacted with a significant measure of success creating a substantial body of experience for Title IX. And, although many institutions of higher learning in our nation did not like being told they could not discriminate on the basis of sex, and still others spent a great deal of time trying to skirt the law, they knew what the regulations said and what they were legally required to do.

The gutting of Title IX was not done by a faint-hearted Congress. It was done by an executive branch that thought the government should be allowed to fund discrimination and that went to the Court to get a ruling allowing it to do so.

Ultimately, it was the Supreme Court that reversed the remedial effects of Title IX: in the face of clear Congressional intent to eliminate sex discrimination in education; in the face of a legislative and regulatory history that showed over a decade of progress in this area; and in the face of majority support in this nation for the elimination of sex discrimination in education.

Mr. Chairperson, members of the Committee, Judge Scalia has demonstrated that he is more than happy to go on the record with his beliefs about sex discrimination and about racial discrimination, even though he actually has had few opportunities to rule in these areas as a Judge.

He could not be more clear in his belief that these areas of law are, at best, a nuisance, and at worst, unworthy of his consideration.

We ask this committee, on behalf of the women of this nation and on behalf of the minority members of our society to reject a nominee to the U.S. Supreme Court who has no intention of using the Constitution and laws of this nation to help move this country toward equal rights and equal opportunities for all its citizens. In fact, reviewing his record and writings on affirmative action, discrimination law and individual rights, he is willing to use the Constitution to obstruct the advancement of equal rights.

We ask this Committee to reject the nomination of Antonin Scalia as Associate Justice of our U.S. Supreme Court.

Thank you.

NOMINATION OF ANTONIN SCALIA TO BE ASSOCIATE JUSTICE OF THE UNITED STATES SUPREME COURT

SEPTEMBER 8, 1986.—Ordered to be printed

Mr. THURMOND, from the Committee on the Judiciary, submitted the following

REPORT

The Committee on the Judiciary, to which was referred the nomination of Antonin Scalia, of Virginia, to be an Associate Justice of the Supreme Court of the United States, having considered the same, by a unanimous vote of 18 yeas, reports favorably thereon, with the recommendation that the nomination be confirmed by the U.S. Senate.

The Committee has concluded that Judge Scalia is exceptionally well qualified for the position to which he has been nominated.

O

71-119 O

S. Hrg. 99 1067

NOMINATION OF JUSTICE WILLIAM HUBBS REHNQUIST

HEARINGS

BEFORE THE

COMMITTEE ON THE JUDICIARY
UNITED STATES SENATE

NINETY-NINTH CONGRESS

SECOND SESSION

ON THE

NOMINATION OF JUSTICE WILLIAM HUBBS REHNQUIST TO BE CHIEF
JUSTICE OF THE UNITED STATES

JULY 29, 30, 31, AND AUGUST 1, 1986

Serial No. J-99-118

Printed for the use of the Committee on the Judiciary

American Bar Association

July 29, 1986

Honorable Strom Thurmond
    Chairman
Committee on the Judiciary
United States Senate
Washington, D.C.   20510

Dear Mr. Chairman:

  This letter is in response to the invitation
to the Standing Committee on Federal Judiciary of the
American Bar Association (the "Committee") to submit
its opinion regarding the nomination of the Honorable
William Hubbs Rehnquist of Washington, D.C. to be
Chief Justice of the United States.

  The Committee's investigation of Justice
Rehnquist covered his professional competence,
judicial temperament and integrity. Because the
nominee is a sitting Justice of the Supreme Court and
is being nominated for the position of Chief Justice,
we were particularly interested in his administrative
abilities, leadership qualities and collegiality.
Consistent with its long standing tradition, the
Committee has not concerned itself with Justice
Rehnquist's general political ideology or his views on
issues except to the extent that such matters might
bear on judicial temperament and integrity.

  The Committee's investigation of Justice
Rehnquist included the following inquiries:

  (1) Members of the Committee interviewed all
of the Associate Justices of the Supreme Court and a
large number of other federal and state judges
throughout the United States.

  (2) Committee members interviewed a cross
section of practicing lawyers throughout the United
States.

STANDING COMMITTEE ON FEDERAL JUDICIARY
750 NORTH LAKE SHORE DRIVE • CHICAGO, ILLINOIS 60611 • TELEPHONE (312) 988-5000

(3) Committee members interviewed many deans and faculty members of law schools throughout the country, including a number of constitutional and Supreme Court scholars.

(4) A group of practicing attorneys reviewed approximately 200 of the written opinions authored by Justice Rehnquist.

(5) Three members of the Committee interviewed Justice Rehnquist.

Professional Background

Justice Rehnquist's career has included service as a practicing lawyer, an Assistant Attorney General with the United States Department of Justice, and as an Associate Justice of the United States Supreme Court. He received A.B. and M.A. degrees from Stanford University in 1948, an M.A. degree from Harvard University in 1949, and an LL.B. from Stanford Law School in 1952. He was a distinguished student in the law school, ranking first in his class. His military experience includes service as a non-commissioned officer in the U.S. Army Air Force during the period from 1943 to 1946.

Justice Rehnquist served as a law clerk to Associate Justice Robert H. Jackson of the Supreme Court of the United States from 1952 to 1953. He then commenced the private practice of law in Phoenix, Arizona. From 1953 to 1955 he was an associate in the firm of Evans, Kitchel & Jencks. During 1956 and 1957 he was a partner in the firm of Ragan & Rehnquist and from 1957 to 1960 he was a partner in the firm of Cunningham, Carson & Messenger. In 1960 he formed with James Powers the Phoenix firm of Powers & Rehnquist, where he practiced until 1969. From 1969 to 1971 he was an Assistant Attorney General, Office of Legal Counsel, United States Department of Justice in Washington, D.C. In 1971 he was nominated by President Nixon as Associate Justice of the United States Supreme Court, and this nomination was confirmed by the Senate in that year.

Through interviews of those who worked with Justice Rehnquist during various stages of his professional career, both prior and subsequent to his appointment to the United States Supreme Court, the Committee learned that he has demonstrated a high degree of competence and integrity, and has displayed excellent judicial temperament.

Honorable Strom Thurmond   -3-   July 29, 1986

Interviews with Judges

In its investigation, the Committee interviewed over 300 persons, including all of the current Associate Justices of the Supreme Court, and more than 180 federal and state judges. Members of the judiciary who know him describe him as "a true scholar, collegial, genial and low key," "unbelievably brilliant," "a very capable individual in every respect". Generally, judges across the country who have become familiar with Justice Rehnquist have expressed admiration and respect for him as an able, hard working, conscientious individual. On the whole, the judicial community was high in its praise of Justice Rehnquist's abilities and qualifications. Of great importance, he enjoys the respect and esteem of his colleagues on the Court.

Interviews with Lawyers

The Committee contacted approximately 65 practicing lawyers throughout the United States. We interviewed a cross section of the legal community, including women and minority lawyers. Many who know Justice Rehnquist, including many who disagree with him politically and philosophically, speak of warm admiration for him and describe him as "very talented," "a bright and able man," "always well prepared," and one who "brings out the best in people and will facilitate the work of the Court."

Interviews with Deans and Professors of Law

The Committee spoke to more than 50 deans and faculty members of a number of law schools throughout the country. Some of these have known Justice Rehnquist personally. We found that he has visited and delivered speeches at several of the law schools. Many of these individuals spoke highly of his writing and analytical ability. The vast majority had strong praise for his professional qualifications.

Survey of Justice Rehnquist's Opinions

Approximately 200 of Justice Rehnquist's opinions were examined for the Committee by a group of practicing attorneys. From that review it can be concluded that the Justice's legal analysis and writing ability are of the highest quality.

Honorable Strom Thurmond   -4-   July 29, 1986

Interview with Justice Rehnquist

Justice Rehnquist was interviewed by three members of the Committee. The Committee members have found him to be extremely intelligent, articulate, friendly, and committed to the fair and proper administration of justice. He has demonstrated outstanding qualities as a jurist, and is approaching the position of Chief Justice with enthusiasm, determination and dedication.

Based on the investigation described above, the Committee unanimously has found that Justice Rehnquist meets the highest standards of professional competence, judicial temperament and integrity, is among the best available for appointment as Chief Justice of the United States, and is entitled to the Committee's highest evaluation of the nominees to the Supreme Court -- Well Qualified.

This report is being filed at the commencement of the Senate Judiciary Committee's hearing. We will review our report at the conclusion of the hearings, and notify you if any circumstances have developed that may require modification of our views.

Respectfully submitted,

ROBERT B. FISKE, JR.
Chairman

The CHAIRMAN. Justice Rehnquist, in 1976, an article which you authored entitled, "The Notion of a Living Constitution," appeared in the May 1976 edition of the Texas Law Review. This article addressed the issue of how the Constitution is to be interpreted by judges.

In recent years, the debate on this subject has increased, and a number of questions have been raised, such as: Are the words of the Constitution to be narrowly construed? What weight is to be given to the intent of the framers of the Constitution? Should the instrument be interpreted to conform with or adjust to conventional societal behavior or attitudes, and so forth.

Of course, a judge's philosophy on this type of issue obviously has a direct and substantial bearing on his or her decision.

Justice Rehnquist, would you please briefly summarize for the committee your views concerning constitutional interpretation by the judiciary?

Justice REHNQUIST. Mr. Chairman, I will certainly do the best I can within the limits of the constraints which I feel are on me.

As a sitting Justice of the Court, I may certainly refer to cases and perhaps try to describe them from memory, and I feel I can also perhaps, where I am informed, speak in fairly general terms. But I could not, of course, express any view on a question that might come before the Court or I could not attempt to say, well, you know, this case that was decided in 1980 will soon be interpreted, or maybe later be interpreted to mean such and such.

This may seem an overly simplistic answer to your question, but it is the kind of question that has to be answered either very shortly or ad infinitum because there are so many nuances.

I think a judge has the obligation, when sitting in a Federal system like ours under a written Constitution, to attempt to use every bit of information and every method he can in order to find out what the Constitution means.

Certainly a large part of this is the written word that the framers used, not the undisclosed intentions of the framers, but the words that they used.

Other useful things are the previous decisions of the Court which have always represented a decision by nine people—or at least nine since some time in the 1830's—who have taken the same oath of office that the then-sitting Justice had, and who presumably have done their best to figure out what it means.

And I think that is as good a short answer as I can give you.

The CHAIRMAN. Justice Rehnquist, a fundamental principle of American judicial review is respect for precedent, for the doctrine of stare decisis. This doctrine promotes certainty in the administration of the law, and yet at least 182 times in its history, the Supreme Court has overruled one or more of its precedents. More than half of these overruling opinions have been issued since 1950. Actually, 96 since 1950.

Justice Rehnquist, would you tell the committee what factors you believe attribute to this increase in overruling previous opinions?

Justice REHNQUIST. I will certainly venture my opinion, Mr. Chairman, although I have not done the research that I would like to do in order to make a more careful answer.

I think the biggest thing about the caseload of the Supreme Court in 1950 and the caseload today is the vast increase in the number of decisions involving constitutional questions. The principle followed by the Court following Justice Brandeis' opinion, I believe, in either the *Ashwander* or the *Burnett* case, is that stare decisis is a very fine rule of law, and it should virtually be unanimously adhered to when you are talking about construing a statute. But when you are talking about construing a provision of the Constitution where Congress cannot come back and change it if it feels the Court has made a mistake, then there is more latitude for overruling precedent.

I think that probably the reason there have been so many more overrulings since 1950 is that a much larger percentage of the Court's docket has involved constitutional cases.

Senator BIDEN. Now, as I understand it, your theory as to what latitude a Justice has in interpreting the Constitution and provisions of this Constitution really relates to one that is much more in line with that recently enunciated by the administration of original intent, that it is very important to look back at what the original intent of the framers of the Constitution or the amendment was in order for you to know how it should be interpreted; is that correct?

Justice REHNQUIST. I am not sure it is entirely correct. I think original intent manifested in the words that the people that drafted the document used is a very important factor in deciding what the provision means.

Senator BIDEN. OK. Now——

The CHAIRMAN. Senator, your time is up.

Senator BIDEN. OK. I will come back to this.

The CHAIRMAN. The distinguished Senator from Maryland.

Senator MATHIAS. Let me pick up, Mr. Chairman, on this original intent question, because I think it is an interesting one. It is one that has engaged the attention of the country in recent months. I suppose that the debate that has been going on can be summarized in two terms that are meant to capsulize the contrasting approaches to Constitutional cases; judges who seek to apply "original intent," and those who engage in "judicial activism," one of the Chairman's favorite phrases.

It is a frequent experience for us on this committee to have nominees who come up and say that if confirmed, they would interpret the Constitution pursuant to the original intent of the framers. That is almost a matter of rote with nominees these days. And most of them are willing to take a pledge to resist judicial activism when they look at the Chairman.

The CHAIRMAN. They have good judgment, don't they? [Laughter.]

Senator MATHIAS. Well, they have prudence in any event.

But if we can get beyond those labels that I think distort the issue, as a practical matter, judges and even legislators are from time to time called to apply the Constitution to an issue that could not possibly have confronted the framers.

There were virtually no public schools in 1787. Issues of prayer in school, school integration, the rights of handicapped students—all of which present difficult Constitutional problems—flow out of the public school system, that system did not exist either physically or, I am sure, in the minds of the framers at the time.

How should the Court approach the problem of applying the words of the Constitution to problems that the Founding Fathers simply could not have foreseen?

Justice REHNQUIST. Well, there are a number of provisions in the Constitution that are sufficiently general so that they have applicability far beyond what the framers, the people who ratified the Constitution, had before them at the time.

In 1787, there was not a steamboat, there was not a railroad, there was not an airplane; yet they gave Congress no power over buggies or over post roads; they said Congress shall have power to regulate commerce among the several States. And that provision is obviously broad enough to embrace any number of things that have come after. And there is a due process clause in the fifth amendment to the Constitution and also an equal protection component in the due process clause.

The fact that there were not any public schools in 1787 does not mean that those clauses of broad general applicability would not have application where appropriate to institutions that have come after the Framers.

Senator MATHIAS. Of course, a question arises in some cases as to which branch of Government should undertake the corrective action when the Constitution is silent. That question is illustrated from time to time in problems that require the court to enter the political thicket. For example, the one-man-one-vote decision, might have been decided by State legislatures, as far as congressional districts are concerned, or might have been decided by the Congress, but ultimately had to be decided by the Court.

Is that one result which can flow from this doctrine that you have just commented on?

Justice REHNQUIST. Yes; it certainly is one result that can flow from it.

Senator MATHIAS. What in your judgment is the way to ensure that the decisions of the Court reflect the application of constitutional principles to evolving problems, and to avoid having Justices simply substitute their personal views for the principles that are embodied in the Constitution?

Justice REHNQUIST. Well, I think probably the best answer I can give is to nominate and appoint judges who sense the difficulty involved in judging; that, as Justice Frankfurter said, if putting on a robe does not make any difference to a man—and he put it as a "man" at that time; he would say "to a man or a woman" now, I suppose—then there is something wrong with that person.

Someone who thinks that they are going to be able to go on a court and apply a whole bunch of kind of horseback opinions, the kind that you form from reading the newspapers, for example—and

I remember this experience, and I daresay an awful lot of other people have had it—of simply reading in the newspapers about a court decision, when I was a lawyer, and saying, you know, "How can that be? That sounds ridiculous." And my wife sits across from me now at the breakfast table, and she will be reading something that the court—and she said, "That is ridiculous." And certainly, when you hear a lot of these decisions described, they sound ridiculous. But sometimes you get back into them, and you see that a surface absurdity really is not an absurdity, in fact, and that your initial reaction to a particular case has got to be tempered by study and that sort of thing.

I do not think taking any particular oath is going to get you a better judge.

Senator MATHIAS. Well, I suppose that that is what this nominating process is all about, to winnow out that very issue.

Do I recall correctly that you said that you had never come to any final conclusion about *Brown* v. *the Board of Education* because of the stare decisis effect of *Plessy* v. *Ferguson?*

Justice REHNQUIST. I thought the stare decisis argument in *Plessy* was a strong one.

Senator MATHIAS. Of course, the nine members of the Supreme Court, alone among all of the Federal judiciary, are the only people who can alter a precedent that is established by the Supreme Court. So, your views about precedent would become extremely important.

When you were here in 1971, you answered a question about precedent by stating that, "A precedent might not be that authoritative if it has stood for a shorter period of time, or if it were the decision of a sharply-divided court."

Is that still your view?

Justice REHNQUIST. I think it is, Senator.

Senator MATHIAS. It would follow, then, that precedents with which you have disagreed, or with which you disagreed at the time you joined the court, but which have now been the law of the land for some 15 or more years, have gained in authority?

Justice REHNQUIST. Other things being equal, I would think so, yes.

Senator MATHIAS. So, that as precedents, they are more binding because of the passage of time?

Justice REHNQUIST. Yes; again, other things being equal.

Senator MATHIAS. Is a precedent more authoritative when it is issued, let us say, over your lone dissent than when you have persuaded two or three colleagues to join in it?

Justice REHNQUIST. Yes; I think it is.

Senator MATHIAS. And these are the kinds of considerations that you would have in mind when you were confronted with the possibility of overturning a precedent?

Justice REHNQUIST. Yes.

Senator MATHIAS. I suppose——

The CHAIRMAN. Senator, your time is up.

Senator MATHIAS. Thank you, Mr. Chairman.

99TH CONGRESS
2d Session }

SENATE

{ EXEC. REPT.
99–18

NOMINATION OF WILLIAM H. REHNQUIST TO BE
CHIEF JUSTICE OF THE UNITED STATES

R E P O R T

FROM THE

COMMITTEE ON THE JUDICIARY
UNITED STATES SENATE

TOGETHER WITH

ADDITIONAL, MINORITY, AND SUPPLEMENTAL
VIEWS

SEPTEMBER 8, 1986.—Ordered to be printed

U.S. GOVERNMENT PRINTING OFFICE

63–399 O   WASHINGTON : 1986

Lone Dissenter—Out of the Mainstream

There has been a generalized allegation that Justice Rehnquist is out of the mainstream of constitutional thought. A qualitative and analytical review of his record on the Court will demonstrate that this indeed is not the case.

Ever since Justice Rehnquist's elevation to the U.S. Supreme Court, he has achieved an undeserved reputation as an ideological extremist whose conservative views place him on the fringe of the Court. As evidence of his alleged extremism, critics point to Justice Rehnquist's reputation as a lone dissenter, whose views on issues stand in direct contrast to those of the other eight Justices. A recent Law Journal article claimed that "in the 14 years in which he has served, no other Justice has so often filed lone dissents." Besides the statistical fallibility of such claims, it is interesting to note that the principles of many of the Justice's earlier lone dissents are gaining acceptance with the other Justices in recent terms. In fact, these same arguments have formed the basis for several recent majority opinions of the Court.

In contrast to his popular image as an extremist, Justice Rehnquist is very much in the mainstream of the current Court. In fact, over the last four terms of the Court, no Justice has written more opinions of the Court than Justice Rehnquist. Of course there are some issues on which Justice Rehnquist remains a sole dissenter, but every Justice appears to have his or her particular idiosyncrasies about certain subjects. Despite the Court's holding to the contrary countless times, Justices Brennan and Marshall are well known for their belief that the eighth amendment prohibits capital punishment. Justice White is well known for his dissents in the cases dealing with State aid for parochial schools, despite the longline of cases proscribing such aid. Justice Powell is adamant in his distaste for Court-created implied rights of action. Justice Stevens remains by far the greatest lone dissenter on the current Court with 27 solo dissents over the last four terms of the Court.

To claim that Justice Rehnquist is too far out of the mainstream, is a striking misperception of the thinking of the present Court. Justice Rehnquist has proven himself a leader of majorities, one who believes in equal justice for all, and there is no reason to think he will not continue to do so as Chief Justice.

ADDITIONAL VIEWS OF MR. MATHIAS

No responsibility entrusted to the U.S. Senate is more important than the duty to participate in the process of selecting the judges of the U.S. courts. The nomination of a new Chief Justice of the United States is, of course, particularly consequential. The Senate's decision on this nomination will have a direct effect not only upon the day-to-day operations of the Supreme Court, but upon the work of every Federal court in the land well into the nation's third century.

In my view, the nomination of Justice Rehnquist requires an analysis sensitive to the specific responsibilities of a Chief Justice. We know that Justice Rehnquist has the intellectual ability to be the Chief Justice. The U.S. Reports for the last 15 years amply show it. But this office deserves more. The Chief Justice must provide leadership and direction to an institution that, by its very nature, is often sharply divided. In this regard, it has been comforting to learn that Justice Rehnquist has the support of his colleagues on the Court. They seem to think he has what it takes to be the "first among equals."

Justice Rehnquist also seems prepared to take on the duties reposed in the Chief Justice as head of the Judicial Branch. He has a thoughful approach to a wide range of topics of importance to the administration of justice. Chief Justice Burger set a high standard in this area, but Justice Rehnquist is qualified to meet it.

Of course, it is not possible for a Senator to ignore several issues that clouded the confirmation of this nominee. The allegations that Justice Rehnquist intimidated voters are disturbing. But nearly a quarter of a century after the events at issue, the extensive testimony concerning those events probably tells us more about the uncertainties of human memory than about the nominee's veracity and fitness for office.

The restrictive covenants in Justice Rehnquist's deeds were also troubling. Every allegation concerning Justice Rehnquist's sensitivity toward racial issues would have been less knotty had the Justice instructed his attorneys to have the covenants removed from the Arizona and Vermont deeds before he accepted them. It gave little comfort to hear him testify that the convenants are "obnoxious" and "unenforceable as a matter of law." But many Americans will find a similar blot on deeds that they or their families have given or received. I concluded that inattention, not insensitivity, best explains Justice Rehnquist's situation.

Finally, I address an issue that one of my colleagues raised in the opening moments of this confirmation hearing. Surely our Nation's laws would be quite different had Justice Rehnquist's views—often expressed alone—been joined by a majority of the Court. In my view, the Nation is fortunate that some of Justice Rehnquist's opinions did not command a majority. But my distaste

(64)

for some of his opinions cannot be conclusive of my vote on this nomination, for two reasons.

First, Justice Rehnquist will continue to express his views—in the majority or in dissent—as a member of the Supreme Court. It may make a difference which chair he occupies. But we should not exaggerate how much of a difference it makes.

Second, respect for the principle of judicial independence should make us reluctant to lean too heavily on the decisions a Federal judge has rendered. The framers of the Constitution knew that an independent judiciary is incompatible with any attempt by the political branches of government to hold a judge personally accountable for his rulings. Certainly a judge's behavior on the bench may demonstrate that he is unfit for a more responsible position, whether due to lack of competence, judicial temperament, or respect for the reasonable bounds of constitutional discourse. But none of these factors is present in this case.

The Senate Judiciary Committee voted 13–5 to recommend to the Senate that the nomination be confirmed. Based on the record before the Committee at that time, I concluded that Justice Rehnquist has the ability to serve effectively as Chief Justice, and therefore I voted with the majority of my colleagues.

CHARLES McC. MATHIAS.

SUPPLEMENTAL VIEWS OF MR. BIDEN

The decision to confirm a new Chief Justice of the U.S. Supreme Court will determine the leader of the third and co-equal branch of our Government—a position of awesome responsibility, sensitivity and importance to our future as a Nation. Only 15 men have presided over the Court, and they have shaped our destiny as distinctly as any who have served as President or as leaders in the Congress. It is one of our highest duties as Senators to advise and consent to this nomination.

In any nomination, whether to the Supreme Court or a lower judicial position, a threshold question for me is whether or not the nominee adheres to a judicial philosophy that would unravel the broad fabric of settled constitutional law and practice. From the fight over the nomination of John Rutledge in 1795—which centered on his speeches against the then-controversial Jay Treaty—through more contemporary struggles over the nominations of Louis Brandeis, Judge John Parker and Abe Fortas, the Senate has often considered a nominee's judicial philosophy and vision of the Constitution. I believe that a nominee for Chief Justice, or even Associate Justice, should be rejected if his or her presence on the Court would severely disrupt the delicate process of constitutional adjudication.

While technically Justice Rehnquist's decisions do not indicate that he has rejected the basic fabric of contemporary constitutional law, he made no effort in the confirmation hearings to allay legitimate concerns that he might wish to move the Court away from these fundamental and respected constitutional doctrines.

This is most troublesome in this case because the nominee has not simply been named to a position as Associate Justice, but is instead being elevated to the highest judicial position in the land—that of Chief Justice of the U.S. Supreme Court.

The Chief Justice plays a unique role in our national Government and uniquely symbolizes our image as a Nation. A Chief Justice not only serves longer than a President, but he and his colleagues exercise power limited only by their conscience and principles. And that power goes to the very heart of our Nation as a republic—whether we will be a government of laws or men.

Our national history has confirmed the central role of the Chief Justice in the major changes that have swept our society over the past 200 years. But beyond any one decision or another is the symbolic place the Chief Justice holds in our scheme of constitutional government. More than any other individual, the Chief symbolizes the guarantee of "Equal Justice Under Law" for all Americans. That is not just an arcane legalism; it is the embodiment of the fundamental purpose of our entire judicial system. The Chief Justice stands as a metaphor for justice in our society.

(67)

Unfortunately, in the hearings Justice Rehnquist was personally unconvincing as to whether he would be willing or able to fulfill the symbolic role of Chief Justice. Three requirements seem necessary for the Chief Justice as the leader of the Court and the head of our judicial system.

First, he must exhibit the capability and willingness to forge a consensus for a unanimous opinion in watershed decisions, such as Justice Warren did in *Brown* v. *Board of Education.*

Second, he must demonstrate the flexibility and openmindedness to put aside his own philosophical or legal views when consensus is required, as exemplified by Chief Justice Burger in the *Nixon* tapes case. When questioned about those two important cases, Justice Rehnquist acknowledged that a consensus, indeed a unanimous opinion, was required to insure compliance with the Court's decision and public respect for the law. However, there is nothing in his record as a sitting justice nor in the hearing record to indicate that he would be willing or capable to exercise this kind of leadership.

The third requirement is that the Chief Justice not only be perceived by the American people as fair and openminded, but also candid and forthright. They expect that this individual, above all others, exemplify this characteristic. Unfortunately, Justice Rehnquist's performance in the confirmation hearings did anything but enforce this perception. In areas in which I questioned Justice Rehnquist pertaining to the sensitive issue of race and gender discrimination, his answers on the record are, at best, incomplete.

The first area of concern involves his actions prior to coming to the Court; that is, his clerkship for the late Justice Robert Jackson, his views about the *Brown* v. *Board of Education* case, and the voter intimidation allegations concerning his election-day activities in Phoenix, Arizona. The second area concerns his actions as a member of the Court over the past 15 years, especially whether he has an open mind with regard to the application of the fourteenth amendment in race and gender discrimination cases. In each of these areas, the record is incomplete or his answers were not sufficiently forthcoming to satisfy the burden on every nominee to justify his or her confirmation.

For these reasons, I will vote against the nomination of William Rehnquist to be the 16th Chief Justice of the U.S. Supreme Court. While I am well aware that he will remain on the Court, I believe the Nation would best be served if he remains one among nine, rather than the "first among equals."

JOSEPH BIDEN.

SUPPLEMENTAL VIEWS OF MR. SIMON

Few votes that I cast on this Committee will equal the importance of my vote on Justice Rehnquist nomination to the Supreme Court.

I entered the hearings inclined to confirm this nominee. Now that the evidence has been presented and weighed, I have made my decision.

The two basic questions are: Will this nominee fulfill the responsibilities well? Will this nominee be better than someone else the President might name?

In reaching these decisions, at the Supreme Court, level consideration of political philosophy is not only in order, it is required, if we are to take our responsibilities seriously. William Rehnquist wrote in the Harvard Law Record in 1959:

> Until the Senate restores its practice of thoroughly informing itself on the judicial philosophy of a Supreme Court nominee before voting to confirm him, it will have a hard time convincing doubters that it could make effective use of any additional part in the selection process.

The future Supreme Court Justice was correct.

In the case of Justice Rehnquist he clearly has the capability to continue as a top legal scholar, and I have no question about his ability to administer the Court as its Chief Justice.

I have serious reservations about his ability to fulfill the role of the symbol of justice for all of our people. His record on civil rights and civil liberties going back long before his years on the Court is not strong. His vision of the law alienates large numbers of Americans.

I ask myself the question: Will this nominee be better then someone else the President might name? The reality is that any member of the Court can fulfill the role of Chief Justice as the symbol of justice for all the people better than Justice Rehnquist can.

I oppose his nomination, recognizing the strong probability that he will be approved. If that happens, I hope he will understand the added symbolic responsibilities of his new role.

PAUL SIMON.

O

(114)

22 Weekly Comp. Pres. Doc. 1204
Sept. 17, 1986

United States Supreme Court

Statement by the President on the Senate's Confirmation of William H. Rehnquist as Chief Justice and Antonin Scalia as Associate Justice

I am very pleased that the Senate has voted to confirm my nominations of William Rehnquist to be Chief Justice of the United States and Antonin Scalia as Associate Justice of the Supreme Court. William Rehnquist has served with great distinction as an Associate Justice of the Supreme Court for the last 15 years. Known as an extraordinary legal mind from his early years in law, Justice Rehnquist earned renown in the Court for the brilliance of his reason and the clarity and craftsmanship of his opinions. I have no doubt that William Rehnquist will prove to be a Chief Justice of historic stature.

Judge Scalia is also widely regarded in his profession as a first-class intellect; a persuasive jurist; and a warm, caring person. He will make a superb addition to the Court.

This vote in the full Senate is a bipartisan rejection of the political posturing that marred the confirmation hearings. It's clear to all now that the extraordinary controversy surrounding the hearings had little to do with Justice Rehnquist's record or character -- both are unassailable and unimpeachable. The attacks came from those whose ideology runs contrary to his profound and unshakeable belief in the proper constitutional role of the judiciary in this country. Justice Rehnquist believes, as I do, that our Founding Fathers did not create the Supreme Court as a kind of supralegislature; that judges should interpret the law, not make it; and that victims of crime are due at least as much consideration from our judicial system as criminal offenders.

Both Chief Justice Rehnquist and Associate Justice Scalia will be strong and eloquent voices for the proper role of the judiciary and the rights of victims, and I am confident that they will both serve the Court and their country very well indeed.

3

THE NOMINATION OF ROBERT BORK

The defining moment in the Reagan administration's attack on substantive due process rights in general and *Roe v. Wade* in particular was the July 1987 nomination of Robert Bork to the U.S. Supreme Court. Robert Bork had long maintained a philosophy of judicial restraint which disallowed any constitutionally-based privacy right. For example, in a controversial 1971 law review article, Bork used *Griswold v. Connecticut* to illustrate the problems of judge-made law. Bork thought *Griswold*, the Court's important stepping stone to the *Roe* decision, embodied the Warren Court's tendency to make its own value choices supreme and thereby displace elected government. For Bork, *Griswold* was "an unprincipled decision" which "fails every test of neutrality." Bork, Neutral Principles and Some First Amendment Problems, 47 Ind. L.J. 1 (1971).

Bork was nominated to replace judicial moderate Lewis Powell, the swing vote on a sharply divided Court and the justice who often stymied much of the Reagan revolution through decisive votes on abortion, as well as affirmative action and church-state relations. The Bork nomination, then, threatened to radically redirect the Court's jurisprudential philosophy. Indeed, Senate Judiciary Committee Chairman Joseph Biden (D-Del.) suggested that the Bork controversy was more about the loss of Justice Powell than about Bork himself, remarking that if "Bork were about to replace Rehnquist or . . . Scalia, this would be a whole different ball game." Walsh, Court Change Elevates Biden's Profile, Wash. Post, July 12, 1987, at A7.

While Bork's attack on *Griswold* might have been a grim harbinger for pro-choice groups opposing Bork, those groups instead used Bork's deep-seated opposition to the privacy right as a weapon against his confirmation. Although their principal concern was abortion, the Block Bork Coalition feared that turning the confirmation hearings into a divisive public referendum on abortion would play into White House charges that the Bork opposition was merely a thinly-veiled pro-choice special interest group. The solution was to rally more generalized opposition to Bork by having abortion subsumed into the larger issue of privacy. Ann Lewis, an anti-Bork political consultant, describes how the campaign seized upon "privacy" as the salient issue:

> It was the right to privacy that he had challenged, so it wasn't that we sat around and thought "we can't talk about abortion, what's another word." He had handed us that because his attack was on the right to privacy. In addition, it was the strongest way to make the case, because when you talk about privacy, everyone has their own private ideas for private behavior. M. Pertschuk & W. Schaetzel, The People Rising 257-58 (1989).

This strategy was implemented in a full page ad that appeared in *The Washington Post* and other newspapers on September 14, 1987. Planned Parenthood warned that the stakes of the Bork nomination were "[d]ecades of Supreme Court decisions uphold[ing] your freedom to make your own decisions about marriage and family, childbearing and parenting" and that "[i]f the Senate confirms Robert Bork, it will be too late. Your personal privacy, one of the most cherished and unique features of American life, has never been in greater danger."

Competing reports prepared by the White House and Senate Judiciary Committee Chairman Joseph Biden served as an opening volley in this debate. The White House Report defended Bork's repudiation of privacy. Analogizing the debate over privacy to the *Lochner* era debate over economic substantive due process, the White House characterized Bork's position as a mere demand that judges only interfere with legislative prerogative when given a clear constitutional mandate to do so. In contrast, the Biden Report argued that Bork's rejection of the privacy right indicated an unprincipled disregard for the "text, history and tradition of the Constitution."

The real battle began on September 15, 1987, when Bork and members of the Senate Judiciary Committee went head to head on the privacy issue. Senator Biden pressed Bork on his assertion that "the economic gratification of a utility company is as worthy of as much protection as the sexual gratification of a married couple, because neither is mentioned in the Constitution." Senator Edward Kennedy (D-Mass.) told Bork that he had "serious questions . . . about placing someone on the Supreme Court that . . . find[s] some rationale not to respect [privacy rights]." Bork responded that the founders "banked a good deal upon the good sense of the people [and their elected representatives]" and asked rhetorically: "Privacy to do what[?] . . . to use cocaine in private? Privacy for businessmen to fix prices in a hotel room?" Nomination of Robert H. Bork to Be Associate Justice of the Supreme Court of the United States: Hearings Before the Senate Comm. on the Judiciary, 100th Cong., 1st Sess. (Part I) (1987).

The Senate Judiciary Committee voted 9-5 against Bork's nomination. A cornerstone of the majority report was Bork's refusal to recognize a constitutional right to privacy. Although Senators such as Robert Dole (R-Kan.) labelled this privacy attack as "unfair" and "absurd," the Senate defeated the Bork nomination 58-42, in large measure because of the privacy issue. *See* 133 Cong. Rec. S14930, S14997-15001 (daily ed. Oct. 23, 1987) (floor debate on the Bork nomination).

The Bork nomination proved highly instructive for subsequent Supreme Court nominees. It illustrated the degree to which a nominee could suffer from an unpopular opinion on the privacy issue. Indeed, to a certain extent the Judiciary Committee and pro-choice groups played their trump card with the Bork incident; in later hearings, nominees were on guard against privacy-based attacks, and were able to tailor their answers to ward off such attacks.

The Nomination of Robert Bork
Documents

National
Legal Center
for the Public Interest

JUDICIAL SELECTION: MERIT, IDEOLOGY, AND POLITICS

by

Prof. Henry J. Abraham

Attorney General Griffin B. Bell

Senator Charles E. Grassley

Prof. Eugene W. Hickok, Jr.

Senior Judge John W. Kern III

Stephen J. Markman, Esq.

and

Wm. Bradford Reynolds, Esq.

FOREWORD

by

Attorney General Edwin Meese III

INTRODUCTION

by

Dr. Gary L. McDowell

JUDICIAL SELECTION:
THE REAGAN YEARS*

STEPHEN J. MARKMAN

The debate spawned by [the Reagan] Administration's judicial selection process served a valuable purpose in focusing public attention on the role of the courts in our system of limited, constitutional government. At the same time, exaggerated political rhetoric has led some to misunderstand this Administration's judicial selection process. Part of my statement today examines that process and dispels some of the myths which have become a common staple of public discourse on this issue.

But before I proceed to that discussion, I would like to discuss what [the Reagan] Administration saw as the appropriate scope of judicial power and its implications for the constitutional responsibility of those who appoint individuals to exercise that power.

President Reagan [took seriously] his solemn constitutional obligation to "preserve, protect, and defend the Constitution of the United States." In that regard, one of the most important responsibilities of the President is the exercise of his appointment authority under Article II, Section 2, of the Constitution to determine the character of the federal courts, a co-equal branch of the national government. To ensure that the Constitution is preserved, protected, and defended, President Reagan was determined to appoint to the federal courts only those individuals who are committed to the rule of law and to the enforcement of the Constitution and statutes as those were adopted by "we the people" and their elected representatives. President Reagan would have been derelict of his constitutional duty if he were to have appointed judges who were willing to create new constitutional "rights" out of thin air, usurp legislative and executive functions, or otherwise give short shrift to the will of "we the people" as expressed in the written law.

Judicial office is one of the highest of all public trusts. It demands and deserves the best talent our country has to offer. Consequently, President Reagan sought to appoint to the bench only those who have the intellectual capacity to deal with the difficult legal issues of a complex society, who have the legal training and experience necessary to take on the important duties of the bench, and who are of the highest personal integrity. He sought to appoint individuals who are intensely committed to the American constitutional ideal of equal justice for all under law. In order to find such individuals with the requisite professional and personal qualifications, the President

---

*This article is adapted from Assistant Attorney General Markman's testimony of February 2, 1988, before the Senate Judiciary Committee. The statement has been lightly edited as to verb tense and other matters of style.

33

undertook to consider the broadest possible range of individuals, regardless of race, gender, national origin, or religious affiliation.

In exercising his appointment power, the President also took care that his nominees possessed those important personal qualities that make for a proper judicial temperament. Those intangible qualities include a willingness to listen fully and fairly to all sides of an issue, and never to pre-judge a case; an appreciation of the need to avoid even the appearance of judicial conflict of interest; a sense of compassion; a willingness to work hard to carry out the court's business without delay; and the demeanor necessary to treat every litigant and witness and counsel courteously and respectfully at all times. The President was determined that his appointees would carry out their duties with dignity, propriety, even-handedness and professionalism. Many of these qualities are elusive and difficult to judge in an individual who has not already served in a judicial capacity. Substantial effort was undertaken, however, to identify these to the best of our abilities.

REAGAN'S JUDICIAL PHILOSOPHY

But for a president charged with preserving, protecting, and defending the Constitution, the search for judicial candidates with legal proficiency and judicial temperament, while critical, is not the end of the process. It is also necessary that those to be appointed demonstrate a sound understanding of the proper role of judges under our Constitution, which, by its own terms, is the "supreme law of the land." Such individuals must demonstrate an understanding that federal judges, no less than members of the Congress, executive branch officials, and State and local legislators, are constrained to act always within the bounds set by the Constitution—that federal judges, in President Franklin Roosevelt's words, are charged "to do justice under the Constitution, not over it."

Such an understanding does not require any particular view of public policy, and has nothing to do with a judge's personal political predilections. It is one thing for a judge to think that some particular public policy is wise or foolish, prudent or imprudent. It is quite a different matter, however, for that judge to think it appropriate for him, rather than the people through their elected representatives, to sit in judgment on the wisdom of or necessity for that policy.

The proper role of a judge within our constitutional system is not at all difficult to discern. Our government is based upon the consent of the governed. This was proclaimed as just by the Declaration of Independence and established as law by Article VII and Article V of our Constitution. Article VII provides that the Constitution would become effective when consented to by all of the States to be bound by it. Article V provides that the Constitution may be amended only with the consent of three-fourths of these States. The Constitution, so agreed to, provides for the adoption of federal laws on enumerated subjects only by elected representatives of the

34

people of the United States. Article I, Section 1 establishes that "[a]ll legislative powers herein granted shall be vested in a Congress of the United States."

The Constitution and laws passed pursuant to it, of course, have meanings; otherwise, the very idea of consent—of ratifying or amending the Constitution or voting for or against laws—would be a nullity. Consent must mean knowing consent, and knowing consent is possible only if the constitutional provisions consented to have ascertainable meanings.

It is, in fact, those meanings that are established by Article VI of the Constitution as the supreme law of the land, binding not only on the legislative and executive branches but also on the judges in every state, including federal judges. As Chief Justice John Marshall said in *Marbury* v. *Madison*, "The framers of the Constitution contemplated that instrument as a rule for the government of *courts*, as well as the legislature."

The classical conception of the judge's role in our system of government was guided by a standard of fidelity to the Constitution as written. If a statute was challenged as unconstitutional, the judge's inquiry was limited to whether the statute in question exceeded a power granted in the Constitution or ran afoul of a prohibition contained in the Constitution. At the core of this vision was the belief that judicial power stemmed from the consent of the people and could be used solely to effectuate the will of the people as authoritatively expressed in the Constitution the people ratified. "We the people" were sovereign, and the judge's role was to act as the agent of the sovereign people in insuring adherence to our highest law. What guided a judge in the exercise of the judicial power was a standard established in the four corners of the Constitution.

Thus, the function of judges is to seek out those meanings consented to by the people—as Marshall wrote in *Marbury*, "to say what the law is," rather than what they think it should be—and to apply that law as required by Article III of the Constitution to the facts of particular "cases" or "controversies" presented to them. As President Reagan said at the investiture of Chief Justice Rehnquist and Associate Justice Scalia:

> Hamilton, Jefferson and all the Founding Fathers recognized that the Constitution is the supreme and ultimate expression of the will of the American people. They saw that no one in office could remain above it, if freedom were to survive through the ages. They understood that, in the words of James Madison, if "the sense in which the Constitution was accepted and ratified by the nation is not the guide to expounding it, there can be no security for a faithful exercise of its powers." The Founding Fathers were clear on this issue. For them, the question involved in judicial restraint was not—as it is not—will we have liberal or conservative courts? They knew that the courts, like the Constitution itself, must not be liberal or conservative. The question was and is, will we have government by the people? And this is why the principle of judicial restraint has had an honored place in our tradition. Progressive as well as conservative judges have insisted on its importance—Justice Holmes, for example, and Justice Felix Frankfurter, who once said, "The highest example of judicial duty is to subordinate one's personal will and one's private views to the law."

35

Until as recently as twenty-five years ago, President Reagan's views on the role of courts in our society would have been viewed as self-evident axioms, about which there could be no controversy. Over the last two and a half decades, however, these first principles of our constitutional order have faced increasing challenge. It might be helpful to compare these first principles with some currently fashionable alternatives.

Instead of taking the words of the Constitution as the lodestar for its meaning, a variety of new (and often mutually contradictory) standards have been proposed in the past twenty-five years to guide judges in exercising their functions. Among these standards are those which would evaluate legislative and executive actions in terms of their consistency with "deeply imbedded cultural values,"[1] "moral evolution,"[2] "the well-being of our society,"[3] "the settled weight of responsible opinion" and "judgments of social importance,"[4] "autonomy and equal concern and respect,"[5] "a fusion of constitutional law and moral theory,"[6] "the dignity of full membership in society,"[7] and judges' own "personal preferences and substantive value judgments."[8] What all of these alternatives have in common is that they purport to authorize judges to look outside the Constitution ratified by the people and outside the statutory language adopted by the people's elected representatives to find a source of law. Yet Article V of the Constitution makes the Constitution and the laws and treaties adopted pursuant to it "the supreme Law of the Land."

What each of these alternative proposed standards has in common is a rejection of the belief in popular sovereignty. Under each of these extra-constitutional standards, a judge would be authorized to strike down a duly enacted law not because "we the people" so required in the Constitution, but because the judge looked to some source of "higher law" which did not derive its validity from the consent of the people. President Reagan's judicial philosophy would preserve our cherished national ideal of self-government. The alternatives would not.

Self-government is the essence of the American experiment, but in recent years, observers of all political perspectives have rightly become concerned that the American capacity for self-government has been eroded as the

---

[1] G. White, *Patterns of American Legal Thought* 160 (1978).

[2] Perry, *Noninterpretive Review in Human Rights Cases: A Functional Justification*, 56 N.Y.U. L. Rev. 278 (1981).

[3] Brest, *The Misconceived Quest for the Original Understanding*, 60 B.U.L. Rev. 204, 226 (1980).

[4] Tushnet, *The Newer Property: Suggestions for the Revival of Substantive Due Process*, 1975 Sup. Ct. Rev. 261, 279-80.

[5] Richards, *Commercial Sex and the Rights of the Person: A Moral Argument for the Decriminalization of Prostitution*, 127 U. Pa. L. Rev. 1195, 1228 (1979) (footnote omitted).

[6] R. Dworkin, *Taking Rights Seriously* 149 (1977).

[7] Karst, *The Supreme Court, 1976 Term—Foreword: Equal Citizenship Under the Fourteenth Amendment*, 91 Harv. L. Rev. 1, 5-6 (1977) (footnotes omitted).

[8] Forrester, *Are We Ready for Truth in Judging?*, 63 A.B.A.J. 1212 (1977).

36

federal judiciary has increasingly asserted its control over matters that, under our constitutional scheme, are rightly the province of the coordinate branches of the national government, States, local governments and the private sector. The growth in the power of the courts has correspondingly reduced the power of the elected representatives of the people and thus the ability of individuals to control their destiny by occasionally "throwing the rascals out of office." Concomitantly, the prestige of the judicial branch has increasingly been threatened as it has performed more quasi-legislative functions and become more like just another political body. Indeed, because of this rise of what some have called an "imperial judiciary,"[9] federal judges have arguably become among the most important actors in the determination of domestic social policy in the United States.

We all recognize the constitutional responsibility and duty of the federal courts, however, to uphold the requirements of the Constitution or of federal law, even if this sometimes defeats the policy objectives of the popular branches of the government. This is necessary and inevitable in a system where a written, permanent Constitution reigns as the supreme law of the land. But the special responsibility of the courts to uphold and carry out the mandate of the law does not justify instances where judges clearly have gone beyond the requirements of the Constitution or the laws of the United States and imposed instead a result based upon their own concepts of desirable social policy, however high-minded those policies might seem.

There can be little doubt that some judges have increasingly substituted their own policy judgments for constitutional or statutory rules of decision in cases that have come before them. Through this kind of judicial overreaching—by which I mean a judge's assertion of and exercise of authority constitutionally reserved to other branches of government—judges have involved themselves in American public policy beyond their constitutional warrant. Particularly where such authority is exercised in the name of the Constitution, these decisions have preempted the proper democratic decisionmaking process and withdrawn legitimate issues from debate within the popular legislative arena.

The wisdom of various policy judgments imposed by the judiciary is not the issue here; people can and do take different views of the results in particular cases. Indeed, this kind of judicial overreaching continues precisely because many people approve of the policy results that can be obtained summarily from the courts rather than having to depend upon the more extended give-and-take and negotiation and compromise of the federal, state, or local legislative processes. But the results in particular cases, however visionary, should not blind us to the consequences of transferring the deter-

---

[9]*See e.g.* Glazer, "Towards an Imperial Judiciary," *reprinted in The American Commonwealth* (Kristol, ed. 1976); *see also* C. Wolfe, *The Rise of Modern Judicial Review* (1986); D. Horowitz, *The Courts and Social Policy* (1977); Kurland, "Government by Judiciary," *Modern Age*, Fall, 1976, at 358; and W. Berns, *Taking the Constitution Seriously* (1987).

37

mination of public policy decisions from the representative branches of federal, state, and local governments to the unaccountable federal judiciary. [At this point, Mr. Markman discussed at considerable length examples of judicial decisions that exemplify judges' disregard for the Constitution's guidance. He also discussed the jurisdiction over appointments to the courts of Washington, D.C. These sections have been omitted owing to consideration of space.]

38

INDIANA LAW JOURNAL

| Volume 47 | FALL 1971 | Number 1 |

NEUTRAL PRINCIPLES AND SOME FIRST AMENDMENT PROBLEMS*

ROBERT H. BORK†

A persistently disturbing aspect of constitutional law is its lack of theory, a lack which is manifest not merely in the work of the courts but in the public, professional and even scholarly discussion of the topic. The result, of course, is that courts are without effective criteria and, therefore we have come to expect that the nature of the Constitution will change, often quite dramatically, as the personnel of the Supreme Court changes. In the present state of affairs that expectation is inevitable, but it is nevertheless deplorable.

The remarks that follow do not, of course, offer a general theory of constitutional law. They are more properly viewed as ranging shots, an attempt to establish the necessity for theory and to take the argument of how constitutional doctrine should be evolved by courts a step or two farther. The first section centers upon the implications of Professor Wechsler's concept of "neutral principles," and the second attempts to apply those implications to some important and much-debated problems in the interpretation of the first amendment. The style is informal since these remarks were originally lectures and I have not thought it worthwhile to convert these speculations and arguments into a heavily researched, balanced and thorough presentation, for that would result in a book.

THE SUPREME COURT AND THE DEMAND FOR PRINCIPLE

The subject of the lengthy and often acrimonious debate about the proper role of the Supreme Court under the Constitution is one that preoccupies many people these days: when is authority legitimate? I find it convenient to discuss that question in the context of the Warren Court and its works simply because the Warren Court posed the issue in acute form. The issue did not disappear along with the era of the Warren Court

---

* The text of this article was delivered in the Spring of 1971 by Professor Bork at the Indiana University School of Law as part of the Addison C. Harriss lecture series.
† Professor of Law, Yale Law School.

majorities, however. It arises when any court either exercises or declines to exercise the power to invalidate any act of another branch of government. The Supreme Court is a major power center, and we must ask when its power should be used and when it should be withheld.

Our starting place, inevitably, is Professor Herbert Wechsler's argument that the Court must not be merely a "naked power organ," which means that its decisions must be controlled by principle.[1] "A principled decision," according to Wechsler, "is one that rests on reasons with respect to all the issues in a case, reasons that in their generality and their neutrality transcend any immediate result that is involved."[2]

Wechsler chose the term "neutral principles" to capsulate his argument, though he recognizes that the legal principle to be applied is itself never neutral because it embodies a choice of one value rather than another. Wechsler asked for the neutral application of principles, which is a requirement, as Professor Louis L. Jaffe puts it, that the judge "sincerely believe in the principle upon which he purports to rest his decision."[3] "The judge," says Jaffe, "must believe in the validity of the reasons given for the decision at least in the sense that he is prepared to apply them to a later case which he cannot honestly distinguish."[3] He must not, that is, decide lawlessly. But is the demand for neutrality in judges merely another value choice, one that is no more principled than any other? I think not, but to prove it we must rehearse fundamentals. This is familiar terrain but important and still debated.

The requirement that the Court be principled arises from the resolution of the seeming anomaly of judicial supremacy in a democratic society. If the judiciary really is supreme, able to rule when and as it sees fit, the society is not democratic. The anomaly is dissipated, however, by the model of government embodied in the structure of the Constitution, a model upon which popular consent to limited government by the Supreme Court also rests. This model we may for convenience, though perhaps not with total accuracy, call "Madisonian."[4]

A Madisonian system is not completely democratic, if by "democratic" we mean completely majoritarian. It assumes that in wide areas of life majorities are entitled to rule for no better reason that they are majorities. We need not pause here to examine the philosophical under-

---

1. H. WECHSLER, *Toward Neutral Principles of Constitutional Law,* in PRINCIPLES, POLITICS, AND FUNDAMENTAL LAW 3, 27 (1961) [hereinafter cited as WECHSLER].
2. *Id.*
3. L. JAFFE, ENGLISH AND AMERICAN JUDGES AS LAWMAKERS 38 (1969).
4. *See* R. DAHL, A PREFACE TO DEMOCRATIC THEORY 4-33 (1956).

pinnings of that assumption since it is a "given" in our society; nor need we worry that "majority" is a term of art meaning often no more than the shifting combinations of minorities that add up to temporary majorities in the legislature. That majorities are so constituted is inevitable. In any case, one essential premise of the Madisonian model is majoritarianism. The model has also a counter-majoritarian premise, however, for it assumes there are some areas of life a majority should not control. There are some things a majority should not do to us no matter how democratically it decides to do them. These are areas properly left to individual freedom, and coercion by the majority in these aspects of life is tyranny.

Some see the model as containing an inherent, perhaps an insoluble, dilemma.[5] Majority tyranny occurs if legislation invades the areas properly left to individual freedom. Minority tyranny occurs if the majority is prevented from ruling where its power is legitimate. Yet, quite obviously, neither the majority nor the minority can be trusted to define the freedom of the other. This dilemma is resolved in constitutional theory, and in popular understanding, by the Supreme Court's power to define both majority and minority freedom through the interpretation of the Constitution. Society consents to be ruled undemocratically within defined areas by certain enduring principles believed to be stated in, and placed beyond the reach of majorities by, the Constitution.

But this resolution of the dilemma imposes severe requirements upon the Court. For it follows that the Court's power is legitimate only if it has, and can demonstrate in reasoned opinions that it has, a valid theory, derived from the Constitution, of the respective spheres of majority and minority freedom. If it does not have such a theory but merely imposes its own value choices, or worse if it pretends to have a theory but actually follows its own predilections, the Court violates the postulates of the Madisonian model that alone justifies its power. It then necessarily abets the tyranny either of the majority or of the minority.

This argument is central to the issue of legitimate authority because the Supreme Court's power to govern rests upon popular acceptance of this model. Evidence that this is, in fact, the basis of the Court's power is to be gleaned everywhere in our culture. We need not canvass here such things as high school civics texts and newspaper commentary, for the most telling evidence may be found in the U.S. Reports. The Supreme Court regularly insists that its results, and most particularly its controversial results, do not spring from the mere will of the Justices in the majority

---

5. *Id.* at 23-24.

but are supported, indeed compelled, by a proper understanding of the Constitution of the United States. Value choices are attributed to the Founding Fathers, not to the Court. The way an institution advertises tells you what it thinks its customers demand.

This is, I think, the ultimate reason the Court must be principled. If it does not have and rigorously adhere to a valid and consistent theory of majority and minority freedoms based upon the Constitution, judicial supremacy, given the axioms of our system, is, precisely to that extent, illegitimate. The root of its illegitimacy is that it opens a chasm between the reality of the Court's performance and the constitutional and popular assumptions that give it power.

I do not mean to rest the argument entirely upon the popular under standing of the Court's function. Even if society generally should ultimately perceive what the Court is in fact doing and, having seen, prove content to have major policies determined by the unguided discretion of judges rather than by elected representatives, a principled judge would, I believe, continue to consider himself bound by an obligation to the document and to the structure of government that it prescribes. At least he would be bound so long as any litigant existed who demanded such adherence of him. I do not understand how, on any other theory of judicial obligation, the Court could, as it does now, protect voting rights if a large majority of the relevant constituency were willing to see some groups or individuals deprived of such rights. But even if I am wrong in that, at the very least an honest judge would owe it to the body politic to cease invoking the authority of the Constitution and to make explicit the imposition of his own will, for only then would we know whether the society understood enough of what is taking place to be said to have consented.

Judge J. Skelly Wright, in an argument resting on different premises, has severely criticized the advocates of principle. He defends the value-choosing role of the Warren Court, setting that Court in opposition to something he refers to as the "scholarly tradition," which criticizes that Court for its lack of principle.[6] A perceptive reader, sensitive to nuance, may suspect that the Judge is rather out of sympathy with that tradition from such hints as his reference to "self-appointed scholastic mandarins."[7]

The "mandarins" of the academy anger the Judge because they engage in "haughty derision of the Court's powers of analysis and reason-

---

6. Wright, *Professor Bickel, The Scholarly Tradition, and the Supreme Court*, 84 HARV. L. REV. 769 (1971) [hereinafter cited as Wright].
7. *Id.* at 777.

ing."[8] Yet, curiously enough, Judge Wright makes no attempt to refute the charge but rather seems to adopt the technique of confession and avoidance. He seems to be arguing that a Court engaged in choosing fundamental values for society cannot be expected to produce principled decisions at the same time. Decisions first, principles later. One wonders, however, how the Court or the rest of us are to know that the decisions are correct or what they portend for the future if they are not accompanied by the principles that explain and justify them. And it would not be amiss to point out that quite often the principles required of the Warren Court's decisions never did put in an appearance. But Judge Wright's main point appears to be that value choice is the most important function of the Supreme Court, so that if we must take one or the other, and apparently we must, we should prefer a process of selecting values to one of constructing and articulating principles. His argument, I believe, boils down to a syllogism. I. The Supreme Court should "protect our constitutional rights and liberties." II. The Supreme Court must "make fundamental value choices" in order to "protect our constitutional rights and liberties." III. Therefore, the Supreme Court should "make fundamental value choices."[9]

The argument displays an all too common confusion. If we have constitutional rights and liberties already, rights and liberties specified by the Constitution,[10] the Court need make no fundamental value choices in order to protect them, and it certainly need not have difficulty enunciating

---

8. *Id.* at 777-78.

9. This syllogism is implicit in much of Judge Wright's argument. *E.g.,* "If it is proper for the Court to make fundamental value choices to protect our constitutional rights and liberties, then it is self-defeating to say that if the Justices cannot come up with a perfectly reasoned and perfectly general opinion *now,* then they should abstain from decision altogether." *Id.* at 779. The first clause is the important one for present purposes; the others merely caricature the position of commentators who ask for principle.

10. A position Judge Wright also seems to take at times. "Constitutional choices are in fact different from ordinary decisions. The reason is simple: the most important value choices have already been made by the framers of the Constitution." *Id.* at 784. One wonders how the Judge squares this with his insistence upon the propriety of the judiciary making "fundamental value choices." One also wonders what degree of specificity is required before the framers may realistically be said to have made the "most important value choices." The Warren Court has chosen to expand the fourteenth amendment's theme of equality in ways certainly not foreseen by the framers of that provision. A prior Court expanded the amendment's theme of liberty. Are both Courts to be judged innocent of having made the most important value choices on the ground that the framers mentioned both liberty and equality? If so, the framers must be held to have delegated an almost complete power to govern to the Supreme Court, and it is untrue to say that a constitutional decision is any different from an ordinary governmental decision. Judge Wright simply never faces up to the problem he purports to address: how free is the Court to choose values that will override the values chosen by elected representatives?

principles. If, on the other hand, "constitutional rights and liberties" are not in some real sense specified by the Constitution but are the rights and liberties the Court chooses, on the basis of its own values, to give to us, then the conclusion was contained entirely in the major premise, and the Judge's syllogism is no more than an assertion of what it purported to prove.

If I am correct so far, no argument that is both coherent and respectable can be made supporting a Supreme Court that "chooses fundamental values" because a Court that makes rather than implements value choices cannot be squared with the presuppositions of a democratic society. The man who understands the issues and nevertheless insists upon the rightness of the Warren Court's performance ought also, if he is candid, to admit that he is prepared to sacrifice democratic process to his own moral views. He claims for the Supreme Court an institutionalized role as perpetrator of limited coups d'etat.

Such a man occupies an impossible philosophic position. What can he say, for instance, of a Court that does not share his politics or his morality? I can think of nothing except the assertion that he will ignore the Court whenever he can get away with it and overthrow it if he can. In his view the Court has no legitimacy, and there is no reason any of us should obey it. And, this being the case, the advocate of a value-choosing Court must answer another difficult question. Why should the Court, a committee of nine lawyers, be the sole agent of change? The man who prefers results to processes has no reason to say that the Court is more legitimate than any other institution. If the Court will not listen, why not argue the case to some other group, say the Joint Chiefs of Staff, a body with rather better means for implementing its decisions?

We are driven to the conclusion that a legitimate Court must be controlled by principles exterior to the will of the Justices. As my colleague, Professor Alexander Bickel, puts it, "The process of the coherent, analytically warranted, principled declaration of general norms alone justifies the Court's function . . . ."[11] Recognition of the need for principle is only the first step, but once that step is taken much more follows. Logic has a life of its own, and devotion to principle requires that we follow where logic leads.

Professor Bickel identifies Justice Frankfurter as the leading judicial proponent of principle but concedes that even Frankfurther never found a "rigorous general accord between judicial supremacy and democratic

---

11. A. BICKEL, THE SUPREME COURT AND THE IDEA OF PROGRESS 96 (1970).

theory."[12] Judge Wright responds, "The leading commentators of the scholarly tradition have tried ever since to succeed where the Justice failed."[13] As Judge Wright quite accurately suggests, the commentators have so far had no better luck than the Justice.

One reason, I think, is clear. We have not carried the idea of neutrality far enough. We have been talking about neutrality in the *application* of principles. If judges are to avoid imposing their own values upon the rest of us, however, they must be neutral as well in the *definition* and the *derivation* of principles.

It is easy enough to meet the requirement of neutral application by stating a principle so narrowly that no embarrassment need arise in applying it to all cases it subsumes, a tactic often urged by proponents of "judicial restraint." But that solves very little. It certainly does not protect the judge from the intrusion of his own values. The problem may be illustrated by *Griswold v. Connecticut*,[14] in many ways a typical decision of the Warren Court. *Griswold* struck down Connecticut's statute making it a crime, even for married couples, to use contraceptive devices. If we take the principle of the decision to be a statement that government may not interfere with any acts done in private, we need not even ask about the principle's dubious origin for we know at once that the Court will not apply it neutrally. The Court, we may confidently predict, is not going to throw constitutional protection around heroin use or sexual acts with a consenting minor. We can gain the possibility of neutral application by reframing the principle as a statement that government may not prohibit the use of contraceptives by married couples, but that is not enough. The question of neutral definition arises: Why does the principle extend only to married couples? Why, out of all forms of sexual behavior, only to the use of contraceptives? Why, out of all forms of behavior, only to sex? The question of neutral derivation also arises: What justifies any limitation upon legislatures in this area? What is the origin of any principle one may state?

To put the matter another way, if a neutral judge must demonstrate why principle X applies to cases A and B but not to case C (which is, I believe, the requirement laid down by Professors Wechsler and Jaffe), he must, by the same token, also explain why the principle is defined as X rather than as X *minus*, which would cover A but not cases B and C, or as X *plus*, which would cover all cases, A, B and C. Similarly, he must

---

12. *Id.* at 34.
13. Wright, *supra* note 6, at 775.
14. 381 U.S. 479 (1965).

explain why X is a proper principle of limitation on majority power at all. Why should he not choose *non-X*? If he may not choose lawlessly between cases in applying principle X, he may certainly not choose lawlessly in defining X or in choosing X, for principles are after all only organizations of cases into groups. To choose the principle and define it is to decide the cases.

It follows that the choice of "fundamental values" by the Court cannot be justified. Where constitutional materials do not clearly specify the value to be preferred, there is no principled way to prefer any claimed human value to any other. The judge must stick close to the text and the history, and their fair implications, and not construct new rights. The case just mentioned illustrates the point. The *Griswold* decision has been acclaimed by legal scholars as a major advance in constitutional law, a salutary demonstration of the Court's ability to protect fundamental human values. I regret to have to disagree, and my regret is all the more sincere because I once took the same position and did so in print.[15] In extenuation I can only say that at the time I thought, quite erroneously, that new basic rights could be derived logically by finding and extrapolating a more general principle of individual autonomy underlying the particular guarantees of the Bill of Rights.

The Court's *Griswold* opinion, by Justice Douglas, and the array of concurring opinions, by Justices Goldberg, White and Harlan, all failed to justify the derivation of any principle used to strike down the Connecticut anti-contraceptive statute or to define the scope of the principle. Justice Douglas, to whose opinion I must confine myself, began by pointing out that "specific guarantees in the Bill of Rights have penumbras, formed by emanations from those guarantees that help give them life and substance."[16] Nothing is exceptional there. In the case Justice Douglas cited, *NAACP v. Alabama*,[17] the State was held unable to force disclosure of membership lists because of the chilling effect upon the rights of assembly and political action of the NAACP's members. The penumbra was created solely to preserve a value central to the first amendment, applied in this case through the fourteenth amendment. It had no life of its own as a right independent of the value specified by the first amendment.

But Justice Douglas then performed a miracle of transubstantiation. He called the first amendment's penumbra a protection of "privacy" and

---

15. Bork, *The Supreme Court Needs a New Philosophy*, FORTUNE, Dec., 1968, at 170.
16. 381 U.S. at 484.
17. 357 U.S. 449 (1958).

then asserted that other amendments create "zones of privacy."[18] He had no better reason to use the word "privacy" than that the individual is free within these zones, free to act in public as well as in private. None of these penumbral zones—from the first, third, fourth or fifth amendments, all of which he cited, along with the ninth—covered the case before him. One more leap was required. Justice Douglas asserted that these various "zones of privacy" created an independent right of privacy,[19] a right not lying within the penumbra of any specific amendment. He did not disclose, however, how a series of specified rights combined to create a new and unspecified right.

The *Griswold* opinion fails every test of neutrality. The derivation of the principle was utterly specious, and so was its definition. In fact, we are left with no idea of what the principle really forbids. Derivation and definition are interrelated here. Justice Douglas called the amendments and their penumbras "zones of privacy," though of course they are not that at all. They protect both private and public behavior and so would more properly be labelled "zones of freedom." If we follow Justice Douglas in his next step, these zones would then add up to an independent right of freedom, which is to say, a general constitutional right to be free of legal coercion, a manifest impossibility in any imaginable society.

Griswold, then, is an unprincipled decision, both in the way in which it derives a new constitutional right and in the way it defines that right, or rather fails to define it. We are left with no idea of the sweep of the right of privacy and hence no notion of the cases to which it may or may not be applied in the future. The truth is that the Court could not reach its result in *Griswold* through principle. The reason is obvious. Every clash between a minority claiming freedom and a majority claiming power to regulate involves a choice between the gratifications of the two groups. When the Constitution has not spoken, the Court will be able to find no scale, other than its own value preferences, upon which to weigh the respective claims to pleasure. Compare the facts in *Griswold* with a hypothetical suit by an electric utility company and one of its customers to void a smoke pollution ordinance as unconstitutional. The cases are identical.

In *Griswold* a husband and wife assert tnat they wish to have sexual relations without fear of unwanted children. The law impairs their sexual gratifications. The State can assert, and at one stage in that litigation did assert, that the majority finds the use of contraceptives immoral. Knowl-

---

18. 381 U.S. at 484.
19. *Id.* at 485, 486.

edge that it takes place and that the State makes no effort to inhibit it causes the majority anguish, impairs their gratifications.

The electrical company asserts that it wishes to produce electricity at low cost in order to reach a wide market and make profits. Its customer asserts that he wants a lower cost so that prices can be held low. The smoke pollution regulation impairs his and the company's stockholders' economic gratifications. The State can assert not only that the majority prefer clean air to lower prices, but also that the absence of the regulation impairs the majority's physical and aesthetic gratifications.

Neither case is covered specifically or by obvious implication in the Constitution. Unless we can distinguish forms of gratification, the only course for a principled Court is to let the majority have its way in both cases. It is clear that the Court cannot make the necessary distinction. There is no principled way to decide that one man's gratifications are more deserving of respect than another's or that one form of gratification is more worthy than another.[20] Why is sexual gratification more worthy than moral gratification? Why is sexual gratification nobler than economic gratification? There is no way of deciding these matters other than by reference to some system of moral or ethical values that has no objective or intrinsic validity of its own and about which men can and do differ. Where the Constitution does not embody the moral or ethical choice, the judge has no basis other than his own values upon which to set aside the community judgment embodied in the statute. That, by definition, is an inadequate basis for judicial supremacy. The issue of the community's moral and ethical values, the issue of the degree of pain an activity causes, are matters concluded by the passage and enforcemment of the laws in question. The judiciary has no role to play other than that of applying the statutes in a fair and impartial manner.

One of my colleagues refers to this conclusion, not without sarcasm, as the "Equal Gratification Clause." The phrase is apt, and I accept it, though not the sarcasm. Equality of human gratifications, where the document does not impose a hierarchy, is an essential part of constitutional doctrine because of the necessity that judges be principled. To be perfectly clear on the subject, I repeat that the principle is not applicable to legislatures. Legislation requires value choice and cannot be principled in the sense under discussion. Courts must accept any value choice the legislature

20. The impossibility is related to that of making interpersonal comparisons of utilities. *See* L. ROBBINS, THE NATURE AND SIGNIFICANCE OF ECONOMIC SCIENCE, ch. 4 (2d ed. 1969) ; P. SAMUELSON, FOUNDATIONS OF ECONOMIC ANALYSIS 243-52 (1965).

makes unless it clearly runs contrary to a choice made in the framing of the Constitution.

It follows, of course, that broad areas of constitutional law ought to be reformulated. Most obviously, it follows that substantive due process, revived by the *Griswold* case, is and always has been an improper doctrine. Substantive due process requires the Court to say, without guidance from the Constitution, which liberties or gratifications may be infringed by majorities and which may not. This means that *Griswold's* antecedents were also wrongly decided, *e.g., Meyer v. Nebraska*,[21] which struck down a statute forbidding the teaching of subjects in any language other than English; *Pierce v. Society of Sisters*,[22] which set aside a statute compelling all Oregon school children to attend public schools; *Adkins v. Children's Hospital*,[23] which invalidated a statute of Congress authorizing a board to fix minimum wages for women and children in the District of Columbia; and *Lochner v. New York*,[24] which voided a statute fixing maximum hours of work for bakers. With some of these cases I am in political agreement, and perhaps *Pierce's* result could be reached on acceptable grounds, but there is no justification for the Court's methods. In *Lochner*, Justice Peckham, defending liberty from what he conceived as a mere meddlesome interference, asked, "[A]re we all . . . at the mercy of legislative majorities?"[25] The correct answer, where the Constitution does not speak, must be "yes."

---

21. 262 U.S. 390 (1922).
22. 268 U.S. 510 (1925).
23. 261 U.S. 525 (1923).
24. 198 U.S. 45 (1905).
25. *Id.* at 59.

THE WHITE HOUSE REPORT:
Information on Judge Bork's Qualifications, Judicial Record & Related Subjects[*]

TABLE OF CONTENTS

[* The White House Report was transmitted to Senator Simon on July 31, 1987 by William L. Ball, III, Assistant to the President. The Report has been abridged for publication to avoid duplicating material treated by other Reports in this issue.—ed.]

GENERAL OVERVIEW

- Judge Robert Bork is one of the most qualified individuals ever nominated to the Supreme Court. He is a preeminent legal scholar; a practitioner who has argued and won numerous cases before the Supreme Court; and a judge who for five years has been writing opinions that faithfully apply law and precedent to the cases that come before him.

- As Lloyd Cutler, President Carter's Counsel, has recently said: "In my view, Judge Bork is neither an idealogue nor an extreme right-winger, either in his judicial philosophy or in his personal position on current social issues. . . . The essence of [his] judicial philosophy is self-restraint." Mr. Cutler, one of the nation's most distinguished lawyers and a self-described "liberal democrat and . . . advocate of civil rights before the Supreme Court," compared Judge Bork to Justices Holmes, Brandeis, Frankfurter, Stewart, and Powell, as one of the few jurists who rigorously subordinate their personal views to neutral interpretation of the law.

- As a member of the Court of Appeals, Judge Bork has been solidly in the mainstream of American jurisprudence.
  - Not one of his more than 100 majority opinions has been reversed by the Supreme Court.
  - The Supreme Court has never reversed any of the over 400 majority opinions in which Judge Bork has joined.
  - In his five years on the bench, Judge Bork has heard hundreds of cases. In all of those cases he has written only 9 dissents and 7 partial dissents. When he took his seat on the bench, 7 of his 10 colleagues were Democratic appointees, as are 5 of the 10 now. He has been in the majority in 94 percent of the cases he has heard.
  - The Supreme Court adopted the reasoning of several of his dissents when it reversed opinions with which he had disagreed. Justice Powell, in particular, has agreed with Judge Bork in 9 of 10 cases that went to the Supreme Court.

- Judge Bork has compiled a balanced record in all areas of the law, including the First Amendment, civil rights, labor law, and criminal law. In fact, his views on freedom of the press prompted scathing criticism from his more conservative colleague, Judge Scalia.

- Some have expressed the fear that Judge Bork will seek to "roll back" many existing judicial precedents. There is no basis for this view in Judge Bork's record. As a law professor, he often criticized the reasoning of Supreme Court opinions; that is what law professors do. But as a judge, he has faithfully applied the legal precedents of both the Supreme Court and his own Circuit Court. Consequently, he is almost always in the majority on the Court of Appeals and has never been reversed by the Supreme Court. Judge Bork understands that in the American Legal system, which places a premium on the orderly development of the law, the mere fact that one may disagree with a prior decision does not mean that that decision ought to be overruled.

- Judge Bork is the leading proponent of "judicial restraint." He believes that judges should overturn the decisions of the democratically-elected branches of government only when there is warrant for doing so in the Constitution itself. He further believes that a judge has no authority to create new rights based upon the judge's personal philosophical views, but must instead rely solely on the principles set forth in the Constitution.

- Justice Stevens, in a speech before the Eighth Circuit Judicial Conference, stated his view that Judge Bork was "very well qualified" to be a Supreme Court Justice. Judge Bork, Justice Stevens explained, would be "a welcome addition to the Court."

Qualifications

Any one of Judge Robert Bork's four positions in private practice, academia, the Executive Branch or the Judiciary would have been the high point of a brilliant career, but he has managed all of them. As *The New York Times* stated in 1981, "Mr. Bork is a legal scholar of distinction and principle."

- Professor at Yale Law School for 15 years; holder of two endowed chairs; graduate of the University of Chicago Law School, *Phi Beta Kappa* and managing editor of the *Law Review*.

- Among the nation's foremost authorities on antitrust and constitutional law. Author of dozens of scholarly works, including *The Antitrust Paradox*, a leading work on antitrust law.

- An experienced practitioner and partner at Kirkland & Ellis.

- Solicitor General of the United States, 1973-77, representing the United States before the Supreme Court in hundreds of cases.

- Unanimously confirmed by the Senate for the D.C. Circuit in 1982, after receiving the ABA's highest rating—"exceptionally well qualified"—which is given to only a handful of judicial nominees each year.

- As an appellate judge, he has an outstanding record: *not one of his more than 100 majority opinions has been reversed by the Supreme Court.*

- The Supreme Court adopted the reasoning of several of his dissents when it reversed opinions with which he had disagreed. For example, in *Sims v. CIA*, Judge Bork criticized a panel opinion which had impermissibly, in his view, narrowed the circumstances under which the identity of confidential intelligence sources could be protected by the government. When the case was appealed, all nine members of the Supreme Court agreed that the panel's definition of "confidential source" was too narrow and voted to reverse.

General Judicial Philosophy

Judge Bork has spent more than a quarter of a century refining a careful and cogent philosophy of law.

- His judicial philosophy begins with the simple proposition that judges must apply the Constitution, the statute, or controlling precedent—not their own moral, political, philosophical or economic preferences.
- He believes in neutral, text-based readings of the Constitution, statutes and cases. This has frequently led him to take positions at odds with those favored by political conservatives. For example, he testified before the Senate Subcommittee on Separation of Powers that he believed the Human Life Bill to be unconstitutional; he has opposed conservative efforts to enact legislation depriving the Supreme Court of jurisdiction over issues like abortion and school prayer; and he has publicly criticized conservatives who wish the courts to take an active role in invalidating economic regulation of business and industry.
- He is not a political judge: He has repeatedly criticized politicized, result-oriented jurisprudence of either the right or the left.
- Judge Bork believes that there is a presumption favoring democratic decisionmaking, and he has demonstrated deference to liberal and conservative laws and agency decisions alike.
- He has repeatedly rebuked academics and commentators who have urged conservative manipulation of the judicial process as a response to liberal judicial activism.
- Judge Bork believes judges are duty-bound to protect vigorously those rights enshrined in the Constitution. He does not adhere to a rigid conception of "original intent" that would require courts to apply the Constitution only to those matters which the Framers specifically foresaw. To the contrary, he has written that it is the "task of the judge in this generation to discern how the framers' values, defined in the context of the world they knew, apply to the

world we know." His opinions applying the First Amendment to modern broadcasting technology and to the changing nature of libel litigation testify to his adherence to this view of the role of the modern judge.

- He believes in abiding by precedent: he testified in 1982 regarding the role of precedent within the Supreme Court:

  I think the value of precedent and of certainty and of continuity is so high that I think a judge ought not to overturn prior decisions unless he thinks it is absolutely clear that that prior decision was wrong and perhaps pernicious.

  He also has said that even questionable prior precedent ought not be overturned when it has become part of the political fabric of the nation.

- As *The New York Times* said in a December 12, 1981, editorial endorsing his nomination to our most important appellate court in 1981:

  Mr. Bork . . . is a legal scholar of distinction and principle. . . . One may differ heatedly from him on specific issues like abortion, but those are differences of philosophy, not principle. Differences of philosophy are what the 1980 election was about; Robert Bork is, given President Reagan's philosophy, a natural choice for an important judicial vacancy.

Abortion

- Judge Bork has never stated whether he would vote to overrule *Roe v. Wade*. Some have suggested, however, that Judge Bork ought not to be confirmed unless he commits in advance *not* to vote to overrule *Roe v. Wade*. Traditionally, judicial nominees do not pledge their votes in future cases in order to secure confirmation. This has long been regarded as clearly improper. Indeed, any judicial nominee who did so would properly be accused not only of lacking integrity, but of lacking an open mind.
- In 1981, Judge Bork testified before Congress in opposition to the proposed Human Life Bill, which sought to reverse *Roe v. Wade* by declaring that human life begins at conception. Judge Bork called the Human Life Bill "unconstitutional."
- Judge Bork has in the past questioned only whether there is a right to abortion in the Constitution.
- This view is shared by some of the most notable, mainstream and respected scholars of constitutional law in America:
  - Harvard Law Professors Archibald Cox and Paul Freund.
  - Stanford Law School Dean John Hart Ely.
  - Columbia Law Professor Henry Monaghan.
- Stanford law professor Gerald Gunther, the editor of the leading law school casebook on constitutional law, offered the following comments on *Griswold v. Connecticut*, the precursor to *Roe v. Wade*: "It marked the return of the Court to the discredited notion of substantive due process. The theory was repudiated in 1937 in the economic sphere. I don't find a very persuasive difference in

reviving it for the personal sphere. I'm a card-carrying liberal Democrat, but this strikes me as a double standard."

- Judge Ruth Bader Ginsburg, one of Judge Bork's colleagues on the D.C. Circuit, has written that *Roe v. Wade* "sparked public opposition and academic criticism . . . because the Court ventured too far in the change it ordered and presented an incomplete justification for its action."

- The legal issue for a judge is whether it should be the court, or the people through their elected representatives, that should decide our policy on abortion.

- If the Supreme Court were to decide that the Constitution does not contain a right to abortion, that would not render abortion illegal. It would simply mean that the issue would be decided in the same way as virtually all other issues of public policy—by the people through their legislatures.

Watergate

- During the course of the Cox firing, Judge Bork displayed great personal courage and statesmanship. He helped save the Watergate investigation and prevent disruption of the Justice Department. As Lloyd Cutler has recently written, "[I]t was inevitable that the President would eventually find someone in the Justice Department to fire Mr. Cox, and, if all three top officers resigned, the department's morale and the pursuit of the Watergate investigation might have been irreparably crippled."

- At first, Bork informed Attorney General Elliott Richardson and Deputy Attorney General William Ruckelshaus that he intended to resign his position. Richardson and Ruckelshaus persuaded him to stay. As Richardson has recently said, "There was no good reason for him to resign, and some good reason for him not to." Richardson and Ruckelshaus felt that it was important for someone of Bork's integrity and stature to stay on the job in order to avoid mass resignations that would have crippled the Justice Department.

- After carrying out the President's instruction to discharge Cox, Bork acted immediately to safeguard the Watergate investigation and its independence. He promptly established a new Special Prosecutor's office, giving it authority to pursue the investigation without interference. He expressly told the Special Prosecutor's office that they had complete independence and that they should subpoena the tapes if they saw fit—the very action that led to Cox's discharge.

- Judge Bork framed the legal theory under which the indictment of Spiro Agnew went forward. Agnew had taken the position that a sitting Vice President was immune from criminal indictment, a position which President Nixon initially endorsed. Bork wrote and filed the legal brief arguing the opposite position, *i.e.*, that Agnew was subject to indictment. Agnew resigned shortly thereafter.

- In 1981, *The New York Times* described Judge Bork's decisions during Watergate as "principled."

JUDGE BORK'S JUDICIAL PHILOSOPHY

Judge Bork's writings and judicial opinions illustrate his judicial philosophy that "[t]he courts must be energetic to protect the rights of individuals, but they must also be scrupulous not to deny the majority's legitimate right to govern." *The Constitution, Original Intent, and Economic Rights*, 23 San Diego L. Rev. 823 (1986). This means two things. First, a "judge fails in his judicial duty" if he "provides a crabbed interpretation that robs a [constitutional] provision of its full, fair and reasonable meaning." *Ollman v. Evans*, 750 F.2d 970, 996 (D.C. Cir. 1984) (en banc) (Bork, J., concurring). Second, a judge must view the Constitution as law—"that the words [of the Constitution] constrain judgment" and "control judges every bit as much as they control legislators, executives and citizens." Bork points out that the specific provisions of the Constitution have limits. "They do not cover all possible or even all desirable liberties." "These limits mean that the judge's authority has limits and that outside the designated areas democratic institutions govern." 23 San Diego L. Rev. at 824-25.

I.

Judge Bork has repeatedly demonstrated his conviction that "courts must be energetic to protect the [constitutional] rights of individuals." This conviction is fully consistent with Judge Bork's view that judicial review is legitimate only "if judges interpret the [Constitution's] words according to the intentions of those who drafted, proposed, and ratified its provisions and its various amendments." As James Madison stated:

> I entirely concur in the propriety of resorting to the sense in which the Constitution was accepted and ratified by the nation. In that sense alone is it the legitimate Constitution. And if that not be the guide in expounding it, there can be no security for a consistent and stable, more than for fanciful exercise of its powers.

As Judge Bork points out, however, intentionalism "is not the notion that judges may apply a constitutional provision only to circumstances specifically contemplated by the Framers," but that a judge must be fully willing "to deal with unforeseen threats to an established constitutional value." According to Judge Bork,

> all an intentionalist requires is that the text, structure, and history of the Constitution provide him not with a conclusion but with a major premise. That premise states a core value that the Framers intended to protect. The intentionalist judge must then supply the minor premise in order to protect the constitutional freedom in circumstances the Framers could not foresee. . . .

23 San Diego L. Rev. at 826-27.

Ollman v. Evans illustrates Judge Bork's application of a core constitutional value to changed circumstances. In *Ollman*, a Marxist history professor sued columnists Evans and Novak for making allegedly defamatory statements about him in a column, particularly, the statement that the professor was "without status" in his profession. Applying a four-factor test, a plurality of the en banc court concluded that under the Supreme Court's cases, the allegedly defamatory material deserved absolute protection under the first amendment because it constituted "opinion" rather than "fact."

Judge Bork wrote a separate concurring opinion, concluding that the plurality relied on a "rigid doctrinal framework . . . inadequate to resolve the sometimes contradictory claims of the libel laws and the freedom of the press." He believed instead that the context and totality of circumstances surrounding the statement about Professor Ollman's status in his profession made it clear that the remark amounted to constitutionally protected "rhetorical hyperbole" uttered in the course of political debate. Judge Bork's analysis was animated by a concern that "in the past few years, a remarkable upsurge in libel actions, accompanied by a startling inflation of damage awards, has threatened to impose a self-censorship on the press which can as effectively inhibit a debate and criticism as would overt governmental regulation that the first amendment would most certainly prohibit."

Judge Bork's opinion in *Ollman* was the subject of a scathing dissent by Judge (now Justice) Scalia, who criticized Judge Bork's attempt to adapt libel law to contemporary circumstances, stating that the concurring opinion had "embark[ed] upon an exercise of, as it puts it, constitutional 'evolution,' with very little reason and very uncertain effect upon the species." Judge Scalia insisted that concerns that developing libel law threatened freedom of the press were better left to legislatures.

Responding to Judge Scalia, Judge Bork wrote:

> On a case like this, it is the task of the judge in this generation to discern how the framers' values, defined in the context of the world they knew, apply to the world we know. The world changes in which unchanging values find their application. The fourth amendment was framed by men who did not foresee electronic surveillance. But that does not make it wrong for judges to apply the central value of that amendment to electronic invasions of personal privacy.
>
> The commerce power was established by men who did not foresee the scope and intricate interdependence of today's economic activities. But that does not make it wrong for judges to forbid states the power to impose burdensome regulations on the interstate movement of trailer trucks. The first amendment's guarantee of freedom of the press was written by men who had not the remotest idea of modern forms of communication. But that does not make it wrong for a judge to find the values of the first amendment relevant to radio and television broadcasting.
>
> So it is with defamation actions. . . . Perhaps the framers did not envision libel actions as a major threat to that freedom. I may grant that, for the sake of the point to be made. But if, over time, the libel action becomes a threat to the central meaning of the first amendment, why should not judges adapt their doctrines? Why is it different to refine and evolve doctrine here, so long as one is faithful to the basic meaning of the amendment, than it is to adapt the fourth amendment to take account of electronic surveillance, the commerce clause to adjust to interstate motor carriage, or the first amendment to encompass the electronic media? I do not believe there is a difference. To say that such matters must be left to the legislature is to say that changes in circumstances must be permitted to render constitutional guarantees meaningless. . . .
>
> . . . The important thing, the ultimate consideration, is the constitutional freedom that is given into our keeping. A judge who refuses to see new threats to an established constitutional value, and hence provides a crabbed interpretation that robs a provision of its full, fair and reasonable meaning, fails in his judicial duty. That duty, I repeat, is to ensure that the powers and freedoms the framers specified are made effective in today's circumstances. The evolution of doctrine to accomplish that end contravenes no postulate of judicial restraint.

750 F.2d at 995-96.

Thus, the objection to Judge Bork's reliance on original intent cannot be that existing constitutional protections would be eroded. Plainly, they would not be. Rather, the objection must be that Judge Bork would be unwilling to invalidate laws to which the Constitution does not speak, but which the critics find objectionable.

II.

Although Judge Bork thus affords broad protection of those rights specified in the Constitution, he firmly believes that the Supreme Court acts illegitimately when it relies on personal preferences with no clear warrant in the text, history, or structure of the Constitution to invalidate laws made by the people's elected representatives. Bork terms the latter "judicial imperialism." Moreover, Bork rejects the claim that judicial imperialism, or noninterpretivism, is a means by which courts only add to, but never subtract from, constitutional freedoms:

> That is wrong. Among our constitutional freedoms or rights, clearly given in the text, is the power to govern ourselves democratically. Every time a court creates a new constitutional right against government or expands, without warrant, an old one, the constitutional freedom of citizens to control their lives is diminished. . . . The claim of noninterpretivists, then, that they will expand rights and freedoms is false. They will merely redistribute them.

The Struggle Over the Role of the Court, National Review 1137, 1139 (Sept. 17, 1982).

Bork's view that majorities are entitled to govern through democratic institutions when the Constitution is silent leads him to reject the creation of so-called "new rights" — rights enforced against government in the name of the Constitution but which have no demonstrable connection with that document. This method of constitutional decisionmaking is commonly referred to as "substantive due process." Although the Supreme Court's decisions invalidating state laws as inconsistent with undefined, nontextual rights of "privacy" provide the clearest recent examples, Judge Bork has been equally critical of the Supreme Court's willingness in the past to invalidate federal and state economic regulations in the name of substantive due process rights to economic liberty and property.

Privacy Rights

In 1971, Professor Bork criticized the Supreme Court's decision in *Griswold* v. *Connecticut*, 381 U.S. 479 (1965), invalidating Connecticut's ban on the use of contraceptives, on the ground that the decision could not be justified in terms of the existing Constitution. Bork noted that a right to use contraceptive devices is not "covered specifically or by obvious implication in the Constitution." Accordingly, he concluded: "Where the Constitution does not embody a moral or ethical choice, the judge has no basis other than his own values upon which to set aside the community judgment embodied in the statute. That, by definition, is an inadequate basis for judicial supremacy." *Neutral Principles and Some First Amendment Problems*, 47 Ind. L.J. 1, 14-15 (1971). Justice Black's dissent, joined by Justice Stewart, made precisely the same point:

> While I completely subscribe to the [view] that our Court has constitutional power to strike down statutes, state or federal, that violate commands of the Federal Constitution, I do not believe that we are granted power by the Due Process Clause or any other constitutional provisions to measure constitutionality by our belief that legislation is arbitrary, capricious or unreasonable, or accomplishes no justifiable purpose, or is offensive to our own notions of "civilized standards of conduct." Such an appraisal of the wisdom of legislation is an attribute of the power to make laws, not of the power to interpret them.

381 U.S. at 513.

Bork's criticisms of *Roe v. Wade*, 410 U.S. 113 (1973), proceed along similar lines. In testifying against the Human Life Bill, Professor Bork stated that *"Roe v. Wade* is, itself, an unconstitutional decision, a serious and wholly unjustifiable judicial usurpation of State legislative authority." Similarly, criticizing noninterpretivism in 1982, Bork stated, "I suppose the most striking example of [noninterpretivism] occurred in the era of the Burger Court, the supposedly conservative Court, with the decision in *Roe v. Wade*. The Court decided with no constitutional warrant that I can see, that the states' statutes regulating abortions were unconstitutional. Nobody has ever been able to locate any authority for a judge to do that in conventional constitutional materials." See *The Legitimacy of the Supreme Court*, An Interview with Robert H. Bork and Burke Marshall, in The Supreme Court and Human Rights 237, 239-41 (1982). Expressing a similar objection, Justice White, joined by Justice Rehnquist, dissented in *Roe* on the ground that there is "nothing in the language or history of the Constitution to support the Court's judgment," which he termed "an exercise of raw judicial power."

Many of the most respected constitutional law scholars have expressed profound disagreement with the reasoning and holding of *Roe v. Wade*, including Harvard Law School Professors Archibald Cox and Paul Freund, Stanford Law School Dean John Hart Ely, and Columbia Law School Professor Henry Monaghan. Dean Ely, a former law clerk to Chief Justice Earl Warren, stated in 1973 that "what is frightening about *Roe* is that this super-protected right is not inferable from the language of the Constitution, the Framers' thinking respecting the specific problem in issue, any general value derivable from the provisions they included or the nation's governmental structure." Similarly, Stanford Law School Professor Gerald Gunther, editor of the leading law school casebook on constitutional law, offered the following related comments on *Griswold v. Connecticut*: "It marked the return of the Court to the discredited notion of substantive due process. The theory was discredited in 1937 in the economic sphere. I don't find a very persuasive difference in reviving it for the personal sphere. I'm a card-carrying liberal Democrat, but this strikes me as a double standard."

As a circuit judge, Bork's approach to substantive due process is illustrated by his opinion, joined by Judge Scalia, in *Dronenburg v. Zech*, 731 F.2d 1388 (D.C. Cir. 1984), declining to extend the right to "privacy" to homosexual sodomy in the Navy. After a thorough review of the Supreme Court's privacy cases, Judge Bork concluded that the Court had neither stated nor applied a principle that would cover a right to engage in homosexual conduct. Citing Justice White's dissent in *Moore v. City of East Cleveland*, 431 U.S. 494 (1977), for the proposition that the creation of new constitutional rights "comes closest to illegitimacy" when judges make "law having little or no cognizable roots in the language or even the design of the Constitution," Judge Bork stated: "If it is in any degree doubtful that the Supreme Court should freely create new constitutional rights, we think it certain that lower courts should not do so." In addition, Judge Bork observed that both the absence of guidance from the Constitution or from articulated Supreme Court principle and the volume of lower court decisions that evade Supreme Court review counsel against the creation of new constitutional rights by lower courts. Judge Bork wrote:

> If the revolution in sexual mores that appellant proclaims is in fact ever to arrive, we think it must arrive through the moral choices of the people and their elected representatives, not through the ukase of this court.

Consistent with Judge Bork's decision in *Dronenburg*, the Supreme Court held two years later in an opinion joined by Justice Powell that the right to privacy does not confer upon homosexuals a fundamental right to engage in sodomy. See *Bowers v. Hardwick*, 106 S.Ct. 2847 (1986).

Liberty and Property Rights

Judge Bork's rejection of substantive due process and the creation of new constitutional rights, of course, includes rejection of economic rights not fairly indicated by the Constitution. For example, after discussing and criticizing the Court's decision and methodology in *Griswold*, Judge Bork rejected as equally illegitimate the invalidation of economic regulations under a generalized notion of laissez faire economic philosophy said by some to pervade the Constitution.

> As Judge Learned Hand understood, economic freedoms are philosophically indistinguishable from other freedoms. Judicial review would extend, therefore, to all economic regulations. The burden of justification would be placed on the government so that all such regulations would start with a presumption of unconstitutionality. Viewed from the standpoint of economic, philosophy, and of individual freedom, the idea has many attractions. But viewed from the standpoint of constitutional structures, the idea works a massive shift away from democracy and toward judicial rule.

The Constitution, Original Intent, and Economic Rights, 23 San Diego L. Rev. 823, 829 (1986). Similarly, speaking of the recent right to privacy cases and the substantive economic due process decisions of the 1930's, Bork has stressed that "in both of these cases, there is no way anyone can point to a provision or a historical meaning of the Constitution which gives the Court any guidance in deciding those cases; therefore, the Court is legislating freely." *The Legitimacy of the Supreme Court*, at 241-42 (1982).

Just as Judge Bork's rejection of the privacy cases leads him to reject the substantive economic due process decisions of the 1930's, one who advocates judicial creation of new constitutional rights must be prepared to accept the creation of rights with which he disagrees. By definition, such rights are not limited by the text of the Constitution, and therefore there is no means other than the individual preferences of the Justices for distinguishing among nontextual rights. Thus, those who insist that Judge Bork should embrace the creation of new rights must be prepared to endorse decisions such as *Lochner v. New York*, 198 U.S. 45 (1905), *Adair v. United States*, 208 U.S. 161 (1908), and *Adkins v. Children's Hospital*, 261 U.S. 525 (1923). *Lochner* struck down a New York liable law limiting the hours of bakery employees to 60 per week, *Adair* invalidated a federal law prohibiting interstate railroads from requiring that its employees agree as a condition of employment not to participate in labor organizations, and *Adkins* held unconstitutional a District of Columbia law requiring the payment of a minimum wage. The reasoning in *Adair* is representative of the Court's substantive due process approach:

> [I]t is not within the function of government [to] compel any person in the course of his business [to] retain the personal services of another. [The] right of a person to sell his labor upon such terms as he deems proper [is] the same as the right of the purchaser of labor to prescribe the conditions. [T]he employer and employe[e] have equality of right, and any legislation that disturbs that equality is an arbitrary interference with the liberty of contract.

Although the constitutional right created in these cases is the right to contract, the Court's analysis could easily be substituted for that employed in *Griswold* simply by replacing "the liberty of contract" with "the right to privacy."

Regardless of his personal preferences, Judge Bork approves of neither form of substantive due process, stating that the doctrine "is and always has been" improper, and that "*Griswold*'s antecedents were also wrongly decided." "With some of these cases I am in political agreement, and perhaps [the] results [in *Pierce* v. *Society of Sisters*, 268 U.S. 510 (1925) (invalidating an Oregon law requiring children to attend public schools)] could be reached on acceptable grounds, but there is no justification for the Court's methods." *Neutral Principles*, 47 Ind. L.J. at 11.

Today's debate over the legitimacy of the Supreme Court's creation of new constitutional rights is remarkably similar to the debate of the *Lochner* era. For instance, in 1937, Assistant Attorney General (later Justice) Robert H. Jackson charged that many of the Supreme Court's decisions were rooted not in the Constitution, but in "the reactionary personal views of individual Supreme Court justices":

> Let us squarely face the fact that today we have two Constitutions. One was drawn and adopted by our forefathers as an instrument of statesmanship and as a general guide to the distribution of powers and the organization of government. . . . The second Constitution is the one adopted from year to year by the judges in their decisions. . . . The due process clause has been the chief means by which the judges have written a new Constitution and imposed it upon the American people.

In short, Judge Bork's judicial philosophy is that of Justices Robert Jackson and Hugo Black: without a clear constitutional warrant, judges may not displace the considered judgments of elected officials.

STATISTICAL ANALYSIS OF JUDGE BORK'S VOTING RECORD

This memorandum reflects an analysis of every case in which

Judge Bork participated while a member of the United States Court Appeals for the District of Columbia Circuit. The analysis includes 423 appellate cases and 3 cases where Judge Bork sat as a trial judge on a three judge appeal.

As the following analysis will demonstrate, Judge Bork is an open-minded judge who is well within the mainstream of contemporary jurisprudence. He has agreed with the other judges on the D.C. Circuit—including what some would consider to be both "liberal" and "conservative" judges—in an overwhelming majority of the cases. In fact, the statistics prove that Judge Bork voted with the majority in over 94% of those cases.

Judge Bork's record on appeal is impeccable. The Supreme Court has *never* reversed any of the majority opinions written by Judge Bork, which total over 100. Indeed, the Supreme Court has never reversed any of the over 400 majority opinions in which Judge Bork has joined in one way or another. Moreover, in a number of cases where Judge Bork dissented, the Supreme Court has adopted Judge Bork's view as its own. Justice Powell, in particular, has agreed with Judge Bork in 9 out of 10 relevant cases that went to the Supreme Court, agreeing and disagreeing with Judge Bork on various issues in the other case.

These statistics concerning Judge Bork's voting record demonstrate that Judge Bork is precisely the kind of judge that President Reagan has described him to be—"a fair-minded jurist who believes his role is to interpret the law, not make it."

Judge Bork's Voting Record Vis-a-Vis Other Judges

A study of Judge Bork's voting recording all of the cases in which he participated (except for cases concerning motions for rehearing, which do not directly involve the merits of the case) reveals that Judge Bork agrees with his colleagues the great majority of the time.

For example, the statistics show that Judge Bork has voted with Judge Scalia—who was confirmed by the Senate for the Supreme Court last year—98% of the time. Judge Bork voted with Judge Ruth Bader Ginsburg almost as often—90% of the time. Indeed, Judge Bork voted together with Judge J. Skelly Wright—who some view as one of the most "liberal" judges on the D.C. Circuit—74% of the time. Table A on the following page provides a fuller account of the statistics in this regard with respect to various judges.

TABLE A

Other Judges	Total Cases	Voted With Bork	Voted Against
Scalia	86	84--98%	2--2%
R. Ginsburg	82	74--90%	8--10%
Wald	86	68--79%	18--21%
Mikva	84	70--83%	14--17%
Edwards	102	82--80%	20--20%
Wright	70	52--74%	18--26%

Judge Bork's Voting Record Vis-a-Vis Justice Powell

Statistics concerning how many times Justice Powell has agreed with Judge Bork's position in D.C. Circuit cases that went to the Supreme Court show a remarkable identity between Justice Powell's views and those of Judge Bork. In the 10 such cases that have occurred to date, Justice Powell "agreed" with Judge Bork 9 times, or 90% of the time. In the other cases, or 10% of the time, Justice Powell agreed with Judge Bork on some issues and disagreed with him on others.

Judge Bork's Majority/Dissent Voting Record

Statistics concerning how many times Judge Bork voted with the majority or the dissent confirm that Judge Bork is well within the mainstream of contemporary jurisprudence. As the following statistics demonstrate, Judge Bork voted with the majority in over 94% of the cases in which he participated, included cases concerning motions for rehearing.

TABLE B

Total Cases 426
Total Cases in Majority .... 401 -- 94% of total cases
   Majority Opinions (Author) .... 106 -- 25% of total cases
   Joined Majority .... 295 -- 69% of total cases
Total Cases in Dissent (includes full
   dissents and dissents in part) .... 25 -- 6% of total cases

Judge Bork's Record on Appeal

Judge Bork's record on appeal has been flawless. In the 106 majority opinions he has written, he has *never* been reversed by the Supreme Court. Perhaps even more remarkably, of the 401 cases in which Judge Bork joined the majority, none were reversed by the Supreme Court, and only one was reversed by the D.C. Circuit *en banc*. In addition, in a number of cases where Judge Bork dissented, either the D.C. Circuit *en banc* or the Supreme Court eventually adopted Judge Bork's position.

TABLE C

Total Cases
Majority Opinions (Author) 426
    Number of cases .... 106 -- 25% of total
    Reversed by Supreme Court 0
    Reversed by D.C. Circuit *en banc* ...... 1[1]
Total Majority Opinions Joined
    Number of cases .... 401 -- 94% of total
    Reversed by Supreme Court 0
    Reversed by D.C. Circuit *en banc* ...... 1 (see footnote 1)
Dissenting Opinions (Authored or Joined)
    Number of cases .... 25 -- 6% of total
    Adopted by Supreme Court............ 6
    Adopted by D.C. Circuit *en banc* ...... 1[2]

Conclusion

The foregoing statistics provide impressive support for President Reagan's statement that "[a]s a member of the U.S. Court of Appeals, Judge Bork has always heard each case with an open mind, following the law and legal precedent, not his personal preferences." As those statistics demonstrate, Judge Bork is the model of a principled and open-minded judge.

---

[1] *See Brown v. United States*, 742 F.2d 1498 (D.C. Cir. 1984) (en banc).
[2] *See Jersey Central Power and Light Co. v. FCC*, 810 F.2d 1168 (D.C. Cir. 1984) (*en banc*).

RESPONSE PREPARED TO WHITE HOUSE ANALYSIS OF JUDGE BORK'S RECORD*

STATEMENT OF COMMITTEE CONSULTANTS

SEPTEMBER 2, 1987

The White House statement, "Materials on Robert H. Bork," released on August 3, 1987, significantly distorts the issues posed for the Senate and the nation by President Reagan's nomination of Judge Bork to fill the Supreme Court vacancy created by the resignation this July of Associate Justice Lewis Powell. Although there is room for debate and disagreement over the ultimate issue—whether the Senate should grant or withhold its consent to the pending nomination—the record of Judge Bork's public pronouncements and actions over the past quarter-century paint a picture of Judge Bork as an extremely conservative activist rather than a genuine apostle of judicial moderation and restraint.

The attempt by the White House to depict Judge Bork as a mainstream moderate simply does not comport with his record. Bruce Fein, a former Reagan Administration official and a conservative legal scholar, made much the same point earlier this week in a radio interview. He remarked:

> Judge Bork, even if he's portrayed as a moderate and is confirmed is not going to alter his vote that way. . . . I think when you try to be a little too cute as the President is being I believe, that no one is deceived. . . . They chose Bob Bork because they wanted him to make changes in the law.

---

* The Chairman of the Senate Judiciary Committee requested a review of the White House briefing paper, released August 3, 1987, on the nomination of Judge Robert Bork to be an Associate Justice of the Supreme Court. The background research was conducted by Committee consultants Jeffrey Peck, a member of the District of Columbia Bar, and Christopher Schroeder, Professor of Law at Duke University. Their research was reviewed and approved by Floyd Abrams, member of the New York Bar, Clark Clifford, member of the District of Columbia Bar; Walter Dellinger, Professor of Law, Duke University Law School; and Laurence H. Tribe, Tyler Professor of Constitutional Law at Harvard Law School.

[This Report is reprinted in full, with the exception of the Report's two appendices.—ed.]

219

III. CONTRARY TO THE POSITION PAPER'S PORTRAYAL, THE
NOMINEE IS A JUDICIAL ACTIVIST

The White House position paper emphasizes a number of generalizations about Judge Bork's adherence to "judicial restraint" and his "faithful application" of the precedent of the Supreme Court and of his own court. According to the White House position paper, for example, Judge Bork "is among the most eloquent and principled proponents of judicial restraint." (Chapter 2, at 1.) In support of its claim, the White House position paper asserts that, "as a judge, [Bork] has faithfully applied the legal precedents of both the Supreme Court and his own Circuit Court." (Chapter 3, at 2.) To demonstrate that "faithful application," the position paper relies on a "statistical analysis of Judge Bork's voting record." This analysis, it claims, shows that the nominee "is an open-minded judge who is well within the mainstream of contemporary jurisprudence." (Chapter 6, at 1.)

These statements are too general and abstract to provide any meaningful sense of Judge Bork's philosophy. As generalizations, moreover, they avoid the more important questions of whether Judge Bork, while sitting on the D.C. Circuit, has practiced restraint, and whether his writings evince a willingness to do so. Or do Judge Bork's opinions and other writings indicate that he has engaged in precisely the same kind of "activism" for which he has chided other jurists, including members of the Warren and Burger Courts?

Attention to specific decisions and writings shows that the picture painted by the White House position paper is inaccurate and incomplete. Among the omissions are clear examples of Judge Bork's advocacy and implementation of conservative activism, which demonstrate that he is not the apostle of judicial restraint and moderation described in the White House position paper.

A. *The Position Paper's Compilation Of Statistics Seriously Distorts
Judge Bork's Record*

1. The Statistical Analysis Is Uninformative Since The Nominee,
As A Circuit Court Judge, Has Been Constitutionally
And Institutionally Bound To Follow Supreme
Court Precedent

As an intermediate court judge, the nominee has been constitutionally and institutionally bound to respect and apply Supreme Court precedent. Indeed, Judge Bork has explicitly recognized that duty in some of his decisions. *Franz v. United States*, 712 F.2d 1428 (D.C. Cir. 1983); *Dronenburg v. Zech.* 741 F.2d 1388 (D.C. Cir. 1984).) Relying on Judge Bork's lack of reversals to show his "faithful application" of Supreme Court precedents thus says nothing about his potential for activism if confirmed as an Associate Justice on the Supreme Court, where he would be free of such restraints. The "statistical analysis," therefore, is uninformative.

   2.   The Position Paper's Statistics Ignore The Rejection By A
        Unanimous Supreme Court Of Judge Bork's Dissent In A
              Recent Leading Case On Sexual Harassment In
                            The Workplace

   The focus in the White House position paper on the lack of reversals of Judge Bork's majority opinions ignores the rejection of one of Judge Bork's dissents by a unanimous Supreme Court. In a factually inaccurate and misleading description, the White House position paper claims that the Supreme Court "adopted positions similar to those of Judge Bork both on the evidentiary issues and on the issue of liability" in the case of *Vinson v. Taylor*. (753 F.2d 141, *rehearing denied*, 760 F.2d 1330 (D.C. Cir. 1985), *aff'd sub nom. Meritor Savings Bank v. Vinson*, 106 S. Ct. 2399 (1986)), the leading case on sexual harassment in the workplace. In fact, Justice Rehnquist's opinion for the full Court took a far more sensitive approach to liability for such harassment than did Judge Bork's dissent.

   Vinson, a bank teller, claimed that her supervisor insisted that she have sex with him, and that she did so because she feared she would be fired if she did not. Vinson claimed that over the next several years, her supervisor made repeated sexual demands, fondled her in front of other employees, exposed himself to her, and forcibly raped her on several occasions. The trial court dismissed the claim, saying that their relationship was "voluntary." The D.C. Circuit reversed, holding that if the supervisor made "Vinson's toleration of sexual harassment a condition of her employment," her voluntariness "had no materiality whatsoever."

   The D.C. Circuit was asked to rehear the case, and the full court declined. Judge Bork dissented from the denial of the rehearing. Attacking the original decision, Judge Bork argued that "voluntariness" should be a complete defense in a sexual harassment case. He said that "[t]hese rulings seem plainly wrong. By depriving the charged person of any defenses, they mean that sexual dalliance, however voluntarily engaged in, becomes harassment whenever an employee sees fit, after the fact, to so characterize it." (760 F.2d at 1330.)

   Judge Bork's holding on the voluntariness issue was flatly rejected by a unanimous Supreme Court, with Justice Powell joining the opinion. (The Court did agree with Judge Bork on the evidentiary issue.) Justice Rehnquist wrote the Court's opinion, and held that the correct test for sexual harassment was whether the employer created "an intimidating, hostile, or offensive working environment." He concluded that "[t]he correct inquiry is whether [plaintiff] by her conduct indicated that the alleged sexual advances were unwelcome, not whether her actual participation in sexual intercourse was voluntary." (106 S. Ct. at 2406.)

The White House position paper's statements about the *Vinson* case thus fail to comport with the clear factual record. And by distorting the facts, the position paper inflates Judge Bork's record with respect to review by the Supreme Court.

3. The Position Paper's Analysis Of Judge Bork's Supposed "Agreement" With Majority Opinions Often Distorts His More Substantive Rejection Of The Majority's Position

Throughout the White House position paper, Judge Bork is identified as having agreed with the majority opinion in a number of cases that purport to show his moderation and restraint. Typical of such attribution is the statement, made in connection with *Planned Parenthood Federation v. Heckler* (712 F.2d 650 (D.C. Cir. 1983)):

> Judge Bork showed his respect for statutory requirements by agreeing with a decision that the Health and Human Services Department violated the law in its attempts to require federally-funded family planning grantees to notify parents when contraceptives were provided to certain minors. Thus, the Department's so-called 'squeal' rule was overturned by the court. (Chapter 2, at 2.)

This description distorts the true nature of Judge Bork's opinion, which is anything but deferential and non-activist.

In *Planned Parenthood*, the plaintiffs challenged a federal regulation that required all family-planning centers to give notice to parents that their teenagers sought contraceptives. Because Congress explicitly stated that it did not intend to "mandate" family involvement in the delivery of services, but rather wanted the centers to "encourage" teenagers to bring their families into the process, the court held that the parental notification requirement was inconsistent with Congress's intent.

Although Judge Bork agreed that Congress intended that notification be voluntary on the teenager's part (*id.* at 665, 667), he concluded that Congress did not clearly prohibit the regulations. He conceded that HHS had misinterpreted the relevant law, but argued nonetheless that the authority necessary for the regulation might be found elsewhere. Noting that the regulations pertained to a "vexed and hotly controverted area of morality and prudence," (*id*. at 665), Judge Bork urged that the case be remanded to search for this unknown authority. The majority argued that a remand would be gratuitous, since it was clear that the Executive had violated the law.

4.　None Of Judge Bork's Majority Opinions Has Ever Been *Reviewed* By The Supreme Court

One "statistic" cited by the White House position paper is that Judge Bork, author of more than 100 majority opinions, has never been reversed. It is more accurate to say, however, that no majority opinion of Judge Bork's has ever been reviewed. Until recently, in all of Judge Bork's majority opinions review had not been sought by either party (100 cases) or review had been denied. (9 cases). While the Supreme Court has recently granted certiorari in one case in which he wrote a majority opinion (*Finzer v. Barry*, (798 F.2d 1450 (D.C. Cir. 1986), *cert. granted*, 107 S. Ct. 1282 (1987)), the Court has still never addressed the merits of any of Judge Bork's majority opinions.

5.　Since Judge Bork Concedes That 90% Of His Docket Has Been Non-Ideological, His Circuit Court Record Says Nothing About His Suitability For The Supreme Court, Whose Docket Is Far More Controversial

The White House position paper goes to great pains to argue that because Judge Bork has never been reversed, he is entitled to sit on the nation's highest court. Its statistical assessment relies on more than 400 cases from the D.C. Circuit. Most of those cases, however, have little relevance to the Bork nomination. As noted by Judge Bork, the D.C. Circuit "is an ideologically divided court" but this "[m]akes no difference on 9/10's of [our] cases. (Notes for Untitled Speech, *Federal Legal Council*, Oct. 16, 1983, at 2.) (Emphasis added.)

Judge Bork himself has acknowledged that the caseload of the Supreme Court is quite different from that of the D.C. Circuit:

> [The Supreme Court] certainly has a distinct set of responsibilities. Everybody has an appeal as of right to this court and any circuit court. So we are much more in the business of settling disputes just because they are disputes. The Supreme Court, which has a discretionary jurisdiction, can't conceivably settle all of the disputes that come up through the federal courts or up through the state courts, and so it must pick and choose, and it picks and chooses bearing in mind its obligation to settle important, un-

resolved questions of law and to lay down guidelines. (*District Lawyer Interview* 1985) at 31-32.)

According to Judge Bork, therefore, 90% of his cases on the D.C. Circuit are non-ideological and, consequently, non-controversial. Judge Bork's affirmance ratio, as described by the White House position paper, thus says little, if anything, about his suitability for the Supreme Court, which agrees to hear only a small percentage of the cases for which review is sought and whose docket has far more ideological and controversial cases.

6. The Statistics Do Not Demonstrate That Judge Bork And Justice Powell Are Ideologically Similar

The position paper claims that Justice Powell has agreed with Judge Bork in 9 of 10 "relevant" cases that went to the Supreme Court. (Chapter 6, at 1.) It thus continues its transparent effort to depict Judge Bork as the ideological equivalent to the retired Lewis Powell. Such depiction has no basis in fact.

The "9 out of 10" figure, marshalled to show the similarity in the views of the two men, seriously misrepresents some of those cases. In *Vinson v. Taylor*, for example, the position paper reports that Judge Bork and Justice Powell were in agreement. In fact, as discussed above (Section III(A)(2)), the two were on opposite sides, with Judge Bork dissenting from a D.C. Circuit opinion that was unanimously affirmed by the Supreme Court. Furthermore, a careful analysis of the remaining cases cited by the position paper shows that Judge Bork and Justice Powell both wrote opinions in only two. . . . In order to identify the substantive distinctions between Justice Powell and Judge Bork, therefore, casual and selective analysis of statistics simply can not suffice. Rather, it is necessary to delve into the judicial philosophy, judicial method and substantive positions of the individuals, as is done in other sections of this Rebuttal.

B. An Accurate Portrait Of Judge Bork's Record Leaves No Doubt That He Has Been A Conservative Activist And Not A Practitioner of Judicial Restraint

Despite the constitutional and institutional restraints under which Judge Bork operated, his judicial record—far from supporting the position paper's assertions of restraint—is replete with examples of an activist approach. Indeed, Judge Bork's colleagues on the D.C. Circuit have made this quite clear.

1. Judge Bork's Novel Approach To Lower Court Constitutional
    Adjudication In *Dronenburg* Led Four Members Of The
    D.C. Circuit To Remind Him That "Judicial
    Restraint Begins At Home"

In *Dronenburg v. Zech* (741 F.2d 1388 (D.C. Cir. 1984)), Judge
Bork's majority opinion affirmed the dismissal of the Navy's discharge of a nine-year veteran for engaging in consensual homosexual
activity. After a lengthy recitation of the Supreme Court's line of privacy decisions for creating what he deemed as "new rights," (*Id.* at
1395), Judge Bork claimed that he could find no "explanatory principle" in them, and then argued that lower federal courts were required
to give very narrow readings to them because the courts "have no
guidance from the Constitution or . . . from articulated Supreme
Court principle." (*Id.* at 1396.)

Judge Bork's theory of lower court constitutional jurisprudence
in *Dronenburg*—a theory that has never been expressed or endorsed
by the Supreme Court—as well as his criticism of the privacy decisions, led four members of the D.C. Circuit to caution Judge Bork, in
their dissent from the denial of the petition for rehearing en banc,
about the proper role of the court:

> [Judge Bork's] extravagant exegesis on the constitutional right of
> privacy was wholly unnecessary to decide the case before the
> court. . . . We find particularly inappropriate the panel's attempt
> to wipe away selected Supreme Court decisions in the name of judi-
> cial restraint. Regardless whether it is the proper role of lower
> courts to 'create new constitutional rights,' surely it is not their
> function to conduct a general spring cleaning of constitutional law.
> Judicial restaint begins at home. (746 F.2d 1579, 1580.) (Emphasis
> added.)

2. Five Members Of The D.C. Circuit Have Charged Judge Bork
    With Evaluating En Banc Cases According To "Self-
    Serving And Result-Oriented" Criterion

Dronenburg is not the only case in which several members of the
District of Columbia Circuit have charged Judge Bork with pursuing
his own agenda. In a series of recent orders issued by the full Court, a
majority decided to reverse its decisions to grant en banc hearings in
four cases. (Cases before the appeals court are normally heard by
panels of three judges, but a party may seek review of a panel decision
by asking for an en banc hearing before all members of the court.)
Although Reagan nominee Lawrence Silberman disassociated himself, Judge Bork, in dissent, joined in the group attacking the majority's decisions. That dissent led Judge Edwards, writing on behalf of

Chief Judge Wald and Judges Robinson, Mikva and Ginsburg, to charge the group led by Judge Bork with conducting their review of en banc cases according to "self-serving and result-oriented criterion." (*United States v. Meyer*, No. 85-6169, Slip op. at 2 (D.C. Cir. July 31, 1987).) (Emphasis added.)

Judge Edwards also noted that the conduct of the faction headed by Judge Bork had done

> substantial violence to the collegiality that is indispensable to judicial decision-making. Collegiality cannot exist if every dissenting judge feels obliged to lobby his or her colleagues to rehear the case en banc in order to vindicate that judge's position. Politicking will replace the thoughtful dialogue that should characterize a court where every judge respects the integrity of his or her colleagues. (*Id.* at 4.) (Emphasis added.)

C. *Judge Bork's Unbroken Repudiation Of The Doctrines Preventing Unwarranted Governmental Intrusion Into The Intimacies Of Personal Life Ignores The Tradition And Text Of The Constitution*

Since 1971, the nominee has mounted a persistent attack on the long line of Supreme Court decisions protecting the intimacies of personal life from unwarranted governmental intrusion. The intensity and consistency of this attack raises substantial concern about the agenda the nominee might bring to the Court with respect to this line of decisions. It also is indicative of Judge Bork's willingness to discard the text, history and tradition of the Constitution in order to achieve the results he desires.

1. Judge Bork Has Dismissed Many Of The Supreme Court's Landmark Privacy Decisions

Judge Bork's rejection of consitutional protection against unwarranted intrusion into the intimacies of one's personal life is not limited to any one case or any one area of private relations. Rather, Judge Bork has dismissed many of the Court's decisions covering a wide range of personal conduct.

a. Judge Bork Has Opposed The Decision Upholding The Right Of Married Couples To Use Contraceptives

In *Griswold v. Connecticut* (381 U.S. 479 (1965)), the Supreme Court struck down a state law making it a crime for married couples to use contraceptives and for physicians to advise such couples about

VI. STARE DECISIS: RESPECT FOR AND ADHERENCE TO PRECEDENT

Apparently recognizing the longstanding and extensive attack that has been mounted by Judge Bork on a wide range of Supreme Court doctrines, the White House has attempted to portray the nominee as a man who would be humbled by elevation to the nation's highest court. However excessive his views may have been in the past, the White House seems to say, Judge Bork would, upon ascension to the

Supreme Court, be reigned in by respect for the institution and its position as a co-equal branch of government. Simply put, this picture is not borne out by Judge Bork's extensive record.

A basic question that the Senate will face as it considers the nomination is this: What are Judge Bork's views on "stare decisis," the crucial doctrine that counsels respect for and adherence to precedent? According to the White House, while some fear that Bork will "seek to 'roll back' many existing precedents. . .,[t]here is no basis for this view in Judge Bork's record." The position paper also attempts to explain Judge Bork's criticism of "the reasoning of Supreme Court opinions" as something "that law professors do." And, the position paper claims that, "as a judge, [Bork] has faithfully applied the legal precedents of both the Supreme Court and his own Circuit Court." Finally, the position paper contends rather generally that Judge Bork "believes in abiding by precedent." A complete review of the nominee's record demonstrates conclusively the error of each assertion.

A. *Judge Bork Has Conceded, In Clear And Unambiguous Terms, That His Views As A Judge "Have Remained About What They Were" When He Was An Academic*

The suggestions in the White House position paper that Judge Bork's sweeping attacks on landmark decisions of the Supreme Court have simply been the typical musings of an academic seeking to provoke debate are flatly contradicted by Judge Bork's own statements to the contrary. His statements belie any assertion that his writings and speeches criticizing Supreme Court cases are merely abstract academic exercises, divorced from his leanings as a potential Justice.

Less than a year ago—and more than four years after he began sitting as a member of the D.C. Circuit—Judge Bork commented on his roles as an academic and as a jurist. In clear and unambiguous terms, the nominee stated:

> Teaching is very much like being a judge and you approach the Constitution in the same way. (Interview with WQED, Pittsburgh, Nov. 19, 1986.) (Emphasis added.)

In a similar vein, Judge Bork said in a 1985 interview:

> [M]y views have remained about what they were [since becoming a judge]. After all, courts are not that mysterious, and if you deal with them enough and teach their opinions enough, you're likely to know a great deal. So when you become a judge, I don't think your viewpoint is likely to change greatly. (*District Lawyer Interview*, 1985, at 31.) (Emphasis added.)

Any remaining doubts about whether the suggestions in the

White House position paper are disingenuous should be put to rest by Judge Bork's additional comment in the same 1985 interview:

> Obviously, when you're considering a man or woman for a judicial appointment, you would like to know what that man or woman thinks, you look for a track record, and that means that you read any articles they've written, any opinions they've written. That part of the selection process is inevitable, and there's no reason to be upset about it. (*Id.* at 33.) (Emphasis added.)

And, finally, to the extent that one may question whether Judge Bork's 1971 *Indiana Law Journal* article is relevant to the Senate's inquiry, the nominee leaves no doubt: "I finally worked out a philosophy which is expressed pretty much in that 1971 *Indiana Law Journal* piece." *(Conservative Digest Interview,* 1985 at 101.)

Judge Bork's own clear statements, therefore, inform the Senate as to where it should look in determining the nominee's jurisprudential views. Beyond these statements, there are several other reasons for carefully considering the Judge Bork's extra-judicial as well as his judicial record.

First, many of Judge Bork's "musings" have taken the form of testimony before Congress, where he was offering his opinions on issues upon which that body would presumably base legislation. Second, Judge Bork has maintained his drumbeat of criticism in articles, speeches and interviews while sitting as member of the D.C. Circuit; such criticism, in other words, did not cease upon the nominee's departure from academia. Third, the attempt to minimize the effects of Judge Bork's writings gives short shrift to the legal academic community and belittles the important contributions that scholarship has made to the development of the law.

Judge Bork's complete 25-year record, then, is relevant to his nomination. The attempt to limit the Senate's consideration to his opinions on the D.C. Circuit should be rejected.

B. *There Is Considerable Basis In Judge Bork's Record For Concern That He Would Overturn Many Landmark Supreme Court Decisions*

The claim that "no basis" exists in Judge Bork's record for concern that he would overturn precedents if confirmed as an Associate Justice is without merit. In fact, the record is replete with specific statements by the nominee that give great cause for concern.

1. Judge Bork Has Said That The Appointment Power Should Be
Used To Correct "Judicial Excesses"

One indication of Judge Bork's views on stare decisis stems from
his remarks on the appointment power. He has said that the "answer" to "judicial excesses" can "only lie in the selection of judges,
which means that the solution will be intermittent, depending upon
the President's ability to choose well and his opportunities to choose
at all." (" 'Inside' Felix Frankfurter," *The Public Interest*, Fall Book
Supplement, 1981, at 109-110.) During the 1982 hearings on his
nomination to the D.C. Circuit, Judge Bork stated that "[t]he only
cure for a Court which oversteps its bounds that I know of is the
appointment power." ("Confirmation of Federal Judges," *Hearings
Before The Senate Judiciary Committee*, 1982, at 7.) In a 1986 article,
Judge Bork wrote that "[d]emocratic responses to judicial excesses
probably must come through the replacement of judges who die or
retire with judges of different views." ("Judicial Review and Democracy," *Society*, Nov./Dec. 1986, at 6.)

2. Judge Bork Has Said That "Broad Areas Of Constitutional
Law" Ought To Be Reformulated And That An
Originalist Judge Should Have "No Problem"
In Overruling A Non-Originalist Precedent

On several occasions, Judge Bork has expressed a clear willingness to overturn precedent. For example, in a January 1987 speech,
Judge Bork, after describing himself as an "originalist," stated:

> Certainly at the least, I would think that an orginalist judge
> would have no problem whatever in overruling a non-originalist
> precedent, because that precedent by the very basis of his judicial
> philosophy, has no legitimacy. It comes from nothing that the
> framers intended. (Remarks on the Panel "Precedent, the Amend-
> ment Process, and Evolution of Constitutional Doctrine," *First An-
> nual Lawyers Convention of the Federalist Society,* Jan. 31, 1987, at
> 124, 126.) (Emphasis added.)

Judge Bork also asserted in this same speech that:

> [T]he role of precedent in constitutional law is less important than
> it is in a proper common law or statutory model.

> [I]f a constitutional judge comes to a firm conviction that the
> courts have misunderstood the intentions of the founders, . . . he is
> freer than when acting in his capacity as an interpreter of the com-
> mon law or of a statute to overturn a precedent. (*Id.* at 125-26.)

While Judge Bork cautioned that a judge is not "absolutely free" in this regard (*id.*), these statements provide a keen insight into the nominee's views on the role of precedent in our constitutional system.

Also significant are Judge Bork's remarks in his well-known *Indiana Law Journal* article:

> Courts must accept any value choice the legislature makes unless it clearly runs contrary to a choice made in the framing of the Constitution. . . . It follows, of course, that broad areas of constitutional law ought to be reformulated. ("Neutral Principles" at 11.) (Emphasis added.)

Yet another indication of Judge Bork's eagerness for the Supreme Court to revisit certain fundamental issues appears in a 1985 local bar interview. When pressed about whether he could identify those constitutional doctrines he thought ripe for reconsideration by the Supreme Court, Judge Bork stated "Yes I can, but I won't." ("A Talk With Judge Bork," *District Lawyer.* June 1985, at 32.) (Emphasis added.)

One such doctrine may the development of the Bill of Rights. In a 1986 speech, Judge Bork posed the question of "whether, given the state of the precedent, a judge that wanted to return to basic principles could do so." ("Federalism," *Attorney General's Conference*, Jan. 24-26, 1986, at 9.) Judge Bork answered:

> The court's treatment of the Bill of Rights is theoretically the easiest to reform. It is here that the concept of original intent provides guidance to the courts and also a powerful rhetoric to persuade the public that the end to [judicial] imperialism is required and some degree of reexamination is desirable. (*Id.*) (Emphasis added.)

Judge Bork also has said that "constitutional law . . . is at least. . . ., as badly in need of reform as antitrust," (Untitled Speech, *William Mitchell College of Law,* Feb. 10, 1984), about which he has remarked that "[a] great body of wrong, indeed, thoroughly perverse, Supreme Court [law] remains on the books. . . ." (Untitled Speech, *Lexecon Conference,* Oct. 30, 1981.)

3. The Record Strongly Suggests That Judge Bork, If Confirmed, Would Vote To Overturn A Substantial Number Of Supreme Court Decisions

It is at this juncture difficult to identify precisely which doctrines "Justice" Bork would seek to reconsider immediately. The record strongly suggests, however, that the number would be substantial.

In a 1982 speech in which he discussed the debate over the different methods of constitutional interpretation, Judge Bork said:

[N]o writer on either side of the controversy thinks that any large proportion of the most significant constitutional decisions of the past three decades could have been reached through interpretation [of the Constitution]. (Untitled Speech, *Catholic University,* March 31, 1982, at 5.) (Emphasis added.)

Similarly, with respect to the Supreme Court's landmark decisions in such cases as *Griswold v. Connecticut* (381 U.S. 479 (1965)) and *Roe v. Wade* (410 U.S. 113 (1973)), Judge Bork remarked:

In not one of those cases could the result have been reached by interpretation of the Constitution, and these, of course, are only a small fraction of the cases about which that could be said. (*Id.* at 4.) (Emphasis added.)

Judge Bork's 1981 testimony on the Human Life bill also strongly suggests that he might vote to overturn a large number of cases. In the context of criticizing the decision in *Roe v. Wade,* Judge Bork testified that it is "by no means the only example of . . . unconstitutional behavior by the Supreme Court." ("The Human Life Bill," *Hearings Before The Subcommittee on Separation of Powers,* 1981, at 310.) In his written testimony, Judge Bork stated:

The judiciary have a right, indeed, a duty, to require basic and unsettling changes, and to do so, despite any political clamor, when the Constitution fairly interpreted demands it. The trouble is that nobody believes the Constitution allows, much less demands, the decision in *Roe* . . . or in dozens of other cases in recent years. (*Id.* at 315.) (Emphasis added.)

Along these same lines, Judge Bork has commented:

[T]he Court . . . began in the mid-1950s to make . . . decisions for which it offered little or no constitutional argument. . . . Much of the new judicial power claimed cannot be derived from the text, structure, or history of the Constitution. ("Judicial Review and Democracy," *Encyclopedia of the American Constitution,* Vol. 2, at 1062 (1986).)

What are the "large proportion" of significant constitutional cases in the "last three decades" that could not have been reached through interpretation of the Constitution? What are the "dozens of cases" not "allowed" by the Constitution? What are the cases since the mid-1950s that are not supported by the Constitution? These are fundamental questions for the hearings in September, but they may not be answered there. But the Senate need not operate on a blank slate in such a case, because Judge Bork has already told us to look at his "track record," including "any articles" he has written. (*District Lawyer,* "Interview" at 33.)

Accordingly, Senators may turn for valuable insight to the nominee's many attacks on past precedents—precedents that he would likely encounter during the two decades he might serve if confirmed to the Court. These attacks . . . may be the only available window to the "dozens of cases" that Judge Bork believes are not "allowed" by the Constitution.

C. *Judge Bork's Application Of His Academic Views To His Judicial Decisions Is Illustrated By His Attack On The Privacy Cases In* Dronenburg

Judge Bork has not only said that he approaches the Constitution "in the same way" both in academia and on the bench; he has actually done so. Indeed, in contrast to the suggestion in the White House position paper that Judge Bork has limited his criticism of Supreme Court cases to academia, the record shows that such criticism also has been leveled from the bench.

In *Dronenburg v. Zech* (741 F.2d 1388 (D.C. Cir. 1984)), for example, Judge Bork critically evaluated the entire line of the Supreme Court's privacy cases, commencing with *Griswold v. Connecticut.* His attack led four members of the D.C. Circuit, in their dissent from the denial of the petition for rehearing en banc, to caution the nominee that "surely it is not the function [of lower courts] to conduct a general spring cleaning of constitutional law." (746 F.2d 1579, 1580.)

D. *Judge Bork's "Faithful Application" Of Supreme Court Precedent While A Circuit Court Judge Is Irrelevant Since He Has Been Constitutionally And Institutionally Bound To Follow The Supreme Court As A Lower Court Judge*

As discussed previously, that Judge Bork may have "faithfully applied" Supreme Court precedents while on the D.C. Circuit, as claimed by the White House position paper, is irrelevant to his potential actions on the Supreme Court. As an intermediate court judge, he has been constitutionally and institutionally bound to respect and apply that precedent. As a Supreme Court Justice, he would not be so bound.

E. *Judge Bork Has Consistently Given Only One Example Of A Constitutional Doctrine That He Regards As Too Well-Settled To Overturn*

The White House position paper stresses that, according to Judge Bork, even "questionable" precedent should not be overturned if "it has become part of the political fabric of the nation." The position paper may be referring to Bork's statement in a 1985 *District Lawyer* interview that there are certain decisions around which "so many statutes, regulations, governmental institutions, [and] private expectations" have been built that "they have become part of the structure of the nation." Importantly, the sole example Judge Bork has ever given of the type of precedent that would meet this test is the interpretation of the commerce clause. *(See District Lawyer Interview* at 32; *Federalist Society Convention* Speech, Jan. 31, 1987, at 4.) He has never, based on the information reviewed thus far, offered any other example.

Judge Bork's rationale for invoking the commerce clause in this context is quite telling. He is willing to uphold decisions under the commerce clause because of his respect for government and for the institutional arrangements that have been built around the clause. This is far different from arguing that precedent should be upheld because of one's respect for his or her predecessors on the Court and their reasons for reaching a particular decision. Elevation to the Supreme Court should be a humbling experience—but Judge Bork's reasons for upholding decisions expanding the commerce clause suggest that he would feel no such humility.

F. *Judge Bork Has Distinguished Between Precedents From Higher Courts And Those Within The Same Court*

Importantly, Judge Bork has drawn a distinction between a judge's duty with respect to precedents from a higher court and those within the same court. At his 1982 confirmation hearings, Bork stated:

> I think that as a court of appeals judge one has to adhere to [stare decisis] very strongly, and that is to follow the lead of the Supreme Court. It is less clear, for example, about precedent within a single court and whether that court should follow it or not. ("Confirmation of Federal Judges," *Hearings Before the Senate Judiciary Committee*, 1982, at 13.)

This strongly suggests that were the constitutional and institutional constraints that apply to an intermediate court judge removed, Bork would be more willing to overturn precedents.

G. *In Contrast To Judge Bork, Justice Powell Emphasized That Stare Decisis Is A Doctrine That "Demands Respect In A Society Governed By Rule Of Law"*

Respect for precedent was a powerful element of Justice Powell's jurisprudence. In his view, "the doctrine of stare decisis, while perhaps never entirely persuasive on a constitutional question, is a doctrine that demands respect in a society governed by the rule of law." (*City of Akron v. Akron Center For Reproductive Health, Inc.,* 462 U.S. 416, 419-420 (1983).) (Emphasis added.)

Justice Powell also underscored the "especially compelling reasons for adhering to stare decisis in applying the principles of *Roe v. Wade.*" (*Id.* at 420 n. 1.) *Roe,* said Powell,

> was considered with special care. It was first argued during the 1971 Term, and reargued—with extensive briefing—the following Term. The decision was joined by the Chief Justice and six other Justices. Since *Roe* was decided in January 1973, the Court repeatedly and consistently has accepted and applied the basic principle that a woman has a fundamental right to make the highly personal choice whether or not to terminate her pregnancy. (*Id.*)

H.   *Many Commentators Doubt That Judge Bork Would Abide By Precedent*

Several commentators do not agree with the White House's assessment that Judge Bork, if confirmed, would abide by precedent. Owen Fiss, the Alexander Bickel Professor of Public Law at Yale University, has written:

> As if to reassure the liberal coalition on the abortion issue, Mr. [Lloyd] Cutler insists that Judge Bork's 'writings reflect a respect for precedent.' Nothing could be farther from the truth: What Judge Bork's writings—spanning almost 20 years as a professor— reflect is not a concern for precedent but a dogmatic commitment to a comprehensive or general theory and a willingness to deride decisions that do not agree with his theory.
> Judge Bork's performance on the Court of Appeals has not revealed a change in outlook. Indeed, his recent effort to confine the right-to-privacy decisions of the Supreme Court earned him a rebuke by his colleagues, who insisted that 'it is not . . . [the] function [of lower court Judges] to conduct a general spring cleaning of constitutional law.' Elevating Judge Bork to the Supreme Court is not likely to instill within him a new reverence for authority, but rather to give him the power to write his views into law. (Letter to The *New York Times,* July 31, 1987.) (Emphasis added.)

Similarly, Oxford and New York University Professor Ronald Dworkin has recently commented:

> Bork's views do not lie within the scope of the long-standing debate between liberals and conservatives about the proper role of the Supreme Court. Bork is a constitutional radical who rejects a requirement of the rule of law that all sides in that debate had previously accepted. He rejects the view that the Supreme Court must

test its interpretations of the Constitution against principles latent in its own past decisions as well as other aspects of the nation's constitutional history. (Dworkin, "The Bork Nomination," *New York Review of Books,* Aug. 13, 1987.)

I. *The Effects Of Reversing The Important Bodies Of Constitutional Law That Judge Bork Has Criticized Would Be Grave*

The doctrine of stare decisis is a cornerstone of our constitutional and jurisprudential foundations. Like most such doctrines, of course, it is not absolute. As Archibald Cox states in his recently published book, some overruling of precedent is part of our constitutional tradition. (Cox, *The Court and the Constitution* (Houghton Mifflin Co. 1987) at 364.) "[W]hen taken with discretion," the step "is essential to the correction of errors." (*Id.*)

What happens when the step is not taken with discretion? If "Justice" Bork were to act on his criticism of any number of the decisions identified above—were he, in other words, to overrule even the shortest of these lines of settled law—the consequences would be grave. Such action could well carry the suggestion, in Mr. Cox's words, that "constitutional rights depend on the vagaries of individual Justices and the politics of the President who appoints them. . . . Constitutionalism as practiced in the past could not survive if, as a result of a succession of carefully chosen Presidential appointments, the sentiment of a majority of the Justices shifted back and forth . . . so that the rights to freedom of choice [and] freedom from State-mandated prayer . . . were alternately recognized and denied." (*Id.* at 364.)

Congressional Record - Senate
July 1, 1987
P. 9188

NOMINATION OF ROBERT BORK

Mr. KENNEDY. Mr. President, I oppose the nomination of Robert Bork to the Supreme Court, and I urge the Senate to reject it.

In the Watergate scandal of 1973, two distinguished Republicans -- Attorney General Elliot Richardson and Deputy Attorney General William Ruckelshaus -- put integrity and the Constitution ahead of loyalty to a corrupt President. They refused to do Richard Nixon's dirty work, and they refused to obey his order to fire Special Prosecutor Archibald Cox. The deed devolved on Solicitor General Robert Bork, who executed the unconscionable assignment that has become one of the darkest chapters for the rule of law in American history.

That act -- later ruled illegal by a Federal court -- is sufficient, by itself, to disqualify Mr. Bork from this new position to which he has been nominated. The man who fired Archibald Cox does not deserve to sit on the Supreme Court of the United States.

Mr. Bork should also be rejected by the Senate because he stands for an extremist view of the Constitution and the role of the Supreme Court that would have placed him outside the mainstream of American constitutional jurisprudence in the 1960's, let alone the 1980's. He opposed the Public Accommodations Civil Rights Act of 1964. He opposed the one-man one-vote decision of the Supreme Court the same year. He has said that the First Amendment applies only to political speech, not literature or works of art or scientific expression.

Under the twin pressures of academic rejection and the prospect of Senate rejection, Mr. Bork subsequently retracted the most neanderthal of these views on civil rights and the first amendment. But his mind-set is no less ominous today.

Robert Bork's America is a land in which women would be forced into back-alley abortions. blacks would sit at segregated lunch counters, rogue police could break down citizens' doors in midnight raids, schoolchildren could not be taught about evolution, writers and artists would be censored at the whim of government, and the doors of the Federal courts would be shut on the fingers of millions of citizens for whom the judiciary is often the only protector of the individual rights that are the heart of our democracy.

America is a better and freer nation than Robert Bork thinks. Yet in the current delicate balance of the Supreme Court, his rigid ideology will tip the scales of justice against the kind of country America is and ought to be.

The damage that President Reagan will do through this nomination, if it is not rejected by the Senate, could live on far beyond the end of his Presidential term. President Reagan is still our President. But he should not be able to reach out from the muck of Irangate, reach into the muck of Watergate, and impose his reactionary vision of the Constitution on the Supreme Court and on the next generation of Americans. No justice would be better than this injustice.

Mr. President, I ask unanimous consent that a statement by Benjamin L. Hooks and Ralph G. Neas of the Leadership Conference on Civil Rights opposing the nomination may be printed in the Record.

There being no objection, the statement was ordered to be printed in the Record, as follows:

STATEMENT OF BENJAMIN L. HOOKS, CHAIRPERSON, AND RALPH G. NEAS, EXECUTIVE DIRECTOR, LEADERSHIP CONFERENCE ON CIVIL RIGHTS

There is no question that a very substantial majority of the civil rights community will strongly oppose the nomination of Robert Bork to be Associate Justice of the United States Supreme Court.

The confirmation of Robert Bork, an ultra-conservative, would dramatically alter the balance of the Supreme Court, putting in jeopardy the civil rights achievements of the past three decades. Well established law could overnight be substantially eroded or overturned.

This is the most historic moment of the Reagan presidency. Senators will never cast a more important and far-reaching vote. Indeed, this decision will profoundly influence the law of the land well into the 21st century.

S. Hrg. 100-1011, Pt. 1

NOMINATION OF ROBERT H. BORK TO BE ASSOCIATE JUSTICE OF THE SUPREME COURT OF THE UNITED STATES

HEARINGS

BEFORE THE

COMMITTEE ON THE JUDICIARY
UNITED STATES SENATE

ONE HUNDREDTH CONGRESS

FIRST SESSION

ON

THE NOMINATION OF ROBERT H. BORK TO BE ASSOCIATE JUSTICE OF
THE SUPREME COURT OF THE UNITED STATES

SEPTEMBER 15, 16, 17, 18, 19, 21, 22, 23,
25, 28, 29, AND 30, 1987

Part 1 of 5 Parts

Serial No. J-100-64

Printed for the use of the Committee on the Judiciary

U.S. GOVERNMENT PRINTING OFFICE

86-974   WASHINGTON : 1989

For sale by the Superintendent of Documents, U.S. Government Printing Office
Washington, DC 20402

OPENING STATEMENT OF ROBERT H. BORK, TO BE ASSOCIATE JUSTICE OF THE U.S. SUPREME COURT

Judge BORK. Mr. Chairman, thank you very much, and distinguished members of the Judiciary Committee.

I would like first to introduce my family if I may.

The CHAIRMAN. Please. I apologize. I had an opportunity to meet them and the hearing has been going on so long I failed to mention that. Please do.

Judge BORK. Well, one person I cannot introduce to you is my mother, Mrs. Elizabeth Bork, who is, I am confident, watching on television. My wife, Mary Ellen Bork, in the gray suit; my daughter, Ellen Bork in the burgundy, my son Charles, and my son Robert, Jr. And as Senator Hatch mentioned, Mrs. Potter Stewart, who is a neighbor of ours, is with us today.

The CHAIRMAN. Welcome all. Thank you for being here.

Judge BORK. I want to begin by thanking the President for placing my name in nomination for this most important position. I am flattered and humbled to have been selected. If confirmed, I assure the Senate that I will approach the enormous task energetically and enthusiastically and will endeavor to the best of my ability to live up to the confidence placed in me.

I also want to thank President Ford and Senators Dole and Danforth and Congressman Fish for their warm remarks in introducing me to the Senate and to this committee.

As you have said, quite correctly, Mr. Chairman, and as others have said here today, this is in large measure a discussion of judicial philosophy, and I want to make a few remarks at the outset on that subject of central interest.

That is, my understanding of how a judge should go about his or her work. That may also be described as my philosophy of the role of a judge in a constitutional democracy.

The judge's authority derives entirely from the fact that he is applying the law and not his personal values. That is why the American public accepts the decisions of its courts, accepts even decisions that nullify the laws a majority of the electorate or of their representatives voted for.

The judge, to deserve that trust and that authority, must be every bit as governed by law as is the Congress, the President, the State Governors and legislatures, and the American people. No one, including a judge, can be above the law. Only in that way will justice be done and the freedom of Americans assured.

How should a judge go about finding the law? The only legitimate way, in my opinion, is by attempting to discern what those who made the law intended. The intentions of the lawmakers govern whether the lawmakers are the Congress of the United States enacting a statute or whether they are those who ratified our Constitution and its various amendments.

(103)

Where the words are precise and the facts simple, that is a relatively easy task. Where the words are general, as is the case with some of the most profound protections of our liberties—in the Bill of Rights and in the Civil War Amendments—the task is far more complex. It is to find the principle or value that was intended to be protected and to see that it is protected.

As I wrote in an opinion for our court, the judge's responsibility "is to discern how the framers' values, defined in the context of the world they knew, apply in the world we know."

If a judge abandons intention as his guide, there is no law available to him and he begins to legislate a social agenda for the American people. That goes well beyond his legitimate power.

He or she then diminishes liberty instead of enhancing it. That is why I agree with Judge Learned Hand, one of the great jurists in our history, when he wrote that the judge's "authority and his immunity depend upon the assumption that he speaks with the mouths of others: the momentum of his utterances must be greater than any which his personal reputation and character can command if it is to do the work assigned to it—if it is to stand against the passionate resentments arising out of the interests he must frustrate." To state that another way, the judge must speak with the authority of the past and yet accommodate that past to the present.

The past, however, includes not only the intentions of those who first made the law, it also includes those past judges who interpreted it and applied it in prior cases. That is why a judge must have great respect for precedent. It is one thing as a legal theorist to criticize the reasoning of a prior decision, even to criticize it severely, as I have done. It is another and more serious thing altogether for a judge to ignore or overturn a prior decision. That requires much careful thought.

Times come, of course, when even a venerable precedent can and should be overruled. The primary example of a proper overruling is *Brown* v. *Board of Education*, the case which outlawed racial segregation accomplished by government action. *Brown* overturned the rule of separate but equal laid down 58 years before in *Plessy* v. *Ferguson*. Yet *Brown*, delivered with the authority of a unanimous Court, was clearly correct and represents perhaps the greatest moral achievement of our constitutional law.

Nevertheless, overruling should be done sparingly and cautiously. Respect for precedent is a part of the great tradition of our law, just as is fidelity to the intent of those who ratified the Constitution and enacted our statutes. That does not mean that constitutional law is static. It will evolve as judges modify doctrine to meet new circumstances and new technologies. Thus, today we apply the first amendment's guarantee of the freedom of the press to radio and television, and we apply to electronic surveillance the fourth amendment's guarantee of privacy for the individual against unreasonable searches of his or her home.

I can put the matter no better than I did in an opinion on my present court. Speaking of the judge's duty, I wrote: "The important thing. the ultimate consideration, is the constitutional freedom that is given into our keeping. A judge who refuses to see new threats to an established constitutional value and hence provides a crabbed interpretation that robs a provision of its full, fair and reasonable meaning, fails in his judicial duty. That duty, I repeat, is to ensure that the powers and freedoms the framers specified are made effective in today's circumstances."

But I should add to that passage that when a judge goes beyond this and reads entirely new values into the Constitution, values the framers and the ratifiers did not put there, he deprives the people of their liberty. That liberty, which the Constitution clearly envisions, is the liberty of the people to set their own social agenda through the processes of democracy.

Conservative judges frustrated that process in the mid-1930's by using the concept they had invented, the 14th amendment's supposed guarantee of a liberty of contract, to strike down laws designed to protect workers and labor unions. That was wrong then and it would be wrong now.

My philosophy of judging, Mr. Chairman, as you pointed out, is neither liberal nor conservative. It is simply a philosophy of judging which gives the Constitution a full and fair interpretation but, where the Constitution is silent, leaves the policy struggles to the Congress, the President, the legislatures and executives of the 50 States, and to the American people.

I welcome this opportunity to come before the committee and answer whatever questions the members may have. I am quite willing to discuss with you my judicial philosophy and the approach I take to deciding cases. I cannot, of course, commit myself as to how I might vote on any particular case and I know you would not wish me to do that.

I note in closing, though it has been mentioned by President Ford, that I have been fortunate to have a rich variety of experience in my professional career in the major areas of private practice, the academic world, government experience, and the judiciary. I have been an associate junior partner and senior partner in one of the nation's major law firms. I have been a professor at the Yale Law School, holding two named chairs, as Chancellor Kent Professor, once held by William Howard Taft, and as the first Alexander M. Bickel Professor of Public Law.

For almost 4 years I served as Solicitor General of the United States, in which capacity I submitted hundreds of briefs and personally argued about 35 cases before the Supreme Court of the United States.

Finally, for the past 5½ years I have been a judge in the U.S. Court of Appeals for the District of Columbia Circuit, where I have written, according to my count—counts have varied here this morning—about 150 opinions, and participated in over 400 decisions. I have a record in each of these areas of the law and it is for this committee and the Senate to judge that record.

I will be happy to answer the committee's questions.

[The statement of Judge Bork follows:]

The CHAIRMAN. Well, let's talk about another case. Let's talk about the *Griswold* case. Now, while you were living in Connecticut, that State had a law—I know you know this, but for the record—that it made it a crime for anyone, even a married couple, to use birth control. You indicated that you thought that law was "nutty," to use your words and I quite agree. Nevertheless, Connecticut, under that "nutty" law, prosecuted and convicted a doctor and the case finally reached the Supreme Court.

The Court said that the law violated a married couple's constitutional right to privacy. You criticized this opinion in numerous articles and speeches, beginning in 1971 and as recently as July 26th of this year. In your 1971 article, "Neutral Principles and Some First Amendment Problems," you said that the right of married couples to have sexual relations without fear of unwanted children is no more worthy of constitutional protection by the courts than the right of public utilities to be free of pollution control laws.

You argued that the utility company's right or gratification, I think you referred to it, to make money and the married couple's right or gratification to have sexual relations without fear of unwanted children, as "the cases are identical." Now, I am trying to understand this. It appears to me that you are saying that the government has as much right to control a married couple's decision about choosing to have a child or not, as that government has a right to control the public utility's right to pollute the air. Am I misstating your rationale here?

Judge BORK. With due respect, Mr. Chairman, I think you are. I was making the point that where the Constitution does not speak—there is no provision in the Constitution that applies to the case—then a judge may not say, I place a higher value upon a marital relationship than I do upon an economic freedom. Only if the Constitution gives him some reasoning. Once the judge begins to say economic rights are more important than marital rights or vice versa, and if there is nothing in the Constitution, the judge is enforcing his own moral values, which I have objected to. Now, on the *Griswold* case itself——

The CHAIRMAN. Can we stick with that point a minute to make sure I understand it?

Judge BORK. Sure.

The CHAIRMAN. So that you suggest that unless the Constitution, I believe in the past you used the phrase, textually identifies, a value that is worthy of being protected, then competing values in society, the competing value of a public utility, in the example you used, to go out and make money—that economic right has no more or less constitutional protection than the right of a married couple to use or not use birth control in their bedroom. Is that what you are saying?

Judge BORK. No, I am not entirely, but I will straighten it out. I was objecting to the way Justice Douglas, in that opinion, *Griswold* v. *Connecticut*, derived this right. It may be possible to derive an objection to an anti-contraceptive statute in some other way. I do not know.

But starting from the assumption, which is an assumption for purposes of my argument, not a proven fact, starting from the assumption that there is nothing in the Constitution, in any legitimate method of constitutional reasoning about either subject, all I am saying is that the judge has no way to prefer one to the other and the matter should be left to the legislatures who will then decide which competing gratification, or freedom, should be placed higher.

The CHAIRMAN. Then I think I do understand it, that is, that the economic gratification of a utility company is as worthy of as much protection as the sexual gratification of a married couple, because neither is mentioned in the Constitution.

Judge BORK. All that means is that the judge may not choose.

The CHAIRMAN. Who does?

Judge BORK. The legislature.

The CHAIRMAN. Well, that is my point, so it is not a constitutional right. I am not trying to be picky here. Clearly, I do not want to get into a debate with a professor, but it seems to me that what you are saying is what I said and that is, that the Constitution—if it were a constitutional right, if the Constitution said anywhere in it, in your view, that a married couple's right to engage in the decision of having a child or not having a child was a constitutionally-protected right of privacy, then you would rule that that right exists. You would not leave it to a legislative body no matter what they did.

Judge BORK. That is right.

The CHAIRMAN. But you argue, as I understand it, that no such right exists.

Judge BORK. No, Senator, that is what I tried to clarify. I argued that the way in which this unstructured, undefined right of privacy that Justice Douglas elaborated, that the way he did it did not prove its existence.

The CHAIRMAN. You have been a professor now for years and years, everybody has pointed out and I have observed, you are one of the most well-read and scholarly people to come before this committee. In all your short life, have you come up with any other way to protect a married couple, under the Constitution, against an action by a government telling them what they can or cannot do about birth control in their bedroom? Is there any constitutional right, anywhere in the Constitution?

Judge BORK. I have never engaged in that exercise. What I was doing was criticizing a doctrine the Supreme Court was creating which was capable of being applied in unknown ways in the future, in unprincipled ways. Let me say something about *Griswold* v. *Connecticut*. Connecticut never tried to prosecute any married couple for the use of contraceptives. That statute was used entirely through an aiding and abetting clause in the general criminal code to prosecute birth control clinics that advertised. That is what it was about.

The CHAIRMAN. But, in fact, they did prosecute a doctor, didn't they, for giving advice?

Judge BORK. Well, I was at Yale when that case was framed by Yale professors. That was not a case of Connecticut going out and doing anything. What happened was some Yale professors sued to have that—because they like this kind of litigation—to have that statute declared unconstitutional. It got up to the Supreme Court under the name of *Poe* v. *Ullman*. The Supreme Court refused to take the case because there was no showing that anybody ever got prosecuted.

They went back down and engaged in enormous efforts to get somebody prosecuted and the thing was really a test case on an abstract principle, I must say.

The CHAIRMAN. Well, let me say it another way then, without doing it in case. Does a State legislative body, or any legislative body, have a right to pass a law telling a married couple, or anyone else, that behind—let's stick with the married couple for a minute—behind their bedroom door, telling them they can or cannot use birth control? Does the majority have the right to tell a couple that they cannot use birth control?

Judge BORK. There is always a rationality standard in the law, Senator. I do not know what rationale the State would offer or what challenge the married couple would make. I have never decided that case. If it ever comes before me, I will have to decide it. All I have done was point out that the right of privacy, as defined or undefined by Justice Douglas, was a free-floating right that was not derived in a principled fashion from constitutional materials. That is all I have done.

The CHAIRMAN. Judge, I agree with the rationale offered in the case. Let me just read it to you and it went like this. I happen to agree with it. It said, in part, "would we allow the police to search the sacred precincts of marital bedrooms for telltale signs of contraceptives? The very idea is repulsive to the notions of privacy surrounding the marriage relationship. We deal with the right of privacy older than the Bill of Rights. Marriage is a coming together for better or worse, hopefully enduring, and intimate to the degree of being sacred. The association promotes a way of life, not causes. A harmony of living, not political face. A bilateral loyalty, not a commercial or social projects."

Obviously, that Justice believes that the Constitution protects married couples, anyone.

Judge BORK. I could agree with almost every—I think I could agree with every word you read but that is not, with respect, Mr. Chairman, the rationale of the case. That is the rhetoric at the end of the case. What I objected to was the way in which this right of privacy was created and that was simply this. Justice Douglas observed, quite correctly, that a number of provisions of the Bill of Rights protect aspects of privacy and indeed they do and indeed they should.

But he went on from there to say that since a number of the provisions did that and since they had emanations, by which I think he meant buffer zones to protect the basic right, he would find a penumbra which created a new right of privacy that existed where no provision of the Constitution applied, so that he——

The CHAIRMAN. What about the ninth amendment?

Judge BORK. Wait, let me finish with Justice Douglas.

The CHAIRMAN. All right.

Judge BORK. He did not rest on the ninth amendment. That was Justice Goldberg.

The CHAIRMAN. Right. That is what I was talking about.

Judge BORK. Yes. And I want to discuss first Justice Douglas and then I would be glad to discuss Justice Goldberg.

The CHAIRMAN. OK.

Judge BORK. Now you see, in that way, he could have observed, equally well, the various provisions of the Constitution protect individual freedom and therefore, generalized a general right of freedom that would apply where no provision of the Constitution did. That is exactly what Justice Hugo Black criticized in dissent in that case, in some heated terms—and Justice Potter Stewart also dissented in that case.

So, in observing that *Griswold* v. *Connecticut* does not sustain its burden, the judge's burden of showing that the right comes from constitutional materials, I am by no means alone. A lot of people, including Justices, have criticized that decision.

The CHAIRMAN. I am not suggesting whether you are alone or in the majority. I am just trying to find out where you are. As I hear you, you do not believe that there is a general right of privacy that is in the Constitution.

Judge BORK. Not one derived in *that* fashion. There may be other arguments and I do not want to pass upon those.

The CHAIRMAN. Have you ever thought of any? Have you ever written about any?

Judge BORK. Yes, as a matter of fact, Senator, I taught a seminar with Professor Bickel starting in about 1963 or 1964. We taught a seminar called Constitutional Theory. I was then all in favor of *Griswold* v. *Connecticut.* I thought that was a great way to reason. I tried to build a course around that, only I said: we can call it a general right of freedom, and let's then take the various provisions of the Constitution, treat them the way a lawyer treats common law cases, extract a more general principle and apply that.

I did that for about 6 or 7 years, and Bickel fought me every step of the way; said it was not possible. At the end of 6 or 7 years, I decided he was right.

The CHAIRMAN. Judge, let's go on. There have been a number of cases that flow from the progeny of the *Griswold* case, all relying on *Griswold,* the majority view, with different rationales offered, that there is a right of privacy in the Constitution, a general right of privacy, a right of privacy derived from the due process, from the 14th amendment, a right of privacy, to use the Douglas word—the penumbra, which you criticize, and a right Goldberg suggested in the *Griswold* case, from the ninth amendment. It seems to me, if you cannot find a rationale for the decision of the *Griswold* case, then all the succeeding cases are up for grabs.

Judge BORK. I have never tried to find a rationale and I have not been offered one. Maybe somebody would offer me one. I do not know if the other cases are up for grabs or not.

The CHAIRMAN. Wouldn't they have to be if they are based on the same rationale?

Judge BORK. Well, it may be that—I have written that some of these cases were wrongly decided, in my opinion. For some of them I can think of rationales that would make them correctly decided but wrongly reasoned. There may be other ways, that a generalized and undefined right of privacy—one of the problems with the right of privacy, as Justice Douglas defined it, or did not define it, is not simply that it comes out of nowhere, that it does not have any rooting in the Constitution, it is also that he does not give it any contours, so you do not know what it is going to mean from case to case.

The CHAIRMAN. Let's talk about another basic right, at least I think a basic right, the right not to be sterilized by the government. The Supreme Court addressed that right in the famous case, *Skinner* v. *Oklahoma.* Under Oklahoma law, someone convicted of certain crimes faced mandatory sterilization. In 1942, Mr. Skinner had been convicted of his third offense and therefore, faced sterilization, brought his case to the Supreme Court. The Court said that the State of Oklahoma could not sterilize him. Let me read something from the Court's opinion.

"We are dealing with legislation which involves one of the basic civil rights of man. Marriage and procreation are fundamental to the very existence and survival of a race. There is no redemption for the individual whom the law touches. Any experiment which the State conducts is to his irreparable injury. He is forever deprived of a basic liberty."

Judge, you said that Supreme Court decision is improper and intellectually empty. I would like to ask you, do you think that there is a basic right, under the Constitution, not to forcibly sterilized by the State?

Judge BORK. There may well be, but not on the grounds stated there. I hate to keep saying this, Mr. Chairman, much of my objection is to the way some members of the Court, not always the whole Court, has gone about deriving these things. In *Skinner* v. *Oklahoma,* I think it might have been better to say that the statute does not have a reasonable basis because there is no scientific evidence upon which to rest the thought that criminality—that was, not then, I do not know anything about the state of scientific evidence now—that criminality is really genetically carried.

The CHAIRMAN. But if there was, they would be able to sterilize?

Judge BORK. Well, I do not know. The second thing about that statute, in this case, is that Justice Douglas did say something which is quite correct and he did not need to talk about procreation and fundamental rights to do it. That is, he noted that the statute made distinctions, for example, between a robber and an embezzler. The embezzler was not subject to this kind of thing.

Had he gone on and pointed out that those distinctions really sterilized, in effect, blue collar criminals and exempted white collar criminals, and indeed, appeared to have some taint of a racial basis to it, he could have arrived at the same decision in what I would take to be a more legitimate fashion.

The CHAIRMAN. I thought that under the equal protection clause, that was the essence of it and you have written—I may be mistaken—I thought you had written that there is no basis under the equal protection clause for having arrived at that conclusion.

Judge BORK. Not the way he did it. What the Court was doing with the equal protection clause for many years, and to which I objected more generally in this article, is that they would decide whether a whole group was in or out and then they would decide what level of scrutiny they would give to the statute to see whether it was constitutional or not.

I think that derives—and I hate to get into a technical question—but I think it derives from a footnote in the *Carolene Products* case, in which they were supposed to look at groups, as such. It would be much better if instead of taking groups as such and saying this group is in, that group is out, if they merely used a reasonable basis test and asked whether the law had a reasonable basis. I think the statute, in *Skinner* v. *Oklahoma*, the sterilization statute, would have failed under a reasonable basis test.

The CHAIRMAN. So you have to find a reasonable basis. If there is one, you could sterilize. If there is not one, you cannot. It seems to me that it comes down to a basic difference. You do not believe the Constitution recognizes what I consider to be a basic liberty, a basic liberty not to be sterilized.

Judge BORK. I agree that that is a basic liberty, and I agree that family life is a basic liberty and so forth. But the fact is we know that legislatures can, constitutionally, regulate some aspects of sexuality.

The CHAIRMAN. True.

Judge BORK. We know that legislatures do and can constitutionally regulate some aspects of family life. There is no question, I think, that these things are subject to some regulation. We have divorce laws, custody laws, child beating laws and so forth. The question always becomes, under the equal protection clause, has the legislature a reasonable basis for the kind of thing it does here.

The sterilization law would probably require an enormous or perhaps impossible degree of justification.

The CHAIRMAN. I hope so.

Judge, my time is about up, but with regard to the *Griswold* case, you are quoted in 1985—you were a judge at this time, although this statement was not made in your judicial capacity—as saying, "I don't think there is a supportable method of constitutional reasoning underlying the *Griswold* decision."

So obviously, you thought about it, and you at least at that point concluded you could not find one.

It seems to me, Judge—and as I said, there are many more cases I would like to talk to you about, and I appreciate you engaging in this dialogue—that you say that a State can impact upon marital relations and can impact upon certain other relations, and it seems to me that there are certain basic rights that they cannot touch. And what you seem to be saying to me is that a State legislature can theoretically, at least, pass a law sterilizing, and we will see what the courts say. It is not an automatic, it is not basic. Right now, if any State legislature in the country asked counsel for the legislature, "Could we pass a law, sterilizing?" I suspect the immediate response from counsel would be, "No, you cannot do that"— not only politically, but constitutionally.

Have any State legislative bodies said, "Can we decide on whether or not someone can or cannot use contraceptives," not any reasonable basis, I imagine all counsel would say "No" flatly; cannot even get into that area.

And it seems to me you are not saying that. You are saying that it is possible that can happen, and in *Griswold* you are saying that there is no principle upon which they could reach the result—not the rationale, you say; you say the result.

Judge BORK. Well, I think I was talking about the principle underlying that one. But I should say——

The CHAIRMAN. Well, wait, let me stop you there, Judge, because I want to make sure I understand. The principle underlying that one is the basic right to privacy, right, and from that flows all these other cases, all the way down to Franz, which you spoke to; all the way down to *Roe* v. *Wade*. They all are premised upon that basic principle that you cannot find.

I am not saying you are wrong. I just want to make sure I understand what you are saying.

Judge BORK. Well, I do not think all those cases necessarily follow. They used the right of privacy in some of those cases, and it was not clear why it was a right of privacy.

I should say that I think not only Justices Black and Stewart could not find it—and Gerald Gunther, who is a professor at Stanford and an authority in these matters, has criticized the case; and Professor Philip Kurland has referred to *Griswold* v. *Connecticut* as a "blatant usurpation."

The CHAIRMAN. But most did find it; the majority did find it, though, didn't they?

Judge BORK. Yes. But I am just telling you, Senator, that a lot of people have thought the reasoning of that case was just not reasoning.

The CHAIRMAN. My time is up. Judge, I want to make it clear, I am not suggesting there is anything extreme about your reasoning. I am not suggesting it is conservative or liberal. I just want to make sure I understand it. And as I understand what you have said in the last 30 minutes, a State legislative body, a government, can, if it so chose, pass a law saying married couples cannot use birth control devices.

Judge BORK. Senator, Mr. Chairman, I have not said that; I do not want to say that. What I am saying to you is that if that law is to be struck down, it will have to be done under better constitutional argumentation than was present in the *Griswold* opinion.

The CHAIRMAN. Again I will end, to quote you, sir, you said, "The truth is that the Court could not reach the result in *Griswold* through principle." I assume you are talking about constitutional principle.

Judge BORK. I do not know—what is that from?

The CHAIRMAN. I am referring to your 1971 article. That is the quote in the 1971 article. And then you said——

Judge BORK. Do you have a page number for that, Senator?

The CHAIRMAN. I will get the page. Sorry—a 1982 speech while you were Judge, speaking at Catholic University. You said, "The result in *Griswold* could not have been reached by proper interpretation of the Constitution." End of quote. We will dig it out for you here to show you—I believe you all sent it to us, so that is how we got it.

Judge BORK. OK. Yes.

The CHAIRMAN. Well, my time is up. I appreciate it. We will do more of this.

I yield—I see Senator Byrd is here. Did you have an opening statement you wished to make, Senator?

Senator THURMOND. I was just going to say I will yield to Senator Byrd if he wishes to make an opening statement.

The CHAIRMAN. Senator Byrd. We are going to cease the questioning for a moment while Senator Byrd makes his opening statement.

Senator HATCH. Judge, you're doing very fine in your concise and cohesive answers. As a matter of fact, I don't see how anybody watching this could doubt that you're an eminent scholar, with a brilliant mind, who is in the mainstream of judicial life, who in sitting in more than 400 cases on the Circuit Court of Appeals for the District of Columbia has never been reversed, who has been within the mainstream with his liberal colleagues on the Courts, if that's an appropriate term, as you have with your conservative colleagues, having agreed 90 percent of the time with Judge Ruth Bader Ginsburg, 83 percent of the time with Judge Mikva, right on down to Judge Skelly Wright around 75 percent of the time.

That doesn't sound to me like you're outside of the mainstream, since you're agreeing with your liberal colleagues. But they have chosen in some of these critical articles to criticize you on 14 percent of your cases, where there is tremendous controversy. That's unfair, and we have a tendency up here, as Senators, because we don't have the time to go into the nuances of these cases as you judges do, to look at everything in terms of 30-second bites for us on television. That's my point, not you.

Now, in recent years we have heard a great deal of commentary about the problems of judicial activism. How would you define judicial activism, because this seems to be really one of the central core matters here.

Judge BORK. I think I would define it as a judge reading into a statute or into the Constitution his personal policy preferences— and let me be clear about this.

No human being can sit down with words in a statute, with history and the other evidence he uses, and not to some extent get his personal moral view into it, because each of us sees the world, understands facts, through a lens composed of our morality and our understanding.

But there is an enormous difference between that inevitable bias that gets in and a judge who self-consciously tries to keep his biases out and tries to be as impartial on the evidence as he can be. There's an enormous difference between that and a judge who incorporates his idea of wise policy into the Constitution or into a statute and, as a matter of fact, if you're familiar with the academic legal debate, most of those writing in the law schools these days seem to prefer the latter kind of a judge, one who does not confine himself to the historical principles of the Constitution.

Senator HATCH. In other words, in simple terms, judicial activism is when judges make law rather than interpret the law?

Judge BORK. That is a good shorthand description.

Senator HATCH. The fact of the matter is that you, as a federal judge, weren't elected to that position; is that right?

Judge BORK. That is correct.

Senator HATCH. You're not elected to make laws.

Judge BORK. I'm not. If I were, if I were going to make laws, then this hearing should consist of me making campaign promises on how I will vote on various cases.

Senator HATCH. That's what these hearings will be if we continue to politicize——

Judge BORK. I'm afraid of that.

Senator HATCH. This may occur as well when judges make a general statement of law and stretch it to cover instances beyond that which the authors really intended; is that right?

Judge BORK. That is correct.

Senator HATCH. And that's what you mean by original intent?

Judge BORK. That's correct.

Senator HATCH. And it doesn't just mean original intent of the Founding Fathers or the original meaning of what they meant; it means the original intent of us Members of Congress who are elected representatives to make these laws to the people, is that right?

Judge BORK. That is correct, Senator.

Senator HATCH. Now, I realize that you have been long known as a most eloquent, consistent and brilliant exponent of the classic theory of judicial restraint.

What is meant by judicial restraint?

Judge BORK. It means that a judge—I've never liked the word judicial activism. I prefer something else. Because a restrained judge should be active in defending those freedoms and powers that are actually in the Constitution—should give them liberal construction. But he should not go beyond that, and that is judicial restraint. It is the morality of the jurist who self-consciously renounces power and tries to enforce the will of the lawmaker.

Senator HATCH. When courts read into the Constitution or particular pieces of legislation policies and rights that are not there, what happens to the ability of the legislatures of the respective States or of the Congress itself to make laws according to the needs of the people?

Judge BORK. The people and their representatives have suddenly been ousted from an area that was legitimately theirs and the courts begin to set a social agenda instead of the people setting their social agenda.

Senator HATCH. When I talk about judicial activism, you don't like the term, but let me at least use that term because we have defined it here.

Judge BORK. All right. I'll accept it.

Senator HATCH. Can judicial activism be employed just as easily as conservative—to reach illegitimate conservative as well as illegitimate liberal end results?

Judge Bork. Up until the mid-1930s, as we all know, Senator, a conservative majority on the Supreme Court was reading its economic preferences into the Constitution.

Senator Hatch. That's why we had the child labor laws in the Lochner era and all those difficulties.

Judge Bork. Labor laws were being struck down, laws protecting workers were being struck down. That changed. I don't think activism is any more proper for a conservative than it is for a liberal. That's why I don't think my philosophy of judging has anything to do with liberalism or conservatism.

Senator Hatch. The thing that is interesting to me is that you have a reputation for being squarely against both forms of judicial activism.

I remember—and I sat there in the hearings when you testified against the so-called human life bill, or human life amendment. That bill basically would have allowed the Congress of the United States to overrule *Roe* v. *Wade* by simple statute. You came in and testified against that. Why?

Judge Bork. Because I think it is unconstitutional for the Congress to try to change a Supreme Court decision by statute. It has been allowed once or twice by the Supreme Court, but I don't think it's proper.

I criticized *Roe* v. *Wade* at that time, but I also opposed any effort to change it by statute or to take away the Supreme Court's jurisdiction over the subject.

Senator Hatch. I agree with you. At the time I voted to put it out of subcommittee, but I was going to vote against it in full committee but it never came up again, and it was precisely because of your arguments that it was basically defeated. I don't think conservatives are any more justified in trying to impose their conservative activism than liberals are in the courts.

Now, in this context, I think it is helpful to re-examine this case for a few minutes, *Griswold* v. *Connecticut*. And this case, as you defined it, was when the Supreme Court invalidated a Connecticut law banning the use of contraceptives.

In the first place, do you, as a personal matter, have anything against the use of contraceptives of the personal choice of individuals to use them or not?

Judge Bork. Nothing whatsoever. I think the Connecticut law was an outrage and it would have been more of an outrage if they ever enforced it against an individual.

Senator Hatch. But they never did.

Judge Bork. No.

Senator Hatch. You will not be surprised to know that your personal feelings about the Connecticut law are similar to those of Justice Hugo Black, the primary dissenter in the *Griswold* case. He said, "I feel constrained to add that the law is every bit as offensive to me as it is to my brethren in the majority." Nonetheless, Justice Black, who certainly was one of the great all time Justices in our age, who was joined by Justice Stewart, whose wonderful wife is here with us today—and, of course, he was another judicial giant, in my opinion—they both dissented in that case.

Now, can you explain why these great jurists could have allowed that law banning contraceptives to stand?

Judge BORK. Justice Stewart called it an uncommonly silly law, which I think it certainly was, at a minimum. I think they would have allowed it to stand simply because they could find no warrant in the Constitution for them, as judges, to override a legislative enactment.

Senator HATCH. In other words, there was no source of authority within the Constitution to rule the way they ruled?

Judge BORK. That is what they concluded.

Senator HATCH. So these two principal jurists, both of whom derided the particular law, agreed with you—or should I say you agreed with them?

Judge BORK. I think the latter is the better form, Senator.

Senator HATCH. I can certainly understand that there is a privacy protection in the Constitution, in the sense of guarantees against unreasonable searches of one's home, and the prohibition of laws that abridge free speech and the free exercise of religion. Those are areas where there is no question about the right of privacy, is there?

Judge BORK. None whatsoever.

Senator HATCH. But what did Justice Black say about the general right of privacy discussed in that case?

Judge BORK. Well, as I recall, didn't he say it was the old natural law theory of judging? You write your own policy prescriptions into the statute.

Senator HATCH. That's basically what he said.

What did Justice Black say about the scope of the so-called privacy right that is no where found in the Constitution?

Judge BORK. I think he said it was utterly unpredictable. I don't recall his exact words, but nobody knows what the scope is.

Senator HATCH. He indicated that it was incapable of being limited or defined, other than by arbitrary judicial fiat; isn't that correct?

Judge BORK. That's true, and that is——

Senator HATCH. And that's what you were concerned about?

Judge BORK. That's what I meant when I said that, you know, privacy to do what? We don't know. Privacy to take cocaine in private; privacy to fix prices in private; privacy to engage in incest in private? The Supreme Court is not going to do those things, but we don't know why.

Senator HATCH. We all have to agree that privacy is a very attractive concept. We all want privacy, don't we?

Judge BORK. We do.

Senator HATCH. Is the legal doctrine in question here about the kind of privacy we all desire, or is it actually a term used to deal with some questions with very public implications?

Judge BORK. Well, it certainly deals with some cases with public implications, that's right.

Senator HATCH. Once again, what would happen if judges began to discover or create new rights in the Constitution, such as the right to be let alone, or the right to be free of taxation, or the right to a balanced budget?

Judge BORK. That's right. I remember some judges who sued under the Constitution for the right to an indexed salary.

Senator HATCH. I agree that——

Judge BORK. And they quite properly lost.

Senator HATCH. Actually, some of those rights would seem very attractive. A right to be let alone. You know, some judge could just say "well, we all ought to have that right", if he wanted to, but it isn't in the Constitution.

Judge BORK. Judging requires careful thought and the making of close distinctions. Once you just put rhetoric into the constitutional adjudication, you don't know where it will go or what it will do.

Senator HATCH. What happens if the courts start creating rights that are not found in the Constitution?

Judge BORK. In my view, it's illegitimate.

Senator HATCH. Well, we're going to be a government not of laws but of the whimsies of the courts; isn't that right?

Judge BORK. Yes.

Senator HATCH. Isn't that basically your criticism?

Judge BORK. That's basically what I have been objecting to for 16 years, and throughout these hearings.

Senator HATCH. It has got to be a little irritating to you as it has to be to anybody who is fair-minded, to be criticized for having criticized *Griswold* v. *Connecticut* on the grounds that you might possibly have wanted to sustain that statute, any more than it was the desire of Hugo Black or Mr. Justice Potter Stewart to have done that.

Judge BORK. It is, Senator, as you know, a regular form of rhetoric to say that, if you would say a statute is not unconstitutional, that must be because you like the statute. That is not right. The question is never whether you like the statute; the question is, is it in fact contrary to the principles of the Constitution.

Senator HATCH. I think I'm starting to understand why you have never been reversed, Judge. I hope the people in this country are, too, because you're right down the middle on these things. You just want the laws to be made by elected representatives and the judges to interpret those laws in accordance with appropriate constitutional application.

Judge BORK. That is true, Senator.

Senator HATCH. I don't know how anybody could find fault with that. And in every one of these cases, I think when you get into the complexities, I think the American people would basically say "I might disagree with Judge Bork on the philosophy on some of these cases, but I cannot disagree on the jurisprudence or the actual application of law." I think most people would feel that way.

By the way, this discussion leads to another important case governed by the so-called privacy doctrine, and that is the case of *Roe* v. *Wade*. You have been criticized for having been critical of this abortion case called *Roe* v. *Wade*.

Can you explain your apprehensions about this particular case?

Judge BORK. It is not apprehension so much, Senator, as it is—If *Griswold* v. *Connecticut* established or adopted a privacy right on reasoning which was utterly inadequate, and failed to define that right so we know what it applies to, *Roe* v. *Wade* contains almost no legal reasoning. We are not told why it is a private act—and if it is, there are lots of private acts that are not protected—why this one is protected. We are simply not told that. We get a review of the history of abortion and we get a review of the opinions of various groups like the American Medical Association, and then we get rules.

That's what I object to about the case. It does not have legal reasoning in it that roots the right to an abortion in constitutional materials.

Senator HATCH. Well, let me just say this.

By the way, I presume your concerns about the reasoning of the *Roe* v. *Wade* case do not necessarily mean that you would automatically reverse that case as a Justice of the Supreme Court?

Judge BORK. No. If you want to hear me on that, I will tell you exactly what I would consider.

Senator HATCH. We would be glad to hear it.

Judge BORK. If that case, or something like it, came up, and if the case called for a broad up or down, which it may not, I would first ask the lawyer who wants to support the right, "Can you derive a right of privacy, not to be found in one of the specific amendments, in some principled fashion from the Constitution so I know not only where you got it but what it covers."

There are rights that are not specifically mentioned in the Constitution, like the right to travel. You know, it's conceivable he could do that, I don't know. If he could not do that, I would say, "Well, if you can't derive a general right of privacy, can you derive a right to an abortion, or at least to a limitation upon anti-abortion statutes legitimately from the Constitution?"

If after argument, that didn't sound like it was going to be a viable theory, I would say to him, "I would like you to argue whether this is the kind of case that should not be overruled." Because, obviously, there are cases we look back on and say they were erroneous or they were not compatible with original intent, but we don't overrule them for a variety of reasons.

A moment ago, in response to a question, I ran through some of the factors. So I would listen to that argument.

As I have said before, a judge with an original intent philosophy, which goes back, by the way, to Marshall and Joseph Story, needs a strong theory of precedent to keep from getting back into matters that are long settled, even if incorrectly settled.

Senator HATCH. So as a judge, you would have to take into consideration such factors as continuity, predictability of the law, facts of the case and so forth.

Would it be safe for me to assume, or members of this committee to assume, that you do not know yourself how you would rule on an abortion case if it came before the Supreme Court until you have all the facts?

Judge BORK. That is true. I have discovered that, to my chagrin, on my present court. You think you know something about a subject, until you get the briefs and hear the argument and you decide it is much more complex than you thought it was. But I have tried to indicate the general factors that I would look at. There may be some lawyer that will suggest some that I haven't thought of.

Senator HATCH. I would also presume—and correct me if I'm wrong—that you have taken no public position on the political or social merits of abortion?

Judge BORK. The only position I have taken was the opposition to the human life bill and the opposition to taking away the Supreme Court's jurisdiction.

Senator HATCH. I think it would be helpful to examine the character of the legal scholarship that has voiced apprehensions similar to yours on this case, since you have been criticized by some of my colleagues as being outside of the mainstream, because of your criticisms of the so-called *Roe* v. *Wade* case.

For example, Gerald Gunther of the Stanford Law School cites *Roe* as an instance of the "bad legacy of substantive due process and ends-oriented" judging.

Professor Archibald Cox of Harvard notes that the "court failed to establish the legitimacy of the decision by not articulating a precept of sufficient attractiveness to lift the ruling above the level of a political judgment."

By the way, let's pause here. What do you suppose Archibald Cox meant when he said that the decision was not legitimate?

Judge BORK. I suppose he means it comes out of no—so far as he can see—comes out of no legitimate constitutional materials, which are primarily text, history and constitutional structure.

Senator HATCH. Do you agree with that?

Judge BORK. Yes.

Senator HATCH. Let's continue. Dean John Ely of Stanford, who also favors abortion, says along with Archibald Cox "It is not a constitutional principle and the court has no business trying to impose it."

Professor Bickel, who I think is respected by almost everybody, who is studied in the law, also criticized the *Roe* decision for being legislation but not legal action. You're aware of that. In fact, this is the very point made by Justices White and Rehnquist. In fact, in later decisions, Justice O'Connor, the nation's first woman Justice, also criticized harshly the *Roe* opinion.

You could go on. Professor Forrester of Cornell calls the case "interventionist", and Professor Kirland of Chicago calls it "a blatant usurpation".

In your lengthy constitutional studies, is there any Supreme Court decision that has stirred more controversy or criticism amongst scholars and citizens than that particular case?

Judge BORK. I suppose the only candidate for that, Senator, would be *Brown* v. *Board of Education*. It is possible, you know, for the Supreme Court to be—

Senator HATCH. Or possibly the *Dred Scott* case.

Judge BORK. Yes, that's right.

Senator HATCH. Where there might be some parallels.

Judge BORK. But in my lifetime, those two. And it's possible for the Supreme Court to be entirely right and get an enormous amount of heat, and it's possible for it to be wrong and get an enormous amount of heat. So the controversy surrounding it isn't really the way I judge the correctness of the decision.

Senator HATCH. That's right, and I think that's starting to come across. I think that you're refuting your extraordinarily extreme critics, which I think are misrepresenting, in their full-page ads and a whole raft of other things what you stand for and what you do as a judge.

In any event, it is clear to me, and I think to others that listen, that your apprehensions about the reasoning of the *Roe* v. *Wade* case are shared by some of the legal minds of our age on both sides of the issue.

Let me ask one further question on this case, however. If you are confirmed, and the abortion decision comes to you, will you describe how you would approach the case? I'm interested to know whether or not you have already prejudged this issue or whether you will keep an open mind with regard to the case that comes before you.

Judge BORK. I think I have listened to arguments in every case, Senator, and sometimes I don't think somebody is going to be able to make it in an argument, and sometimes they do make it, despite my initial doubts.

But as I have mentioned to you, I would ask for a grounding of the privacy right and a definition of it in a traditional, constitutional reasoning way. As I say, if that can't be done, I will ask for a rooting of the right to an abortion, or some right to an abortion of some scope, in traditional, legal, constitutional materials. And if that can't be done, then I would like to hear argument on stare decisis and whether or not this is the kind of case that should or should not be overruled.

Senator HATCH. I acknowledge that you have encountered only one case similar to *Griswold* and *Roe*—in other words, the contraceptive case and the abortion case—on the D.C. Circuit, and that was the important *Dronenberg* v. *Zech* case.

Now, this is a case that is cited by your critics as evidence for your antipathy to the so-called right of privacy. Could you describe the facts of that case?

Judge BORK. That was a case in which the Navy discharged, honorably, I think it was a petty officer for engaging in homosexual conduct in the barracks with a junior, subordinate. The Navy has a regulation against homosexual conduct, not against the status of homosexuality, but against homosexual conduct in the service.

The discharged sailor sued, alleging, among other things, that he had a right of privacy to engage in homosexual conduct in the Navy, and that that flowed from *Griswold* and *Roe*.

Our panel of the court disagreed. We thought the right of privacy was relatively undefined, but we saw no principle in the Supreme Court's jurisprudence on the subject which would lead us to tell the Navy it could not ban that kind of conduct.

Later the Supreme Court, in *Bowers* v. *Hardwick*, upheld a much more severe regulation. After all, all we said was that the Navy was entitled to discharge this fellow honorably. In *Bowers* v. *Hardwick*, they allowed the criminalizing of civilian homosexual conduct, which is a much larger step than we took.

Senator HATCH. Your holding in that case was basically merely a finding that the doctrine of privacy could not be expanded to cover consensual sodomy; is that right?

Judge BORK. That's correct.

Senator HATCH. And as I understand it, there was unanimous consensus or agreement by the three-judge panel?

Judge BORK. That's correct.

Senator HATCH. Who were the other two judges besides yourself?

Judge BORK. Judge Scalia, and I think it was Judge Williams from the ninth circuit—is that correct?

Senator HATCH. And you say that the Supreme Court later, in a precisely similar case, upheld your particular point of view?

Judge BORK. Yes. Well, it wasn't precisely similar. I think that was a harder case for the court.

Senator HATCH. You're talking about the *Bowers* v. *Hardwick* case?

Judge BORK. Yes.

Senator HATCH. Okay. But it was consistent, though——

Judge BORK. Oh, certainly.

Senator HATCH [continuing]. With your particular decision, is that correct?

Judge BORK. That is correct.

Senator SIMPSON. I think that it is worthwhile to recognize what an extraordinary ally and force you are. One of the quotes from that case was you said, as you were sticking with the decision, the fact that this was an expression of opinion. You said it is the kind of hyperbole that must be accepted in the rough and tumble of political argument. And I agree with that.

And that is one thing the Senator from Ohio and I have always agreed on. It is a rough and tumble but you can do it with civility and we try to do that.

Let us get back to privacy. That is a recurring theme here about privacy and judicial restraint and *Griswold* v. *Connecticut*, and we have now talked about contraception, homosexuality, sterility or else sexual preference, sexual gratification. There is no telling where we will get if we keep struggling along in this area. Those are important things. I do not even belittle that. But it has all been taken out of context, every bit of it.

I do not think you had an appropriate time to respond on the issue of priv   ~·, and especially with regard to the *Griswold* case and the *Skinner* case. I guess I want to be sure because there was a line of questioning which I gathered—and I think it was our Chairman, and it was a good line of questioning—it was, well if you do not embrace these things through some method, how are we going to get to that point? How do you protect?

I want to ask you if it is fair to say that you believe that privacy is protected under the Constitution, but that you just do not believe that there is a general and unspecified right that protects everything including homosexual conduct, incest, whatever—and you mentioned that yesterday. Is that correct?

Judge BORK. That is correct, Senator. I think the fact that I did not get everything I wanted to say out was my fault because I was trying to discuss with Senator Biden and others the constitutional problem. But I think it requires a fuller answer than that and that is this: No civilized person wants to live in a society without a lot of privacy in it. And the framers, in fact, of the Constitution protected privacy in a variety of ways.

The first amendment protects free exercise of religion. The free speech provision of the first amendment has been held to protect the privacy of membership lists and a person's associations in order to make the free speech right effective. The fourth amendment protects the individual's home and office from unreasonable searches and seizures, and usually requires a warrant. The fifth amendment has a right against self-incrimination.

There is much more. There is a lot of privacy in the Constitution. *Griswold,* in which we were talking about a Connecticut statute which was unenforced against any individual except the birth control clinic, *Griswold* involved a Connecticut statute which banned the use of contraceptives. And Justice Douglas entered that opinion with a rather eloquent statement of how awful it would be to have the police pounding into the marital bedroom. And it would be awful, and it would never happen because there is the fourth amendment.

Nobody ever tried to enforce that statute, but the police simply could not get into the bedroom without a warrant, and what magistrate is going to give the police a warrant to go in to search for signs of the use of contraceptives? I mean it is a wholly bizarre and imaginary case.

Now let me say this——

The CHAIRMAN. Would the Senator yield at that point just for clarification?

Senator SIMPSON. Yes, certainly, Mr. Chairman.

The CHAIRMAN. If they had evidence that a crime was being committed——

Judge BORK. How are they going to get evidence that a couple is using contraceptives?

The CHAIRMAN. Wiretap.

Judge BORK. Wiretapping?

The CHAIRMAN. Wiretap.

Judge BORK. You mean to say that a magistrate is going to authorize a wiretap to find out if a couple is using contraceptives?

The CHAIRMAN. They could, could they not, under the law?

Judge BORK. Unbelievable, unbelievable.

The CHAIRMAN. I understand that, but under the law, Judge, could they not have—it was a crime, correct?

Judge BORK. It was a crime on the statute books which was never prosecuted, never.

The CHAIRMAN. Well, the fact that it was not prosecuted did not mean it was not a crime, does it?

Judge BORK. I have more to say about that, whether it was a crime or not.

The CHAIRMAN. Let us assume they were drug dealers. There was evidence that they were involved in some other legal activity, and there was a wiretap.

Judge BORK. And they hear a discussion of contraceptives?

The CHAIRMAN. Yes.

Judge BORK. Nobody is going to get a warrant for that and no prosecution is going to be upheld for that. And I would like to go on to that point because——

The CHAIRMAN. Thank you, Senator.

Senator SIMPSON. Judge, let me come back to another one here.

Judge BORK. Well, okay.

Senator SIMPSON. Go ahead. I want to hear that.

Judge BORK. I want to say that you really could not enforce that thing, and the privacy was not the issue in that case. It was the use of contraceptives, and it is a little hard to locate something about contraceptives in the Constitution.

But be that as it may, let me illustrate my objection to what is generalized right of privacy. Suppose a Senator introduced a bill which said every man and woman and child in this country has a right of privacy, period. I do not think that bill would go anywhere until he had to tell everybody exactly what the right of privacy protected. Did it protect incest? Did it protect beating your wife in private? Did it protect price-fixing in private?

No Congress would ever pass a bill like here, here is a generalized right of privacy; make of it what you will. No court would uphold such a statute because it would be void for vagueness.

Now the Supreme Court or Justice Douglas in effect did the same thing with the Constitution. Nobody knows what that thing means. But you have to define it; you have to define it. And the court has not given it definition. That is my only point.

Now the only reason that Connecticut statute stayed on the statute book—it was an old, old statute, dating back from the days when Connecticut was entirely a Yankee State—the only reason it stayed on the statute book was that it was not enforced. If anybody had tried to enforce that against a married couple, he would have been out of office instantly and the law would have been repealed.

Furthermore, if the prosecutor brought such a case, I do not think any court would uphold a conviction, assuming that you could get a conviction. That law had not been enforced for so long—it is an utterly antique statute; I do not think it was ever enforced—I think you would have a great argument of no fair warning, or sometimes that lawyers call—and I hate to use a word like this—desuetude, meaning it is just so out of date it has gone into limbo.

So no prosecutor is going to bring that prosecution. If he did, the law would disappear and furthermore no court would uphold the prosecution. That is the fact. That law never went anywhere. My objection—I think the law was an utterly silly law, but my objection is simply to the undefined nature of what the court did there. And I have tried to illustrate that for you by asking you whether you would vote for a statute that said nothing more than that everybody has a right of privacy, and the court shall enforce it. I do not think you would.

Senator SIMPSON. Judge Bork, one thing that kind of surprised me yesterday and yet it did not is that you really described that case as being some kind of a law school exercise, a professorial dream, a mess-around kind of a case. Is that right?

Judge BORK. Yes, it was. Some professors found that law in the books and tried to frame a case to challenge it on constitutional grounds. And, as I say, they had trouble getting anybody arrested, and the only person who could get arrested was a doctor who advertised that he was giving birth control information, contraceptive information, and I do not know if they prosecuted him or fined him under the aiding and abetting clause of the Code, and I think both sides regarded it as an interesting test case. The whole case was practically an academic exercise.

Senator SIMPSON. Judge Black and Judge Stewart both dissented.

Judge BORK. They did indeed, and Justice Harlan refused to go along with the right of privacy. He had reasons of his own. He used, I think, the concept of ordered liberty.

Now we go back to the general right of privacy, upon which *Roe* v. *Wade* is based coming out of *Griswold*, and you had two, one Justice Goldberg out of the ninth amendment and the other one from Justice Douglas which is called the penumbra, which is sort of a vague term, but I understand that is something to do with astronomy and various shadows and unclear things, but it comes from the specific mentioning of rights of privacy, as you have enumerated to me in various other amendments.

Now you in your studying it and making a statement like that, do you really believe that you can find anywhere a general right of privacy that you would accept from the Constitution?

Judge BORK. I do not know, Senator. I certainly would not accept emanations and penumbras analysis, which is I think less an analysis than a metaphor. And the ninth amendment part gives me difficulty because it is a little hard to know what category of rights, if any, were supposed to be preserved by the ninth amendment unless it is the State constitutional rights.

But there may be some way to do it. I have heard fairly strong moral arguments for abortion, just as I have hard fairly strong moral arguments against it. Whether those moral arguments could be rooted to the constitutional material, I really do not know.

What I do unfortunately, I suppose, is take Supreme Court opinions that seem to me unsatisfactory as matters of constitutional reasoning and criticize them. And I have not gone back into the history and other things in an attempt to construct a new——

Senator THURMOND. Judge, keep your voice up so we can hear you.

Judge BORK. All right, Senator—a new right of privacy that has some other meaning. Maybe, as I say, one of the moral arguments would apply perhaps only to abortion because *Griswold* and *Roe* are quite different cases in quite different situations, and I do not know if you want me to rehearse some of the moral argumentation I have heard or not, but I do not know—I have not heard anybody yet root it in the Constitution.

Senator HEFLIN. But I am correct in assuming that as of now at this hearing that you know of no theory which could be derived from the Constitution which would grant a general right of privacy.

Judge BORK. Well, certainly not a general right of privacy that is as free-floating as the one we have now because we do not even know what it covers. Privacy to do what? But it is true, Senator, I do not know, I do not have available a constitutional theory which would support a general defined right. But that does not mean that there is not one, and it seems to me I often am surprised to learn that there is an argument in a certain direction that I had not anticipated and I have not tried to anticipate one here.

And I can only say that if somebody has a constitutional theory, I will listen to it attentively.

Senator HEFLIN. Am I correct in saying that you do not expect to seek it and try to find it yourself?

Judge BORK. Well, if a case came before me I would, but, no, now I am in the business of hearing and deciding cases, and I really do not have time to go off and anticipate a question that may or may not ever come before me. But if a case comes before me—sometimes lawyers' arguments give you ideas that the lawyer has not expressed—I would send my clerks out and try to research that.

Senator HEFLIN. All right, now to the second one. If you cannot derive a general right of privacy, can you derive a right to an abortion which is "a" of two and you have "b", which is, can you derive a right to abortion from the Constitution, that is, obviously, that specifically gives somebody a right of privacy? So, we just dismiss—I mean, that I do not think is in the language there that could be construed that says you have a specific, implicit, explicit right to an abortion, in the Constitution.

All right, your "b" part of that is, at least which would provide a limitation upon anti-abortion statutes legitimately from the Constitution. What do you, at this time, see as a possibility of a limitation?

Judge BORK. Well, it would seem to me, Senator, that it would be easier to argue a right to an abortion. I am not saying it would work, but it would be easier to do that than it would be to find this generalized right of privacy. For example, I understand groups are working—I have not seen their work product, but I am told that groups are working on that. For example, some groups, I think, are trying an equal protection argument.

Only women have this specific burden and forcing a woman to carry a baby to term—some of the groups are arguing, I suppose, is a form of gender discrimination. I have not seen that argument worked out, but I know it is being worked on.

Senator HEFLIN. Well, that would be basically difficult from the language of the Constitution, since mostly parts of the Constitution is a conferring power on the federal government with a reservation to the States and to the people for the power that is not specifically granted to the federal government, under the 10th amendment.

Judge BORK. I was referring more to the equal protection clause of the 14th amendment, as the place in which that argument would be rooted. I do not suggest it would succeed. I do not suggest it would not. You asked me if one could begin to talk about where one might root such an argument, and I think the right to an abortion—you might attempt to root it there, successfully or not, I do not pretend to guess, but it is easier than a general right of privacy.

Senator HEFLIN. Well, that would go basically contrary to some of your feelings on the 14th amendment, extending in that area, would it not?

Judge BORK. In the area of women?

Senator HEFLIN. Well, in the area of trying to give it as to a particular right of a limitation upon the States to pass certain laws, which would, in effect, limit the anti-abortion statutes.

Judge BORK. Well, I do not mean, Senator, to try to offer anybody some hope or something that I would find that constitutional right. I am just saying that that is one area in which the argument might take place. And I do not think it is entirely contrary to my constitutional philosophy because I have been saying, this morning, that the equal protection clause applies to women as well as to men—obviously, because it would be ridiculous to say it applies only to men—and that for over 90 years, the Supreme Court has been using this question of is this a reasonable, fair classification.

I would suppose that is where the argument would be built, might be built. But, I can go no further than that. I have not seen the argument. It is not doctrinally absolutely impossible, but I cannot go any further than that.

Senator HEFLIN. All right, so now the third is the stare decisis, which would argue that this is the kind of case that should not be overruled. Do you have any thoughts pertaining to how you would approach the issue of Roe versus Wade from a stare decisis basis?

Judge BORK. Senator, I do not want to get too close to the actual case, but——

Senator THURMOND. Mr. Chairman, it seems to me he is bordering now on a question asking him to express an opinion on a matter that may come before the Supreme Court and I would think that would be improper.

The CHAIRMAN. Well, that is for the Judge to decide, what he thinks he can and cannot answer. Judge, how do you wish to answer that question?

Judge BORK. Well, I was beginning to say, Mr. Chairman, to Senator Heflin, that I do not want to discuss stare decisis in the specific context of Roe v. Wade because that is getting awfully close to how do the factors apply there and therefore, how would you decide. But I will be glad to discuss my general approach to stare decisis and the kinds of factors I would consider. I do not think I can discuss how they might apply in this instance, because that would be too close to committing myself to a particular vote later. If that is satisfactory to you, I will be glad to.

Senator HEFLIN. Yes, go ahead.

Judge BORK. All right. I think it has to be, in the first place, clear that the prior decision was erroneous. I mean, not just shaky but really wrong in terms of constitutional theory, constitutional principle. But that is not sufficient to overrule. I have discussed these factors before, but I will mention them again, and a number of factors counsel against overruling. For example, the development of private expectations on the part of the citizenry. Is this an internalized belief and a right? The growth of institutions, governmental institutions, private institutions around a ruling.

Now, I have given two examples of that. One was the commerce clause and one was the free press clause, in both of which cases many institutions have grown up in dependence upon that and they have become part of the fabric of our national life. The need for continuity and stability in the law, which is certainly always a factor to be weighed. The need for predictability in legal doctrine. I think the preservation of confidence in the Court by not saying that this crowd just does whatever they feel like as the personnel changes. And the respect due to the judgment of predecessors on a legal issue, if they have explained their judgment.

Now, of course, against that is—if it is wrong, and secondly, whether it is a dynamic force so that it continues to produce wrong and unfortunate decisions. I think that was one of the reasons the court in Erie Railroad v. Tompkins overruled Swift v. Tyson—a degenerative force, I think what Brandeis or somebody maybe called dynamic potential. That is the kind of thing you would have to weigh and that is a very fact-based consideration, a very particularistic consideration about whether this is the kind of case that goes one way or the other. I think the Court has got to work out a better theory of stare decisis than it has now articulated.

Senator HEFLIN. Well, is it fair to say that number one, that you think that the reasoning that brought about the decision of *Roe* v. *Wade* is wrong? That the decision, based on that reasoning, was wrong? And that unless some general right of privacy is shown to you to come from the Constitution or unless you can find, in the 14th amendment or somewhere else, some limitation on anti-abortion statutes, then basically you would have to, under your thinking, look to the area of stare decisis in determining whether or not you think *Roe* v. *Wade* ought to be reversed?

Judge BORK. That is correct, Senator. I would have to ask myself what the presumption in favor of preserving a prior precedent meant in this case and whether it was overcome by other factors.

UNITED STATES COURT OF APPEALS
DISTRICT OF COLUMBIA CIRCUIT
WASHINGTON D C 20001

ROBERT H BORK
TED STATES CIRCUIT JUDGE

October 1, 1987

Honorable Joseph R. Biden, Jr.
Chairman
Committee on the Judiciary
United States Senate
Washington, D.C. 20510

Dear Senator Biden:

I would like to thank you and the other members of the Committee for your courteous and insightful questions during my appearance before the Committee. They confirmed my belief that discussion and debate are essential to growth and change in the law. In response to several concerns raised by Senator DeConcini, I would also like to take this opportunity to set out at somewhat greater length my views on the issues of gender discrimination under the Equal Protection Clause and privacy rights.

II. <u>Right to Privacy</u>

Another area you asked about is the Constitution's
protection of individual liberty. As I commented before the
Committee, the Constitution protects numerous and important
aspects of liberty. For instance, the first amendment protects
freedom of speech, press, and religion; the fourth amendment
protects "[t]he right of the people to be secure in their
persons, houses, papers, and effects, against unreasonable
searches and seizures;" and the sixth and seventh amendments
protect the right to trial by jury. All of these freedoms and
more are fundamental. A judge who fails to give these freedoms
their full and fair effect fails in his judicial duty. But to
say that a judge must be tireless to protect the liberties
guaranteed by the Constitution does not mean that one can find a
right to liberty or personal autonomy more expansive than those
found in the Constitution. Once a judge moves beyond the
constitutional text, history, and the structure the Constitution

- 7 -

162

creates, he has only his own sense of what is important or
fundamental to guide his decisionmaking.

More fundamentally, where the constitutional materials do
not specify a value to be protected and has thus left implementation of that value to the democratic process, an unelected judge
has no legitimate basis for imposing that value over the contrary
preferences of elected representatives. When a court does so, it
lessens the area for democratic choice and works a significant
shift of power from the legislature to the judiciary. While the
temptation to do so is strong with respect to a law as "nutty"
and obnoxious as that at issue in Griswold v. Connecticut, 381
U.S. 479 (1965), the invention of rights to correct such a
wholly, misguided public policy inevitably involves the judiciary
in much more difficult policy questions about which reasonable
people disagree, such as abortion or homosexual rights. (In
saying this, I do not preclude the possibility that some cases I
have criticized could be defended on more adequate constitutional
grounds than the opinions offered. I think I made that clear at
the hearings.)

While a legislator obviously can and should make distinctions between such things as the freedom to have an abortion and
the freedom to use contraceptives, a court cannot engage in such
ad hoc policy making. A court cannot invent rights that apply
only in one case and are abandoned tomorrow in a case that cannot
fairly be distinguished. The process of inventing such rights is
contrary to the basic premises of self-government and inconsistent application denies litigants the fairness and impartiality
they are entitled to expect from the judiciary.

This was the basis of my criticism of Justice Douglas'
opinion in Griswold, the case invalidating Connecticut's statute
banning the use of contraceptives. To put the decision in
perspective, it is important to note that Griswold, even in 1965,
was for all practical purposes nothing more than a test case.
The case arose as a prosecution of a doctor who sought to test
the constitutionality of the statute. There is no recorded case
in which this 1879 law was used to prosecute the use of contraceptives by a married couple. The only recorded prosecution was
a test case involving two doctors and a nurse, and in that case
the state itself moved to dismiss.

This point was made by Justice Frankfurter four years before
Griswold in Poe v. Ullman, 367 U.S. 497 (1961), a case rejecting
an earlier attempt to have the Connecticut law invalidated. In
addition, Justice Frankfurter's opinion took judicial notice of
the fact that "contraceptives are commonly and notoriously sold
in Connecticut drug stores," and concluded that there had been an
"undeviating policy of nullification by Connecticut of its anti-
contraceptive laws throughout all the long years that they have
been on the statute books." Id. at 502. Thus, it cannot
realistically be said that failure to invalidate the Connecticut
law would have had any material effect on the ability of married
couples to use contraceptives in the privacy of their homes.

- 8 -

163

My principal objection to the majority opinion in Griswold was the Court's construction of a generalized right of privacy not tied to any particular provision of the Constitution to strike down a concededly silly law which it found offensive. Justice Black's dissent, joined by Justice Stewart, made precisely the same point:

> While I completely subscribe to the [view] that our Court has constitutional power to strike down statutes, state or federal, that violate commands of the Federal Constitution, I do not believe that we are granted power by the Due Process Clause or any other constitutional provision or provisions to measure constitutionality by our belief that legislation is arbitrary, capricious or unreasonable, or accomplishes no justifiable purpose, or is offensive to our own notions of "civilized standards of conduct." Such an appraisal of the wisdom of legislation is an attribute of the power to make laws, not of the power to interpret them.

381 U.S. at 513. Of course, had the state actually sought to enforce the law against a married couple, questions under the fourth amendment as well as under the concept of fair warning would certainly have been presented.

Absent a violation of such a specific, constitutionally granted right of privacy, however, it is difficult to discern the constitutional impediment to the Connecticut law. In my view, Justice Douglas' attempt to do so by creating a free-floating "right to privacy" does not state a principle of constitutional adjudication that was either neutrally derived or which could be neutrally applied in the future.

As I stated in my Indiana Law Review article (page 7):

> If we take the principle of the decision to be a statement that government may not interfere with any acts done in private, we need not even ask about the principle's dubious origin for we know at once that the Court will not apply it neutrally. The Court, we may confidently predict, is not going to throw constitutional protection around heroin use or sexual acts with a consenting minor. We can gain the possibility of neutral application by reframing the principle as a statement that government may not prohibit the use of contraceptives by married couples, but that is not enough. The question of neutral definition arises: Why does the principle extend only to married couples?

- 9 -

> Why, out of all forms of sexual behavior,
> only to the use of contraceptives? Why, out
> of all forms of behavior, only to sex? The
> question of neutral derivation also arises:
> What justifies any limitation upon
> legislatures in this area? What is the
> origin of any principle one may state?

As I went on to note in the article, the "zones of privacy" discussed by Justice Douglas do not really have anything to do with privacy at all. These zones of privacy, I stated,

> protect both private and public behavior and
> so would more properly be labelled "zones of
> freedom". If we follow Justice Douglas' next
> step, these zones would then add up to an
> independent right of freedom, which is to
> say, a general constitutional right to be
> free of legal coercion, a manifest impos-
> sibility in any imaginable society. . . . We
> are left with no idea of the sweep of the
> right of privacy and hence no notion of the
> cases to which it may or may not be applied
> in the future.

Indiana Law Review Article at 9.

With all modesty, my suggestions that the right of privacy was not really about "privacy" as such, that this right would not be applied consistently, and that it would lead the Court into much more difficult moral and social issues, have all proved prophetic.

For example, the "privacy" right recognized in Roe v. Wade, 410 U.S. 113 (1973) -- a right to terminate a pregnancy -- is not really about privacy, but is more accurately described as a right to personal autonomy or liberty. Privacy refers to an interest in anonymity or confidentiality whereas liberty describes freedom to engage in a certain activity. The question in Roe, therefore, is whether any provision of the Constitution recognizes an individual right to terminate pregnancy against state intrusion. The Court's opinion in Roe made no attempt to ground such a right in the Constitution except to say that it was "founded in the 14th Amendment's concept of personal liberty and restrictions upon state action." Id. at 153.

This is my difficulty with the opinion. As Justice White's dissent, joined by Justice Rehnquist, stated, there is "nothing in the language or history of the Constitution to support the Court's judgment," which the dissent termed "an exercise of raw judicial power." The due process clause of the fourteenth amendment provides that "No State shall . . . deprive any person of life, liberty, or property, without due process of law." If the clause is read as written, then it guarantees that life,

- 10 -

liberty, and property will not be taken without the safeguard of fair and adequate legal procedures to challenge the legality of the deprivation. Once such procedures have been given, and the legality of the deprivation established, the due process clause does not establish an independent barrier to the deprivation. If, on the other hand, the clause is read to protect liberty against deprivation regardless of procedures, then the judge must have a theory for deciding which liberties are protected and which are not since no one would suggest that all liberty is immune from state regulation.

So far as I can tell, no one has ever been able to explain why some liberties not specified in the Constitution should be protected and others should not. As far as the Constitution is concerned, when it does not speak to the contrary the state is free to regulate. A judge who uses the due process clause to give substantive protection to some liberties but not others has no basis for decision other than his own subjective view of what is good public policy.

Attempts to read substantive protections of liberty into the due process clause have failed in the past precisely because the clause gives no indication of which liberties are to be preferred to others. In the early part of this century, for example, the Supreme Court read the due process clause of the fifth and fourteenth amendments to protect a generalized liberty of contract, and routinely struck down laws that interfered with that liberty. Thus, in Lochner v. New York, 198 U.S. 45 (1905), the Supreme Court invalidated a New York labor law limiting the hours of bakery employees to 60 hours a week. Similarly, in Adair v. United States, 208 U.S. 161 (1908), the Court struck down a federal law prohibiting interstate railroads from requiring as a condition of employment that its workers agree not to join labor unions. And in Adkins v. Children's Hospital, 261 U.S. 525 (1923), the Court held the District of Columbia's minimum wage law unconstitutional.

As I have said elsewhere, the Supreme Court's modern attempts to use the due process clause as a substantive protection of liberty have also been unconvincing. Although the Court has held in Roe that a woman has a constitutional right to receive an abortion, it has more recently held that consenting adults do not have a constitutional right to engage in homosexual sodomy. See Bowers v. Hardwick, 106 S. Ct. 2841 (1986). Justice White's opinion for the Court in Bowers reasoned as follows:

> It is obvious to us that neither ["the concept of ordered liberty" nor the liberties "deeply rooted in this Nation's history and tradition" formulation] would extend a fundamental right to homosexuals to engage in acts of consensual sodomy. Proscriptions against that conduct have ancient roots.

- 11 -

<u>Id.</u> at 2844.

The difference between these two decisions illustrates my point that it is difficult, if not impossible, to apply the undefined right of privacy in a principled or consistent manner. It is difficult to understand why abortion is a constitutionally protected liberty and homosexual sodomy is not. Neither activity is mentioned in the Constitution, both involve activity between consenting adults, and "[p]roscriptions against [both activities] have ancient roots."

Some have said that the principle may be that individuals have a constitutional right to use their bodies as they wish. Not only is this principle to be found nowhere in the Constitution, but also its application would invalidate laws against prostitution, consensual incest among adults, bestiality, drug use, and suicide, not to mention draft laws and countless safety measures such as laws requiring the use of seat belts and motorcycle helmets. This principle is thus far too general to support a particular decision without sweeping in these other cases.

As I stated before the Committee, it would be inappropriate for me to give any indication of how I would vote as a member of the Supreme Court should the issue arise again. But suffice it to say that the question would be one of searching for an appropriate constitutional basis and precedent. As I have emphasized not every incorrectly decided constitutional decision should be open to reconsideration.

Although I cannot claim to have exhaustively researched the question, I do not think that the ninth amendment provides any basis for a contrary conclusion. The ninth amendment provides: "The enumeration in the Constitution, of certain rights, shall not be construed to deny or disparage others retained by the people." The historical meaning of this amendment is revealed by the circumstances of its adoption. As you are certainly aware, the original Constitution did not contain a Bill of Rights. Rather, it established a national government of enumerated powers. But during the ratification debates, calls were made with increasing frequency by the so-called Anti-Federalists for adoption of a Bill of Rights. The Federalists raised two objections to inclusion of a Bill of Rights. First, it was said to be unnecessary because Congress would have no power to abridge fundamental rights of the people as the general government was one of enumerated, and therefore limited, powers. Second, the Bill of Rights was said to be dangerous because the reservation of certain rights might be read to imply that power was given to the federal government to regulate all others.

Once James Madison became convinced of the need for a Bill of Rights, Madison defended his proposal as follows:

- 12 -

167

> It has been objected also against the bill of
> rights, that, by enumerating particular
> exceptions to the grant of power, it would
> disparage those rights which were not placed
> in that enumeration; and it might follow, by
> implication, that those rights which were not
> singled out, were intended to be assigned
> into the hands of the General Government, and
> were consequently insecure. This is one of
> the most plausible arguments I ever heard
> urged against the admission of rights into
> this system; but, I conceive, that it may be
> guarded against. I have attempted it, as
> gentlemen may see by turning to the last
> clause of the fourth resolution. (1 Annals
> of Congress 456 (J. Gales & W. Seaton ed.
> 1834)).

The clause to which Madison referred was the provision that would
later be adopted in somewhat shorter form as the ninth amendment.
Thus, it appears that the amendment's instruction that the
enumeration "of certain rights, shall not be construed to deny or
disparage others retained by the people" was meant to prevent any
implication, as Madison put it, "that those rights which were not
singled out, were intended to be assigned into the hands of the
General Government."

This means that whenever the Constitution does not grant the
power to regulate conduct to the federal government, the people
have a right to engage in that conduct free from federal
interference even though the conduct is not specified in the Bill
of Rights. It must be emphasized that the "right" protected by
the ninth amendment runs against the federal government when it
undertakes to regulate individuals through an unwarranted expansion of its powers. For this reason, it makes little sense
either textually or historically to speak of ninth amendment
rights enforceable against the states. As I have said elsewhere,
if that were the meaning of the ninth amendment, then surely
there would have been heated debate in the state ratifying
conventions, and litigants and courts would have invoked the
amendment in that capacity. That neither occurred, I think, is
strong evidence that the amendment was not intended to create
federally enforceable rights against the states.

Moreover, even if one agrees with the recent suggestion that
the ninth amendment protects natural rights against state and
federal intrusion, the nature and scope of those rights is
undefined and virtually limitless. For example, John Locke, a
thinker whose writings profoundly influenced the framers' view of
"natural rights," regarded property and contract rights as among
the most important natural rights of men. Accordingly, if the
ninth amendment were to be interpreted as a grant of liberty
against government intrusion, it would necessarily include the
freedom of contract. Of course, this would lead to invalidation

- 13 -

of the worker protection legislation struck down by Lochner and
its progeny, or any other form of economic regulation that
hampers the "right" to contract.

Alternatively, members of the Supreme Court have invoked
their own notions of natural law in the past. For example,
Justice Bradley's concurrence in Bradwell v. State, 83 U.S. 130
(1973), upholding a law forbidding women from practicing law,
states: "The natural and proper timidity and delicacy which
belongs to the female sex evidently unfits it for many of the
occupations of civil life. . . . [The] paramount destiny and
mission of woman are to fulfil the noble and benign offices of
wife and mother. This is the law of the Creator."

But those who now urge reliance on the ninth amendment see a
different set of natural rights emanating from the ninth amendment. For example, Professor Tribe filed a brief with the
Supreme Court in Bowers v. Hardwick suggesting that one of the
rights "retained by the people" under the ninth amendment is the
right to engage in homosexual sodomy. Equally plausible are
claims that the ninth amendment protects drug use, mountain
climbing, and consensual incest among adults. Certainly the text
of the amendment makes no distinction among any of these
"rights." Therefore, unless the ninth amendment is to be read to
invalidate all laws that limit individual freedoms, judges who
invoke the clause selectively will be doing nothing more than
imposing their subjective morality on society.

Although Justice Goldberg's concurrence in Griswold invoked
the ninth amendment, the problems just discussed are, I think,
the reason why the Supreme Court has never rested a decision on
the ninth amendment. For instance, even Justice Douglas, the
author of the majority opinion in Griswold, stated in a
concurring opinion in the companion case to Roe v. Wade, that
"The Ninth Amendment obviously does not create federally
enforceable rights." Doe v. Bolton, 410 U.S. 179, 210 (1973)
(Douglas, J., concurring). Unless someone can find a way both to
read the ninth amendment to apply against the states and to
discover which additional rights are retained by the people, I do
not see any principled way for a judge to rely on the clause to
invalidate state laws.

There is one final matter I wish to mention. There appears
to be some confusion concerning my view of, and the Court's
decision in, Skinner v. Oklahoma, 316 U.S. 535 (1942). Skinner
held that a state statute requiring sterilization of recidivist
robbers but not embezzlers worked "a clear, pointed, unmistakable
discrimination," id. at 541, and therefore violated the equal
protection clause of the fourteenth amendment. It is important
to understand the rationale given by the Court for its decision.
The Court did not rely on a substantive due process right to
privacy. In fact, the Court declined Chief Justice Stone's
invitation in a separate concurrence to decide the case under the
due process clause. Instead, the Court rested its decision

- 14 -

squarely on the equal protection clause: "The equal protection clause would indeed be a formula of empty words if such conspicuously artificial lines could be drawn." Id.

In my 1971 article, I was critical of what I believed to be the Supreme Court's inconsistent application of the equal protection clause. I cited six cases as examples in which the Court both upheld and invalidated challenged classifications. One of the cases I cited was Skinner v. Oklahoma. I did not cite Skinner, or any other case I listed, for the correctness or incorrectness of its holding. Rather, my point was merely that it appeared that "the differing results cannot be explained on any ground other than the Court's preferences for particular values." Indiana Law Review at 12. This was the sum total of my "criticism" of Skinner, and I think it is at best inaccurate to suggest, as some have, that my inclusion of Skinner in a string cite means that I disagree with the decision in the case.

As I stated in my testimony before the Committee, the state's decision to sterilize robbers but not embezzlers may have been indicative of racial bias because the statute operated disproportionately against racial minorities and the poor. If that is true, and if robbery and embezzlement are, as the Court said, "intrinsically the same quality of offense," 316 U.S. at 541, then I think it may be fair to say the state engaged in impermissible discrimination. In addition, I note that sterilization of criminals raises serious and independent questions under the eighth amendment's prohibition on cruel and unusual punishment, questions neither I nor the Court addressed.

I hope that these additional comments prove to be of assistance to you.

Sincerely,

Robert H. Bork

cc: Honorable Dennis DeConcini
     Honorable Strom Thurmond

THE OPPOSITION TO BORK:

NARAL

The Case For Women's Liberty

National
Abortion Rights
Action League

individual integrity would be secure from invasions by the new government.

Second, when he urges that judicial understanding of broad constitutional concepts like liberty and equality ought to be constrained by "original intent,"[36] he would limit twentieth century courts to eighteenth century assumptions about race, sex, and class. In the absence of an Equal Rights Amendment, women are particularly vulnerable to his text-based absolutism.

Third, his view that courts ought to be extremely deferential to legislative and executive authority amounts to a rejection of judicial responsibility to protect individual rights -- especially the rights of those less able to defend themselves in the political process. That responsibility is central to our

20

system of checks and balances and has remained a preeminent theme throughout ou
history.

His devotion to "restraint" does not, however, mean a devotion to legal
continuity or social stability. Although American women now assume that the
rights acknowledged in decisions such as Roe v. Wade and Griswold v. Connecticut
are essential, Judge Bork sees legal "truth" as trumping such assumptions.[37]

His colleagues have pointed out the hypocrisy of Judge Bork's posture as the
apostle of judicial restraint, since Judge Bork has shown little compunction
about asserting his own unusual views aggressively and in dubious contexts.[38]
Judge Bork has even inspired those of his peers who agree with his disposition of
particular cases to disclaim connection with his extreme rhetoric.[39]

Robert Bork believes that courts must be extremely deferential to
legislative activity regarding matters of "morality." He explains that he is a
"value skeptic," by which he means that there is no principled way to decide that
one set of moral values is "better" than another. Therefore, he concludes, a
vote of the majority is the only fair way for society to choose:

> *"[T]here is no uniform national consensus concerning the moral standards
> that are now being imposed by the judiciary . . . the liberty of free men,
> among other things, is the liberty to make laws, which is increasingly being
> denied . . . Roe v. Wade is the classic instance . . . When the court
> nationalizes morality by making up these consitutional rights, it strikes at
> federalism . . . in a central way.*"[40]

After the Founders drafted the Constitution, they designed the Bill of
Rights to check the power of self-interested, and often vicious, majority rule.
When Judge Bork argues that questions of "morality" should remain with local
ballot boxes, even when fundamental individual liberties are being trampled, he
conveniently forgets this basic history.

Likewise, those who define the abortion rights debate as one between "pro-
abortion" groups and "anti-abortion" groups deliberately misstate the point.

21

173

These two groups of advocates do not take equivalent and opposite moral stances. Those who support the "right to choose" do not stand in favor of a particular choice -- such as, abortion instead of gestation. Instead, they stand for individual freedom to wrestle with personal and moral issues, while government keeps a respectful distance. And they assume that, in a pluralistic society, a variety of decisions and behaviors is both inevitable and beneficial despite the degree of discomfort one person's choice may cause to another person.

This norm of individual freedom is antithetical to the "anti-choice" assertion of moral authority to impose a preferred set of values on society as a whole, including minorities with differing moral views. A judge who upholds individual liberty of conscience, especially in hard cases, will find support in every document from the Constitutional Convention. The reverse is true for an imposition by majoritarian vote of moral absolutism.[41]

In a 1984 case wherein he launched a full-scale assault on privacy doctrine, Judge Bork's peers on the D.C. Circuit were not at all convinced by his claim of "value skepticism." On the contrary, his language was so lacking in respect for the Supreme Court that it drew their harsh criticism:

> "[W]e believe that [Judge Bork's opinion] substituted [his] own doctrinal preferences for the constitutional principles established by the Supreme Court."[42]

Judge Bork has criticized directly what he describes as judicial creation of "new rights." He defines these as all rights lacking "explanatory principle [in] existing textual rights suggest[ed] [by] the contours of a value already stated in the document or implied by the Constitution's structure and history."[43] Of these "new rights," the right to privacy has received Judge Bork's most frontal attack:

> "The 'penumbra' [considered to be the source of the right of privacy] was no more than a perception that it is sometimes necessary to protect actions or

22

*associations not guaranteed by the Constitution in order to protect an
activity that is. The penumbral right has no life of its own as a right
independent of its relationship to a first amendment freedom. Where that
relationship does not exist, the penumbral right evaporates.*[44]

Since decision-making regarding personal health and sexual behavior does not

involve first amendment political activity, Judge Bork believes that the Court

created an illegitimate "new right" in Griswold. Quoting Justice White, Judge

Bork has demonstrated the vehemence of his opposition to constitutional privacy

by asserting that judicial protection of such rights makes the Court "most

vulnerable" and brings it "nearest to illegitimacy."[45] Regarding whether a

woman's decision to terminate her pregnancy is protected by the constitutional

right to privacy, Judge Bork has stated that:

> "I am convinced, as I think most legal scholars are, that Roe v. Wade is,
> itself, an unconstitutional decision, a serious and wholly unjustifiable
> judicial usurpation of State legislative authority."[46]

Unlike most members of the bench, Judge Bork believes the Supreme Court ought

not to be reluctant to overrule past precedent in constitutional cases. As a

result, we must take seriously the possibility that, given the chance, Judge Bork

could well disapprove the constitutional right of privacy completely, since

Supreme Court recognition of this most comprehensive of rights is a twentieth

century development. He has expressed similar lack of respect for the line of

cases that recognizes the "fundamental" nature of a host of individual rights,

including marriage, childbearing, and parenting.[47]

Women are especially vulnerable in Bork's textually absolutist world.

Concerning equal protection, he has asserted that, "The Constitution has

provisions that create specific rights. These protect, among others, racial,

ethnic, and religious minorities."[48] Since gender is glaringly absent from this

list, we must wonder whether Bork would take non-passage of the Equal Rights

Amendment as a majoritarian mandate against "equal protection" of women.

23

His lack of interest in or compassion for women is evident in many of his opinions. One dramatic example can be seen in his response to a challenge to American Cyanamid's "fetal protection policy;" that policy bars women of childbearing age from jobs which might involve exposure to dangerous levels of lead unless they consent to be sterilized. Judge Bork declined to apply the worker protection principles of the Occupational Safety and Health Act, construing the statute very narrowly as applying solely to working conditions, not to company policies enacted to govern those conditions. According to his legal philosophy, such a reading is required because the concerns of women workers were not at issue when the Act was written. Moreover, what he saw as a "moral" component of the dispute fortified his conclusion that the court should refuse to offer relief:

> "These are moral issues of no small complexity, but they are not for us. Congress has enacted a statute and our only task is the mundane one of interpreting its language and applying its policy . . . The women involved in this matter were put to a most unhappy choice. But no statute redresses all grievances, and we must decide cases according to law."[49]

Judge Bork's remarkable insensitivity to women's concerns is perhaps most vivid in his 1985 analysis of why sexual harassment ought not be treated as sex discrimination. His views appear in his dissent from the en banc denial of rehearing in Vinson v. Taylor.[50] That he is worse than reactionary is clear from the fact that the circuit court was affirmed 9-0 by the U.S. Supreme Court in an opinion written by Justice Rehnquist. Judge Bork claims to have a "doctrinal difficulty" in classifying harassment as discrimination. In his view, a woman's claim cannot accurately be called "sex discrimination" because unwelcome sexual advances are not made solely and without exception to members of the opposite sex. He concludes that because a bisexual supervisor could conceivably use his, or her, authority to solicit sexual favors from male and female employees

24

interchangeably, the cause of action is "artificial."[51]

Considering that his supporters assert that his "neutrality" is one of the judge's most important virtues, it also seems worth noting that Bork employs a blatant double standard when assessing the damage that sexual harassment does to workplace morale. When a male superior harasses a female employee, Judge Bork admits that the behavior is "reprehensible," but he is troubled by the difficulty of determining when a woman's participation may be voluntary. He concludes that the court ought not to recognize her claim. Conversely, with respect to men who engage in sexual activity with men over whom they have supervisory authority, Judge Bork has no trouble condemning the behavior:

> "common sense and common experience demonstrate . . . [that] [e]pisodes of this sort are certain to be deleterious to morale and discipline, to call into question the even-handedness of superiors' dealings with lower ranks, to make personal dealings uncomfortable where the relationship is sexually ambiguous . . . ."[52]

Judge Bork may or may not have a legitimate concern that military discipline would suffer if sexual behavior between servicemen were to be sanctioned. Yet anyone who desires to see our society plagued less systematically by sexual abuse of women must be appalled at the contrast between, on the one hand, his eagerness to mete out swift and uncompromising punishment in Dronenburg and, on the other, his protestations of confusion and judicial helplessness in Vinson.

Many judges, like Justice Powell, do see the judicial role as limited. Yet, they nonetheless approach their duties with compassion and an ability, when appropriate, to respond to the plight of those who have been and persistently continue to be powerlessness in the legislative process. Judge Bork has rejected this responsibility:

> "[U]nless the Constitution . . . says this minority is protected in these ways, then I think the judge must remit this minority to the democratic process. I think this is a very civilized and fair nation; I don't think being remitted to the democratic process is a sad fate for most people."[53]

25

F. CONCLUSION: NARAL OPPOSES ROBERT BORK

The Reagan administration has nominated Robert Bork to the U.S. Supreme Court because he is a creative and effective legal reactionary. Using the language of "original intent" and "judicial restraint," he sets forth an approach to constitutional law that voids personal privacy as well as women's claim to equal protection. Like most arch-conservatives, he presumes that the marketplace works, that the political system is fair, that democratically enacted legislation is constitutional, and that government agencies generally act in good faith. What makes Bork unusually dangerous, however, is that his prescription of very deferential judicial behavior and fidelity to eighteenth century assumptions would unbalance our three-part system of government. He would dismantle the mechanism that has throughout our history kept these various power-brokering systems accountable to constitutional principles.

Since his July 1, 1987 nomination to the Supreme Court, much attention has been paid to Judge Bork's expressed hostility to constitutional privacy, especially as it protects a woman deciding to choose abortion. Predictably, when this history of hostility inspired close questioning by members of the Senate Judiciary Committee, the harshest edges appeared to have been smoothed from his theory. Yet, his suggestions that he would be receptive to new arguments in favor of constitutional privacy and women's equal rights are unconvincing. The radical jurisprudence he has been expounding forcefully for years from both the bench and the podium leaves no doubt about the crabbed contours of the rights he would be willing to vindicate were he to sit on the Supreme Court. In all fairness to their female constituents, the Senators must reject this nomination.

###

26

| 100TH CONGRESS | SENATE | EXEC. REPT. |
| 1st Session | | 100-7 |

NOMINATION OF ROBERT H. BORK TO BE AN ASSOCIATE JUSTICE OF THE UNITED STATES SUPREME COURT

OCTOBER 13, 1987.—Ordered to be printed

Mr. BIDEN, from the Committee on the Judiciary,
submitted the following

REPORT

together with

ADDITIONAL, MINORITY, AND SUPPLEMENTAL VIEWS

The Committee on the Judiciary, to which was referred the nomination of Judge Robert H. Bork to be an Associate Justice of the United States Supreme Court, having considered the same reports unfavorably thereon, a quorum being present, by a vote of nine yeas and five nays, with the recommendation that the nomination be rejected.

PART ONE: BACKGROUND AND QUALIFICATIONS

I. BACKGROUND

The committee received the President's nomination of Judge Robert H. Bork to be an Associate Justice of the United States Supreme Court on July 7, 1987. The hearings on Judge Bork's nomination were held on September 15, 16, 17, 18, 19, 21, 22, 23, 25, 28, 29, and 30. The nominee completed 30 hours of testimony, extending over four-and-a-half days, before the committee. The 12 days of hearings lasted approximately 87 hours, and during that time the committee heard from 112 witnesses.

The testimony of public witnesses was organized so as to encourage as full and complete a discussion as possible of the various subjects relevant to this nomination. An effort was made to bring before the committee some of this nation's most eminent legal scholars and most distinguished lawyers and public servants to testify both in favor of and against the nominee. Where appropriate, witnesses testified in panels organized by subject matter, facilitating thorough questioning and debate of each issue. The committee was particularly privileged to receive testimony from President Gerald Ford, former Chief Justice Warren Burger and five former Attorneys General of the United States. Set forth as Appendix I to this Report is a complete witness list for these hearings, organized by date of appearance and briefly indicating biographical data where appropriate.

The committee carefully and thoroughly scrutinized the nominee's qualifications and credentials, his five-year record as a Judge on the United States Court of Appeals for the District of Columbia Circuit, and his extensive written and spoken record. On October 6, a quorum being present, the committee took two roll call votes. The first vote was on a motion to report the nomination with a favorable recommendation. The committee voted, 9 to 5 against that motion:

NAYS	AYES
Mr. Biden	Mr. Thurmond
Mr. Kennedy	Mr. Hatch
Mr. Byrd	Mr. Simpson
Mr. Metzenbaum	Mr. Grassley
Mr. DeConcini	Mr. Humphrey
Mr. Leahy	
Mr. Heflin	
Mr. Simon	
Mr. Specter	

(2)

The second roll call vote was on a motion to report the nomination with a negative recommendation. The committee voted, 9 to 5, in favor of the motion:

AYES	NAYS
Mr. Biden	Mr. Thurmond
Mr. Kennedy	Mr. Hatch
Mr. Byrd	Mr. Simpson
Mr. Metzenbaum	Mr. Grassley
Mr. DeConcini	Mr. Humphrey
Mr. Leahy	
Mr. Heflin	
Mr. Simon	
Mr. Simpson	

II. THE NOMINEE

Judge Bork was born on March 1, 1927, in Pittsburgh. He attended the University of Pittsburgh for a short time and then enlisted in the United States Marine Corps in 1945. He served until 1946, when he was honorably discharged. Following military service, he attended the University of Chicago, where he received a Bachelor of Arts degree. During his first year at the University of Chicago Law School, Judge Bork enlisted in the Marine Corps Reserves. He was called back to duty in 1950 and served in active military duty until 1952. He received his law degree from the University of Chicago Law School in 1953. From 1953-1954, he was a research associate with the University of Chicago Law School's Law and Economics Project.

From 1954-1962, the nominee engaged in the private practice of law. He practiced first with the New York firm of Wilkie, Owen, Farr, Gallagher & Watson and then later was an associate and partner at the Chicago firm of Kirkland, Ellis, Hodson, Chaffetz & Masters.

From 1962-1973, the nominee was a member of the faculty of the Yale Law School. He was an associate professor from 1962-1965 and a full professor from 1965-1973.

From 1973-1977, Judge Bork served as Solicitor General of the United States. In this capacity, he argued a number of cases before the Supreme Court. Judge Bork briefly served as Acting Attorney General from 1973-1974.

In 1977, Judge Bork returned to the faculty of the Yale Law School. He served as the Chancellor Kent Professor of Law from 1977-1979 and as the Alexander Bickel Professor of Public Law from 1979-1981. His book, *The Antitrust Paradox: A Policy At War With Itself,* was published in 1978.

In 1981, Judge Bork returned to private practice as a partner in Kirkland & Ellis, working out of the Washington office.

From 1982 to the present, Judge Bork has served as a judge on the U.S. Court of Appeals for the District of Columbia Circuit.

III. THE AMERICAN BAR ASSOCIATION'S EVALUATION

For the first time since the American Bar Association's (ABA) Standing Committee on Federal Judiciary began evaluating Supreme Court nominees, a substantial minority of the Standing Committee found a Supreme Court nominee to be "not qualified" to serve on the nation's highest court. In evaluating the nomination of Judge Bork, Harold R. Tyler, Jr., Chairman of the Standing Committee (and a former federal district court judge), testified that "ten members voted well-qualified; one, not opposed, and four, not qualified." (Comm. Print Draft, Vol. 1, at 902.)

Prior to the Bork nomination, the only time that the ABA Standing Committee did not initially return a unanimously well-qualified evaluation was in 1971, when Chief Justice Rehnquist was first appointed to the Court. In that case, while the Standing Committee was unanimously of the view that Chief Justice Rehnquist was "qualified" for the appointment, three members found that his qualifications did not establish his eligibility for the committee's highest rating and, therefore, said that they were "not opposed" to his confirmation.

When Judge Clement F. Haynsworth, Jr. was nominated to the Court in 1969, the Standing Committee's initial unanimous evaluation was that he was "qualified professionally;" this was later changed to an 8 to 4 vote after evidence came to light of an alleged financial conflict of interest. Even Judge G. Harrold Carswell (nominated in 1970), whose professional competence was an issue before the Senate, received unanimous approval by the ABA. The nominations of Judge Haynsworth and Judge Carswell were rejected by the Senate.

No Supreme Court nominee who has received even a single "Not Qualified" vote from the Standing Committee has ever been confirmed by the Senate.

A. The ABA Standing Committee Uses Three Categories to Rate Supreme Court Nominees

The Standing Committee now uses three categories to describe its evaluations of Supreme Court nominees. "Well qualified" is reserved for those nominees who "meet the highest standards of professional competence, judicial temperament and integrity. . . . The persons in this category must be among the best available for appointment to the Supreme Court." "Not opposed" is the second category, applying to persons who, while "minimally qualified," are not among the best available for appointment and are not endorsed by the committee. The third category is "not qualified"—those who are not qualified "with respect to professional qualifications" for appointment to the Supreme Court. This rating system is somewhat different from that used for federal district court and appellate court judgeships.

The Standing Committee rates candidates on the basis of a limited set of criteria. As stated in a September 21 letter from Judge Tyler to Chairman Biden: "The Committee's evaluation of Judge Bork is based upon its investigation of his professional competence, judicial temperament and integrity. Consistent with its longstanding tradition, the Committee's investigation did not cover Judge Bork's political or ideological philosophy except to the extent that such matters might bear on judicial temperament or integrity." (Comm. Print Draft, Vol. 1, at 954.) The handbook of the ABA

Standing Committee directs its members, when investigating temperament, to consider the prospective nominee's "compassion, decisiveness, open-mindedness, sensitivity, courtesy, patience, freedom from bias and commitment to equal justice, among other factors."

In a September 4 letter to Senator Metzenbaum, Judge Tyler advised that because of the limited scope of the Standing Committee's evaluation, "this committee should not specifically recommend to the Senate how it should vote on confirmation of a given nominee," and that although some might construe a "well qualified" rating as "equivalent to a firm recommendation to the Senate," such a construction "would not be justified." (Comm. Print Draft, Vol. 1, at 970.)

B. The ABA Conducted an Extensive Investigation of Judge Bork

The 15 members of the ABA Standing Committee conducted an extensive investigation of Judge Bork, including interviews with five members of the Supreme Court, with many of his colleagues on the D.C. Circuit Court of Appeals, and with approximately 170 other federal and state court judges, including female and minority members of the bench, throughout the United States. The ABA Committee also interviewed approximately 150 practicing attorneys, 79 law school deans and professors, 11 of Judge Bork's former law clerks and a number of present or former lawyers who served under Judge Bork in the office of the Solicitor General when he headed that office.

Judge Bork's opinions were examined by the dean and 10 professors at the University of Michigan Law School. The Standing Committee reviewed and considered written submissions from a number of institutions and groups, including the White House, the Lawyers Committee for Civil Rights Under Law, the past chairmen of the Antitrust Section of the ABA, the NAACP Legal Defense and Education Fund, Inc., the American Civil Liberties Union, the National Women's Law Center, Public Citizen Litigation Group and People for the American Way.

Finally, Judge Bork was personally interviewed on two separate occasions, for a total of about six hours, by three members of the ABA Standing Committee. A second interview was unprecedented for a Supreme Court nominee, but was considered necessary because of "some additional questions" that arose from discussion among members of the ABA Committee and submissions of various groups. (Comm. Print Draft, Vol. 1, at 903.)

C. The ABA Committee Was Split in Its Evaluation of Judge Bork

Based on the criteria identified above, a majority of the ABA Committee concluded that Judge Bork is "well qualified" for appointment to the Supreme Court. Five members of the committee concluded that Judge Bork did not merit such a rating because of their concerns about his judicial temperament. Such concerns were related to Judge Bork's "compassion, open-mindedness, his sensitivity to the rights of women and minority persons or groups and comparatively extreme views respecting constitutional principles or their application, particularly within the ambit of the Fourteenth Amendment." In addition, one dissenting member also expressed reservations about what that member termed inconsistent and possibly misleading recollections by Judge Bork of the events surrounding the resignations of Attorney General Elliot Richardson and Deputy Attorney General William Ruckelshaus during the Watergate episode.

The interviews of Judge Bork's colleagues, other federal and state court judges, practicing attorneys and academics revealed praise for the nominee's intellectual and professional attainments and admiration for his experience and analytical abilities. Those persons who considered Judge Bork either highly qualified or qualified praised his integrity, scholarship and professional competence. A number of those interviewed expressed concerns, however, about the nominee's judicial temperament, most often relating to doubts about his compassion, open-mindedness and sensitivity to women and minorities.

The Standing Committee also reviewed allegations made by Judge James F. Gordon, a senior federal district court judge from Kentucky, relating to preparation of the written opinion in *Vander Jagt* v. *O'Neill*, 699 F.2d 1166 (D.C. Cir.), *cert. denied*, 464 U.S. in which Judge Gordon sat by designation on the D.C. Circuit. Judge Gordon had written a letter to Chairman Biden, dated August 24, 1987, which was transmitted to the ABA Standing Committee. The letter alleged that Judge Bork had wrongfully attempted to make his view of the case the majority opinion, when the other two judges on the panel disagreed with his reasoning. *(See generally* Part Three, Section VIII, *infra.)* Chairman Tyler testified that, given the circumstances, the Standing Committee had felt that this "was [not] something that should weigh for or against [Judge Bork] at all." (Comm. Print Draft, Vol. 1, at 910.)

IV. THE LEGAL COMMUNITY'S EVALUATION OF JUDGE BORK

A. The Negative Evaluation of Judge Bork by the Academic Community Is Unprecedented

The committee has received letters from approximately 2,000 members of the legal academic community in opposition to Judge Bork's confirmation. Simply put, the extent of this opposition is unprecedented. Prior to this nomination, the maximum number of law professors voicing their disapproval of a judicial nominee had been 300, in connection with the nomination of Judge Carswell.

The committee received letters signed by 1,925 law professors opposing Judge Bork's confirmation. (Comm. Print Draft, Vol. 3, at 1899.) This figure represents nearly 40 percent of the full-time law faculty at American Bar Association-accredited law schools in 47 states and the District of Columbia. (There are no ABA-accredited law schools in Alaska, Nevada and Rhode Island.) The signatories to these letters also represent faculty from 90 percent of the ABA-accredited law schools (153 schools out of a total of 172).

The committee also received a letter signed by 32 law school deans.[1] (Comm. Print Draft, Vol. 2, at 91-97.) This letter stated:

> Judge Bork has developed and repeatedly expressed a comprehensive and fixed view of the Constitution that is at odds with most of the pivotal decisions protecting civil rights and liberties that the Supreme Court has rendered over the past four decades. . . . If Judge Bork were to be confirmed, his vote could prove determinative in turning the clock back to an era when constitutional rights and liberties, and the role of the judiciary in protecting them, were viewed in a much more restrictive way. (Comm. Print Draft, Vol. 2, at 92.)

Finally, the committee received a letter from 71 constitutional law professors, the text of which was identical to that signed by the law school deans. Three persons signed both this letter and the deans' letter. (Comm. Print Draft, Vol. 2, at 80-90.)

B. Opposition to Judge Bork's Confirmation Also Came from Other Professional Legal Groups

A large number of practicing lawyers and organized bar groups have also expressed their opposition to Judge Bork's confirmation. One such group is the Association of the Bar of the City of New York, through its Executive Committee, testified against the confirmation. The Association, which is one of the oldest and most prestigious bar organizations in the country and which at present has almost 17,000 members, stated that Judge Bork's "fundamental judicial philosophy . . . appears to this Association to run counter to many of the fundamental rights and liberties protected by the Constitution." (Comm. Print Draft, Vol. 2, at 845.)

The Committee also heard testimony from John Clay, representing Lawyers for the Judiciary, a Chicago-based organization with more than 700 members, which opposes Judge Bork's confirmation. The statement of Lawyers for the Judiciary concludes that "Judge Bork's philosophy . . . puts him outside the mainstream of constitutional jurisprudence and would deny what our citizens regard as their basic, fundamental rights." (Comm. Print Draft, Vol. 3, at 2212.)

---

[1] In a September 28 letter to the Chairman and ranking Member, James Vorenberg, Dean of the Harvard Law School, stated that while he was opposed to Judge Bork's confirmation, he did not intend to be listed as a signatory to the letter.

PART TWO: THE CONSTITUTION'S UNENUMERATED RIGHTS

I. JUDGE BORK'S VIEW OF THE CONSTITUTION DISRE-GARDS THIS COUNTRY'S TRADITION OF HUMAN DIGNITY, LIBERTY AND UNENUMERATED RIGHTS

The Bork hearings opened on the eve of the celebration of the 200th anniversary of our Constitution. The hearings proved to be about that Constitution, not just about a Supreme Court nominee.

The hearings reaffirmed what many understand to be a core principle upon which this nation was founded: Our Constitution recognizes inalienable rights and is not simply a grant of rights by the majority. Chairman Biden's opening statement identified these fundamental principles:

> I believe all Americans are born with certain inalienable rights. As a child of God, I believe my rights are not derived from the Constitution. My rights are not derived from any government. My rights are not derived from any majority. My rights are because I exist. They were given to me and each of my fellow citizens by our Creator, and they represent the essence of human dignity. (Comm. Print Draft, Vol. 1, at 68.)

This image of human dignity has been associated throughout our history with the idea that the Constitution recognizes "unenumerated rights." These are rights beyond those specifically mentioned in the Constitution itself, rights that are affirmed by the grand open-ended phrases of the document: "liberty," "due process," "equal protection of the laws" and others. The sober responsibility of preserving the meaning and content of these rights has fallen to the judiciary, and especially to the Supreme Court.

Against this understanding of the Constitution, and of human dignity, Judge Bork offers an alternative vision—that Americans have no rights against government, except those specifically enumerated in the Constitution. The contrast was stated cogently by Professor Philip Kurland:

> I think it makes all the difference in the world whether you start with the notion that the people have all the liberties except those that are specifically taken away from them, or you start with the notion, as I think Judge Bork now has, that they have no liberties except those which are granted to them. (Comm. Print Draft, Vol. 3, at 1391.)

As Professor Kurland concluded: "I do not know of anything more fundamental in our Constitution" than the idea that the people have all the liberties except those specifically relinquished.

(8)

A. Judge Bork's Judicial Philosophy Does Not Recognize the Concept of Unenumerated Rights and Liberties

1. Judge Bork's Core Theory

Judge Bork has consistently described his constitutional theory as "intentionalist," meaning that he considers it the function of a judge to determine the intentions of the body that wrote the laws and to apply those intentions to the case brought before the court. Interpreting law is thus a matter of discerning the original intent of those responsible for making it.

Judge Bork reaffirmed this view in his opening statement before the committee:

> The judge's authority derives entirely from the fact that he is applying the law and not his own personal values . . . . How should a judge go about finding the law? The only legitimate way is by attempting to discern what those who made the law intended. The intentions of the lawmakers govern, whether the lawmakers are the Congress of the United States enacting a statute or those who ratified our Constitution and its various amendments. (Comm. Print Draft, Vol. 1, at 78-79.)

At the end of four and one-half days of testimony, Judge Bork confirmed that he had not altered his basic philosophy:

> [T]here is much in my earlier writings—most particularly, my views on the proper role of judges and the need for faithful adherence to the text and the discernible intentions of the ratifiers of the Constitution and statutes—that I subscribe to just as fully today as I did before. . . . If the Members of the Committee are looking, as you have said you are, for predictability, it is certainly predictable that I will adhere to my judicial philosophy as I have described it in these hearings and elsewhere. (Comm. Print Draft, Vol. 1, at 721.) [2]

2. Judge Bork's Judicial Philosophy Leads Him to Conclude that the Constitution "Specified Certain Liberties and Allocates All Else to Democratic Processes"

The implications of Judge Bork's theory of original intent are quite clear from his writings, speeches and testimony. The most dramatic consequence of his theory is the rejection of the concept of unenumerated rights and liberties. He has consistently held to the view, both before and during the hearings, that the Constitution should not be read as recognizing an individual right unless

---

[2] Judge Bork did not always rely on orginal intent and the text of the Constitution for the resolution of constitutional controversies. As he wrote in 1968:

The text of the Constitution, as anyone experienced with words might expect, is least precise where it is most important. Like the Ten Commandments, the Constitution enshrines profound values, but necessarily omits the minor premises required to apply them . . . . History can be of considerable help, but it tells us much too little about the specific intentions of the men who framed, adopted, and ratified the great clauses. The record is incomplete, the men involved had vague or even conflicting intentions, and no one foresaw or could have foreseen, the disputes that changing social conditions and outlooks would bring before the Court. . . . ("The Supreme Court Needs a New Philosophy," Fortune 138, 141 (Dec. 1968).)

that right can be specifically found in a particular provision of the document.[3]

In particular, Judge Bork has repeatedly rejected the well-established line of Supreme Court decisions holding that the "liberty" clauses of the Fifth and Fourteenth Amendments protect against governmental invasion of a person's substantive personal liberty and privacy. He has said, for example, that:

> [T]he choice of "fundamental values" by the Court cannot be justified. Where constitutional materials do not clearly specifiy the value to be preferred, there is no principled way to prefer any claimed human value to any other. The judge must stick close to the text and the history, and their fair implications, and not construct new rights. ("Neutral Principles and Some First Amendment Problems," 47 *Indiana Law Journal* 1, 8 (1971).)

Judge Bork has also disregarded the text of the Ninth Amendment, which provides that "[t]he enumeration in the Constitution, of certain rights, shall not be construed to deny or disparage others retained by the people." In Judge Bork's view, while there are alternative explanations for the Amendment,

> if it ultimately turns out that no plausible interpretation can be given, the only recourse for a judge is to refrain from inventing meanings and ignore the provision, as was the practice until recently. ("Interpretation of the Constitution," 1984 Justice Lester W. Roth Lecture, University of So California, October 25, 1984, at 16; emphasis added.) [4]

This suggested disregard for the Amendment is consistent with Judge Bork's general recommendation about a judge's role "when his studies leave him unpersuaded that he understands the core of what the Framers intended" with respect to a particular constitutional provision:

> [The judge] must treat [the provision] as nonexistent, since, in terms of expression of the framers' will, it is nonexistent. . . . When the meaning of a provision . . . is unknown, the judge has in effect nothing more than a water blot on the document before him. He cannot read it; any meaning he assigns to it is no more than judicial invention

---

[3] In response to a question by Senator DeConcini, Judge Bork testified that he believed there were "some rights that are not enumerated but are found because of the structure of the Constitution and government." (Comm. Print Draft, Vol. 1, at 224.) These "structural" rights, which "the individual [has] for the sake of a governmental process that the Constitution outlines" ("Neutral Principles" at 17), are wholly distinct from "unenumerated rights" as that phrase is ordinarily used. These latter rights preserve individual liberties in the face of government's desire to override them, and are rights retained by the people, rather than rights given to them by the majority. It is the tradition recognizing these rights that is the subject of this Section.

[4] Judge Bork did not always believe that the Ninth Amendment should be ignored. In 1968, he argued:

"Legitimate activism requires, first of all, a warrant for the court to move beyond the range of substantive rights that can be derived from the traditional sources of constitutional law. The case for locating this warrant in the long-ignored 9th Amendment was persuasively made by Justice Arthur Goldberg [in *Griswold* v. *Connecticut,* 381 U.S. 479 (1965)]. . . . This seems to mean that the Bill of Rights is an incomplete, open-ended document, and that the work of completion is, at least, in major part, a task for the Supreme Court. There is some historical evidence that this is substantially what Madison intended." ("The Supreme Court Needs a New Philosophy" at 170.)

of a constitutional prohibition; and his proper course is to ignore it. (*Id.* at 11-12; emphasis added.) [5]

According to Judge Bork, "[t]he Constitution specified certain liberties and allocates all else to democratic processes." ("Judicial Review and Democracy," *Society,* Nov./Dec. 1986 at 7; emphasis added.) Thus, under Judge Bork's view, the court interferes with the "democratic process" whenever it recognizes a right that is not specified in the Constitution. As he said in a 1985 speech and reaffirmed at the hearings, the Constitution is essentially a zero-sum system, in which rights for some necessarily come only at the expense of others:

> Senator SIMON. One point, at a speech at Berkeley in 1985, you say . . .' [When] a court adds to one person's constitutional rights it subtracts from the rights of others.' Do you believe that is always true?
>
> Judge BORK. Yes, Senator. I think it's a matter of plain arithmetic. . . .
>
> Senator SIMON. I have long thought it is kind of fundamental in our society, that when you expand the liberty of any of us, you expand the liberty of all of us.
>
> Judge BORK. I think, Senator, that is not correct. (Comm. Print Draft, Vol. 1, at 289, 421; emphasis added.)

B. This Nation Was Conceived with the Recognition of Pre-existing Inalienable Rights that the Constitution Does Not Specifically Enumerate But Nonetheless Acknowledges and Protects

The founding documents of American constitutionalism—the Declaration of Independence, the Constitution and the Bill of Rights—were accepted not because they exhausted the protection of basic rights but because they expressly protected unenumerated rights as well. Indeed, the Constitution was conceived to create a national government that although sufficiently powerful to bind together diverse states, "would not threaten the individual liberty that the people retained and did not cede to any level of government." (Written statement of Professor Laurence H. Tribe, Comm. Print Draft, Vol. 2, at 18-19.)

The broad purposes of this plan are clear from the language of the founding documents. As former Congresswoman and Professor Barbara Jordan testified: "The Declaration of Independence preceded the Constitution, and the Declaration of Independence speaks of inalienable rights endowed by our Creator . . . , among them life, liberty, [and the] pursuit of happiness." (Comm. Print Draft, Vol. 1, at 787.) The Fifth Amendment states that no person shall be deprived of liberty." The Ninth Amendment mandates that "[t]he enumeration in the Constitution, of certain rights, shall not be construed to deny or disparage others retained by the people." Finally, the Fourteenth Amendment—with its specific protection of "liber-

---

[5] These statements cannot be squared with either Judge Bork's own framework for interpreting the Constitution or the clear statements of the Supreme Court. Indeed, they are in direct conflict with the position of the revered Chief Justice, John Marshall, who stated in *Marbury v. Madison,* 1 Cranch 137, 174 (1803): "It cannot be presumed that any clause in the Constitution is intended to be without effect."

ty"—was added with a similar purpose: To restrain the power of the states to infringe the fundamental rights of any person.

The intent to protect inalienable, unenumerated rights is clear from the history of the Bill of Rights. Originally, many opposed a Bill of Rights, fearing that the express protection of certain rights would justify an inference that rights not specifically identified were subject to governmental control. The fear that the Bill of Rights would be used in a way inimical to unenumerated rights was best expressed by James Iredell at the North Carolina ratifying convention:

> A bill of rights, as I conceive, would not only be incongruous, but dangerous. No man, let his ingenuity be what it will, could enumerate all the individual rights not relinquished by this Constitution. Suppose, therefore, an enumeration of a great many, but an omission of some, and that long after all traces of our present disputes were at an end, any of the omitted rights should be invaded, and the invasion complained of; what would be the plausible answer of the government to such a complaint? Would they naturally say, "We live at a great distance from the time when this Constitution was established. We can judge of it much better by the ideas of it entertained at the time, than by any ideas of our own. The bill of rights, passed at that time, showed that the people did not think every power retained which was not given, else this bill of rights was not only useless but absurd. But we are not at liberty to charge an absurdity upon our ancestors, who have given such strong proofs upon their good sense, as well as their attachment to a liberty. So long as the rights enumerated in the bill of rights remain unviolated, you have no reason to complain. This is not one of them." Thus a bill of rights might operate as a snare rather than a protection. (Jonathan Elliot, *Debates in the Several State Conventions on the Adoption of the Federal Constitution,* Vol. IV, at 149 (1836).)

Despite fears such as those expressed by Iredell, a number of states were very much concerned about the absence of a Bill of Rights. These states ratified the Constitution on the understanding that a Bill of Rights, including a general provision that there should be no negative inference from the express protection of certain rights that unenumerated rights are not also protected, would shortly be added to the Constitution. (Written statement of David A. J. Richards, Comm. Print Draft, Vol. 3, at 1584–85.)

The Ninth Amendment, of course, expressly rebuts the negative inference feared by many of the Founders. As Madison said when he introduced the Amendment:

> It has been objected also against a bill of rights, that, by enumerating particular exceptions to the general grant of power, it would disparage those rights which were not placed in that enumeration; and it might follow by implication, that those rights which were not singled out, were intended to be assigned into the hands of the General Gov-

ernment, and were consequently insecure. This . . . may
be guarded against. I have attempted it . . . [referring to
the Ninth Amendment]. (1 Annals of Congress 439 (Gales
and Seaton 1834).)

The Supreme Court has recently underscored Madison's rationale. In *Richmond Newspapers* v. *Virginia*, 448 U.S. 555 (1980), the
Court stated:

The Constitution's draftsmen . . . were concerned that
some important rights might be thought disparaged because not specifically guaranteed.
Madison's efforts, culminating in the Ninth Amendment,
served to allay the fears of those who were concerned that
expressing certain guarantees could be read as excluding
others. (*Id.*; emphasis added.)

Thus, the history surrounding the drafting and ratification of the
Bill of Rights indicates that there had to be an express guarantee
that unenumerated rights would be fully protected. The Ninth
Amendment is at the core of both the Constitution and the ratification debates. The concept of unenumerated rights illustrates the
depth of the tradition that the Founders meant to protect by the
Ninth Amendment.

C. Judge Bork's Approach to Liberty and Unenumerated Rights Is Outside the Tradition of Supreme Court Jurisprudence

Judge Bork's approach to liberty and unenumerated rights sets
him apart from every other Supreme Court Justice. Indeed, not one
of the 105 past and present Justices of the Supreme Court has ever
taken a view of liberty as narrow as that of Judge Bork. As Professor Tribe testified:

If [Judge Bork] is confirmed as the 106th Justice, [he]
would be the first to read liberty as though it were exhausted by the rights . . . the majority expressly conceded
individuals in the Bill of Rights. He would be the first to
reject an evolving concept of liberty and to replace it with
a fixed set of liberties protected at best from an evolving
set of threats. (Tribe statement, Comm. Print Draft, Vol. 2,
at 7.)

In particular, Judge Bork's philosophy is outside the mainstream of
such great judicial conservatives as Justices Harlan, Frankfurter
and Black, as well as such recent conservatives as Justices Stewart,
Powell, O'Connor and Chief Justice Burger. Each of these members
of the Court accepted and applied some concept of liberty, substantive due process and unenumerated rights.

As summarized by former Secretary of Transportation William
T. Coleman, Jr.:

There can be no question that privacy and substantive individual liberty interests are clearly within the Constitution as written. Moreover, for more than half a century,
the Supreme Court, by recognizing the constitutional basis
for the protection of such fundamental liberties, has been
able to respond in a principled fashion to the . . . prob-

lems and abuses which the framers could not have foreseen and thus cannot plausibly be said to have intended to
immunize from constitutional protection. . . . Judge Bork
. . . simply refuses to use the specific text "liberty" and
over sixty years of Supreme Court jurisprudence or, if necessary (which it is not), the open-textured language of the
Due Process Clause, to afford them constitutional protection from any intrusion in addition to mere physical restraint. (Written statement of William T. Coleman, Jr., at
21–22.) (Mr. Coleman's statement is attached as Appendix
II to this report.)

1. In the 19th Century, the Supreme Court Recognized the Concept of Unenumerated Rights

From the earliest days of the Republic, "the Supreme Court has
consistently and unanimously recognized that in adopting the Constitution, the people of the United States did not place the bulk of
their hard-won liberty in the hands of government, save only for
those rights specifically mentioned in the Bill of Rights or elsewhere in the document." (Tribe statement, Comm. Print Draft, Vol.
2, at 19; emphasis in original.)

In *Fletcher* v. *Peck*, 10 U.S. (6 Cranch.) 87, 135, 139 (1810), for example, Chief Justice Marshall barred a state's revocation of a
series of land grants by relying, in part, on "general principles
which are common to our free institutions." The Chief Justice
noted that the "nature of society and government [may limit the]
legislative power." Justice Story, in *Terret* v. *Taylor*, 13 U.S. (9
Cranch.) 43 (1815), struck down a state's attempt to divest a church
of its property simply by declaring that the statute violated "principles of natural justice" and the "fundamental laws of every free
government," as well as the "spirit and letter" of the Constitution.

The Court was even clearer in its recognition of certain fundamental rights in *Hurtado* v. *California*, 110 U.S. 516 (1884). It rejected the view that the Fourteenth Amendment—commanding
that "[n]o State shall deprive any person of life, liberty, or property,
without due process of law"—addressed only the fairness of legal
procedures. The Court stated that the concept of limited government
underlying the Constitution "guarantee[s] not particular forms of
procedure, but the very substance of individual rights to life, liberty
and property," protecting "those fundamental principles of liberty
and justice which lie at the base of all our civil and political
institutions. . . ." *(Id.* at 532, 535.)

2. The Justices of This Century, Including the Leading Conservative Justices, Have Recognized Unenumerated Rights

a. Justices Frankfurter and Harlan

Some witnesses have supported Judge Bork on the ground that
his expressions of "judicial restraint" put him in the tradition of
Felix Frankfurter and John Marshall Harlan. As stated by Secretary Coleman, former law clerk to Justice Frankfurter, "[i]n light
of [Judge Bork's] views on substantive liberty and privacy, it is

clear that this characterization is 100% wrong." (Coleman statement at 20–21.)

Justice Frankfurter summarized his views on the liberty clause of the Fourteenth Amendment in *Rochin* v. *California*, 342 U.S. 165, 169 (1952):

> These standards of justice are not authoritatively formulated anywhere as though they were specifics. Due process of law is a summarized constitutional guarantee of respect for those personal immunities which, as Mr. Justice Cardozo twice wrote for the Court, are "so rooted in the traditions and conscience of our people as to be ranked as fundamental," *Snyder* v. *Massachusetts*, 291 U.S. 97, 105 (1934), or are "implicit in the concept of ordered liberty." *Palko* v. *Connecticut*, 302 U.S. 319, 325 (1937).

In Justice Frankfurter's view, the due process clause "expresses a demand for civilized standards . . . [which] neither contain the peculiarities of the first eight amendments nor are . . . confined to them." *Louisiana ex rel. Francis* v. *Resweber*, 329 U.S. 459, 468 (1947) (Frankfurter, J., concurring). The clause, he said, possessed "independent potency." *Adamson* v. *California*, 332 U.S. 46, 66 (1947) (Frankfurter, J., concurring). And with respect to decisions applying the guarantees of the First Amendment to the states, Justice Frankfurter said they were based on the

> reasoning that the Fourteenth [Amendment] prevents state intrusion upon "fundamental personal rights and liberties," that among those rights and liberties are free speech, press, etc., which the First Amendment explicitly protects against federal encroachment, and that, because they are fundamental (not because they are contained in the First Amendment), they fall within the scope of the prohibitions of the Fourteenth [Amendment]. (F. Frankfurter, "Memorandum on 'Incorporation' of the Bill of Rights Into The Due Process Clause of the Fourteenth Amendment," 78 *Harv. L. Rev.* 746, 749 (1965).)

Like Justice Frankfurter, Justice Harlan argued for a conception of the due process clause that was flexible and was independent of, but drawing support from, the Bill of Rights. The clearest and most expansive expositions of Justice Harlan's views on liberty and due process are found in *Poe* v. *Ullman*, 367 U.S. 497 (1961) (Harlan, J., dissenting), and *Griswold* v. *Connecticut*, 381 U.S. 479 (1965) (Harlan, J., concurring in the judgment).

In *Poe*, Justice Harlan disagreed with the dismissal on procedural grounds of a challenge to Connecticut's ban on the use of contraceptives. He argued that the law should be struck down as "an intolerable and unjustifiable invasion of privacy in the conduct of the most intimate concerns of an individual's personal life." (367 U.S. at 539.) Justice Harlan then set forth his view of the appropriate constitutional framework:

> Due process has not been reduced to any formula; its content cannot be determined by reference to any code. The best that can be said is that through the course of this Court's decisions it has represented the balance which our

Nation, built upon postulates of respect for the liberty of the individual, has struck between that liberty and the demands of organized society. If the supplying of content to this constitutional concept has of necessity been a rational process, it certainly has not been one where judges have felt free to roam where unguided speculation might take them. The balance of which I speak is the balance struck by this country, having regard to what history teaches are the traditions from which it developed as well as the traditions from which it broke. **That tradition is a living thing.** A decision of this Court which radically departs from it could not long survive, while a decision which builds on what has survived is likely to be sound. No formula could serve as a substitute, in this area, for judgment and restraint. (367 U.S. at 542 (Harlan, J., dissenting); emphasis added.)

Justice Harlan concluded:

> [Our] "liberty" is not a series of isolated points pricked out in terms of the taking of property; the freedom of speech, press, and religion, the right to keep and bear arms; the freedom from unreasonable searches and seizures; and so on. It is a rational continuum which, broadly speaking, includes a freedom from all substantial and arbitrary impositions and restraints. . . . (Id. at 543.)

In *Griswold,* the Court struck down the Connecticut law. Justice Harlan stated that the proper constitutional analysis required an examination of whether the law "infringes the Due Process Clause of the Fourteenth Amendment because the enactment violated basic values 'implicit in the concept of ordered liberty,' *Palko* v *Connecticut,* 302 U.S. 319, 325." (*Griswold,* 381 U.S. at 500.)

Justice Harlan consistently advanced his view of "liberty" and "due process" articulated in his dissenting opinion in *Poe.* Dissenting in *Duncan* v. *Louisiana,* 391 U.S. 145 (1968), for example, he stated that "the very breadth and generality of the [Fourteenth] Amendment's provisions suggest that its authors did not suppose that the Nation would always be limited to mid-19th century conceptions of 'liberty' and 'due process of law' but that the increasing experience and evolving conscience of the American people would add new 'intermediate premises.' " *(Id.* at 175; (Harlan, J., dissenting).) To restrict due process to "rules fixed in the pas[t] . . . 'would be to deny every quality of the law but its age, and to render it incapable of progress or improvement.' " *(Id.* at 176–77; footnote omitted.)

b. Justice Brandeis

Justice Brandeis expressed his conception of liberty in slightly different, albeit no less eloquent, terms. In a dissent now recognized as expressing the Court's majority view, he said:

> The makers of the Constitution undertook to secure conditions favorable to the pursuit of happiness. They recognized the significance of man's spiritual nature, of his feelings and of his intellect. They knew that only a part of the

pain, pleasure and satisfactions of life are to be bound in material things. They sought to protect Americans in their beliefs, their thoughts, their emotions and their sensations. They conferred, as against the Goverment, **the right to be let alone**—the most comprehensive of rights and the right most valued by civilized man. (*Olmstead* v. *United States*, 277 U.S. 438, 478 (1928); emphasis added.)

c. Justice Black

While Justice Black's views on "liberty" were far different from those of Justice Frankfurter and Justice Harlan, they were still more expansive than those espoused by Judge Bork.

In *Loving* v. *Virginia*, 388 U.S. 1 (1967), for example, Justice Black joined the opinion of the Court striking down a state law prohibiting interracial marriage. The Court held not only that the law violated the Equal Protection Clause, but also that it deprived the petitioners of "liberty" within the meaning of the Due Process Clause. The Court said: "The freedom to marry has long been recognized as one of the vital personal rights essential to the orderly pusuit of happiness by free men." (*Id.* at 12.)

In *Bolling* v. *Sharpe*, 347 U.S. 497 (1954), Justice Black joined the opinion of the Court holding that segregation by law in District of Columbia public schools deprived children of their "liberty" under the Fifth Amendment. The Court reasoned that the term "liberty" cannot be "confined to mere freedom from bodily restraint" but "extends to the full range of conduct which the individual is free to pursue . . . ." (*Id.* at 499–500.)

Justice Black also joined the Court's opinion in *Skinner* v. *Oklahoma*, 316 U.S. 535 (1942), which held that a law permitting the sterilization of habitual criminals violated the Equal Protection Clause of the Fourteenth Amendment. Central to the Court's analysis was the decision to subject the law to strict scrutiny because it affected "one of the basic civil rights of man. Marriage and procreation are fundamental to the very existence of the human race." (*Id.* at 541.)

Professor Walter Dellinger, former law clerk to Justice Black, testified that Judge Bork "does . . . [not] accept the enthusiastic approach of Justice Black, which fills in the liberty clause by a complete and total incorporation of the Bill of Rights." (Comm. Print Draft, Vol. 2, at 732.) And as summarized by Professor Stephen Schulhofer, who also clerked for Justice Black, in a letter to the committee:

> Justice Black often joined opinions that recognized fundamental liberties not explicitly enumerated. . . . [E]ven the restrictive theory that Justice Black sometimes espoused is far different from Judge Bork's position, because of the broader context of constitutional doctrine to which Justice Black passionately subscribed. (Comm. Print Draft, Vol. 3, at 2350.)

d. Justice Stewart

Justice Stewart also agreed that "liberty" in the Constitution has substantive content. Although he dissented in *Griswold*, his concurring opinion in *Roe* v. *Wade*, 410 U.S. 113 (1973), clearly accepted the long line of substantive due process decisions:

> *Griswold* stands as one in a long line of . . . cases decided under the doctrine of substantive due process, and I now accept it as such. . . . The Constitution nowhere mentions a specific right of personal choice in matters of marriage and family life, but the "liberty" protected by the Due Process Clause of the Fourteenth Amendment covers more than those freedoms explicitly named in the Bill of Rights. (*Id.* at 168.)

e. Justice Powell

Justice Powell has echoed the same themes as Justices Frankfurter and Harlan. He wrote in *Moore* v. *East Cleveland*, 431 U.S. 494 (1977), for example, that fundamental liberties were those that are "deeply rooted in this Nation's history and tradition." The right of privacy, he said, must be elaborated through "careful 'respect for the teaching of history [and] solid recognition of the basic values that underlie our society.' " (*Id.* at 503.)

Summarizing Justice Powell's opinion in *Moore*, Professor Dellinger testified:

> As Justice Powell said in *Moore* . . ., this court has long recognized that freedom of choice and marriage and family life is one of the liberties protected by the Fourteenth Amendment. With that sweeping text, with that as history, how can one decline to exercise the responsibility that is given, a responsibility which as Justice Powell says must be exercised with caution and restraint, but exercised nonetheless if the guarantees of the Fourteenth Amendment are not to become an empty set. (Comm. Print Draft, Vol. 2, at 725.)

f. Chief Justice Burger

Chief Justice Burger, while testifying in support of Judge Bork's confirmation, differs sharply from the nominee on the question of recognition of unenumerated rights. Writing for the Court in *Richmond Newspapers* v. *Virginia*, 448 U.S. 555 (1980), in which the Court held that the right of the public and press to attend criminal trials is guaranteed under the First and Fourteenth Amendments, he stated:

> [A]rguments such as the state makes have not precluded recognition of important rights not enumerated. Notwithstanding the appropriate caution against reading into the Constitution rights not explicitly defined, the Court has **acknowledged that certain unarticulated rights are implicit in enumerated guarantees. For example, the rights of association and privacy** . . . appear nowhere in the Constitution or the Bill of Rights. Yet these important but unarticulated rights have nonetheless been found to share constitutional protection with explicit guarantees. The concerns expressed by Madison have thus been resolved; **fundamental rights, even though not expressly guaranteed,**

have been recognized by the Court as indispensable to the enjoyment of rights explicitly defined. (*Id.* at 580–81; emphasis added.)

It is not only in his *Richmond Newspapers* opinion that Chief Justice Burger differs from Judge Bork on the question of unenumerated rights; the difference is also apparent from the Chief Justice's testimony. When asked about his defense of unenumerated rights in *Richmond Newspapers,* the Chief Justice said he "would be astonished if Judge Bork would not subscribe to it." (Comm. Print Draft, Vol. 2, at 699.) As discussed above, Judge Bork clearly does not subscribe to a theory of unenumerated rights as articulated by Chief Justice Burger in *Richmond Newspapers.*

g. Judge Bork's Views Stand Apart from Those of Other Justices

Across the range of cases that Judge Bork has criticized, some of the Justices identified above have dissented from individual decisions. None comes close, however, to sharing the nominee's judicial philosophy. As Senator Kennedy remarked at the hearing: "[W]hat we are basically talking about is just not one particular area of decisions, but we are talking about a[n] [ac]cumulation." (Comm. Print Draft, Vol. 1, at 782.)

When those cumulative views are considered, Judge Bork stands apart. As Professor Wechsler, who is sometimes referred to as sharing Judge Bork's views, has remarked: "In all the things Judge Bork has written, I've never seen any recognition on his part that the open-ended language of the 14th Amendment was not simply a way of describing the admission of Negroes to the polity but was understood to be a broad reference to freedoms. I think that it means it is legitimate for judges, within this realm of duty, to articulate untouchable areas of autonomy or freedom." (Lewis, "Bork on Liberty," *New York Times,* September 6, 1987.)

Every one of the Justices reviewed above has recognized the concept of fundamental rights and liberties—a concept Judge Bork steadfastly refuses to accept. (*See* Testimony of Paul Gewirtz, Comm. Print Draft, Vol. 2, at 1246; Tribe testimony, Comm. Print Draft, Vol. 2, at 55.)

3. Each Member of the Current Court Accepts the Notion of Fundamental Rights

As revealed by *Turner* v. *Safley,* 107 S. Ct. 2254 (1987), in which the Court unanimously struck down a ban on marriage by prison inmates, every current Justice accepts the view that the substantive "liberty" in the Constitution encompasses at least some fundamental personal matters. Justice O'Connor, in an opinion joined by every Justice (including Chief Justice Rehnquist and Justice Scalia), noted "that the decision to marry is a fundamental right" even for prisoners. (107 S. Ct. at 2265, *citing Zablocki* v. *Redhail,* 434 U.S. 374 (1976) and *Loving* v. *Virginia, 388 U.S. 1 (1967).)*

4. Prominent Constitutional Scholars Who Have Often Held Widely Different Views Reject Judge Bork's Philosophy of the Constitution

Two prominent constitutional scholars who otherwise often hold widely different constitutional views are Philip Kurland and Laurence Tribe. On the issue before the committee, however, both are in agreement. Both Professor Kurland and Professor Tribe testified against Judge Bork's confirmation, relying on an assessment of Judge Bork's views of the history and tradition from which this nation was conceived.

Professor Kurland said:

> My concern is very much that by providing as narrow a construction of the Constitution as possible with regard to individual rights and liberties, Judge Bork would be denying the essence of the purpose behind the Constitution's origins 200 years ago, which was the preservation of all the liberties that the English legal tradition had created and were in the process of creating and were expected to continue to create. (Comm. Print Draft, Vol. 3, at 1390.)

Similarly, Professor Tribe testified:

> He [Judge Bork] reads the entire Constitution as though the people who wrote and ratified it gave up to government all of the fundamental rights that they fought a revolution to win unless a specific reservation of rights appears in the text. . . . I am proud that we have . . . a 200-year-old tradition establishing that people retain certain unspecified fundamental rights that courts were supposed to discern and to defend. (Comm. Print Draft, Vol. 2, at 6–7.)

* * * * * * *

Judge Bork's narrow definition of liberty sets him apart from the tradition and history from which this nation was conceived. As Professor Kurland testified:

> Judge Bork's judicial philosophy . . . reveals an unwillingness to recognize that the principal objective of the framers of our Constitution two hundred years ago was the preservation and advancement of individual liberty. Liberty was indeed the watchword of the national convention and of the state ratifying conventions as well. The Constitution did not create individual rights; the people brought them to the Convention with them and left the Convention with them, some enhanced by constitutional guarantees. The Bill of Rights in guaranteeing more, made sure that none was adversely affected. (Comm. Print Draft, Vol. 3, at 1387.)

Judge Bork's definition of liberty also sets him apart from every Justice who has ever sat on the Supreme Court. Indeed, it is because of the Court that "an established part of our legal tradition [is] to view the Constitution as forbidding government abuses which, in the words of Justice Frankfurter, 'offend those canons of decency and fairness which express the notions of justice of English-speaking peoples.'" (Coleman Statement at 12, *quoting Adamson* v. *California*, 332 U.S. 46, 59, 66–67 (1947) (Frankfurter, J., concurring).)

II. THE THEORY OF PRECEDENT OR "SETTLED LAW" HELD BY JUDGE BORK CANNOT TRANSFORM HIS JUDICIAL: PHILOSOPHY INTO AN ACCEPTABLE ONE FOR THE SUPREME COURT

A. While Judge Bork's Theory of Precedent Appears to Lessen the Friction Between His Philosophy of Original Intent and Accepted Supreme Court Decisions, It Leaves Many Uncertainties and Concerns

Judge Bork has applied his theory of the Constitution to attack a large number of Supreme Court decisions, including many landmark cases. Reconsidering these cases would reopen debate on many significant issues. Perhaps this is why Judge Bork said in response to a question by Senator Thurmond, "anybody with a philosophy of original intent requires a theory of precedent." (Comm. Print Draft, Vol. 1, at 101.) While a theory of precedent appears to lessen the friction between Judge Bork's philosophy and accepted Supreme Court decisions, it creates in the end many uncertainties and concerns of its own.

Prior to the hearings, Judge Bork had occasionally expressed the view that some decisions ought now to be upheld, even though wrong under his theory of original intent. The hearings, however, provide by far the most extended discussions by Judge Bork of his theory of precedent.

Under questioning by Senator Thurmond, for example, Judge Bork said:

> What would I look at [before overruling a prior decision]? Well, I think I would look and be absolutely sure that the prior decision was incorrectly decided. That is necessary. And if it is wrongly decided—and you have to give respect to your predecessors' judgment on these matters—the presumption against overruling remains, because it may be that there are private expectations built up on the basis of the prior decision. It may be that governmental and private institutions have grown up around that prior decision. There is a need for stability and continuity in the law. There is a need for predictability in legal doctrine. (Comm. Print Draft, Vol. 1, at 101.)

In other places, Judge Bork encapsulated these thoughts by saying that law, even erroneous law, can become "settled," meaning it should not be overruled. (*See, e.g.,* Comm. Print Draft, Vol. 1, at 84, 414.)

Later, in response to a question from Senator Heflin, Judge Bork added countervailing considerations—considerations that argued in favor of overruling a precedent:

> Now, of course, against [upholding a precedent] is—if it is wrong, and secondly, whether it is a dynamic force so that it continues to produce wrong and unfortunate decisions. I think that was one of the reasons the court in Erie Rail-

road against Tompkins overruled Swift against Tyson, a degenerative force, but I think what Brandeis or somebody can maybe call dynamic potential. (Comm. Print Draft, Vol. 1, at 268.)

An exchange with Chairman Biden produced a further statement on these countervailing considerations:

[A] case should not be overruled unless it was clearly wrong and perhaps pernicious, "pernicious" . . . meant there in the sense of capable of having dynamic force, generative force, that would produce new wrong decisions. (Comm. Print Draft, Vol. 1, at 297.)

Finally, Judge Bork concluded his testimony by emphasizing his respect for precedent:

[T]here are views I have testified to here that reaffirm my acceptance of a body of jurisprudence as established and no longer judicially assailable, notwithstanding, that [it] has developed in a manner different from a direction I had suggested . . . . [W]hen I say [the result in a case is required by] "the law,' I regard precedent as an important component of the law. As I have described many times here, there are a number of important precedents that are today so woven into the fabric of our system that to change or alter them would be, in my view, unthinkable. (Comm. Print Draft, Vol. 1, at 721–22.)

The committee finds that Judge Bork's ideas concerning precedent or settled law, in both their general terms as well as the manner in which Judge Bork applies them to particular cases, raise a number of serious concerns.

B. **Judge Bork's Combination of Original Intent and Settled Law Creates an Irresolvable Tension Between His Oft-Repeated Desire to Reformulate Constitutional Law and His Willingness to Follow a Decision He Believes To Be Profoundly Wrong**

1. **Judge Bork Has Often Announced His Firm Conviction that Many Supreme Court Decisions Are Flatly Wrong and Ought To Be Overruled**

Judge Bork's embrace of precedent sets up a sharp tension with his often repeated proclamations of the ease with which a judge with his views can overrule erroneous decisions. Judge Bork's record, in fact, strongly suggests a willingness to "reformulate" "broad areas of constitutional law." ("Neutral Principles" at 8.)

In January of this year, for example, Judge Bork claimed:

Certainly at the least, I would think that an originalist judge would have no problem whatever in overruling a non-originalist precedent, because that precedent by the very basis of his judicial philosophy, has no legitimacy. (remarks to the *First Annual Lawyers Convention of the Federalist Society*, January 31, 1987, at 126.)

In a speech delivered before an Attorney General's conference in 1986, he observed:

> The Court's treatment of the Bill of Rights is theoretically the easiest to reform. It is here that the concept of original intent provides guidance to the courts and also a powerful rhetoric to persuade the public that the end to [judicial] imperialism is required and some degree of reexamination desirable. ("Federalism," *Attorney General's Conference Speech*, January 24-26, 1986, at 9.)

Prior to the hearings, Judge Bork seemed to elevate his views of original intent over respect for precedent: "Supreme Court justice[s] can always say . . . their first obligation is to the Constitution, not to what their colleagues said 10 years before." ("Justice Robert H. Bork: Judicial Restraint Personified," *California Lawyer*, May 1985, at 25.) During the hearings, Senator Kennedy played an audio tape of the question and answer period following a 1985 speech in which Judge Bork made perhaps his clearest declaration to that effect:

> I don't think that in the field of constitutional law precedent is all that important. I say that for two reasons. One is historical and traditional. The court has never thought constitutional precedent was all that important. The reason being that if you construe a statute incorrectly, the Congress can pass a law and correct it. If you construe the Constitution incorrectly Congress is helpless. Everybody is helpless. **If you become convinced that a prior court has misread the Constitution I think it's your duty to go back and correct it.** Moreover, you will from time to time get willful courts who take an area of law and create precedents that have nothing to do with the name of the Constitution. And if a new court comes in and says, 'Well, I respect precedent,' what you have is a ratchet effect, with the Constitution getting further and further away from its original meaning, because some judges feel free to make up new constitutional law and other judges in the name of judicial restraint follow precedent. **I don't think precedent is all that important. I think the importance is what the Framers were driving at, and to go back to that.** (*Canisius College Speech*, October 8, 1985, *quoted in* Comm. Print Draft, Vol. 1, at 523-24, emphasis added.)

Following the playing of this tape, the following exchange took place:

> Senator KENNEDY. Those statements speak for themselves. Your own words cast strong doubt upon your adherence to precedent that you think is wrong.
>
> Judge BORK. Senator, you and I both know that it is possible, in a give and take question and answer period, not to give a full and measured response. You and I both know that when I have given a full and measured response, I have repeatedly said there are some things that are too settled to be overturned . . . .

It is not the kind of thing that ought to be weighed against my more considered statements when I am not just engaging in give and take. (Comm. Print Draft, Vol. 1, at 527.)

The committee finds that even accepting this explanation, Judge Bork's views pose a serious dilemma. Judge Bork has strongly suggested a reformation in constitutional law, one that will bring a "second wave in constitutional theory." Although perhaps open to differing interpretations, the committee is concerned that the "second wave" is aimed at reform in the courts —in the decisions courts reach, not just in the classroom as some academic exercise. (*See* "The Crisis in Constitutional Theory: Back to the Future," *Speech to the Philadelphia Society.* April 3, 1987, at 10–15, *quoted in* Comm. Print Draft, Vol. 1, at 672–77.) Against this drive to pursue his views on original intent, and to "sweep the elegant, erudite, pretentious, and toxic detritus of non-originalism out to sea" (Comm. Print Draft, Vol. 1, at 677), Judge Bork has erected the breakwater of his theory of precedent. The question is: How much will it hold back?

At the very least, Judge Bork's opposing forces pose a dilemma for litigants. As Robert Bennett, Dean of the Northwestern University School of Law, testified:

A moment's reflection will show that it will not do to say that a case was wrong but I will not vote to overrule it. What are lawyers and litigants to do with that case when the next one arises that is a little bit different? Are they to appeal to what the judge says is constitutionally right or to the precedent he says he will tolerate, even though it is wrong?

To be sure, all judges suffer from this dilemma to a degree, but few insist that they know the route to constitutional truths with the vehemence that Judge Bork does. For that reason, I remain baffled and concerned about Judge Bork's likely approach to the use of precedent, despite the assurances he has offered. (Comm. Print Draft, Vol. 3, at 1224.)

The committee believes there is a substantial risk that Judge Bork would resolve this dilemma by reading a prior decision very narrowly, so that it had little, if any, substantial effect on future decisions, notwithstanding that it is never overruled. In Judge Bork's terms, a prior decision can lose its "dynamic" or "generative" force through another kind of barren reading, this time of the past decision itself. As Professor Gewirtz testified:

[M]ost lawyers recognize that precedents are generally capable of either a broad or restrictive reading. . . . Given the leeway that judges inevitably have . . . I think it's reasonable to conclude that Judge Bork will read decisions he disagrees with restrictively, and that means, of course, that in the closely contested cases, that are the sort of cases that come to the Supreme Court, it is likely that Judge Bork would decide the earlier decisions he believes were wrongly decided simply don't control the matter in question. (Testimony of Paul Gewirtz, Comm. Draft Print,

Vol. 2, at 1171; *see also* Remarks of Senator Specter, Comm. Print Draft, Vol. 1, at 255; Testimony of Burke Marshall, Comm. Print Draft, Vol. 1, at 832; Tribe statement, Comm. Print Draft, Vol. 2, at 32–34.)

The committee finds that there are substantial uncertainties in the extent to which Judge Bork's respect for settled law would operate as a serious curb on his pursuit of his idea of original intent. All that is necessary is to understand what one witness called the "lens effect:" Judge Bork would simply see future cases through a lens that embodied his own strong views about original intent and would thereby be highly likely to see the erroneous, but settled decisions, as inapplicable to new situations. (*See* statement of Thomas Grey, Comm. Print Draft, Vol. 2, at 1106.)

2. Judge Bork's Testimony on the First Amendment's Clear and Present Danger Standard Demonstrates that a Judge Who "Accepts" Precedent with Which He Disagrees May Well Read that Precedent Narrowly

In the early part of this century, Justices Holmes and Brandeis argued in now-famous dissents that speech critical of the government may be punished only when it presents a "clear and present danger.". (*See Abrams* v. *United States,* 150 U.S. 616 (1919) and *Gitlow* v. *New York,* 268 U.S. 652 (1925).) The Supreme Court has accepted these dissents as expressing the correct view of the First Amendment and has articulated its most recent formulation of the "clear and present danger" standard in *Brandenburg* v. *Ohio,* 395 U.S. 444 (1969). Judge Bork's testimony on *Brandenburg* provides an excellent insight into the uncertainties associated with his theory of precedent.

As Senator Specter said, *Brandenburg* "essentially state[s] the Holmes' clear and present danger doctrine" (Comm. Print Draft, Vol. 1, at 254), and prohibits a state from punishing speech advocacy unless it involves "incitement to imminent lawless action." Prior to the hearings, Judge Bork had criticized *Brandenburg* as "fundamentally wrong." ("The Individual, the State, and the First Amendment," *University of Michigan* (1979), at 19.) Before the committee, however, he first testified: "I think *Brandenburg* is fine. I am not concerned about it." (Comm. Print Draft, Vol. 1, at 255.) The next day, in response to a question by Senator Thurmond, Judge Bork expanded on his position concerning *Brandenburg*:

> I had really said, I did say that I thought theoretically the advocacy of law violation in . . . circumstances [not involving a claim that the law being challenged was unconstitutional] could have been punished under the First Amendment. What *Brandenburg* did was say there must be a closer nexus between the advocacy and the lawless action. It said the advocacy of law violation must be in circumstances where there is the likelihood of imminent lawless action. So it added one factor to what I said, the closeness of the danger.
>
> Now, I have not changed my mind about what I said upon this subject. I could have accepted a First Amend-

ment law that developed the way I thought in 1971 it ought to have from the beginning. I could accept that.

The law did not develop that way. It developed to require a closer nexus between the advocacy and the violent action or the lawless action, imminent lawless action. . . .

I accept the fact that the Supreme Court has added an additional safeguard to the position that I took in 1971 for speech advocating lawlessness. As an academic, I thought that was not theoretically justified. As a judge, I accept it, and that is all there is to that. (Comm. Print Draft, Vol. 1, at 311.)

Later the same day, responding to Senator Specter, Judge Bork said of *Brandenburg*, "I accept *Brandenburg* as a judge and I have no desire to overturn it. I am not changing my criticism of the case. I just accept it as settled law." (Comm. Print Draft, Vol. 1, at 409.)

Senator Specter then identified the difficulty with Judge Bork's views:

[T]hat brings up the subject down the line as to original intent and how firmly committed you are to accepting stare decisis, and there are some strong statements which you have made that an originalist ought not to accept cases which have been established. . . .

One, the next case will have a shading and a nuance and I am concerned about your philosophy and your approach. And, secondly, I am concerned about your acceptance of these cases. If you say you accept this one, so be it. But you have written and spoken, ostensibly as an original interpretationist, of the importance of originalists not allowing the mistakes of the past to stand. (Comm. Print Draft, Vol. 1, at 410-11.)

Professor Gewirtz made the same point, albeit in different terms:

Brandenburg is usually said to hold that advocacy may be punished only if it involved "incitement to imminent lawless action." But the Supreme Court concluded that the Ohio statute was unconstitutional on its face; read narrowly, *Brandenburg's* "holding" could be limited to that, and not read as a rule about what particular degree or kind of proximate danger is constitutionally required. Furthermore, . . . if Judge Bork does not accept the "intellectual and historic and traditional underpinning" of the clear-and-present-danger requirement—if he does not genuinely accept the premises for protecting extreme speech—then he may end up applying clear-and-present-danger standards in a more restrictive way than others would. He might, for example, "accept" *Brandenburg* in the sense of requiring more than mere advocacy to sustain a conviction, but nevertheless uphold a conviction based on jury instructions that require a somewhat lesser degree of imminence of harm than other readings of *Brandenburg* might suggest. (Statement of Paul Gewirtz, Comm. Print Draft, Vol. 2, at 1185-86.)

These statements were not made only in the abstract. In *Hess v. Indiana,* 414 U.S. 105 (1973), the Supreme Court reviewed the conviction of an anti-war demonstrator for using a vulgar word in promising a return to the streets after he had been removed by the police. The Court reversed the conviction on the ground that because the lawless action was not imminent, the demonstrator's advocacy could not be proscribed. The Court treated the case as one controlled by *Brandenburg.*

In the hearings, however, Judge Bork did not find that *Brandenburg* controlled the facts presented by *Hess.* In an exchange with Senator Specter, he said that in his view, *Hess* was an "obscenity in the public streets" case, not a case involving dissident political speech, and he was not "so wild about it." (Comm. Print Draft, Vol. 1, at 411.)

Judge Griffin Bell, who testified on Judge Bork's behalf, seems to concur with this analysis. After Senator Specter described the facts of *Hess,* Judge Bell stated:

> Well, I am not familiar with the *Hess* case, but that would bother me if somebody said they would do something and then they immediately figure a way to get around it . . . . I do not think you could make an obscenity case out of the facts as you stated them. I mean, I do not think that could be seriously argued that that was an obscenity case. It is a speech case. (Comm. Print Draft, Vol. 3, at 1377.)

Judge Bork's colloquy with Senator Specter, and the analysis of his remarks by Senator Specter and Professor Gewirtz, illustrate the uncertainties and risks with Judge Bork's theory. If *Hess v. Indiana* had not yet been decided, and Judge Bork were confirmed, it is clear that he would be able to dissent in *Hess,* treating it as an obscenity case—and yet remain faithful to everything he said in the hearings about precedent generally, and everything he said about his faithfulness to *Brandenburg* specifically.

This is only one example of the ways in which the statements Judge Bork made in the hearings leave substantial uncertainties about how he would "follow precedent," on the one hand, and how he would pursue his version of original intent, on the other hand. (*See also* Gewirtz statement, Comm. Print Draft, Vol. 2, at 1183–1186.)

C. Judge Bork's Theory of Settled Law Applies Less to Cases Extending Individual Liberties than to Cases Making Structural or Institutional Changes in Government, And Thus Would Not Protect Those Individual Rights Cases that Judge Bork Has Criticized

Judge Bork has said that "the Court's treatment of the Bill of Rights is theoretically the easiest to reform." (*Attorney General's Conference Speech,* Jan. 24–26, 1986, at 9.) Decisions involving the Bill of Rights largely involve the expansion of individual rights. As such, complex social institutions and economic structures do not usually build up around them. They are thus typically different from cases like those expanding the power of Congress to regulate commerce or the power of the U.S. government to issue paper money as legal tender. These latter cases have become, in Judge

Bork's words, "the basis for a large array of social and economic institutions, [therefore] overruling them would be disastrous." (Comm. Print Draft, Vol. 1, at 102.) If such institutions have not grown up around Bill of Rights cases, they are to that extent easier to reform. As Professor Grey explained:

> These examples [of the Commerce Clause and the Legal Tender Cases] illustrate the very weak character of the constraints imposed by precedent on the overruling of "erroneous" constitutional precedent. **In both cases, the protected precedents expanded governmental power.** In both cases, any attempt to overrule them would involve social upheavals of vast dimensions, and would be completely impractical. **Decisions defining and protecting individual constitutional rights rarely if ever are so socially entrenched. It is difficult to think of any individual rights decision or line of decisions that, if overruled, would present the intractable practical difficulties posed by the cases Judge Bork has used as examples. Indeed, I have not found any example in his pre-nomination discussions of the doctrine of precedent of any constitutional decision protecting individual rights that he identifies as even presumptively immune from overruling.** (Grey Statement, Comm. Print Draft, Vol. 2, at 1108; emphasis added.)

During the committee hearings, Judge Bork for the first time made some specific references to individual rights decisions that were, in his view, "settled." They were *Brandenburg, Shelley v. Kraemer* and *Bolling v. Sharpe,* and some of the freedom of the press cases. Each is, to varying degrees, difficult to square with Judge Bork's announced criteria for refusing to overrule a decision. Even putting that aside, however, there still is a tremendous area—in which the Court has given content to unenumerated rights and liberties—where his prior stated positions are not in the least constrained by his statements before the committee concerning settled law.

D. Judge Bork's Statements About the Application of Settled Law to Old Conflicts Say Little About His Willingness To Apply the Tradition of Unenumerated Rights to New Conflicts Between Government and the Individual that May Arise

The Supreme Court's prior decisions, whether settled or not, cannot cover all new situations, under even the broadest reading of those cases. It is in the context of these new cases that Judge Bork's theory of original intent would stand without any of the constraining influence of precedent. Thus, that "Judge Bork's record is . . . a source of concern because of what it reveals about how he is likely to approach novel issues of liberty and equality that will emerge in the years ahead, issues where a Justice has a leeway that is not closely channelled by precedent." (Gewirtz statement, Comm. Draft Print, Vol. 2, at 1186.)

In the committee's view, respect for precedent, as Judge Bork expressed it, does not alleviate the concern that the nominee would pursue his particular theory of original intent. It does not remove the risk that important precedents preserving individual liberties and human dignity would be robbed of their generative force. And it in no way compensates for his rejection of the tradition of unenumerated rights, a tradition that must be maintained to deal with new issues as they arise in the future.

PART THREE: A CRITICAL ANALYSIS OF JUDGE BORK'S POSITIONS ON LEADING MATTERS

I. THE RIGHT TO PRIVACY—THE RIGHT TO BE LET ALONE

A. Before the Hearings, the Right to Privacy Had Been a Principal Part of Judge Bork's Attack on the Supreme Court

The constitutional right to privacy or, in Justice Brandeis's words, the right to be let alone, has been a major part of Judge Bork's attack on the jurisprudence of the Supreme Court. In 1971, for example. he denounced the first modern privacy decision, *Griswold* v. *Connecticut,* 381 U.S. 479 (1965), as "unprincipled" and "intellectually empty." *Griswold* concerned a law making it a crime for anyone to use birth control. Judge Bork said that the desire of a "husband and wife to have sexual relations without unwanted children" was indistinguishable, for constitutional purposes, from the desire of an electric utility company to "void a smoke pollution ordinance." "The cases," he said, "are identical." ("Neutral Principles" at 8–9.)

Judge Bork reiterated his attack on *Griswold* after becoming a federal court judge. In a 1982 speech, he said that "the result" in the case could not "have been reached by interpretation of the Constitution." (*Catholic University Speech* at 4.) In 1985, he announced that there was no "supportable method of reasoning underlying" *Griswold.* (*Conservative Digest* Interview, October 1985, at 97.) In 1986, he declared that replacing the approach in *Griswold* with a "concept of original intent" is "essential to prevent courts from invading the proper domain of democratic government." ("The Constitution, Original Intent, and Economic Rights," 23 *San Diego L. Rev.,* 823, 829 (1986).)

In an interview given after he was nominated to the Supreme Court, Judge Bork was asked: "But your core views on privacy expressed in [the 1971 *Indiana Law Journal* article]—you still believe?"

> Answer. "Yes. I agreed with Justice Black, who dissented in that case, *Griswold* v. *Connecticut.*" (July 29, 1987, *St. Louis Post-Dispatch.*)

Judge Bork's attacks on the privacy right have extended to the principal cases upon which *Griswold* relied, and would extend, presumably, to all the cases subsequent to *Griswold,* although Judge Bork has identified only *Roe* v. *Wade* by name. (*Hearings Before the Subcommittee on Separation of Powers of the Senate Judiciary Committee,* 97th Cong., 1st Sess., June 10, 1981, at 310.)

One of the cases relied upon by the Court in *Griswold* was *Skinner* v. *Oklahoma.* 316 U.S. 535 (1942). There, the Supreme Court unanimously set aside a state law that imposed sterilization upon

(30)

certain common criminals, but not upon embezzlers or other white collar criminals. Said the Court: "We are dealing here with legislation which involves one of the basic rights of man. Marriage and procreation are fundamental to the very existence and survival of the race." (*Id.* at 541.) Judge Bork has analyzed *Skinner* as follows:

All law discriminates and thereby creates inequalities. The Supreme Court has no principled way of saying which non-racial inequalities are impermissible. What it has done, therefore, is to appeal to simplistic notions of "fairness" or to what it regards as "fundamental interests," in order to demand equality in some cases but not in others, thus choosing values and producing a line of cases [such as] *Skinner.* ("Neutral Principles" at 11-12.)

In speeches and writings after he became a judge, the nominee has also said that the " 'right of procreation' . . . is another made-up constitutional right . . . Neither it [nor the right] to privacy are to be found anywhere in the Constitution.[6] ("Foundations of Federalism: Federalism and Gentrification," *Yale Federalist Society,* April 24, 1982, at 9 of the Question and Answer Period; *see also* "The Struggle Over the Role of the Courts," *National Review,* September 17, 1982, 1137, 1138; "A Conference on Judicial Reform," *Free Congress and Education Foundation,* June 14, 1982, at 6.)

Judge Bork addressed the Supreme Court's line of privacy decisions in two opinions on the Court of Appeals. In *Dronenburg* v. *Zech,* 741 F.2d 1388 (D.C. Cir. 1984). he wrote that the Supreme Court had created "new rights" in the privacy cases. Judge Bork recited the holdings in a number of those cases, and concluded that since they lacked an "explanatory principle," (*Id.* at 1395-96), lower court judges could not determine how to apply them in new cases.

In *Franz* v. *United States,* 707 F.2d 582 (D.C. Cir. 1983), Judge Bork went out of his way in his concurring opinion to criticize the majority opinion for finding that the privacy decisions of the Supreme Court implied some constitutional protection for the right of a non-custodial father to maintain visitation rights with his child. Judge Bork argued that the right of privacy was "ill-defined," and that "[s]ince the Constitution itself provides neither textual nor structural guidance to judges embarked upon this chartless sea, it behooves us to be cautious rather than venturesome." (707 F.2d at 1438.)

As a lower court judge, the nominee was, of course, bound to abide by *Griswold* and its progeny. Judge Bork acknowledged this very point in *Dronenburg,* stating that his arguments against *Griswold* and the other privacy cases were "completely irrelevant to the function of a circuit judge. The Supreme Court has decided that it may create new constitutional rights and, as judges of constitutionally inferior courts, we are bound absolutely by that determination." (*Dronenburg,* 741 F.2d at 1396 n. 5.) In the committee's view,

---

[6] During the hearings, Judge Bork suggested that he might have reached the same result the Court did in *Skinner* by applying a "reasonableness test" under the Equal Protection Clause. Whether or not he would do so, however, Judge Bork has made clear that he rejects the right of procreation in *Skinner.*

however, Judge Bork's opinions in *Dronenburg* and *Franz* suggest that there is a significant risk that he would to overrule *Griswold* and the other privacy cases if freed of the constitutional and institutional constraints that limit a lower court judge.

Judge Bork's strong attack on the Court's line of privacy decisions left no doubt before the hearings about his position. In an interview given just before coming before the committee, however, Judge Bork interjected into his discussion of *Griswold* what might be construed as a qualification:

> The court did not dispose of it in a logical way, on the basis of sound constitutional reasons. A lot of cases in which the court's reasoning isn't adequate might conceivably come out the same way on adequate reasons. I [once] said something rather harsh about *Roe* v. *Wade*, but [what I said] really applied more to the line of reasoning that was followed. ("Sentences From the Judge," *Newsweek*, September 14, 1987, at 36.)

This proferred distinction between the Court's reasoning and the result it reaches was a major topic at the hearings.

B. At the Hearings, Judge Bork Confirmed His Pre-Hearing Views About a Right to Privacy

At the hearings, Judge Bork repeated in various ways the claim that although "[t]here is a lot of privacy in the Constitution," (Comm. Print Draft, Vol. 1, at 217), there is no "generalized" right to privacy of the kind necessary to support *Griswold* and its progeny. He testified that in the Constitution there is no "unstructured, undefined right of privacy [such as the right] that Justice Douglas elaborated [in Griswold]." (Comm. Print Draft, Vol. 1, at 87.) Senator Simpson and Judge Bork engaged in the following exchange:

> Senator SIMPSON. I want to ask you if it is fair to say that you believe that privacy is protected under the Constitution, but that you just do not believe that there is a general and unspecified right that protects everything. . . . Is that correct?
>
> Judge BORK. That is correct, Senator. (Comm. Print Draft, Vol. 1, at 217.)

When Senator Hatch queried him about Justice Black's view of the "so-called privacy right," Judge Bork seemed to endorse the view that the right "was utterly unpredictable." (Comm. Print Draft, Vol. 1, at 157.) He described his objection to a "generalized" right to privacy:

> Nobody knows what that thing means. But you have to define it; you have to define it. And the court has not given it definition. That is my only point. (Comm. Print Draft. Vol. 1, at 218.)

At this juncture, Judge Bork's objection seemed to be that the Court had not defined the privacy right sufficiently, so that it is "utterly unpredictable."

It became clear, however, that Judge Bork also believes that there is no constitutional right extending privacy protections beyond those provided by specific amendments. As summarized by Chairman Biden:

> Yesterday you indicated that although you did not like the generalized right of privacy or use of substantive due process, you time and again pointed out that certain core ideas were protected and they were protected by the First Amendment, you pointed out. Privacy. First Amendment, Fourth Amendment, Fifth Amendment, Eighth Amendment. You went down the list.
>
> Now, what I would like to ask you is this. If Justices Harlan, Powell, Frankfurter, Jackson, Cardozo had found a fundamental right of privacy or a fundamental right to be protected under another specific amendment to the Constitution, there would not have been any occasion to see that the Constitution also contains the basic right of privacy.
>
> Obviously they could not find it in any single amendment. Therefore, my question is, putting aside all the specific amendments you have mentioned either now or during the past several days, do you believe that the Constitution recognizes a marital right to privacy? (Comm. Print Draft, Vol. 1, at 300.)

Judge Bork responded: "I do not know. It may well . . . But I have never worked on a constitutional argument in that area." (*Id.*) In a colloquy with Senator DeConcini, Judge Bork suggested that the equal protection clause might be an alternative basis for reaching the same result as the Court did in *Griswold*. (Comm. Print Draft, Vol. 1. at 300.)

In his testimony before the committee, therefore, Judge Bork returned to the distinction, first articulated in his September 14. 1987 *Newsweek* interview, between reasons and results. This distinction ultimately failed, however, to leave any prospect that a rationale for the right to privacy satisfactory to Judge Bork could ever be found.

First, Judge Bork testified that *Griswold* did not contain a correct understanding of the liberty and due process clauses of the Fourteenth Amendment: "Well, if they apply the due process clause that way . . . . Why not in *Griswold* v. *Connecticut* and why not in all kinds of cases? You are off and running with substantive due process which I have long thought is a pernicious constitutional idea." (Comm. Print Draft, Vol. 1, at 262.) Second, he testified that the Ninth Amendment provided no justification for the result in *Griswold*. (Comm. Print Draft. Vol. 1, at 102–03; 224–25; 241.) Third, he said he would have dissented in *Griswold*. (Comm. Print Draft. Vol. 1. at 573.) Finally, in response to Senator Heflin, Judge Bork testified, "I do not have available a constitutional theory which would support a general, defined right [of privacy]." (Comm. Print Draft, Vol. 1, at 266.)

Thus, Judge Bork has rejected all the offered rationales for a right to privacy of the sort necessary to support *Griswold* and its progeny, as well as the entire constitutional tradition of unenumerated rights upon which it rests. It appears that Judge Bork adheres to his earlier view that "the result" in *Griswold* could not be reached by "interpretation" of the Constitution. (*Catholic University Speech* at 4.) At the same time, he left open the possibility that "maybe somebody would offer" him a new argument for the right that he would accept. (Comm. Print Draft, Vol. 1, at 90.)

In the committee's view, it is unlikely that a successful new argument will be proffered. As several witnesses testified, the arguments in support of a right to privacy have in the course of our constitutional history been presented; indeed, they were all summarized or alluded to in the *Griswold* case itself. (*See* Comm. Print Draft, Vol. 3. at 1611–13; Tribe testimony, Comm. Print Draft, Vol. 2, at 45 ("I do not think that constitutional law is a game of hide and seek. The idea that there might be a right hiding there from Judge Bork to be discovered in the next decade . . . is not very plausible").) Given Judge Bork's extensive experience in analyzing these matters, his steadfast rejection of the tradition of unenumerated rights and his professed inability thus far to find any constitutional warrant for such a right, there is little, if any, prospect that a new argument will be presented that is both unique and convincing to him.

As Chairman Biden concluded after two-and-a-half weeks of hearings:

> Will [Judge Bork] be part of the progression of 200 years of history of every generation enhancing the right to privacy and reading more firmly into the Constitution protection for individual privacy? Or will he come down on the side of government intrusion? I am left without any doubt in my mind that he intellectually must come down for government intrusion and against expansion of individual rights. (Comm. Print Draft, Vol. 3, at 1615.)

C. Judge Bork's Denial of the Right to Privacy Places the Entire Line of Privacy Decisions at Risk, and Is Likely to Prevent Any Subsequent Development and Extension of It

During the hearings, Judge Bork expounded on his theory of "settled law"—of accepting past cases even though they were wrong. He offered to the committee new examples of cases with which he still disagreed, but which he would not overrule because they had become, in his view, settled law. (*See* Part Two, Section II, *supra.*) Judge Bork did not include within his examples any of the privacy decisions. Accordingly, Judge Bork left the committee with the clear impression that he feels free to overrule any or all of the privacy decisions. And given his conclusion that the doctrine of substantive due process is "pernicious." (Comm. Print Draft, Vol. 1, at 262), there is a substantial risk of overruling.

The committee recognizes that Judge Bork testified that he would entertain arguments that these cases were the sort that should not be overruled. (*See e.g.,* Comm. Print Draft, Vol. 1, at 268.) At the very least, however, he can be expected to limit them to their narrow facts. To do otherwise would mean that they would continue to operate as a "generative" force in the law, producing new erroneous decisions. (*See* Part Two, Section II, *supra.*) Thus, if he did not overrule these cases, there is a substantial risk that he would certainly leave the right to privacy inapplicable to future cases. The manner in which he analyzed the privacy cases in *Dronenburg* and *Franz* provides a partial insight into how he might eviscerate the right to privacy.

As Professor Sullivan testified, Judge Bork's views on privacy place him in a lonely position:

> On the scope of the right to privacy, good and reasonable, fair-minded men and women differ greatly, and in good faith, and that has happened, it is happening now, and I expect it to continue as long as there is a right of privacy to argue about.
>
> **But there has been no disagreement on the Supreme Court, for 75 years, that there exists some right to privacy, and it is that disagreement of Judge Bork that we are focusing on.**
>
> There are two sides to the issue on its scope, but there have not been, in our jurisprudence, two sides of the issue as to its existence, and that is what puts Judge Bork outside the mainstream. (Comm. Print Draft, Vol. 3, at 1621; emphasis added.)

After this testimony, Senators Biden and Simpson engaged in the following colloquy:

> The CHAIRMAN. I want to make it clear, that as I understand what Judge Bork has said, he disagreed with the existence of a generalized right to privacy, and in that sense he is all by himself in the line of justices for the past 75 years. . . . That is the debate. If I am wrong about that, I would like to be corrected now. . . . [T]his is so fundamental a point.
>
> Senator SIMPSON. Mr. Chairman, it is, indeed, and in one sentence let me say that Judge Bork—and he said it so clearly—his problem with the abstract constitutional right of privacy is that it has no inherent limits. . . .
>
> The CHAIRMAN. You are correct that Judge Bork said that there are no inherent limits. **Ergo, he has concluded, because he cannot find a way to put limits upon it, like other judges have, because he does not want to be subjective, which he says he rejects out of hand and worries about. Because he cannot place—there are no inherent limits—he chooses to deny the existence of the right in the first instance.** (Comm. Print Draft, Vol. 3, at 1621-22; emphasis added.)

The Chairman's conclusion suggests that by rejecting the tradition of unenumerated rights, including the right to privacy, Judge Bork may place his desire to minimize the influence of judges in society above his own first principle, faithfulness to the original intent.

In the committee's view, one additional point about the Supreme Court's privacy cases merits brief mention. The Court in these decisions has not been floating, as Judge Bork has said, on a "chartless sea," (*Franz*, 707 F.2d at 1438), constructing unpredictable rights that strike without warning. It has been constrained and guided by the text, history and structure of the Constitution, together with the history, tradition and collected wisdom expressed in the Supreme Court's decisions. As Professor Sullivan testified, "[the Justices] have said look to our traditions, look to our values." In doing that, the Court has articulated a right that "doesn't strike without warning. It has been an extraordinarily limited right as expounded by the Supreme Court so far." (Comm. Print Draft, Vol. 1, at 1634, 1640.)

* * * * * *

The rights recognized by the Supreme Court have been tremendously important, and promise to continue to be so into the future. Consider what our nation would have been like had the Court not implemented the history and tradition of the Constitution:

It would not have affirmed a right "to marry, establish a home and bring up children." (*See Meyer* v. *Nebraska*, 262 U.S. 390 (1923).)

It would not have prevented the government from making it a crime to send children to private school. (*See Pierce* v. *Society of Sisters*, 268 U.S. 510 (1925).)

It would not have prohibited the government from sterilizing a selected group of criminals; nor could it protect other citizens from interferences with reproduction. (*See Skinner* v. *Oklahoma*, 316 U.S. 535 (1942).)

It would not have intervened to stop a government from outlawing the use of birth control by married couples (*See Griswold* v. *Connecticut*, 381 U.S. 479 (1965)), or by others. (*See Eisenstadt* v. *Baird*, 405 U.S. 438 (1972).)

It would have to stand idly by while a government prevented a grandmother from taking an orphaned grandson into her home. (*See Moore* v. *City of East Cleveland*, 431 U.S. 494 (1977).)

It would not have recognized marriage as a fundamental right to be protected against unjustified laws interfering with its exercise by the poor or those in prison. (*See Zablocki* v. *Redhail*, 434 U.S. 374 (1976); *Turner* v. *Safley*, 107 S. Ct. 2254 (1987).)

The committee believes that Judge Bork's position on the right to privacy exposes a fundamentally inappropriate conception of what the Constitution means. Judge Bork's failure to acknowledge the "right to be let alone" illuminates his entire judicial philosophy. If implemented on the Supreme Court, that philosophy would place at risk the salutary developments that have already occurred under the aegis of that right and would truncate its further elaboration.

MINORITY VIEWS

INTRODUCTION

The hearings on Judge Bork were some of the most far-ranging, probing, and exhaustive ever undertaken by the Committee. The nominee was the most open and forthright to appear before the Committee. The hearings focused on several basic areas: the qualifications of the nominee; the nominee's view of the Constitution; the nominee's view of the role of the judiciary; the nominee's views on specific issues such as civil rights, the right of privacy; First Amendment rights, antitrust issues, and criminal law issues; his view of precedents; and his role in dismissing Watergate special prosecutor Archibald Cox. In each instance, Judge Bork's record and thoughtful responses place him well within the conservative mainstream of American jurisprudence.

As for qualifications, no one seriously questions that Judge Bork is eminently qualified by virtue of his ability, integrity and experience. Therefore, opponents attacked Judge Bork in other areas, such as his view of the judiciary's role in our democracy. However, Judge Bork's belief that judges should merely interpret, and not make, law is clearly the accepted view of most Americans. Additionally, Judge Bork's understanding of Constitutional principles of limited federal power is both intellectually honest and comports with historical and contemporary analysis of this great document.

The major criticisms leveled at Judge Bork are the result of misunderstandings by his critics: First, a misunderstanding of the difference between the role of a professor and that of a judge, and second, a misunderstanding of Judge Bork's position on substantive issues. Despite sloganeering and misrepresentations to the contrary, Judge Bork is well within the judicial mainstream on such issues as individual liberties, civil rights, the First Amendment, criminal law issues, antitrust matters, and the value of precedent.

Along with a vast number of judges and legal scholars, Judge Bork disapproves of a Court-created generalized "right of privacy." What this means is that Judge Bork does not believe that judges are free, at their whims, to create new "rights." His view that Constitutional rights must have a basis in the Constitution is being portrayed by some as extremism, as an unpredictable philosophy. In reality, Judge Bork's comprehensive theory of jurisprudence is firmly based in our judicial history, and is at least as predictable as any other judicial philosophy, and certainly more so than one which strains to "create" new rights.

Despite a unanimous Senate confirmation to serve as Court of Appeals Judge since Watergate, some opponents tried to rekindle

(215)

controversy over Judge Bork's role in dismissing Archibald Cox. Testimony by Former Attorney General Elliott Richardson should now put this issue to rest forever. Additionally, egregious misrepresentations of specific decisions or comments by Judge Bork have been promoted and repeated by his opponents. It takes very little to create an incorrect perception, but tedious work to set the record straight; that explains the lengthy discussions which follows in these views.

Judge Bork has proved to be a forceful intellect, and a man of unquestioned integrity. He is the victim of the misunderstandings of his critics, who confused the roles of Robert Bork as a legal commentator and Robert Bork, the Judge; critics who do not truly understanding his substantive positions, and who launched an aggressive public relations campaign based on what they thought to be Judge Bork's views. In reality, Judge Bork has excelled at all experiences an attorney can have: as private practitioner, as a law professor, as a government lawyer, and as a judge. An objective review of this nominee and his record must lead one to concur with the assessment of Chief Justice Burger who said that in the past 50 years no nominee to the Supreme Court has "had better qualifications."

RIGHT TO PRIVACY

Another area Judge Bork discussed was the Constitution's protection of individual liberty. As Judge Bork's testimony before, and subsequent letters to the Committee indicated, the Constitution protects numerous and important aspects of liberty. For instance, the First Amendment protects freedom of speech, press, and religion; the Fourth Amendment protects "[t]he right of the people to be secure in their persons, houses, papers, and effects, against unreasonable searches and seizures;" and the Sixth and Seventh amendments protect the right to trial by jury. All of these freedoms and more are fundamental. Judge Bork has made it quite plain that, in his view, a judge who fails to give these freedoms their full and fair effect fails in his judicial duty. But Judge Bork has also stated that merely because a judge must be tireless to protect the liberties guaranteed by the Constitution does not mean that judges should make up a right to liberty or personal autonomy not found in the Constitution. Once a judge moves beyond the constitutional text, history, and the structure the Constitution creates, he has only his own sense of what is important or fundamental to guide his decisionmaking. We believe, as Judge Bork does, that a judge has no greater warrant to depart from the Constitution than does Congress or the President. In other words, judges, even of the Supreme Court, are not above the law.

This means that where the constitutional materials do not specify a value to be protected and have thus left implementation of that value to the democratic process, an unelected judge has no legitimate basis for imposing that value over the contrary preferences of elected representatives. When a court does so, it lessens the area for democratic choice and works a significant shift of power from the legislative to the judicial branch. While the temptation to do so is strong with respect to a law as "nutty" and obnoxious as that at issue in *Griswold* v. *Connecticut*, 381 U.S. 479 (1965), the invention of rights to correct such a wholly, misguided public policy inevitably involves the judiciary in much more difficult policy questions about which reasonable people disagree, such as abortion or homosexual rights.

As Judge Bork has told us, while a legislator obviously can and should make distinctions between such things as the freedom to have an abortion and the freedom to use contraceptives, a court cannot engage in such *ad hoc* policymaking. A court cannot invent rights that apply only in one case and are abandoned tomorrow in a case that cannot fairly be distinguished. The process of inventing such rights is contrary to the basic premises of self-government and inconsistent application denies litigants the fairness and impartiality they are entitled to expect from the judiciary.

This was the basis of Judge Bork's criticism of Justice Douglas' opinion in *Griswold*, the case invalidating Connecticut's statute banning the use of contraceptives. To put the decision in perspective, Judge Bork noted that *Griswold*, even in 1965, was for all practical purposes nothing more than a test case. The case arose as a prosecution of a doctor who sought to test the constitutionality of the statute. There is no recorded case in which this 1879 law was used to prosecute the use of contraceptives by a married couple. The only recorded prosecution was a test case involving two doctors and a nurse, and in that case the state itself moved to dismiss.

This point was made by Justice Frankfurter 4 years before *Griswold* in *Poe* v. *Ullman*, 367 U.S. 497 (1961), a case rejecting an earlier attempt to have the Connecticut law invalidated. In addition, Justice Frankfurter's opinion took judicial notice of the fact that "contraceptives are commonly and notoriously sold in Connecticut drug stores," and concluded that there had been an "undeviating policy of nullification by Connecticut of its anticontraceptive laws throughout all the long years that they have been on the statute books." *Id.* at 502. Thus, it cannot realistically be said that failure to invalidate the Connecticut law would have had any material effect on the ability of married couples to use contraceptives in the privacy of their homes.

Judge Bork's principal objection to the majority opinion in *Griswold* was the Court's construction of a generalized right of privacy not tied to any particular provision of the Constitution to strike down a concededly silly law which it found offensive. Justice Black's dissent, joined by Justice Stewart, made precisely the same point:

> While I completely subscribe to the [view] that our Court has constitutional power to strike down statutes, state or federal, that violate commands of the Federal Constitution, I do not believe that we are granted power by the Due Process Clause or any other constitutional provision or provisions to measure constitutionality by our belief that legislation is arbitrary, capricious or unreasonable, or accomplishes no justifiable purpose, or is offensive to our own notions of "civilized standards of conduct." Such an appraisal of the wisdom of legislation is an attribute of the power to make laws, not of the power to interpret them.

381 U.S. at 513.

Justice Black proceeded to declare this unequivocal rejection of the existence of a general right of privacy based on the Constitution:

> The Court talks about a constitutional "right of privacy" as though there is some constitutional provision or provisions forbidding any law ever to be passed which might abridge the "privacy" of individuals. But there is not.

381 U.S. at 508.

At the hearings Lloyd Cutler pointed out the similarities between this passage and Judge Bork's view: "He [Bork] does not agree intellectually with a generalized right of privacy. I believe that Justice Stewart did not agree intellectually with a generalized right of privacy." (Hearings, 9/23/87 at 144.)

Of course, Judge Bork has stated repeatedly that had the state actually sought to enforce the law against a married couple, questions under the Fourth Amendment as well as under the concept of fair warning would certainly have been presented.

Absent a violation of such a specific, constitutionally granted right of privacy, however, it is difficult to discern the constitutional impediment to the Connecticut law. In Judge Bork's view, Justice Douglas' attempt to do so by creating a free-floating, "right to privacy" does not state a principle of constitutional adjudication that was either neutrally derived or which would be neutrally applied in the future.

As Judge Bork noted in his Indiana Law Review article, the "zones of privacy" discussed by Justice Douglas do not really have anything to do with privacy at all. These zones of privacy, he stated,

> protect both private and public behavior and so would more properly be labelled "zones of freedom". If we follow Justice Douglas' next step, these zones would then add up to an independent right to freedom, which is to say, a general constitutional right to be free of legal coercion, a manifest impossibility in any imaginable society. . . . We are left with no idea of the sweep of the right of privacy and hence no notion of the cases to which it may or may not be applied in the future.

Indiana Law Review article at 9.

In fact, Judge Bork's suggestions that the right of privacy was not really about "privacy" as such, that this right would not be applied consistently, and that it would lead the Court into much more difficult moral and social issues, have all proved prophetic.

For example, Judge Bork explained that the "privacy" right recognized in *Roe* v. *Wade*, 410 U.S. 113 (1973)—a right to terminate a pregnancy—is not really about privacy, but is more accurately described as a right to personal autonomy or liberty. Privacy refers to an interest in anonymity or confidentiality whereas liberty describes freedom to engage in a certain activity. The question in *Roe*, therefore, is whether any provision of the Constitution recognizes an individual right to terminate pregnancy against State intrusion. As Judge Bork testified, the Court's opinion in *Roe* made no attempt to ground such a right in the Constitution except to say that it was "founded in the 14th Amendment's concept of personal liberty and restrictions upon state action." *Id.* at 153.

This is Judge Bork's difficulty with the opinion. As Justice White's dissent, joined by Justice Rehnquist, stated, there is "nothing in the language or history of the Constitution to support the Court's judgment,' which the dissent termed "an exercise of raw judicial power." The Due Process Clause of the Fourteenth Amendment provides that "No State shall . . . deprive any person of life, liberty, or property, without due process of law." If the clause is read as written, then it guarantees that life, liberty, and property will not be taken without the safeguard of fair and adequate legal procedures to challenge the legality of the deprivation. Once such procedures have been given, and the legality of the deprivation established, the Due Process Class does not establish an independent barrier to the deprivation. If, on the other hand, the clause is read to protect liberty against deprivation regardless of procedures, then the judge must have a theory for deciding which liberties are protected and which are not since no one would suggest that all liberty is immune from state regulation.

Justice Scalia has also rejected the generalized substantive due process right to privacy. Significantly, as a Circuit Judge, Justice Scalia jointed Judge Bork's opinion in *Dronenburg* v. *Zech*, 741 F.2d 1388 (D.C. Cir. 1984), which held that there was no privacy right to homosexual conduct in the Navy, and which sharply criticized the Supreme Court's privacy decisions. The *Dronenburg* opinion stated:

> [W]hen the [Supreme] court creates new rights, as some
> Justices who have engaged in the process state that they
> have done, lower courts have none of the [ ] [constitutional
> and historical] materials available and can look only to
> what the Supreme Court has stated to be the principles in-
> volved.

741 F.2d at 1395.

And Justice O'Connor has also been consistently opposed to the
expansive, generalized privacy right that some Justices have found
in the Constitution. In her dessenting opinion in *City of Akron* v.
Akron Center for Reproductive health, a case invalidating certain
regulations on abortion procedures, she wrote:

> Irrespective of what we may believe is wise or prudent
> policy in this difficult area, "the Constitution does not con-
> stitute us as 'Platonic Guardians' nor does it vest in this
> Court the authority to strike down laws because they do
> not meet our standards of desirable social policy, 'wisdom,'
> or 'common sense.' "

Similarly, just last year in *Thornburgh* v. *American College of Obstetricians,* another case in which state regulations on abortion
were invalidated, Justice O'Connor forcefully dissented, asserting
that "[t]he Court's abortion decisions have already worked a major
distortion in the Constitution." Moreover, her refusal to accept the
privacy right is not limited to the abortion context. She also joined
in Justice White's opinion in *Bowers* v. *Hardwick,* 103 S. Ct. 2481,
2505–06 (1983), finding that there is no constitutional right to privacy, consensual homosexual conduct. Thus, Justice O'Connor has
never endorsed any application of a right to privacy in any context.

As Judge Bork stated before the Committee, it would be inappropriate for him to give any indication of how he would vote as a
member of the Supreme Court should the issue arise again. But
suffice it to say that the question would be one of searching for an
appropriate constitutional basis and precedent. And as Judge Bork
has stated, not every incorrectly decided constitutional decision
should be open to reconsideration.

As Judge Bork has explained, no one has ever been able to explain why some liberties not specified in the Constitution should be
protected and others should not. As far as the Constitution is concerned, when it does not speak to the contrary the State is free to
regulate. A judge who uses the Due Process Clause to give substantive protection to some liberties but not others has no basis for decision other than his own subjective view of what is good public
policy. That is what the debate is really about. Should unelected
judges stick to their constitutionally assigned role of neutrally interpreting and applying the law, or should they bend and ignore
the law according to their policy preferences in order to reach results they like?

We are not without historical precedents that show what happens when unelected judges attempt to encroach upon the legislature's proper sphere. Attempts to read substantive protections of
liberty into the Due Process Clause have failed in the past precisely because the clause gives no indication of which liberties are to

be preferred to others. In the early part of this century, for example, the Supreme Court read the due process clause of the Fifth and Fourteenth Amendments to protect a generalized liberty of contract, and routinely struck down laws that interfered with that liberty. Thus, in *Lochner* v. *New York*, 198 U.S. 45 (1905), the Supreme Court invalidated a New York labor law limiting the hours of bakery employees to 60 hours a week. Similarly, in *Adair* v. *United States*, 208 U.S. 161 (1908), the Court struck down a Federal law prohibiting interstate railroads from requiring as a condition of employment that its workers agree not to join labor unions. and in *Adkins* v. *Children's Hospital*, 261 U.S. 525 (1923), the Court held the District of Columbia's minimum wage law unconstitutional.

If the hearings former Secretary of HUD Carla Hills pointed out that Judge Bork's criticism of *Roe* and *Griswold* is based on his fear of a reneual of *Lochnerian* activism.

> Judge Bork with Justice Black and a great number of other distinguished constitutional scholars who have criticized the logic, not the result, in *Roe* and the *Griswold* cases, seek to avoid precisely that type [i.e. *Lochnerian* of activism.

As Judge Bork points out, the Supreme Court's modern attempts to use the Due Process Clause as a substantive protection of liberty have also been unconvincing. Although the Court has held in *Roe* that a woman has a constitutional right to receive an abortion, it has more recently held that consenting adults do not have a constitutional right to engage in homosexual sodomy. See *Bowers* v. *Hardwick*, 106 S. Ct. 2841 (1986). Justice White's opinion for the Court in *Bowers* reasoned as follows:

> It is obvious to us that neither ["the concept of ordered liberty" nor the liberties "deeply rooted in this Nation's history and tradition" formulation] would extend a fundamental right to homosexuals to engage in acts of consensual sodomy. Proscriptions against that conduct have ancient roots.

Id. at 2844.

The difference between these two decisions illustrates Judge Bork's point that it is impossible to apply the undefined right of privacy in a principled or consistent manner. It is difficult to understand why abortion is a constitutionally protected liberty but homosexual sodomy is not. Neither activity is mentioned in the Constitution, both involve activity between consenting adults, and "[p]roscriptions against [both activities] have ancient roots."

Judge Bork said it this way at the hearings:

> [L]et me repeat about this created, generalized, and undefined right to privacy in *Griswold*. Aside from the fact that the right was not derived by Justice Douglas in any traditional mode of constitutional analysis, there is the: . . . we do not know what it is. We do not know what it covers. It can strike at random. *For example the Supreme Court has not apply the right of privacy consistently and I think it is safe to predict that the Supreme Court will not.* For exam-

ple, if it really is a right of sexual freedom in private, as some have suggested, then *Bowers* v. *Hardwick,* which upheld a statute against sodomy as applied to homosexuals, is wrongly decided. Privacy to do what, Senators? You know, privacy to use cocaine in private? Privacy for businessmen to fix prices in a hotel room? We just do not know what it is. (Emphasis added.)

Some have said that the principle may be that individuals have a constitutional right to use their bodies as they wish. Not only is this principle to be found nowhere in the Constitution, but also its application would invalidate laws against prostitution, consensual incest among adults, bestiality, drug use, and suicide, not to mention draft laws and countless safety measures such as laws requiring the use of seat belts and motorcycle helments. This principle is thus far too general to support a particular decision without sweeping in these other cases. Unless the American people decide that judges should be given far more authority and responsibility for running our society, the Construction requires that they follow the law.

As Carlos Hills said at the hearings:

I know that his criticism of *Griswold* was based upon its rationale. I know that he is concerned as a judicial activist with a vast undefined right of privacy, fearing that it removes the discretion from the elected bodies to a small group of judges who are unelected.

Many of the most respected constitutional law scholars have expressed profound disagreement with the reasoning and holding of *Roe* v. *Wade,* the leading example of substantive due process. These include Harvard Law School Professors Archibald Cox and Paul Freund, Stanford Law School Dean John Hart Ely, and Columbia Law School Professor Henry Monaghan. Dean Ely, a former law clerk to Chief Justice Earl Warren, stated in 1973 that

what is frightening about *Roe* is that this super-protected right is not inferable from the language of the Constitution, the Framers' thinking respecting the specific problem in issues, any general value derivable from the provisions they included or the nation's governmental structure.

Similarly, Stanford Law School Professor Gerald Gunther, editor of the leading law school casebook on constitutional law, offered the following related comments on *Griswold* v. *Connecticut*:

It marked the return of the Court to the discredited notion of substantive due process. The theory was discredited in 1937 in the economic sphere. I don't find a very persuasive difference in reviving it for the personal sphere. I'm a card-carrying liberal Democrat, but this strikes me as a double standard.

Some witnesses have urged the Ninth Amendment as a basis for invalidating State laws that restrict liberty or privacy not otherwise protected in the Constitution. As Judge Bork has explained, the Ninth Amendment provides no basis for doing so. The Ninth Amendment provides: "The enumeration in the Constitution, of certain rights, shall not be construed to deny or disparage others retained by the people." The historical meaning of this amendment is revealed by the circumstances of its adoption. The original Constitution did not contain a Bill of Rights. Rather, it established a National Government of enumerated powers. But during the ratification debates, calls were made with increasing frequency by the so-called Anti-Federalists for adoption of a Bill of Rights. The Federalists raised two objections to inclusion of a Bill of Rights. First, it was said to be unnecessary because Congress would have no power to abridge fundamental rights of the people as the general government was one of enumerated, and therefore limited, powers. Second, the Bill of Rights was said to be dangerous because the reservation of certain rights might be read to imply that power was given to the Federal Government to regulate all others.

When James Madison became convinced of the need for a Bill of Rights, he defended his proposal as follows:

> It has been objected also against the bill of rights, that, by enumerating particular exceptions to the grant of power, it would disparage those rights which were not placed in that enumeration; and it might follow, by implication, that those rights which were not singled out, were intended to be assigned into the hands of the General Government, and were consequently insecure. This is one of the most plausible arguments I ever heard urged against the admission of rights into this system; but, I conceive, that it may be guarded against. I have attempted it, as gentlemen may see by turning to the last clause of the fourth resolution. (1 Annals of Congress 456 (J. Gales & W. Seaton ed. 1834)).

The clause to which Madison referred was the provision that would later be adopted in somewhat shorter form as the Ninth Amendment. Thus, it appears that the amendment's instruction that the enumeration "of certain rights, shall not be construed to deny or disparage others retained by the people" was meant to prevent any implication, as Madison put it, "that those rights which were not singled out, were intended to be assigned into the hands of the General Government."

This means that whenever the Constitution does not grant the *power to regulate* conduct to the Federal Government, the people have a right to engage in that conduct free from *Federal* interference even though the conduct is not specified in the Bill of Rights. It must be emphasized that the "right" protected by the Ninth Amendment runs against the Federal Government when it undertakes to regulate individuals through an unwarranted expansion of its powers. For this reason, it makes little sense either textually or historically to speak of Ninth Amendment rights enforceable against the *States*. As Judge Bork has said elsewhere, if that were the meaning of the Ninth Amendment, then surely there would have been heated debate in the State ratifying conventions, and litigants and courts would have invoked the amendment in that capacity. That neither occurred is strong evidence that the amendment was not intended to create federally enforceable rights against the States.

Moreover, Judge Bork correctly states that even if one agrees with the recent suggestion that the Ninth Amendment protects natural rights against State and Federal intrusion, the nature and scope of those rights is undefined and virtually limitless. For example, John Locke, whose writings profoundly influenced the framers' view of "natural rights," regarded property and contract rights as among the most important natural rights of men. Accordingly, if the Ninth Amendment were to be interpreted as a grant of liberty against Government intrusion, it would necessarily include the freedom of contract. Of course, this would lead to invalidation of the worker protection legislation struck down by *Lochner* and its progeny, or any other form of economic regulation that hampers the "right" to contract.

Alternatively, members of the Supreme Court have invoked their own notions of natural law in the past. For example, Justice Bradley's concurrence in *Bradwell* v. *State*, 83 U.S. 130 (1873), upholding a law forbidding women from practicing law, states:

> The natural and proper timidity and delicacy which belongs to the female evidently unfits it for many of the occupations of civil life. . . . [The] paramount destiny and mission of woman are to fulfil the noble and benign offices of wife and mother. This is the law of the Creator.

But those who now urge reliance on the Ninth Amendment see a different set of natural rights emanating from the Ninth Amendment. For example, Professor Tribe filed a brief with the Supreme Court in *Bowers* v. *Hardwick* suggesting that one of the rights "retained by the people" under the Ninth Amendment is the right to engage in homosexual sodomy. Equally plausible are claims that the Ninth Amendment protects drug use, mountain climbing, and consensual incest among adults. Certainly the text of the amendment makes no distinction among any of these "rights." Therefore, unless the Ninth Amendment is to be read to invalidate all laws that limit individual freedoms, judges who invoke the clause selectively will be doing nothing more than imposing their subjective morality on society. The Constitution nowhere authorizes them to do so.

Although Justice Goldberg's concurrence in *Griswold* invoked the Ninth Amendment, Judge Bork has explained that the problems just discussed are probably the reason why the Supreme Court has *never* rested a decision on the Ninth Amendment. For instance, even Justice Douglas, the author of the majority opinion in *Griswold*, stated in a concurring opinion in the companion case to *Roe* v. *Wade*, that "The Ninth Amendment obviously does not create federally enforceable rights." *Doe* v. *Bolton*, 410 U.S. 179, 210 (1973) (Douglas, J., concurring). Unless someone can find a way both to read the Ninth Amendment to apply against the States and to discover which additional rights are retained by the people, there is no principled way for a judge to rely on the clause to invalidate State laws.

There is an additional matter that requires mentioning. There appears to be some confusion concerning Judge Bork's view of, and the Court's decision in, *Skinner* v. *Oklahoma*, 316 U.S. 535 (1942). *Skinner* held that a State statute requiring sterilization of recidivist robbers but no embezzlers worked "a clear, pointed, unmistakable discrimination," *id.* at 541, and therefore violated the equal protection clause of the Fourteenth Amendment. It is important to understand the rationale given by the Court for its decision. The Court did *not* rely on a substantive due process right to privacy. In fact, the Court declined Chief Justice Stone's invitation in a separate concurrence to decide the case under the due process clause. Instead, the Court rested its decision squarely on the Equal Protection Clause: "The equal protection clause would indeed be a formula of empty words if such conspicuously artificial lines could be drawn." *Id.*

In his 1971 article, Judge Bork was critical of what he believed to be the Supreme Court's inconsistent application of the Equal Protection Clause. He cited six cases as examples in which the Court both upheld and invalidated challenged classifications. One of the cases Judge Bork cited was *Skinner* v. *Oklahoma.* He did not cite *Skinner,* or any other case listed, for the correctness or incorrectness of its holding. Rather, Judge Bork's point was merely that it appeared that "the differing results cannot be explained on any ground other than the Court's preferences for particular values." (Indiana Law Review at 12.) This was the sum total of Judge Bork's "criticism" of *Skinner,* and it is a mischaracterization to suggest that Judge Bork's inclusion of *Skinner* in a string cite means that he disagrees with the decision in the case:

> In his testimony, Judge Bork pointed out that the statute in question made a distinction between a robber and an embezzler and, with respect to that distinction, if the *Skinner* decision "had gone on and pointed out those distinctions really sterilized, in effect, blue-collar criminals and exempted white-collar criminals, and indeed, appeared to have some taint of a racial bias to it, [Douglas] could have arrived at the same decision in what I would take to be a more legitimate fashion."

In addition, Judge Bork noted that sterilization of criminals raises serious and independent questions under the Eighth Amendment's prohibition on cruel and unusual punishment, questions neither Judge Bork nor the Court addressed. In short, there is no reason to believe that Judge Bork would have any disagreement with the result reached by the Court in *Skinner.*

24 Weekly Comp. Pres. Doc. 38
Jan. 14, 1988

Letter Accepting the Resignation of Robert H. Bork as United
States Circuit Judge

Dear Bob:

It is with deep sadness that I accept your decision to resign as
United States Circuit Judge for the District of Columbia Circuit,
effective February 5, 1988. In my many appointments to the Federal
bench, I have attempted to select men and women of uncommon
intellect, unimpeachable integrity, and a strong, steady temperament
-- men and women with special gifts for communication and reasoning
and with an abiding courage of conviction. You, Bob, epitomize these
virtues at their very finest -- which is why I turned to you to fill
Justice Lewis Powell's seat on the Supreme Court.

The unprecedented political attack upon you which resulted in the
regrettable Senate action was a tragedy for our country. All Americans
are the poorer today for not having your extraordinary talents and
legal skills on the High Court.

And yet, as I read your letter of resignation, I cannot help but feel
a warm admiration for the difficult decision you have made. There is,
as you state, a lively public debate brewing in this country, fueled in
no small part by your confirmation hearings -- a debate over the
proper role of the judiciary in our system of representative self-government. That debate has advocates who view the courts and the
Constitution as mere instruments for political advantage. Effective
advocacy of a more traditional approach to the judicial function occurs
too infrequently. Your recent experience, against a background of
unswerving commitment to the doctrine of judicial restraint, makes
you uniquely well suited to carry that debate forward.

For your many years of dedicated public service, especially the last
six on the Court of Appeals, your country and I thank you. For your
courageous adherence to conviction and refusal to forsake your ideals,
your country and I salute you. For daring to embark on this new
course in selfless service of the cause of truth and justice in the public
arena, your country and I remain in your debt.

While your public service on the Court of Appeals will be sorely
missed, I am confident that your writings and other contributions as

a private citizen are destined to have a most profound and lasting impact on the Nation.

Best wishes for success in your future endeavors.

Sincerely,

Ronald Reagan

[The Honorable Robert H. Bork, United States Circuit Judge for the District of Columbia Circuit, Washington, D.C. 20001]

January 7, 1988

Dear Mr. President:

Six years ago you appointed me to the United States Court of Appeals for the District of Columbia Circuit. That was a great honor and I continue to be grateful to you for it. The task of serving the law and the ends of justice has made the last six years absorbing and fulfilling.

It is, therefore, with great reluctance, and only after much thought and discussion with my family, that I have now decided to step down from the bench. This decision is the more difficult because of what I owe to you, to the many Americans who have written to me in the last six months to express their support, and, indeed, to all Americans our system of justice serves. Because I recognize these debts and obligations, I want to explain the course I have chosen.

The crux of the matter is that I wish to speak, write, and teach about law and other issues of public policy more extensively and more freely than is possible in my present position. As a sitting judge on a very busy court, I cannot devote the time and energy I wish to public discourse. Moreover, constraints of propriety and seemliness limit the topics a federal judge may address and the public positions he may advocate. My experience as your nominee for Associate Justice of the Supreme Court of the United States made me acutely aware of the restrictions on my ability to address issues. For several months, various highly vocal groups and individuals systematically misrepresented not only my record and philosophy of judging but, more importantly, the proper function of judges in our constitutional democracy. This was a public campaign of miseducation to which, as a sitting federal judge, I felt I could not publicly respond. What should have been a reasoned national debate about the role of the courts under the Constitution became an essentially unanswered campaign of misinformation and political slogans. If, as a judge, I cannot speak out against this attempt to alter the traditional nature of our courts, I think it important to place myself where I can.

You nominated me to my present court and to the Supreme Court precisely because I do speak for the traditional view of the judge's role under the Constitution. It is a view that goes back to the founding of our nation and was ably articulated by, among others, James Madison, Thomas Jefferson, Alexander Hamilton, and Joseph Story. It has been espoused by the greatest judges in our history. That view, simply put, is that a judge must apply to modern circumstances the principles laid down by those who adopted our Constitution but must not invent new principles of his own.

A few years ago I said:

In a constitutional democracy the moral content of law must be given by the morality of the framer or the legislator, never by the morality of the judge. The sole task of the latter -- and it is a task quite large enough for anyone's wisdom, skill, and virtue -- is to translate the framer's or the legislator's morality into a rule to govern unforeseen circumstances. That abstinence from giving his own desires free play, that continuing and self-conscious renunciation of power, that is the morality of the jurist.

That was my view then. It is my view now. Though there are many who vehemently oppose it, that philosophy is essential if courts are to govern according to the rule of law rather than whims of politics and personal preference. That view is essential if courts are not to set the social agenda for the nation, and if representative democracy is to maintain its legitimate spheres of authority. Those who want political judges should reflect that the political and social preferences of judges have changed greatly over our history and will no doubt do so again. We have known judicial activism of the right and of the left; neither is legitimate.

My desire to participate in the public debate on these matters is what prompts my decision to leave the bench at this time. I had considered this course in the past but had not decided until the recent confirmation experience brought home to me just how misfocused the public discourse has become. A great many supporters have written to urge that I continue in public service. The decision I have made will, I believe, allow me to do just that. My views on these matters are of long standing. Because of my experience as your nominee, I am now in a better position to address the issues than ever before.

Though I am sure this decision is the correct one, I find, as the time of my departure draws near, that the prospect of leaving the federal judiciary fills me not merely with reluctance but with sadness. Any lawyer should be deeply honored to be a federal judge and to serve with a nationwide corps of the most dedicated men and women one is likely ever to meet. The work of an appellate judge may be the aspect of the legal profession for which I am best suited. I have actively enjoyed the day-to-day work of judging -- the exchanges with lawyers at oral argument, the discussions with colleagues and clerks in arriving at a correct decision, and the effort to craft the best opinion one can. Trying with all one's capacities to do justice according to law is a deeply satisfying experience, both intellectually and emotionally. I will miss it more than I can say. I find some consolation in leaving behind a record of which I believe I may be proud, and one by which I am content to be judged.

In choosing a date for my departure, I have considered, among other factors, the desirability of leaving time for the nomination and confirmation of my successor as well as the importance of beginning my new work without undue delay. It will, however, take a few weeks to complete work on hand. I ask, therefore, that you accept my resignation as Circuit Judge, United States Court of Appeals for the District of Columbia Circuit, effective at the close of business, Friday, February 5, 1988.

With deep gratitude for your confidence in me, for appointing me to this court and nominating me to the Supreme Court, I will always remain

Yours truly,

Robert H. Bork

4

JUSTICE ANTHONY KENNEDY

The confirmation hearings of Anthony Kennedy were "the first to be defined by the post-Bork model"; the Senate Judiciary Committee's focus was now on the overall approach the candidate took to constitutional interpretation. Wermiel, Confirming the Constitution, 56 Law and Contemporary Problems 122, 131 (1993). As a result, unlike the O'Connor hearings, where the Senators had focused on O'Connor's personal and legal views on abortion per se, the confirmation hearings of Anthony Kennedy took their cue from the sweeping jurisprudential inquiry of Robert Bork. The Kennedy hearings focused on the nominee's overall view on the right to privacy. Yet, Kennedy was, not surprisingly, a bit less forthcoming in his responses than his unsuccessful predecessor had been.

Kennedy repeatedly admitted that he believed that the protection of the value of privacy was included in the word liberty. Yet when Senator Dennis DeConcini (D-Az.) asked Kennedy point blank whether or not he believed that there was a fundamental right to privacy, and whether that right was a freestanding one which deserved similar consideration as those rights that were enumerated in the constitution, Kennedy hedged. He responded only that this was a "generally correct" statement. Later during his exchange with DeConcini, Kennedy admitted that there was no doubt in his mind as to the existence of a fundamental right to privacy. But when Senator Leahy tried to pin Kennedy down on the same issue, Kennedy would only say that his views on the right to privacy were still evolving. Nomination of Anthony M. Kennedy to Be Associate Justice of the Supreme Court of the United States: Hearings Before the Senate Comm. on the Judiciary, 100th Cong., 2d Sess. (1988).

Kennedy was similarly opaque in his statements on *stare decisis*. He was asked why he thought there had been an increase in the number of cases that the Court had overruled. Pointing to the rise in the overall number of cases the Court hears as well as an increase in the number of public law cases, Kennedy claimed that because of the number of precedents the Court has to deal with was constantly rising, statistically it was becoming more probable that the shaping of the law would require many of them to be overturned. With regard to the centrality of *stare decisis*, Kennedy did note that the doctrine ensures impartiality and stability in the law, but he failed to illuminate the extent of his personal commitment to the principle.

Abortion and *Roe v. Wade* only came up a few times in the hearings. Kennedy was called upon to clarify a statement he allegedly made to Senator Jesse Helms (R-N.C.) that, as a practicing Catholic, Kennedy opposed abortion. In the hearing, however, Kennedy mildly stated that he would, as he would expect any Justice to, leave his own personal religious beliefs out of decision-making. The Committee members declined to press the issue further or to directly question Kennedy on how he might vote in an abortion case. Reluctant to harp upon the divisive abortion issue, the Committee chose instead to look only to the broad issues of privacy and *stare decisis*.

Ultimately, Kennedy had learned his lessons well from the Bork debacle; "[h]e set a mild-mannered tone that was neither evasive nor belligerent . . . [and h]e declined to get . . . specific, not only about *Roe*, but also about the foundational privacy case, *Griswold v. Connecticut*." Wermiel at 133. His approach was successful. Anthony Kennedy was confirmed by a unanimous 97-0 vote in the Senate.

Justice Anthony Kennedy
Documents

S. Hrg. 100-1037

NOMINATION OF ANTHONY M. KENNEDY TO BE ASSOCIATE JUSTICE OF THE SUPREME COURT OF THE UNITED STATES

HEARINGS

BEFORE THE

COMMITTEE ON THE JUDICIARY
UNITED STATES SENATE

ONE HUNDREDTH CONGRESS

FIRST SESSION

ON

THE NOMINATION OF ANTHONY M. KENNEDY TO BE ASSOCIATE JUSTICE OF THE SUPREME COURT OF THE UNITED STATES

DECEMBER 14, 15 AND 16, 1987

Serial No. J-100-67

Printed for the use of the Committee on the Judiciary

U.S. GOVERNMENT PRINTING OFFICE
WASHINGTON : 1989

The CHAIRMAN. Judge, let me explain to you, and to my colleagues, how the ranking member and I would like to proceed today. That is, as has been the custom in the recent past, we will allow each Senator to question you up to a half an hour, hopefully to have some continuity to the questions, and allow both you full time to answer the questions and they to flesh out the line of questioning they wish to pursue.

It is my hope, although not my expectation, that we will complete one round of questioning today. We will stop, though, at 6 o'clock, or as close to 6 o'clock as we can get. And at approximately 3:15, we will take a break for 15 minutes or so to give you an opportunity to stretch your legs and maybe get a cup of coffee or whatever you would like.

Judge, I will begin my first round here by telling you at the outset that I would like to pursue or touch on three areas in my first round. One is the question of unenumerated rights, and if there are such, if they exist under our Constitution. Secondly, as a matter, quite frankly, more of housekeeping and for the record, with you under oath, I would like to question you about your meetings with Justice Department, White House and other officials, and whether or not any commitments were elicited or made. I quite frankly must tell you at the outset I have had long discussions and full cooperation from the White House in this matter, and I am satisfied; but I think we should have it under oath what transpired and what did not.

Thirdly, if time permits—which it probably will not—I would like to discuss with you a little bit about your views on the role of precedent as a Supreme Court Justice. Ofttimes, it is mentioned here that we unanimously voted for you when you came up as a circuit court appointee, and that is an honor. You are to be congratulated. But as you well know, we unanimously vote for almost everybody who comes up. Ninety-eight percent of all those that come before the Congress are unanimously approved of. That is in no way to denigrate the support shown to you by us in your previous appearance here, but it is to indicate that, as you know better than most of us, the role of a lower court judge and the role of a Supreme Court judge are different. They are both to seek out and find justice under the Constitution, but lower court judges are bound by precedent. They do not have the authority, the constitutional authority to alter Supreme Court decisions. But as a Supreme Court Justice, you obviously will have that authority, and I would like at some point to discuss to what extent you think that authority resides in a member of the court.

Judge Kennedy, let me begin, though, with the unenumerated rights question, which occupied a great deal of our time in the prior hearing—not your prior hearing, but the prior hearing with Judge Bork.

Judge Kennedy, in your 1986 speech on unenumerated rights which, if I am not mistaken—I have a copy of it here—was entitled "Unenumerated Rights and the Dictates of Judicial Restraint," in that speech you place great emphasis on the specific text of the Constitution as a guidepost for the court. You said, for example— and I quote from the concluding page of that speech—

I recognize, too, that saying the constitutional text must be our principal reference is in a sense simply to restate the question what that text means. But uncertainty over precise standards of interpretation does not justify failing to attempt to construct them, and still less does it justify flagrant departures.

What we find out today, or at least I do, is how you go about attempting to construct such standards of interpretation. As I read your speech, you were concerned that unenumerated rights articulated by the Supreme Court, such as the right of privacy, but not exclusively limited to that, in your words "have a readily discernible basis in the Constitution." But you also recognize, Judge Kennedy, that the text of the Constitution is not always, to use your phrase, I believe, "a definitive guide."

On two separate occasions, in August of 1987 and February of 1984, you have described the Due Process Clause, which, of course, contains the word "liberty," the 14th amendment. You described that as a spacious phrase. That seems to—well, let me not suggest what it suggests.

The point I want to raise with you is there seems to be an underlying tension here; that you talk about liberty as being a spacious phrase, and you insist at the same time that the constitutional text must be our principal reference.

Although I have my own view of what you mean by that—and they are not incompatible, those two phrases, as I see it—I would like you to give us your view of the liberty clause. Do you believe that the textual reference to liberty in the 5th and 14th amendments and in the Preamble of the Constitution provides a basis for certain fundamental unenumerated rights?

Judge KENNEDY. Senator, of course, the great tension, the great debate, the great duality in constitutional law—and this has been true since the court first undertook to interpret the Constitution 200 years ago—has been between what the text says and what the dictates of the particular case require from the standpoint of justice and from the standpoint of our constitutional tradition. The point of my remarks—and we can talk about the Canadian speech in detail, if you choose—was that it is really the great role of the judge to try to discover those standards that implement the intention of the framers.

The framers were very careful about the words they used. They were excellent draftsmen. They had drawn 11 constitutions for the separate states. This, they recognized, was a unique undertaking.

But the words of the Constitution must be the beginning of our inquiry.

Now, how far can you continue that inquiry away from the words of the text? Your question is whether or not there are unenumerated rights. To begin with, most of the inquiries that the Supreme Court has conducted in cases of this type have centered around the word "liberty." Now, the framers used that, what I call "spacious phrase," both in the fifth amendment, almost contemporaneous with the Constitution, and again in the 14th amendment they reiterated it.

The framers had an idea which is central to Western thought.

The CHAIRMAN. Western thought?

Judge KENNEDY. Thought. It is central to our American tradition. It is central to the idea of the rule of law. That is there is a zone of liberty, a zone of protection, a line that is drawn where the individual can tell the Government: Beyond this line you may not go.

Now, the great question in constitutional law is: One, where is that line drawn? And, two, what are the principles that you refer to in drawing that line?

The CHAIRMAN. But there is a line.

Judge KENNEDY. There is a line. It is wavering; it is amorphous; it is uncertain. But this is the judicial function.

The CHAIRMAN. It is not unlike, as I understand what you have said, one of your predecessors—if you are confirmed—discussing shared traditions and historic values of our people in making that judgment, and another of your predecessors suggesting that there is a right to be let alone, left alone.

Let me ask you, Judge Kennedy, Justice Harlan, one of the great true conservative Justices, in my view, of this century, had a similar concern; and as I understand it—correct me if I am wrong—expressed it not dissimilarly to what you are saying when he said no formula could serve as a substitute in this area for judgment and restraint, and that there were not any "mechanical yardsticks" or "mechanical answers."

Do you agree with the essence of what Justice Harlan was saying?

Judge KENNEDY. It is hard to disagree with that. That was the second Mr. Justice Harlan. Remember, though, Senator, that the object of our inquiry is to use history, the case law, and our understanding of the American constitutional tradition in order to determine the intention of the document broadly expressed.

One of the reasons why, in my view, the decisions of the Supreme Court of the United States have such great acceptance by the American people is because of the perception by the people that the Court is being faithful to a compact that was made 200 years ago. The framers sat down in a room for three months. They put aside politics; they put aside religion; they put aside personal differences. And they acted as statesmen to draw a magnificent document. The object of our inquiry is to see what that document means.

The CHAIRMAN. Judge, it will come as no surprise to you that one of the storm centers of our last debate and discussion was whether or not there were unenumerated rights and whether the document was expansive.

Would you agree with Justice Harlan that, despite difficult questions in this area, the Court still has a clear responsibility to act to protect unenumerated rights, although where it draws that line depends on the particular Justice's view?

Judge KENNEDY. Yes, although I am not sure that he spoke in exactly those terms.

The CHAIRMAN. No, I am not quoting him.

Judge KENNEDY. I am not trying to quibble, but it may well be the better view, rather than talk in terms of unenumerated rights to recognize that we are simply talking about whether or not liberty extends to situations not previously addressed by the courts, to protections not previously announced by the courts.

The CHAIRMAN. Let us be more fundamental than that. There are certain rights that the courts over the years have concluded that Americans have either retained for themselves or have been granted that do not find specific reference in the Constitution—the right of privacy being one, as you pointed out in your speech, the right to travel.

So what we are talking about here, what I am attempting to talk about here and you are responding, is that whether or not in the case of the 14th amendment the word "liberty" encompasses a right that maybe heretofore has not been articulated by the court and does not find residence in some text in the Constitution, and whether or not the ninth amendment means anything.

Could you tell me what the ninth amendment means to you? And for the record, let me read it. I know you know it well. "The enumeration in the Constitution of certain rights shall not be construed to deny or disparage others retained by the people."

Can you tell me what you think the framers meant by that?

Judge KENNEDY. I wish I had a complete answer. The ninth amendment has been a fascination to judges and to students of the Constitution for generations.

When Madison—and he was the principal draftsman of the Bill of Rights—wrote the Bill of Rights, he wanted to be very sure that his colleagues, the voters, and the world understood that he did not have the capacity to foresee every verbal formulation that was necessary for the protection of the individual. He was writing and presenting a proposal at a time when State constitutions were still being drafted, and he knew that some State constitutions, for instance the Virginia Bill of Rights went somewhat further than the Constitution of the United States.

In my view, one of his principal purposes, simply as a statesman, was to give assurance that this was not a proclamation of every right that should be among the rights of a free people.

Now, going beyond that, I think the sense of your question is: Does the ninth amendment have practical significance——

Senator THURMOND. Please keep your voice up so we can hear you.

Judge KENNEDY. Does the ninth amendment have practical significance in the ongoing determination of constitutional cases?

As you know, the Court has rarely found occasion to refer to it. It seems to me the Court is treating it as something of a reserve clause, to be held in the event that the phrase "liberty" and the other spacious phrases in the Constitution appear to be inadequate for the Court's decision.

The CHAIRMAN. Judge, I do not want to hurt your prospects any, but I happen to agree with you, and I find comfort in your acknowledgement that it had a purpose.

There are some who argue it has no purpose. Some suggest it was a water blot in the Constitution. But I read it as you do. It does not make either of us right, but it indicates that there is some agreement, and I think the historical text, and the debate surrounding the Constitution sustains the broad interpretation you have just applied.

And is it fair to say that in the debate about unenumerated rights, and the right of privacy in particular, that there is a question of crossing the line, acknowledging the existence of unenumerated rights, and the existence of the right of privacy? The real debate for the last 40 years has been on this side of the line, among those who sit on the bench and the Supreme Court, who acknowledge that there is, in fact, for example, a right to privacy, but argue vehemently as to how far that right extends.

Some believe that extends only to a right of privacy to married couples. Others would argue, and will argue, I assume at some point, that that right of privacy extends to consensual homosexual activity. But the debate has been on this side of the line, that is, as to how far the right extends, not if the right exists.

Do you have any doubt that there is a right of privacy? I am not asking you where you draw the line, but that it does exist and can be found, protected within the Constitution?

Judge KENNEDY. It seems to me that most Americans, most lawyers, most judges, believe that liberty includes protection of a value that we call privacy. Now, as we well know, that is hardly a self-defining term, and perhaps we will have more discussions about that.

The CHAIRMAN. Well, I would like to go back to that, if my colleagues have not covered it. I only have about 10 minutes under my own rules, and I would like to settle, if we can at the outset here, the question of whether or not any commitments were given, or were asked for.

In your questionnaire, you identified at least seven different sets of meetings, and a number of phone calls that you had with White House staff, or Justice Department personnel before you were actually nominated by the President.

Let me ask you this first. Since completing your questionnaire, have you recalled any other meetings, or conversations of any type, that have not already been identified, and that took place before your actual nomination?

Judge KENNEDY. No, I have not recalled any such additional instances.

The CHAIRMAN. To be absolutely clear, I am asking you here about direct communications of any type with the White House or Justice Department, as well as indirect communications such as through some third party or intermediary. That is, someone coming to you, asking your view, and that view being transmitted through that person back to anyone connected with the Administration.

Judge KENNEDY. I understood that question in the sense that you describe when I answered the questionnaire, and I understand it that way now. The conversations that I described were the only conversations that occurred.

The CHAIRMAN. Judge, I appreciate your cooperating in this matter, but I hope you understand why it is important.

Let's look at, if you will, the October 28th meeting that you identified. According to your questionnaire, that meeting was attended by Howard Baker, Kenneth Duberstein, A. B. Culvahouse, Mr. Meese, and Assistant Attorney General William Bradford Reynolds.

Were you asked at that meeting how you would rule on any legal issue?

Judge KENNEDY. I was not; I was asked no question which came even close to the zone of what I would consider infringing on judicial independence. I was asked no question which even came close to the zone of what I would consider improper. I was asked no question which came even close to the zone of eliciting a volunteered comment from me as to how I would rule on any particular case, or on any pending issue.

The CHAIRMAN. Judge, were you asked about your personal opinion on any controversial issue?

Judge KENNEDY. I was not.

The CHAIRMAN. Did anyone ask you what, as a personal matter, you thought of any issue or case?

Judge KENNEDY. No such questions were asked, and I volunteered no such comments.

The CHAIRMAN. And were you asked anything about cases currently before the Court?

Judge KENNEDY. No, sir.

The CHAIRMAN. I realize there is some redundancy in those questions, but is important, again, for the record.

Now, Judge, there was—if I can move to the end here—there was some newspaper comment about a meeting that took place after you had been nominated.

Let me ask you the question. Did you meet with any sitting United States Senators prior to your being nominated by the President?

Judge KENNEDY. No.

The CHAIRMAN. Now let me turn to that period, now, after the nomination.

Judge KENNEDY. Now let's be precise, however. I think the nomination was sent to the Senate some weeks after it was announced.

The CHAIRMAN. I beg your pardon. From the time the President had announced his intention——

Judge KENNEDY. At the time I had already met with you and a number of Senators, but if the demarcation in your question is as to the time the President made the announcement in the White House——

The CHAIRMAN. That is what I mean.

Judge KENNEDY. The answer is no, I had not met with any United States Senators prior to that time.

The CHAIRMAN. Now I would like to speak with you about the same issues, subsequent to the President standing with you and announcing to all of the world that you were going to be his nominee.

Have you made any commitments or promises to anyone in order to obtain their support for your nomination?

Judge KENNEDY. I have not done so, and I would consider it highly improper to do so.

The CHAIRMAN. So just to make the record clear, you made no promise to any Member of the Senate on anything?

Judge KENNEDY. Other than that I would be frank and candid in my answers.

The CHAIRMAN. Judge, I am not doubting you for a minute. As I am sure you are aware, though, one of my colleagues is reported to have spoken with you about the issue of abortion on November the 12th at a meeting at the White House.

Let me read to you—and I am sure you have seen the text—from a newspaper article by a columnist named Cal Thomas. And Mr. Thomas says the following happened. I am quoting from his article.

Republican Senator Jesse Helms of North Carolina told me that he and Judge Kennedy met in a private room at the White House on November the 12th.

Then a quote within a quote.

"I think you know where I stand on abortion," Mr. Helms said to Judge Kennedy. Judge Kennedy smiled and answered, "Indeed I do, and I admire it. I am a practicing Catholic."

The article then goes on to say:

Judge Kennedy did not elaborate, but Mr. Helms interpreted the response to mean that Judge Kennedy is opposed to abortion and would look favorably on any case in which the Court's earlier decisions striking down the abortion laws of all 50 States might be overturned.

A bit later in the column, Mr. Thomas continued:

"I am certain as I can be," said Mr. Helms, "without having heard him say I shall vote to reverse *Roe* v. *Wade*—which of course he wasn't going to say—on what he called this 'privacy garbage'—recent Supreme Court decisions involving not only abortion but civil rights, protections for homosexuals—Mr. Helms indicated a certain collegiality with what he believes to be Judge Kennedy's views."

Ultimately though, said, Mr. Helms, quote, "Who knows?," but, quote, "That's where we are with any of the nominees." End of quote. End of column.

Could you, for the record, characterize for us how accurate or inaccurate you think that column is.

Judge KENNEDY. I have not seen that column, but I have absorbed it from what you have said, Senator.

To begin with, I think it is important to say that if I had an undisclosed intention, or a fixed view on a particular case, an absolutely concluded position on a particular case or a particular issue, perhaps I might be obligated to disclose that to you.

I do not have any such views with reference to privacy, or abortion, or the other subjects there mentioned, and therefore, I was not attempting, and would not attempt to try to signal, by inference, or by indirection, my views on those subjects.

The conversation that you referred to was wide-ranging, and of a personal nature. The Senator asked me about my family and my character, and I told him, as I have told others of you, that I admire anyone with strong moral beliefs.

Now it would be highly improper for a judge to allow his, or her, own personal or religious views to enter into a decision respecting a constitutional matter. There are many books that I will not read, that I do not let, or these days do not recommend, my children read. That does not prohibit me from enforcing the first amendment because those books are protected by the first amendment.

A man's, or a woman's, relation to his, or her, God, and the fact that he, or she, may think they are held accountable to a higher power, may be important evidence of a person's character and temperament. It is irrelevant to his, or her, judicial authority. When we decide cases we put such matters aside, and as—I think it was—Daniel Webster said, "Submit to the judgment of the nation as a whole."

The CHAIRMAN. So Judge, when you said—if it is correct—to Senator Helms: "Indeed I do, and I admire it, I am a practicing Catholic," you were not taking, at that point a position on the constitutional question that has been and continues to be before the Court?

Judge KENNEDY. To begin with, that was not the statement.

The CHAIRMAN. Will you tell us what——

Judge KENNEDY. We had a wide-ranging discussion and those two matters were not linked.

The CHAIRMAN. Those two matters were not linked. So the article is incorrect?

Judge KENNEDY. In my view, yes.

The CHAIRMAN. That is fine. I thank you. My time is up. I yield to my colleague from South Carolina.

Senator THURMOND. Thank you, Mr. Chairman.

Judge Kennedy, a fundamental principle of American judicial review is respect for precedent, for the doctrine of stare decisis. This doctrine promoted certainty in the administration of the law, yet at least over 180 times in its history, the Supreme Court has overruled one or more of its precedents, and more than half of these overruling opinions have been issued in the last 37 years.

Judge Kennedy, would you tell the committee what factors you believe attribute to this increase in overruling previous opinions.

Judge KENNEDY. That is a far-ranging question, Senator, which would be an excellent law review article, but let me suggest a few factors.

First, there is a statistical way to fend off your question, by pointing out that the Supreme Court hears many more cases now than it formerly did. You will recall, in the early days of the Republic, when some cases were argued for days.

The CHAIRMAN. He may be the only one able to recall the early days of the Republic, here, on the committee. [Laughter.]

Judge KENNEDY. I was using "you" in the institutional sense, Senator. And that has changed.

Secondly, the Court has taken many more public-law cases on its docket.

And thirdly, there are simply many, many more precedents for the Court to deal with, and so the adjustment, the policing, the shaping of the contours of our law simply require more over ruling, as a statistical matter.

That does seem, though, to be not quite a complete answer to your question, because your question invites at least exploration of the idea whether or not the Supreme Court has changed its own role, or its own view of, its role in the system, or has changed the substantive law, and it has.

In the last 37 years, the Supreme Court has followed the doctrine of incorporation by reference, so that under the Due Process Clause of the 14th amendment, most of the specific provisions of the first eight amendments have been made applicable to the States, including search and seizure, self-incrimination, double jeopardy, and confrontation. Many of these cases, many of these decisions, involved overruling. So there was a substantive change of doctrine that did cause an increase in the number of overruled cases, Senator.

Senator THURMOND. Incidentally, Judge, if I propound any question that you feel would infringe upon the theory that you should not answer questions in case it might come before the Supreme Court, just speak out, because I do not want you to feel obligated to answer if I do.

Judge KENNEDY. Thank you very much, Senator.

Senator THURMOND. Judge Kennedy, we have recently celebrated the 200th anniversary of the Constitution of the United States.

Many Americans expressed their views about the reason for the amazing endurance of this great document. Would you please share with the committee your opinion as to the success of our Constitution, and its accomplishment of being the oldest existing Constitution in the world today.

Judge KENNEDY. Well, the reasons for its survival, and its success, Senator, are many fold. The first is the skill with which it was written. Few times in history have men sat down to control their own destiny before a government took power; in the age of Pericles, and in the Roman empire, just before Augustus, and again, in 1789. The framers wrote with great skill, and that is one reason for the survival of the Constitution, for the survival of the Constitution despite a horrible civil war, a war arguably, and I think probably, necessary to cure a defect in the Constitution.

Then there is the respect that the American people have for the rule of law. We have a remarkable degree of compliance with the law in this country, because of the respect that the people have for the Constitution and for the men who wrote it.

My third suggestion for why there has been a great success in the American constitutional experience is the respect that each branch of the government shows to the other. This is a vital part of our constitutional tradition. It has remained true since the founding of the Republic.

Senator LEAHY. I want to ask you questions in three different areas, primarily. One is in the privacy area; one is in the criminal law area—I spent about a third of my adult life as a prosecutor, so I have an interest there, and you have written a number of cases there; and then lastly in the first amendment area

Normally, in these things, I take first amendment first, but a number of your comments to me privately, a number of decisions you have made in the past, give me a lot more comfort in those areas than a number of other nominees have.

To begin in the area of privacy, I wonder if I might just follow up on a couple of questions. Senator Biden asked you a number of questions in this area yesterday. In response to one, you said that you think, "most Americans, most lawyers, most judges, believe that liberty includes protection of a value we call privacy."

You did not state your own view at that point. But slightly later you said that you had no fixed view on the right of privacy. Senator DeConcini followed up on that. And in response to a question from him, you said that you had no doubt about the existence of a right to privacy, although you prefer to think of it as a value of privacy.

Is this a semantic difference? Or is there a difference between right and value? And if there is a difference, what is your view?

Judge KENNEDY. I pointed out at one time in yesterday's hearings that I am not sure whether it is a semantic quibble or not. I think that the concept of liberty in the due process clause is quite expansive, quite sufficient, to protect the values of privacy that Americans legitimately think are part of their constitutional heritage. It seems to me that sometimes by using some word that is not in the Constitution, we almost create more uncertainties than we solve. It is very clear that privacy is a most helpful noun, in that it seems to sum up rather quickly values that we hold very deeply.

Senator LEAHY. But you understand——

The CHAIRMAN. Will the Senator yield on that point?

Senator LEAHY. Certainly.

The CHAIRMAN. And this may save some time, because I had a whole round of questions on this.

Let me put it to you very bluntly. Do you think *Griswold* was reasoned properly?

Judge KENNEDY. I really think I would like to draw the line and not talk about the *Griswold* case so far as its reasoning or its result.

I would say that if you were going to propose a statute or a hypothetical that infringed upon the core values of privacy that the Constitution protects, you would be hard put to find a stronger case than *Griswold*.

The CHAIRMAN. That doesn't answer the question. Is there a marital right to privacy protected by the Constitution?

Judge KENNEDY. Yes—pardon, is there a——

The CHAIRMAN. Marital right to privacy.

Judge KENNEDY. Marital right to privacy; that is what I thought you said. Yes, sir.

The CHAIRMAN. Thank you.

Senator LEAHY. Well, if I might follow on that, have you had any cases so far when you have been in the Court of Appeals where you have had to follow the *Griswold* case?

Judge KENNEDY. The *Beller* v. *Middendorf* case was one where we examined it and discussed it extensively. The case we discussed yesterday.

And I'm tempted to say that is the only one.

Senator LEAHY. But in that, what reference did you make to *Griswold*?

Judge KENNEDY. We tried, I tried, in the *Beller* case, to understand what the Supreme Court's doctrine was in the area of substantive due process protection, and came to the conclusion, as stated in the opinion, that the Supreme Court has recognized that there is a substantive component to the due process clause.

I was willing to assume that for the purposes of that opinion. I think that is right. I think there is a substantive component to the due process clause.

Senator LEAHY. And that is your view today?

Judge KENNEDY. Yes.

Senator LEAHY. When you first——

Judge KENNEDY. And I think the value of privacy is a very important part of that substantive component.

Senator LEAHY. The reason we spend so much time on this is that it is probably the area where we hear as much controversy and as much debate in the country about Supreme Court decisions as any single issue. Certainly I do in my own State, and I am sure others do. It is a matter that newspaper debates will go on, editorial debates will go on.

And in a court that often seems tightly divided, everybody is going to be looking at you. None of us are asking you to prejudge cases. But I think also, though, if we are going to respond to our own responsibility to the Senate, we have to have a fairly clear view of what your views are before we vote to confirm you.

I should also just add—something that obviously goes without saying—we expect you to speak honestly and truthfully to your views, and nobody doubts but that you will. Some commentators and some Senators seem to make the mistake of thinking that a view expressed by a nominee here at these confirmation hearings must, by its expression, become engraved in stone, and that a nominee can never change that view. You do not have that view, do you?

Judge KENNEDY. Well, I would be very careful about saying that a judge should make representations to the committee that he immediately renounces when he goes on the court.

Senator LEAHY. That is not my point, Judge Kennedy. What I am saying is that I would assume that your own views on issues have evolved over the years.

Judge KENNEDY. Yes.

Senator LEAHY. What I am suggesting is that even as to views expressed here, should you go on the Supreme Court, there is nothing to stop an evolution of your views in either direction, or in any direction?

Judge KENNEDY. I think you would expect that evolution to take place. And with reference to the right of privacy, we are very much in a stage of evolution and debate.

I think that the public and the legislature have every right to contribute to that debate. The Constitution is made for that kind of debate.

The Constitution is not weak because we do not know the answer to a difficult problem. It is strong because we can find that answer.

Now it takes time to find it, and the judicial method is slow.

Senator LEAHY. It is also an evolutionary method, is it not?

Judge KENNEDY. It is the gradual process of inclusion and exclusion, as Mr. Justice Cardozo called it. And it may well be that we are still in a very rudimentary state of the law so far as the right of privacy is concerned.

If you had a nominee 20 years ago for the Supreme Court of the United States, and you asked him or her what does the first amendment law say with reference to a State suit based on defamation against a newspaper, not the most gifted prophet could have predicted the course and the shape and the content of the law today.

And we may well be there with reference to some of these other issues that we are discussing.

Senator LEAHY. I would hope that all Members of the Senate will listen to that answer. I think that the fallacy that has come up, in some of the debate on Supreme Court nominees—one that has probably been heard across the political spectrum—is that we can somehow take a snapshot during these hearings that will determine for all time how Judge Anthony Kennedy or Judge Anybody is going to then vote on the Supreme Court on every issue. And that just cannot be done, and in fact, should not be done. That is not the purpose of these hearings.

Senator HUMPHREY. I have a speaking engagement off the Hill at 12, so I cannot take too much time. I am sure you will be glad to hear that, Mr. Chairman.

I want to go back to the ninth amendment, Judge Kennedy. If I understood some of the questions correctly, some Senators seem to be trying to get you to say that there are some privacy rights hiding there in the ninth amendment waiting to come out, come out, wherever you are. That seems to me to be a very generous reading of the intent of the authors and ratifiers of the ninth amendment. Wouldn't you agree?

Would you give us your understanding of the historical intent of the ninth amendment?

Judge KENNEDY. Well, as I have indicated, the intent is really much in doubt. My view was that Madison wrote it for two reasons. Well, they are really related. He knew, as did the other framers, that they were engaged on an enterprise where they occupied the stage of world history; not just the stage of legal history, but the stage of world history. These were famous, famous men even by the standards of a day unaccustomed to celebrities. And he was very, very careful to recognize his own fallibilities and his own limitations.

So he first of all wanted to make it clear that the first eight amendments were not an exhaustive catalogue of all human rights. Second, he wanted to make it clear that State ratifying conventions, in drafting their own constitutions, could go much further than he did. And the ninth amendment was in that sense a recognition of State sovereignty and a recognition of State independence and a recognition of the role of the States in defining human rights. That is why it is something of an irony to say that the ninth amendment can actually be used by a federal court to tell the State that it cannot do something. But the incorporation doctrine may lead to that conclusion, and that is the tension.

Senator HUMPHREY. May lead to that conclusion.

Judge KENNEDY. May. May lead to that conclusion.

Senator HUMPHREY. Well, let me ask you this, finally. I do hope we will have an opportunity to think about matters further and ask further questions of you. Let me just ask you this, finally, with regard to privacy rights.

What standards are there available to a judge, a Justice in this case, to determine which private consensual activities are protected by the Constitution and which are not?

Judge KENNEDY. There are the whole catalogue of considerations that I have indicated, and any short list or even any attempt at an exhaustive list, I suppose, would take on the attributes of an argument for one side or the other.

A very abbreviated list of the considerations are the essentials of the right to human dignity, the injury to the person, the harm to the person, the anguish to the person, the inability of the person to manifest his or her own personality, the inability of a person to obtain his or her own self-fulfillment, the inability of a person to reach his or her own potential.

On the other hand, the rights of the State are very strong indeed. There is the deference that the Court owes to the democratic process, the deference that the Court owes to the legislative process, the respect that must be given to the role of the legislature, which itself is an interpreter of the Constitution, and the respect that must be given to the legislature because it knows the values of the people.

Senator HUMPHREY. Those, especially the first category, sound like very subjective judgments.

Judge KENNEDY. The task of the judge is to try to find objective referents for each of those categories.

Senator HUMPHREY. Thank you, Mr. Chairman. Thank you, Judge.

Senator HUMPHREY. Yes.

In your Stanford speech you point out that in the post-*Griswold* privacy cases the debate shifts to the word "privacy" rather than to the constitutional—to a constitutional term such as "liberty."

What is the significance in that statement? What are you trying to say?

Judge KENNEDY. Well, I was trying to indicate that simply because we find a new word we don't avoid a whole lot of very difficult problems. It is not clear to me that substituting the word "privacy" is much of an advance over interpreting the word "liberty," which is already in the Constitution.

And I indicated that, to illustrate that, that the Convention on Human Rights, which contains the word "private," produced a case which had many of the same issues in it that we would have to confront, and so that the word "privacy" should not be something that convinces us that we have much certainty in this area.

Senator HUMPHREY. Are you saying that these privacy cases would be better dealt with under the liberty clause?

Judge KENNEDY. That is why I have indicated that I think liberty does protect the value of privacy in some instances.

Senator HUMPHREY. You would prefer then to deal with privacy cases under the liberty clause?

Judge KENNEDY. Yes.

Senator HUMPHREY. As opposed to dealing with them under emanations of penumbrae?

Judge KENNEDY. Yes, sir.

Senator HUMPHREY. Ever seen an emanation? That is a real term of art, isn't it? I am not a lawyer. Had that ever been used before?

Judge KENNEDY. Certainly not in a constitutional case.

Senator HUMPHREY. That is really a, that one is really a shameless case of——

The CHAIRMAN. Senator, excuse me.

Senator HUMPHREY. Yes?

The CHAIRMAN. The Senator from West Virginia would like to ask you a question.

Senator BYRD. Did you say emanation? To emanate? What is the word you are referring to?

Judge KENNEDY. Emanations.

Senator BYRD. Emanations?

Judge KENNEDY. Emanations, yes. "Penumbras and emanations" was the phrase used in the *Griswold* case.

Senator BYRD. Thank you. That word is not in the Constitution, though, is it?

Judge KENNEDY. Not at all. And I have indicated it is not even in any previous—the Senator indicated it was not even in any previous cases.

Senator BYRD. But the word "liberty" is in the Constitution?

Judge KENNEDY. Yes, sir.

Senator BYRD. I like that word "liberty" in the Constitution.

Senator HUMPHREY. Do you think there are a whole lot more emanations from this penumbra?

Judge KENNEDY. I don't find the phrase very helpful.

Senator HUMPHREY. Good. Well, two hopes. Hope number one is that you will at least once a year read your Stanford speech. Hope number two is that you will not intrude on our turf. Thank you.

Judge KENNEDY. Thank you, Senator. I will certainly commit to the former, and I will try to comply with the latter.

NOMINATION OF ANTHONY M. KENNEDY TO BE AN ASSOCIATE JUSTICE OF THE UNITED STATES SUPREME COURT

REPORT

OF THE

COMMITTEE ON THE JUDICIARY UNITED STATES SENATE

together with

ADDITIONAL AND SUPPLEMENTAL VIEWS

FEBRUARY 1, 1988.—Ordered to be printed

U.S. GOVERNMENT PRINTING OFFICE

19-119

WASHINGTON : 1988

V. JUDGE KENNEDY'S TESTIMONY SUGGESTS THAT HE HAS AN ABIDING RESPECT FOR PRECEDENT

As Senator Thurmond stated, "a fundamental principle of American judicial review is respect for precedent, for the doctrine of *stare decisis.*" (Tr., 12/14/87, at 105.) In neither his opinions on the court of appeals nor in his speeches has Judge Kennedy commented on the value of precedent in our constitutional tradition or on the factors upon which he would rely in determining whether a decision should be overruled. His testimony on this all-important issue was thus critical to gaining a thorough understanding of his judicial philosophy.

Judge Kennedy's most extensive testimony on this issue came in response to questioning by Senator Heflin. With respect to his approach generally to stare decisis and to its role in our system of law, Judge Kennedy stated:

> Stare decisis is really a description of the whole judicial process which proceeds on a case-by-case basis as judges slowly and deliberately decide the facts of a particular case and hope that their decision in this case yields a general principle that may be of assistance to themselves and to later courts.

> Stare decisis insures impartiality. . . . It ensures that from case to case, from judge to judge, from age to age, the law will have a stability that the people can understand and rely upon. . . .

> Now there have been discussions that stare decisis should not apply as rigidly in the constitutional area as in other areas, and the argument is that there is no other overruling body in the constitutional area. . . . On the

other hand, . . . it seems to me that when judges have announced that a particular rule is found in the Constitution that is entitled to very great weight, the Court does two things. It interprets history and it makes history, and it has got to keep those two roles separate. Stare decisis helps them do that. (Tr., 12/14/87, at 211-12.)

Judge Kennedy also identified for Senator Heflin the factors upon which he would rely in determining whether a case should be overruled:

In any case . . . the role of the judge is to approach the subject with an open mind, to listen to the counsel, and to look at the facts of the particular case to see what the injury is, see what the hurt is, to see what the claim is; and then to listen to his or her colleagues, and then to research the law. What does the most recent decision, the decision that is before the Court if it is subject to being examined for possible overruling, if that is the case, what does that decision say? What is its logic? What is its reasoning? What has been its acceptance by the lower courts? Has the rule proven to be workable? Does the rule fit with what the judge deems to be the purpose of the Constitution as we have understood it over the last 200 years? And history is tremendously important in this regard. (*Id.* at 211.)

And under questioning from Senator Leahy, Judge Kennedy added that courts should "look to see how the great Justices that have sat on the court for years have understood and interpreted the Constitution, and from that you get a sense of what the Constitution really means." (Tr., 12/15/87, at 58-59.)

In his testimony, Judge Kennedy also indicated that he does not have any list of cases that he believes should be overruled. The following exchange is informative on this point:

Senator HUMPHREY. Quoting . . . from your Stanford speech, Judge, you said: The unrestrained exercise of judicial authority ought to be recognized for what it is—the raw exercise of political power.

* * * * *

. . . Is Anthony Kennedy concerned that judges have sometimes overreached? . . . Is it your view that at times in our history, the Supreme Court has overreached, has exercised, rawly exercised political power?

Judge KENNEDY. There are a few cases where it is very safe to say that they did, the *Dred Scott* case being the paradigmatic example of judicial excess.

Senator HUMPHREY. . . . How about in modern times? . . .

Judge KENNEDY. I did not really have a list of cases in mind. I had more in mind an approach, an attitude that I sometimes see reflected on the bench.Jacket 019-119 Folios 750-751 Extensions A013er.013

The CHAIRMAN. If I understand the answer to the question the Senator asked, is that there are no specific cases which you had in mind when you referred to the unrestricted exercise——

Judge KENNEDY. That is correct. None come immediately to mind. But that concern always underlies the examination by a judge of his own writings. . . .

* * * * *

Senator HUMPHREY. This approach and attitude which caused you to make the statement cautioning against unrestrained exercise of judicial authority . . . is that something that bothers you, professionally?

Judge KENNEDY. Well, I do not think the judiciary of the United States, as a whole, has departed from its mandate or its authority, but I simply think it is a concern that must always remain . . . in the open, so that judges are aware of the limitations on their authority. (Tr., 12/15/87, at 66–70; emphasis added.)

Judge Kennedy's testimony shows a respect for precedent. While he may from time to time seek further movement in the law, there is no evidence of a desire for abrupt departures from carefully developed doctrines or established lines of decisions. As summarized by Professor Tribe:

Judge KENNEDY . . . has both expressed in his speeches, and exemplified in his judicial work, a commitment to gradual evolution of doctrine and precedent, within the context of a principled exposition of constitutional text, history and structure that is not tied down by any doctrinaire and backward-looking philosophy of an originalist sort.

* * * * *

[To Judge Kennedy,] stare decisis is less a method or doctrine than a summary of how courts, building their understanding of texts and traditions in part upon the perceptions of their judicial predecessors, inevitably operate in a system such as ours. . . . Ideally, in the judicial world envisioned by Judge Kennedy, it is the ongoing process of refining and perfecting the vision of the future implicit in the work of the past that marks the judge's vision. (Answer of Professor Laurence Tribe to written question from Chairman Biden.)

* * * * *

Judge Kennedy's testimony about this over-all judicial philosophy and approach to constitutional interpretation was informative, enlightening and encouraging. It is clear that he has no definitive, overarching theory to explain the Constitution but is instead still searching for a better understanding of the document and the difficult questions it often presents. His view that "New generations add new insights"—that our capacity to understand the basic principles established by the Framers improves with time—is distinctive and is likely to contribute to our evolving understanding of the Constitution.

PART THREE: JUDGE KENNEDY'S VISION OF LIBERTY UNDER THE CONSTITUTION

I. JUDGE KENNEDY'S APPROACH TO LIBERTY AND FUNDAMENTAL RIGHTS IS WITHIN THE TRADITION OF SUPREME COURT JURISPRUDENCE

The established jurisprudence of the Supreme Court holds that the "liberty" clauses of the 5th and 14th Amendments protect against governmental invasion of a person's substantive liberty and privacy. Each of the 105 previous and current Justices has endorsed the view, expressed in a variety of ways, that the Constitution protects some rights that are not spelled out in the text and has not interpreted the Constitution as a narrow code of enumerated rights. The second Justice Harlan, for example, recognized that liberty "is not a series of isolated points pricked out" in terms of specific consitutional provisions but is instead "a rational continuum which, broadly speaking, includes a freedom from all substantial and arbitrary impositions and restraints." (*Poe* v. *Ullman*, 367 U.S. 497, 543 (1961) (Harlan, J., dissenting).)

Judge Kennedy's views, particularly as set forth in his testimony, appear to be within this 200-year tradition establishing that the people retain certain fundamental rights that courts are to discern and protect. This is evident, for example, from an exchange between Senator Heflin and Judge Kennedy, in which the nominee was asked about his statement (*see* Canadian Institute speech, at 18–20) that most rights in the Constitution are enforced as negatives or prohibitions, rather than an affirmative grants:

> Senator HEFLIN. . . . You seem to view these prohibitions in the Constitution as limiting the expansion of judicial power. Are they also, though, a means of preventing Government from denying individuals their fundamental rights?
>
> Judge KENNEDY. I would agree that they certainly are, Senator. . . . (Tr. 12/14/87, at 209–10; emphasis added.)

Judge Kennedy's record also makes clear that he rejects the view that the people have no liberties except those specifically granted to them by their Government. As he said in a recent speech, "[a]s the Framers progressed with their studies, [republican government] came to mean . . . a government that emanates from the people, rather than being a concession to the people from some overarching sovereign." ("Federalism: The Theory and the Reality," Historical Society for the United States District Court for the Northern District of California, October 26, 1987, at 3.) This is consistent with an acceptance of our Constitution as establishing a system by which the people have all the liberties except those specifically relinquished to the Government.

The committee agrees with Judge Kennedy that the "underpinning of our Constitution is a great heritage that ensures our written Constitution is a living reality, not, in Madison's phrase, a mere 'parchment barrier.'" (Answer to written question No. 5 from Senator Simon.)

II. JUDGE KENNEDY PLACES GREAT WEIGHT ON THE PRESERVATION AND ADVANCEMENT OF INDIVIDUAL LIBERTY

One approach to liberty and fundamental rights is that taken by the second Justice Harlan, one of the great judicial conservatives of this century. He argued for a conception of the due process clause that was flexible and was independent of, but drawing support from, the Bill of Rights. The clearest exposition of his view is in *Poe* v. *Ullman, supra,* in which he said:

> Due process has not been reduced to any formula; its content cannot be determined by reference to any code. The best that can be said is that through the course of this Court's decisions it has represented **the balance which our Nation, built upon the postulates of respect for the liberty of the individual, has struck between that liberty and the demands of organized society.** . . . The balance of which I speak is the balance struck by this country, having regard to what history teaches are the traditions from which it developed as well as the traditions from which it broke. **That tradition is a living thing.** (*Poe*, 367 U.S. at 542 (Harlan, J., dissenting).)

And in *Griswold* v. *Connecticut,* 381 U.S. 479 (1965), Justice Harlan stated that proper consitutional analysis required an examination of whether the law "infringes the Due Process Clause of the Fourteenth Amendment because the enactment violated basic values **implicit in the concept of ordered liberty.'**" (381 U.S. at 500; emphasis added, Harlan, J., concurring.) [3]

Judge Kennedy's views appear to be within the tradition exemplified by Justice Harlan. In his testimony, for example, the nominee emphasized the relationship between order and liberty and the role of the court in finding the proper balance. He said in response to a question from Senator Hatch that "I do not think that there is a choice between order and liberty. We can have both. Without **ordered liberty, there is no liberty at all.**" (Tr., 12/14/87, at 157; emphasis added; *see also* Tr., 12/15/87, at 146 ("You may have order and liberty, and without both you only have anarchy.").)

Judge Kennedy's testimony also reveals a recognition on his part that a principal objective of this Nation's founders was the preservation and advancement of individual liberty. Indeed, the term "liberty" in the 5th and 14th Amendments is a key watchword for Judge Kennedy. This is clear from an exchange with Chairman Biden:

> Judge KENNEDY. The Framers had an idea which is central to Western thought. . . . It is central to the idea of the rule of law. **That is that there is a zone of liberty, a zone of protection, a line that is drawn where the individual**

---

[3] Justice Harlan relied here on Justice Cardozo's often-cited statement that there are certain "principle[s] of justice so rooted in the traditions and conscience of our people as to be ranked as fundamental" and thus "implicit in the concept of ordered liberty." (*Palko* v. *Connecticut,* 302 U.S. 319, 325 (1937).)

can tell the Government: Beyond this line you may not
go.

Now the great question in constitutional law is: One,
where is the line drawn? And, two, what are the principles
that you refer to in drawing this line?

The CHAIRMAN. But there is a line.

Judge KENNEDY. There is a line. It is wavering; it is
amorphous; it is uncertain. But this is the judicial function. (Tr., 12/14/87, at 93; emphasis added.)

Importantly, Judge Kennedy does not view the Constitution as
essentially a zero-sum system, in which the rights for some necessarily come only at the expense of others. He agreed with Senator
Simon's statement that "in our society . . . when you expand the
liberty of any of us, you expand the liberty of all of us," and noted
that when the Supreme Court has extended the liberty of some,
"all of our freedoms have been enhanced." (Answer to written
question No. 2 from Senator Simon.)

In Judge Kennedy's view, therefore, the core question is how far
liberty extends and not whether it exists in the first instance.
Judge Kennedy looks for the "wavering line" between the state
and the individual so that he may mark the boundaries of the
"zone of liberty." And a right protected by the liberty clause need
not be specifically mentioned in the text of the Constitution, since
"liberty," as that term is understood by this nominee, "extends
beyond the substantive points that are marked out in the Bill of
Rights." (Tribe testimony, Tr., 12/16/87, at 98.)

III. JUDGE KENNEDY'S UNDERSTANDING OF THE DUE PROCESS CLAUSE PROTECTS THE VALUES OF PRIVACY

A. Judge Kennedy's Concept of Liberty Encompasses the Values of Privacy, Including the Right to Marital Privacy

Judge Kennedy testified that the due process clause protects the
values of privacy. This was clear in an exchange with Senator
DeConcini:

Senator DECONCINI. . . . [I]t appears from reading your
[Canadian Institute] speech, that you have concluded, without question, that there is a fundamental right to privacy.
And I think the Chairman had you state that, and that is
your position, correct?

Judge KENNEDY. Well, I have indicated that that is essentially correct. I prefer to think of the value of privacy
as being protected by the clause, liberty, and maybe that is
a semantic quibble, maybe it is not.

Senator DECONCINI. But it is there, is that——

Judge KENNEDY. Yes, sir.

Senator DECONCINI. No question about it being in existence?

Judge KENNEDY. Yes, sir. (Tr., 12/14/87, at 176; emphasis added.)

Senator Leahy pursued this point further, asking Judge Kennedy
whether in fact he had only a semantic quibble. (Tr., 12/15/87, at
41.) Judge Kennedy responded:

> . . . I think that the concept of liberty in the due process clause is quite expansive, quite sufficient, to protect the values of privacy that Americans legitimately think are part of their constitutional heritage. . . . It is very clear that privacy is a most helpful noun, in that it seems to sum up rather quickly values that we hold very deeply. (*Id.* at 42; emphasis added.) [4]

Then, in an exchange with Chairman Biden, Judge Kennedy stated that in his view, the Constitution protects a marital right to privacy:

> The CHAIRMAN. . . . Do you think *Griswold* was reasoned properly?
>
> Judge KENNEDY. I really think I would like to draw the line and not talk about the *Griswold* case so far as its reasoning or result.
>
> I would say that if you were going to propose a statute or a hypothetical that infringed upon the core values of privacy that the Constitution protects, you would be hard put to find a stronger case than *Griswold*.
>
> The CHAIRMAN. . . . Is there a marital right to privacy protected by the Constitution?
>
> * * * * *
>
> Judge KENNEDY. . . . Yes, sir. (*Id.* at 42–43; emphasis added.)

B. Judge Kennedy's Dissent in *United States* v. *Penn* Demonstrates His Respect for Privacy and Family Rights and His Willingness to Apply Existing Decisions to Novel Situations

Judge Kennedy's dissent in *United States* v. *Penn*, 647 F.2d 876 (9th Cir.), *cert. denied*, 449 U.S. 903 (1980), demonstrates his respect for fundamental rights involving privacy and the family. He argued that the police violated the Fourth Amendment by offering $5 to a 5-year-old child in order to get him to inform them where his mother kept her heroin. In Judge Kennedy's view:

> The existence of the parent-child union and the fundamental place it has in our culture require no citation, but it is perhaps appropriate to note that courts have protected it where the threat of disruption is in some respects more attenuated than in the circumstances of the case before us. *See Moore* v. *City of East Cleveland*, 431 U.S. 494 (1977), *Wisconsin* v. *Yoder*, 406 U.S. 205 (1972), *Pierce* v. *Society of Sisters*, 268 U.S. 510 (1925).
>
> . . . [W]e have the authority, and the duty, to protect the relation between a mother and child from such manipulation.
>
> . . . I view the police practice here as both pernicious in itself and dangerous as precedent. Indifference to personal

---

[4] Judge Kennedy reiterated this point in response to a written question from Senator Simon, noting that "I believe that the liberty protected by the Fifth and Fourteenth Amendments includes protection for the value that we call privacy." (Answer to written question No. 12 from Senator Simon.)

liberty is but the precursor of the state's hostility to it. (*Id.* at 888–89.)

This statement shows respect for the parent-child relationship. Furthermore, it illustrates Judge Kennedy's support for the view expressed in the Supreme Court decisions cited that the Constitution protects aspects of that relationship. Judge Kennedy's willingness to apply these cases to a novel situation also demonstrates a genuine commitment to the idea of a living and evolving Constitution.

IV. IN JUDGE KENNEDY'S VIEW, PRIVACY IS AN IMPORTANT PART OF THE SUBSTANTIVE COMPONENT OF THE DUE PROCESS CLAUSE

During his appearance before the committee, Judge Kennedy was asked by Senator Leahy about his opinion in *Beller* v. *Middendorf, supra,* Part Two, Section IV. The following exchange took place:

> Judge KENNEDY We . . . came to the conclusion, as stated in the opinion, that the Supreme Court has recognized that there is a substantive component to the due process clause.
>
> And I was willing to assume that for the purposes of [the] opinion. **And I think that is right; I think there is a substantive component to the due process clause.**
>
> Senator LEAHY. And that is your view today?
>
> Judge KENNEDY. Yes. . . . **And I think the value of privacy is a very important part of that substantive component.** (Tr., 12/15/87, at 43–44; emphasis added.)

V. JUDGE KENNEDY HAS A REASONED AND BALANCED APPROACH TO THE NINTH AMENDMENT, ONE THAT IS FULLY CONSISTENT WITH HIS UNDERSTANDING OF "LIBERTY" IN THE DUE PROCESS CLAUSE

Judge Kennedy was quite careful in expressing his views about the Ninth Amendment, which provides that "[t]he enumeration in the Constitution, of certain rights, shall not be construed to deny or disparage others retained by the people." One view was that the Amendment was designed to protect the ability of the States to confer rights beyond those in the Bill of Rights. (*See, e.g.,* Tr., 12/14/87, at 96; Tr., 12/15/87, at 79.) A second view is that the Amendment shows a belief by the Framers "that the first eight amendments were not an exhaustive catalogue of all human rights." (Tr., 12/15/87, at 79.) In fact, Judge Kennedy testified that "the Court is treating [the Ninth Amendment] as something of a **reserve clause,** to be held in the event that that the phrase 'liberty' and the other spacious phrases in the Constitution appear to be inadequate for the Court's decision." (Tr., 12/14/87, at 97; emphasis added.)

Chairman Biden raised the Ninth Amendment with Judge Kennedy in the context of Chief Justice Burger's majority opinion in *Richmond Newspapers* v. *Virginia,* 448 U.S. 555 (1980). Writing that "the concerns expressed by Madison and others have . . . been resolved; fundamental rights, even though not expressly guaranteed, have been recognized by the court as indispensable to the enjoyment of rights not explicitly defined," the Chief Justice cited the Ninth Amendment. (*Id.* at 580.) And he referred to it as a "constitutional savings clause," (*id.* at 579, n.15), a term quite similar to the "reserve clause" idea invoked by Judge Kennedy. Most importantly, Judge Kennedy responded to the chairman's reference to *Richmond Newspapers* by noting that the Court has not found it necessary to rely on the Ninth Amendment because "liberty can support" the Chief Justice's conclusions about fundamental rights. (Tr., 12/15/87, at 219.)

VI. JUDGE KENNEDY ACCEPTS A CLEAR ROLE FOR THE COURTS IN THE FUNDAMENTAL RIGHTS AREA

The hearings made clear that Judge Kennedy favors an appropriate role for the courts in defining the contours of "liberty" and in determining whether it extends to situations not previously addressed. The nominee testified, for example, that despite the difficult questions in this area, the courts have a clear responsibility to act. (Tr., 12/14/87, at 95.) Furthermore, referring to the line between protection for the individual and governmental interference, Judge Kennedy said: "The Supreme Court's role is to determine where that line is drawn and to determine what principles are to be used in defining the protections contained within the zone of liberty." (Answer to written question No. 1 from Senator Simon.)

When asked by Senator DeConcini "[h]ow would you define the enforcement power given to the judiciary," (Tr., 12/14/87, at 178), Judge Kennedy responded:

> Well, the enforcement power of the judiciary to ensure that the word liberty in the Constitution is given its full and necessary meaning, consistently with the purposes of the document as we understand it. (*Id.* at 178.)

Judge Kennedy added in response to a question from Senator Humphrey that "[t]he Framers had . . . a very important idea when they used the word 'person' and when they used the word 'liberty.' And these words have content in the history of Western thought and in the history of our law and in the history of the Constitution, and I think judges can give that content." (Tr., 12/15/87, at 204.)

In Judge Kennedy's view, however, liberty and privacy are not boundless or unlimited. When Senator Humphrey asked whether the due process clause is "a blank check," for example, Judge Kennedy said, "[c]ertainly not." (*Id.* at 64.) Judge Kennedy's position is that the contours and limits of liberty are debatable and that it is the role of the courts to decide cases within the confines of that debate. With respect to the right of privacy, Judge Kennedy said, "we are very much in a stage of evolution and debate . . . [W]e are still in a very rudimentary state of the law so far as the right of privacy is concerned." (*Id.* at 45-46.) And Judge Kennedy stressed that "the Constitution is made for that kind of debate. The Constitution is not weak, because we do not know the answer to a difficult problem. It is strong because we can find that answer." (*Id.*)

Judge Kennedy provided the committee with some criteria he would use to define the contours of liberty in a particular case. Responding to a question from Senator Humphrey about the standards available to the court "to determine which private consensual activities are protected by the Constitution and which are not," (Tr., 12/15/87, at 80), Judge Kennedy identified the following factors:

> [T]he essentiality of the right to human dignity, the injury to the person, the harm to the person, the anguish to the person, the inability of the person to manifest his or her own personality, the inability of a person not to obtain his or her own self-fulfillment, the inability of a person not to reach his or her own potential. (*Id.* at 80.)

And in response to a question from Senator Leahy, Judge Kennedy said:

> [E]ssentially, we look to see the concept of individuality and liberty and dignity that those who drafted the Constitution understood . . . We see whether or not the right has been accepted as part of the rights of a free people in the historical interpretation of our own Constitution and the intention of the Framers. (*Id.* at 57.)

Judge Kennedy also indicated that these factors must be balanced against the interests asserted by the state. Those interests, he said,

> are very strong. . . . There is the deference that the court owes to the democratic process, the deference that the court owes to the legislative process, the respect that must be given to the role of the legislature, which itself is an interpreter of the Constitution, the respect that must be given to the legislature because it knows the values of the people. (*Id.* at 80–81.)

*   *   *   *   *

The committee did not ask for, of course, nor did it receive, any guarantees as to how a "Justice" Kennedy would resolve future cases involving liberty and privacy issues. Nevertheless, the committee was encouraged by Judge Kennedy's testimony on the liberty protected by the Constitution. Indeed, his evolving understanding of the commands of the 5th and 14th Amendments that no person shall be deprived of "life, liberty, or property, without due process of law;" his recognition that the liberty clause is a "spacious phrase;" his belief that it protects the values of privacy; and his clear acceptance of a role for the courts in outlining the contours of liberty—no matter how difficult such questions might be—all suggest that, if confirmed as the 106th Justice, he would be within the 200-year tradition of Supreme Court jurisprudence.

PART SIX: JUDGE KENNEDY TESTIFIED THAT HE MADE NO COMMITMENTS TO THE ADMINIS-TRATION OR TO ANY OTHER PARTY IN CON-NECTION WITH HIS NOMINATION OR CONFIR-MATION

Under questioning by Chairman Biden, Judge Kennedy testified that he made no commitments to the Administration or to any other party in connection with either his nomination or confirmation. With respect to an October 28, 1987 meeting among Judge Kennedy and officials of the White House and Justice Department, for example, the following exchange took place:

> The CHAIRMAN. . . . Were you asked at that meeting how you would rule on any legal issue?
>
> Judge KENNEDY. I was not, and I was asked no question which came even close to the zone of what I would consider infringing on judicial independence.
>
> I was asked no question which even came close to the zone of what I would consider improper. I was asked no question which came even close to the zone of eliciting a volunteered comment from me as to how I would rule on any particular case, or on any pending issue.
>
> The CHAIRMAN. Judge, were you asked about your personal opinion on any controversial issue?
>
> Judge KENNEDY. I was not.
>
> The CHAIRMAN. Did anyone ask you what, as a personal matter, you thought of any issue or case?
>
> Judge KENNEDY. No such questions were asked, and I volunteered no such comments.
>
> The CHAIRMAN. And were you asked anything about cases currently before the Court?
>
> Judge KENNEDY. No, sir. (Tr., 12/14/87, at 100.)

Chairman Biden also asked about meetings subsequent to the President's announcement of Judge Kennedy's selection:

> The CHAIRMAN. Now I would like to speak with you about the same issues, subsequent to the President . . . announcing . . . that you were going to be his nominee.
>
> Have you made any commitments or promises to anyone in order to obtain their support for your nomination?
>
> Judge KENNEDY. I have not done so, and I would consider it highly improper to do so.
>
> The CHAIRMAN. So just to make the record clear, you made no promise to any member of the Senate on anything?
>
> Judge KENNEDY. Other than that I would be frank and candid in my answers. (*Id.* at 101–02.)

Finally, Chairman Biden inquired about a newspaper column that recounted a meeting between Judge Kennedy and Senator Helms, in which Judge Kennedy was reported to have given some signal about his views on abortion. Judge Kennedy indicated that the column was incorrect (*Id.* at 105), and stated:

> . . . I think it is important to say that if I had an undisclosed intention, or a fixed view, on a particular case, an absolutely concluded position on a particular case or a particular issue, perhaps I might be obligated to disclose that to you.
>
> I do not have any such views with reference to privacy, or abortion, or the other subjects there mentioned [in the column], and therefore, I was not attempting, and would not attempt to try to signal, by inference, or by indirection, my views on those subjects. (*Id.* at 103–04.)

As Senator Metzenbaum said with respect to the column: "We certainly know that Judge Kennedy specifically disavowed the facts as claimed in that article. . . . And he was very categorical and very unequivocal in saying it just did not happen that way." (Tr., 12/16/87, at 199.)

CONCLUSION

Under Article II of the Constitution, the President has the right to name justices to the Supreme Court—with the "advice and consent" of the Senate. Since Justice Powell resigned in June 1987, this committee has held hearings on two nominees. During each set of hearings, the committee examined the nominee's judicial philosophy and approach to interpreting the Constitution. It has in each occasion probed the nominee's views on the Constitution's fundamental law, his commitment to our constitutional scheme and his vision of the Supreme Court's role in interpreting the supreme law of the land. That examination, as the committee's vote on the two nominees makes unequivocally clear, does not necessarily guarantee a particular outcome. Rather, it is the means through which the committee develops the record on which the Senate exercises its constitutional duty of advice and consent.

The committee has concluded that Judge Kennedy's judicial philosophy and approach to constitutional interpretation is consistent with the history and tradition of this Nation and of the Supreme Court. The nominee's testimony established that he respects a continuous evolution of constitutional doctrine. His vision of constitutional interpretation seems to invoke Justice Holmes's reminder that cases "must be considered in the light of our whole experience and not merely in that of what was said [two] hundred years ago." (*Missouri* v. *Holland*, 252 U.S. 416, 433 (1920).) Indeed, Judge Kennedy does not insist on certitudes where none exist or on simple keys to unlock constitutional meaning; rather, he accepts both the built-in ambiguities of the Constitution—"spacious phrases," in Judge Kennedy's terms—and the role of the courts in trying to resolve them. And the courts are to fulfill this task, in his view, with the benefits of history and experience and with the accumulated wisdom of those who have confronted the challenges of times past.

Characteristic of Judge Kennedy's approach is his view on liberty under the Constitution. He recognizes a tradition of liberty and privacy—a tradition that creates a zone of protection against unwarranted governmental intrusion into intimate family matters, such as the right to marital privacy. And he embraces the view, as he put it, that "the American people do have a shared vision. . . . I think important in that shared vision is the idea that each man and woman has the freedom and the capacity to develop to his or her own potential." (Tr., 12/15/87, at 49.)

The committee is not without its concerns about Judge Kennedy, particularly in the area of civil rights protection for women and minorities. These concerns arise from several of Judge Kennedy's opinions. But none of these opinions suggest an agenda to diminish the role of the Federal courts in protecting individual rights. Furthermore, the nominee's testimony demonstrated that his views on civil rights issues have evolved and developed over time, as he has become more sensitive to the conditions under which some in our society have labored. Several witnesses attested to this evolution and to Judge Kennedy's open-mindedness, and to the fact that his development process is continuing. He is a grown man who will grow more, said Nathaniel Colley. And as Dean Praeger concluded:

> Because Anthony Kennedy is both open to discussion and open-minded, I am sure that the concerns expressed during these hearings will be taken in and reflected upon by him over a long period of years. . . . [He is] genuinely open, . . . [he] loves the study of law but also has a real world sense of the impact of the law on individual people, and . . . [he] is deeply concerned about fairness. . . . (Praeger written statement, at 2.)

The transition from circuit court judge to Supreme Court justice is one, in Michael Martinez's words, "from follower to leader." (Tr., 12/16/87, at 270.) It is a transition from following precedents to setting precedents, from reacting to history to charting a course of history. And, at this particular time in history, with the Supreme Court closely divided on many of the critical issues of the day, it is a transition with great significance. In the view of the committee, Judge Kennedy's record and views expressed at the hearings warrant that the Senate confirm his nomination to the Supreme Court.

VIEWS OF MESSRS.
JOSEPH R. BIDEN, Jr.
EDWARD M. KENNEDY.
ROBERT C. BYRD.
HOWARD M. METZENBAUM.
DENNIS DeCONCINI.
PATRICK J. LEAHY.
HOWELL HEFLIN.
PAUL SIMON.
ARLEN SPECTER.

5

JUSTICE DAVID SOUTER

When Justice William Brennan announced his retirement from the Supreme Court, pro-choice interests held their breath in anticipation of a powerful blow. Brennan had long been the viewed as the guardian of individual liberties on the Court; his capacity to build consensus and sway opinions had been a rallying point for the liberal position. Moreover, his position on the bench would be filled by President George Bush, who had proven to be at least as fierce an advocate for the pro-life position as his predecessor Ronald Reagan. With this thought and this threat in mind, pro-choice groups and Senators prepared to do battle with whichever person Bush nominated.

If the Senate Judiciary Committee had prepared for a fierce debate on the abortion issue, they were to be disappointed. Bush's nominee, David Souter, came to his confirmation hearings without any hint about his position in evidence. The Senate and the media were consistently stymied as they searched Souter's meager paper trail for some indication of pro-life or anti-privacy leanings. The hearings themselves proved similarly unenlightening. Despite a virtual barrage of pointed questions on abortion, *Roe*, and privacy, Souter refused to be pinned down. While the Senators were as relentless with Souter as they had been with O'Connor, Souter--unlike O'Connor--had no record on the abortion issue, making it easier for Souter to equivocate.

Much to the chagrin of many members of the Senate Judiciary Committee, Souter was adamant in his refusal to answer questions regarding his personal views on abortion. His consistent refusal to commit either way on the abortion issue stands in dramatic contrast to his willingness to express his views on other controversial topics, including the death penalty. Yet Souter seemed to recognize the litmus-test quality of the abortion questions; moreover, he maintained that discussion of his personal beliefs on abortion, even in the context of the hearing, would contradict his statement that he would keep his personal beliefs out of the abortion decision.

Souter came closest to directly discussing abortion when he related an anecdote about his years as a residential advisor at Harvard. He had counseled a freshman couple on what to do when the young girl became pregnant. Souter related this story to demonstrate his appreciation of the difficulty of the choice to have an abortion; he refused, however, to reveal in exactly which direction he instructed the couple.

On the issue of *Roe*, Souter was similarly vague. He insisted that expressing an opinion about the propriety of the decision would later compromise his objectivity on the Court. While gladly conceding that a general liberty interest did exist, Souter argued that the specific rights it protected and the weight it should be given were matters for case-by-case analysis.

The questioning Senators scored a small victory on the privacy issue. Souter admitted that he believed that the due process clause of the Fourteenth Amendment did recognize an unenumerated right of privacy. In fact, when pressed, Souter said that he believed that the marital right to privacy was fundamental. Nevertheless, the Senators were unable to push him to extend his analysis to abortion per se. Indeed, the Senators who ultimately voted against Souter admittedly did so not because they disagreed with Souter's stated positions but because Souter remained an unknown — especially on the abortion issue. Senator Edward Kennedy (D-Mass.) voiced his concern over Souter's reticence: "[t]o a large extent, in spite of the hearings we have held, the Senate is still in the dark about this nomination, and all of us are voting in the dark." Senate Comm. on the Judiciary, 101st Cong., 2d Sess, Report on the Nomination of David H. Souter to be an Associate Justice of the United States Supreme Court (Exec. Rept. 101-32), at 90 (minority views of Senator Kennedy).

Souter played his cards well at his confirmation hearing. He was candid on certain issues--even some highly controversial issues--so he could not be accused of being uncooperative. Yet he managed to refrain from giving the Judiciary Committee any abortion-rope with which to hang him. The result is that Souter was confirmed as much because the Senators couldn't find fault as because they found actual favor.

Justice David Souter
Documents

Congressional Record - Senate
Sept. 11, 1990
Pp. 12771-12772

NOMINATION OF JUDGE DAVID SOUTER

Mr. SPECTER. Mr. President, 2 days from now, on September 13, the Judiciary Committee will commence hearings on Judge David Souter for the position of Associate Justice of the Supreme Court of the United States.

Since the opening statements at the committee hearings are necessarily limited, I think it is useful to take the floor today to discuss in some greater length two very important issues which are before the Judiciary Committee and will be before the Senate on Judge Souter's nomination.

The public discussion today, Mr. President, is focused largely on a way questions appropriately may be formulated to determine Judge Souter's views on abortion. That proposition, I suggest, encompasses two principal topics. First, should one issue, however important, dominate the selection of a Supreme Court Justice? And, second, has the Supreme Court's increasing activity in deciding major public policy issues as contrasted with their traditional interstitial interpretation of constitutional and statutory provisions given the public and the Senate the right to know the nominee's ultimate positions? I answer both of those questions in the negative.

Mr. President, it is understandable that there is deep concern in this country on the abortion question. I think it fair to say that no issue has so divided our Nation, with the exception of slavery, since its inception.

In my open house town meetings, as I believe in yours, Mr. President, this issue dominates the agenda, and each year, on January 22, Washington is the site of numerous demonstrations on the anniversary of Roe versus Wade, and hundreds and sometimes more than a thousand of my constituents from Pennsylvania come to talk about the issue.

With the Court evenly split and the next Justice in a position to perhaps cast the deciding vote on this tremendously important matter, there has been virtually exclusive focus on what Judge Souter may or may not do on this subject. But I suggest that beyond what the news media has covered and beyond what has been discussed on cocktail

tion is being widely discussed at all levels in our society -- there are many, many other issues of tremendous importance.

Judge Souter dominated the news in late July, but by August Saddam Hussein replaced Judge Souter, and at the present time there is a deployment of tens of thousands, perhaps more than 100,000 -- the exact number not being publicized -- as to how many United States troops are present in Saudi Arabia.

It may well be that the critical questions under the War Powers Resolution deciding whether the President has the authority to send those troops without congressional consent may be before the Court. The War Powers Act provides that unless Congress gives specific authorization within 60 days troops must be withdrawn if they are in a position of peril or there are hostilities. Of course, there are complex legal issues as to whether the War Powers Resolution is applicable. But an even more complicated subject is the constitutionality of the War Powers Resolution.

Balancing perhaps the two most important parts of the Constitution or, as important as any, is the exclusive prerogative of the Congress to declare war and the authority of the President as Commander in Chief to dispatch U.S. troops. That issue has not been decided, but it might well be decided by the Supreme Court, and it might well be that Justice Brennan's replacement will cast the critical vote.

There are enormously important questions on the death penalty, with a long series of decisions being decided five to four, and in the balance hangs our society's right to a very important measure for deterrence in law enforcement and, obviously, very important interests on the part of the accused who faces the death chamber, and again Justice Brennan's replacement may cast the decisive vote.

Similarly, in the civil rights area and on quotas, there is a long series of decisions, five to four, this year in the Metro Broadcasting case, the rights of minorities prevailing by a thin 5-to-4 vote, contrasted with Croson, the decision striking down the minority set-asides, very recently. Again, Justice Brennan's replacement is in a critical position.

This year the Supreme Court decided, in a surprising adjudication, that district courts can order that taxes be imposed, again by 5-to-4 decision. It may be there is no more controversial decision in the history of the Court than that one. And that comes on the heels of the decision on holding legislators, councilmen, the city of Yonkers in contempt of court, an extraordinary application of judicial authority given the traditional separation of legislative responsibilities in taxing authority.

So these are just a few of the critical issues before the Court. And there are many other 5-to-4 decisions, as in the right-to-die case. So I suggest, as forcefully as I can, that there not be overemphasis on any single issue, and I do believe that abortion has unreasonably dominated the agenda as we look to what Justice Brennan's successor may be called upon to decide.

Mr. President, there is another very vexing question that is pending before the Senate and that is how far may Senators go in their questions? Or perhaps more accurately stated, what must a nominee answer if he is to be confirmed? There are no hard and fast rules on this subject. During the course of the past 10 years we have seen a fascinating series of nominations. We saw Justice O'Connor decline to answer many, many questions on the ground that the issue might come before the Supreme Court. Her confirmation candidly was never in doubt and she was confirmed.

Chief Justice Rehnquist declined to answer many questions. He finally did answer some on the issue of the authority of Congress to take away court jurisdiction on first amendment issues. He finally said, after extensive interchanges, that the Congress did not have that authority. But he refused to answer many other questions. There is a sense that goes through these Supreme Court nomination processes, at least as I see it, that the Justices, the nominees, tend to answer as many questions as they feel necessary for confirmation. Of course, that is a hard factor to evaluate. It was reported that Chief Justice Rehnquist felt he ought not to appear before the Judiciary Committee at all, as a sitting Justice coming before the Senate seeking the higher position as Chief Justice.

When Justice Scalia came before the Judiciary Committee, he answered virtually no questions, and following that proceeding, Senator DeConcini and I had prepared a resolution to try to set a minimum standard, if that is possible -- perhaps it is not possible, given the individuality of the 100 Senators -- which would try to establish a minimum standard as to what a Supreme Court nominee would have to answer.

Before we could proceed, Judge Bork was nominated, and his proceedings, I think, established a standard or an attitude that a nominee has to answer very wide-ranging questions on judicial philosophy.

Interesting, Mr. President, as we now debate whether Judge Souter has to answer fundamental questions as to how he is going to decide the next case on abortion, overrule or sustain Roe versus Wade, that 3 years ago there was considerable debate as to whether we could even inquire into Judge Bork's judicial ideology. That was the first question I asked when he came to my office on the so-called courtesy call. I said, "Judge, do you think it appropriate to discuss judicial ideology?" He said, "I don't like the term ideology, but I think it is appropriate to answer questions on judicial philosophy." And of course there were wide-ranging questions.

Again, I think Judge Bork's proceedings illustrated the proposition, at least in my sense, that he had to answer wide-ranging questions, because he had written and spoken extensively on so many subjects, if he were to have any chance of confirmation.

Justice Kennedy, although his confirmation was never in doubt, also answered a wide range of questions.

So I think there has been established a Senate standard, perhaps a Senate attitude that could be generalized that a nominee does have to answer questions on judicial philosophy and specific questions on his writings, his speeches, and opinions if he is a lower court judge, unless they go to his inclination or his decisionmaking function in a case likely to come before the Court.

S. Hrg. 101-1263

NOMINATION OF DAVID H. SOUTER TO BE ASSOCIATE JUSTICE OF THE SUPREME COURT OF THE UNITED STATES

HEARINGS

BEFORE THE

COMMITTEE ON THE JUDICIARY UNITED STATES SENATE

ONE HUNDRED FIRST CONGRESS

SECOND SESSION

ON

THE NOMINATION OF DAVID H. SOUTER TO BE ASSOCIATE JUSTICE OF THE SUPREME COURT OF THE UNITED STATES

SEPTEMBER 13, 14, 17, 18, AND 19, 1990

Serial No. J-101-95

Printed for the use of the Committee on the Judiciary

U.S. GOVERNMENT PRINTING OFFICE

39-454   WASHINGTON : 1991

The CHAIRMAN. But he has indicated that one of the Supreme Court Justices you most admire was the second Justice Harlan, who served on the Supreme Court between 1955 and 1971, and who was widely regarded, is widely regarded as one of the great conservative Justices ever to serve on the Court.

Now, Justice Harlan concurred in the Court's landmark decision of *Griswold*. That is the Connecticut case that said that the State of Connecticut, the legislature and the Governor couldn't pass a law that—constitutionally—said that married couples could not use birth control devices to determine whether or not they wished to procreate.

Justice Harlan indicated that that Connecticut law violated the due process clause of the 14th amendment which says that no State can deprive any person of life, liberty, or property without process of law.

Now, my question is this, Judge: Do you agree with Justice Harlan's opinion in *Griswold* that the due process clause of the 14th amendment protects a right of a married couple to use birth control to decide whether or not to have a child?

Judge SOUTER. I believe that the due process clause of the 14th amendment does recognize and does protect an unenumerated right of privacy. The——

The CHAIRMAN. And that—please continue. I didn't mean to interrupt. I like what you are saying.

Judge SOUTER. The only reservation I have is a purely formal reservation in response to your question, and that simply is: No two judges, I am sure, will ever write an opinion the same way, even if they share the same principles. And I would not go so far as to say every word in Justice Harlan's opinion is something that I would adopt. And I think for reasons that we all appreciate, I would not think that it was appropriate to express a specific opinion on the exact result in *Griswold,* for the simple reason that as clearly as I will try to describe my views on the right of privacy, we know that the reasoning of the Court in *Griswold,* including opinions beyond those of Justice Harlan, are taken as obviously a predicate toward the one case which has been on everyone's mind and on everyone's lips since the moment of my nomination—*Roe* v. *Wade,* upon which the wisdom or the appropriate future of which it would be inappropriate for me to comment.

But I understand from your question, and I think it is unmistakable, that what you were concerned about is the principal basis for deriving a right of privacy, and specifically the kind of reasoning that I would go through to do so. And in response to that question, yes, I would group myself in Justice Harlan's category.

The CHAIRMAN. Well, Judge, let me make it clear, I am not asking you about how you would decide or what you even think about *Roe* v. *Wade.*

Judge SOUTER. I understand that.

The CHAIRMAN. Now, in the *Griswold* case, I am curious what proposition you think it stands for. Do you believe it is a case in a long line of cases, establishing an unenumerated right to privacy, a right the Constitution protects, even though it is not specifically mentioned in the document?

Judge SOUTER. I think probably it would be fairest to say that it is a case in a confused line of cases and it is a case which, again referring to the approach that Justice Harlan took, it is a case which to me represents at least the beginnings of the modern effort to try to articulate an enforceable doctrine.

My own personal approach to that derivation begins with, I suppose, the most elementary propositions about constitutional government, but I do not know of any other way to begin. I am mindful not only of the national Constitution of 1787, but of the history of State constitution-making in that same decade.

If there is one generalization that we can clearly make, it is the generalization about the intended limitation on the scope of governmental power. When we think of the example of the national Constitution, I think truly we are at the point in our history when every schoolchild does know that the reason there was no Bill of Rights attached to the draft submitted to the States in the first instance after the convention recessed, was the view that the limitations on the power to be given to the National Government was so clearly circumscribed, that no one really needed to worry about the possible power of the National Government to invade what we today group under the canon of civil liberties, and we know the history of that response.

We know that there were States like my own which were willing to ratify, but were willing to ratify only on the basis of requesting that the first order of business of the new Congress would be to propose a Bill of Rights in New Hampshire, like other States, who was not bashful about saying would not be in it.

The CHAIRMAN. Did you wish to continue?

Judge SOUTER. If I may. This attitude did not sort of spring up without some antecedent in 1787. I am not an expert on the constitutions of all of the original States, but I do know something about my own.

One of the remarkable things about the New Hampshire Constitution, which began its life at the beginning of that same decade, is the fact that it began with an extraordinarily jealous regard for civil rights, for human rights. The New Hampshire Constitution did not simply jump in and establish a form of government. They did not get to the form of government until they had gotten to the Bill of Rights first.

They couched that Bill of Rights with an extraordinary breadth and a breadth which, for people concerned with principles of interpretation, requires great care in the reading. But the New Hampshire constitutionalists of 1780 and 1784 were equally concerned to protect a concept of liberty, so-called, which they did not more precisely define.

So, it seems to me that the starting point for anyone who reads the Constitution seriously is that there is a concept of limited governmental power which is not simply to be identified with the enumeration of those specific rights or specifically defined rights that were later embodied in the bill.

If there were any further evidence needed for this, of course, we can start with the ninth amendment. I realize how the ninth amendment has bedeviled scholars, and I wish I had something novel to contribute to the jurisprudence on it this afternoon, which I do not.

The CHAIRMAN. It is novel that you acknowledge it, based on our past hearings in this committee. [Laughter.]

One of the last nominees said it was nothing but a waterblot on the Constitution, which I found fascinating. At any rate, go ahead.

Judge SOUTER. Well, I think it is two things—maybe it is more. I have no reason to question the scholarship which has interpreted one intent of the ninth amendment as simply being the protection or the preservation of the State bills of rights which preceded it.

Neither, quite frankly, do I find a basis for doubting that, with respect to the national bill of rights, it was something other than what it purported to be, and that was an acknowledgment that the enumeration was not intended to be in some sense exhaustive and in derogation of other rights retained.

The CHAIRMAN. Is that the school to which you would count yourself a graduate?

Judge SOUTER. I have to count myself a member of that school, because, in any interpretive enterprise, I have to start with the text and I do not have a basis for doubting that somewhat obvious and straightforward meaning of the text.

The CHAIRMAN. Let me ask you another question here, and I realize this is somewhat pedantic, but it is important for me to understand the foundation from which you build here.

You have made several references appropriately to the Bill of Rights and the Federal Government. Do you have any disagreement with the incorporation doctrine that was adopted some 70 years ago applying the Bill of Rights to the States? Do you have any argument with that proposition?

Judge SOUTER. No; my argument with the incorporation doctrine would be with the proposition that that was meant to exhaust the meaning of enforceable liberty. That, in point of fact, as you know, I mean that was Justice Harlan's concern.

The next really—I mean that brings to the fore sort of the next chapter in American constitutional history that bears on what we are talking about, because one cannot talk about the privacy doctrine today, without talking about the 14th amendment.

The CHAIRMAN. Judge, I am truly interested in us going back through in an orderly fashion the evolution of constitutional doctrine, but as my colleague sitting behind you will tell you, I only have a half hour to talk to you and I want to ask you a few more specific questions, if I may.

The 14th amendment, as you know, was designed explicitly to apply to the States. Speaking to the liberty clause of the 14th amendment, Justice Harlan said:

The full scope of the liberty guaranteed by the Due Process Clause cannot be found in or limited by the precise terms of the specific guarantees elsewhere provided in the Constitution,

Which is totally consistent with what you have been saying thus far.

Judge SOUTER. Yes.

The CHAIRMAN. Now, do you agree with Justice Harlan that the reference to liberty in the 5th and 14th amendments provide a basis for certain—not all, but certain—unenumerated rights, rights that the Constitution protects, even though they are not specifically enumerated within the Constitution?

Judge SOUTER. I think the concept of liberty as enforceable under the due process clause is, in fact, the means by which we enforce those rights. It is sterile, I think, to go into this particular chapter of constitutional history now, but you will recall that Justice Black was a champion at one point of the view that the real point of the fourth amendment, which was intended to apply unenumerated substantive rights, was the privileges of immunities clause, and not due process. Well, as a practical matter, that was read out of the possibility of American constitutionalism, at least for its time, and it has remained so by the slaughterhouse cases.

What is left, for those who were concerned to enforce the unenumerated concepts of liberty was the liberty clause and due process, and by a parity of reasoning by the search for coherence in constitutional doctrine, we would look to the same place and the same analysis in the fifth amendment when we are talking about the National Government.

The CHAIRMAN. Now, let us follow on. We recognize, you recognize, you have stated that *Griswold* and the various means of reasoning to arrive at the conclusion that there was a constitutionally protected right of a married couple to determine whether or not to procreate, to use birth control or not, is a constitutionally sound decision.

Now, shortly thereafter there was a similar case in Massachusetts, although in this case it did not apply to married couples, there was a Massachusetts statute, in the *Eisenstadt* case, that said unmarried couples, and the rationale was that there is reason to not be out there allowing unmarried couples to buy birth control, because it would encourage sexual promiscuity, and the Supreme Court struck that down, as well, saying that it violated a right to privacy, having found once again, most Justices ruled that way, in the 14th amendment.

Now, do you agree that that decision was rightly decided?

Judge SOUTER. Well, my recollection—and I did not reread *Eisenstadt* before coming in here, so I hope my recollection is not faulty, but my recollection is that *Eisenstadt* represented a different approach, because the reliance on the Court there was on equal protection. I know that my recollection is——

The CHAIRMAN. Yes, the——

Judge SOUTER. I am sorry.

The CHAIRMAN. Go ahead. I am sorry.

Judge SOUTER. My recollection is that the criticism of *Eisenstadt* at the time was whether the Supreme Court was, in fact, reaching rather far to make the equal protection argument. But I think there is one point that is undeniable, without specifically affirming or denying the wisdom of *Eisenstadt*, and that is there is going to be an equal protection implication from whatever bedrock start privacy is derived under the concept of due process, and I think that then leads us back to the essentially difficult point of interpretation, and that is how do you go through the interpretive process to find that content which is legitimate as a concept of due process.

The CHAIRMAN. Also, to what extent you find it legitimate. Is it a fundamental right, or is it an ordinary right? In the case of *Griswold*, in the *Griswold* case, it was discerned and decided that there was a fundamental right to privacy relating to the right of married couples to use contraceptive devices. Do you believe they were correct in that judgment, that there is a fundamental right?

Judge SOUTER. I think the way, again, I would express it without getting myself into the position of endorsing the specifics of the cases, is that I believe on reliable interpretive principles there is certainly, to begin with, a core of privacy which is identified as marital privacy, and I believe it can and should be regarded as fundamental.

I think what we also have to recognize is that the notion of protected privacy, which may be enforceable under the 14th amendment, has a great potential breadth and not every aspect of it may rise to a fundamental level.

The CHAIRMAN. I agree. That is why I am asking you the question, because as you know as well as I do, if the Court concludes that there is a fundamental right, then for a State to take action that would extinguish that right, they must have, as we lawyers call, it is required they look at it through the prism of strict scrutiny. Another way of saying it, for laymen, is that they must have a pretty darn good reason. If it is not a fundamental right and it is an ordinary right, they can use a much lower standard to determine whether the State had a good enough reason to preempt that right.

So, as we talk about this line of cases, in *Griswold* and in *Eisenstadt*—let me skip, in *Moore* v. *East Cleveland,* where the Court ruled, extending this principle of privacy from the question of procreation, contraception and procreation, to the definition of a family. As you know, East Cleveland had an ordinance defining a family that did not include a grandmother and grandson, and so East Cleveland, under that ordinance, said that a grandmother and her two grandchildren could be evicted from a particular area in which they lived, because they were not a family, as defined by the local municipality in zoning ordinance.

Now, the Court came along there and it made a very basic judgment. It said—if I can find my note, which I cannot find right now, and I think it is important to get the exact language, if I can find it—I just found it. [Laughter.]

Justice Powell said, "freedom of personal choice in matters of marriage and family life is one of the liberties protected by the Due Process Clause of the 14th amendment."

Now, my question, Judge, is do you believe that that assertion by Justice Powell is accurate?

Judge SOUTER. I think that assertion by Justice Powell represents a legitimate judgment in these kinds of problems with respect to *Moore* just as in the discussion with *Griswold*. I am going to ask you to excuse me from specifically endorsing the particular result, because I recognize the implications from any challenge that may come from the other privacy case that is on everyone's mind.

But the one thing that I want to make very clear is that my concept of an enforceable marital right of privacy would give it fundamental importance. What the courts are doing in all of these cases is saying—although we speak of tiers of scrutiny—what the courts are saying, it seems to me in a basically straightforward way—is that there is no way to escape a valuation of the significance of the particular manifestation to privacy that we are concerned with, and having given it a value we, indeed, have to hold the State to an equally appropriate or commensurate reason before it interferes with that value.

The CHAIRMAN. That is exactly what I am trying to find out in your answering. So the valuation applied to a definition of family, is fundamental. The valuation applied to whether a married couple can use contraception is fundamental. The valuation applied to whether or not an unmarried couple can use contraception is fundamental.

Now, I would like to ask you, as I move along here, as you look at this line of cases we have mentioned—and I will not bother to go through a couple of others that I have anticipated—is my time up? I saw the light go off and I thought my time was about up and the one thing these fellows are not likely to forgive me for—they will forgive me for a lot of things but not for going over my time.

That when it comes to personal freedom of choice, as Justice Powell put it, in family and in marriage, one basic aspect of that freedom is the right to procreate. Now, early in the 1940's, in the

Skinner case, the Supreme Court said that criminals could not be sterilized. The Court made it very clear and it said, "Marriage and procreation are fundamental" and that sterilization affected "one of the basic civil rights of man."

I assume that some of the civil rights that you are referring to that those who wrote the New Hampshire Constitution referred to.

Do you agree that procreation is a fundamental right?

Judge SOUTER. I would assume that if we are going to have any core concept of marital privacy, that would certainly have to rank at its fundamental heart.

The CHAIRMAN. Now, the reason I am pursuing this is not merely for the reason you think, I suspect. It is because you have been categorized as—I believe you have described yourself as an interpretivist.

Judge SOUTER. I did and I have, yes.

The CHAIRMAN. You have begun—and I thank you for it—you have begun to flesh out for me on which part of the spectrum of the interpretivists you find yourself.

Let me, in the interest of time, move on here. I am trying to skip by here.

Let me ask you this, Judge. The value that the Court places on certain alleged, by many, privacy rights will dictate, as we said earlier, the burden placed upon a State in the circumstance when they wish to extinguish that right, or impact on that right.

Judge SOUTER. Yes, sir.

The CHAIRMAN. Now, you have just told us that the right to use birth control, to decide whether or not to become pregnant is one of those fundamental rights—the value placed on it is fundamental.

Now, let us say that a woman and/or her mate uses such a birth control device and it fails. Does she still have a constitutional right to choose not to become pregnant?

Judge SOUTER. Senator, that is the point at which I will have to exercise the prerogative which you were good to speak of explicitly. I think for me to start answering that question, in effect, is for me to start discussing the concept of *Roe* v. *Wade.* I would be glad—I do not think I have to do so for you—but I would be glad to explain in some detail my reasons for believing that I cannot do so, but of course, they focus on the fact that ultimately the question which you are posing is a question which is implicated by any possibility of the examination of *Roe* v. *Wade.* That, as we all know, is not only a possibility, but a likelihood that the Court may be asked to do it.

The CHAIRMAN. Judge, let me respectfully suggest the following to you: That to ask you what principles you would employ does not, in any way, tell me how you would rule on a specific fact situation.

For example, all eight Justices, whom you will be joining, all eight of them have found there to be a liberty interest that a woman retains after being pregnant. That goes all the way from Justice Brennan—who is no longer on the Court—who reached one conclusion from having found that liberty interest, to Justice Scalia who finds a liberty interest and yet, nonetheless says, explicitly he would like to see *Roe* v. *Wade,* he thinks *Roe* v. *Wade* should be overruled.

So the mere fact that you answer the question whether or not a woman's liberty interest, a woman's right to terminate pregnancy exists or does not exist, in no way tells me or anyone else within our earshot how you would possibly rule on *Roe* v. *Wade*.

Judge SOUTER. I think to explain my position, I think it is important to bear in mind there are really two things that judges may or may not be meaning when they say there is a liberty interest to do thus and so, whatever it may be. They may mean simply that in the whole range of human interests and activities the particular action that you are referring to is one which falls within a broad concept of liberty. If liberty means what it is, we can do if we want to do it. Then obviously in that sense of your question, the answer is, yes.

The CHAIRMAN. It is more precise, Judge, than that. I mean liberty interest has a constitutional connotation that most lawyers and all justices have ascribed to it in varying degrees. For example, Justices Blackmun, Brennan, Marshall, and Stevens, they have said a woman has a strong liberty interest, although Justice Stevens has phrased it slightly differently. Justice O'Connor has made it clear that she believes a woman has some liberty interest. Even Justices Rehnquist, White, Kennedy, and Scalia, all of whom criticized the Court's rulings in this area have said that a woman has at least some liberty interest in choosing not to remain pregnant.

Now, each of these Court members has acknowledged what we lawyers call a liberty interest after conception. So my question to you is, is there a liberty interest retained by a woman after conception?

Judge SOUTER. I think, Senator, again, we have got to be careful about the sense of the liberty interest. There is the very broad sense of the term which I referred to before and then there is the sense of an enforceable liberty interest. That is to say, one which is enforceable against the State, based upon a valuation that it is fundamental. It seems to me that that is the question which is part of the analysis, of course, upon which *Roe* v. *Wade* rests.

The CHAIRMAN. Well, all liberty interests have following all liberty interest is a right. The question is, how deeply held and rooted that right is; and what action the State must take and how serious that action must be—the rationale for that action—to overcome that interest?

But once we acknowledge there is a liberty interest, there is a right.

Judge SOUTER. But what—I am sorry.

The CHAIRMAN. So I am not asking you to tell me—I am just told my time is up—I am not asking you to tell me what burden of proof the State must show in order to overcome that. I am asking you is there a liberty interest and your answer is what, yes, or no?

Judge SOUTER. My answer is that the most that I can legitimately say is that in the spectrum of possible protection that would rank as an interest to be asserted under liberty, but how that interest should be evaluated, and the weight that should be given to it in determining whether there is in any or all circumstances a sufficiently countervailing governmental interest is a question with respect, I cannot answer.

The CHAIRMAN. Now, let me turn to my colleague from Ohio Senator Metzenbaum, for his questioning.

Senator Metzenbaum.

Senator METZENBAUM. Thank you, Mr. Chairman.

Judge Souter, I want to focus on your view of really what is at stake in the abortion debate. Now, we write the laws in Congress, the Court interprets the laws, but we all must be aware that the laws affect the personal lives and the hopes and the dreams of the people who must live with the laws we make.

I want to start to talk with you on a personal level, not as a constitutional scholar nor as a lawyer. This year, I held hearings on legislation that would codify the principles of *Roe* v. *Wade*. I heard stories from two women who had had illegal abortions prior to 1973. They were women about your age. They told horrifying stories.

One woman was the victim of a brutal rape and she could not bear raising a child from that rape along side her own two children. Another woman, who was poor and alone, self-aborted. It is a horrible story, just a horrible story, with knitting needles and a bucket.

I heard from a man whose mother died from an illegal abortion when he was 2 years old, after doctors told her that she was not physically strong enough to survive the pregnancy.

I will tell you, Judge Souter, that the emotion that those people still feel, after more than 20 years, is very real, sufficiently strong to have conveyed it to those of us who heard their testimony. Each woman risked her life to do what she felt she had to do. One of those women paid the price.

My real question to you is not how you would rule on *Roe* v. *Wade* or any other particular case coming before the Court. But what does a woman face, when she has an unwanted pregnancy, a pregnancy that may be the result of rape or incest or failed contraceptives or ignorance of basic health information, and I would just like to get your own view and your own thoughts of that woman's position under those circumstances.

Judge SOUTER. Senator, your question comes as a surprise to me. I was not expecting that kind of question, and you have made me think of something that I have not thought of for 24 years.

When I was in law school, I was on the board of freshmen advisers at Harvard College. I was a proctor in a dormitory at Harvard College. One afternoon, one of the freshmen who was assigned to me, I was his adviser, came to me and he was in pretty rough emotional shape and we shut the door and sat down, and he told me that his girlfriend was pregnant and he said she is about to try to have a self-abortion and she does not know how to do it. He said she is afraid to tell her parents what has happened and she is afraid to go to the health services, and he said will you talk to her, and I did.

I know you will respect the privacy of the people involved, and I will not try to say what I told her. But I spent 2 hours in a small dormitory bedroom that afternoon, in that room because that was the most private place we could get so that no one in the next suite of rooms could hear, listening to her and trying to counsel her to approach her problem in a way different from what she was doing, and your question has brought that back to me.

I think the only thing I can add to that is I know what you were trying to tell me, because I remember that afternoon.

Senator METZENBAUM. Well, I appreciate your response. I think it indicates that you have empathy for the problem. In your writings, as a matter of fact, you reveal real empathy for those who are morally opposed to abortion.

For instance, in 1986, as a State supreme court justice, you wrote a special concurrence in a wrongful birth case called *Smith* v. *Coat*, outlining, in your words, how a physician with conscientious scruples against abortion—this is a quote:

How a physician with conscientious scruples against abortion and the testing and counseling that may inform an abortion decision can discharge his professional obligation, without engaging in procedures that his religious or moral principles condemn.

As a matter of fact, that was sort of dictum. That was dictum in the case, it was not necessary.

As attorney general, you filed a brief in *Coe* v. *Hooker*, which emphasized that,

Thousands of New Hampshire citizens possess a very strongly held and deepseeded moral belief that abortion is the killing of unborn children.

That brief went on to conclude,

It is not accurate to say that the moral feelings of other individuals and groups, both public and private, may not constitutionally interfere with a woman's otherwise unrestricted right to decide to have an abortion.

I start off saying it is not accurate to say that. Now, you obviously indicated a concern for the doctor with conscientious scruples against abortion, you indicated your concern about feelings of individuals and groups, both public and privately. My concern is do you have the same degree of empathy for the woman who must make a difficult decision when faced with an unwanted pregnancy. That is really the thrust of my concern, and I think the thrust of the concern, frankly, Judge Souter, of millions of American women, not really wanting to know how you will vote on a particular case, but wanting to know whether you can empathize with their problem.

Judge SOUTER. If they were to ask me whether I could, I would ask them to imagine what it was like to be in that room that fall afternoon that I described to you. That is an experience which has not been on my mind, because it has not had to be, but I learned that afternoon what was at stake.

I hope I have learned since that afternoon what is at stake on both sides of this controversy. You mentioned my opinion in the *Smith* v. *Cody* case. I do not know whether that was dictum or not. I did not think it was at the time.

What I thought I was addressing at the time was as moral dilemma which had been created not unnecessarily, but which had necessarily been raised by the majority opinion of my court.

If I were to generalize from that concurrence in *Smith* v. *Cody*, it would be that I believe I, indeed, can empathize with the moral force of the people whom I addressed, and I can with equal empathy appreciate the moral force of people on the other side of that controversy.

Senator METZENBAUM. My staff just points out to me that each year almost 3.5 million women face that problem of an unwanted pregnancy, much like the woman that you mentioned.

Everybody talks about *Roe* v. *Wade* as a case. I do not think of it as a case. I think of it as those witnesses who came before my committee. I think of it as women generally. I think of it as my own daughters, who are married, and I can imagine a situation where they might need to have or want to have an abortion. Other women less fortunate than they would not be able to go to a different State, if there were no law.

I think about what would happen if there were no constitutional protection, and I ask you not how you vote on the case, but what are your thoughts as to what would happen to those women in this country who might be able to go, if they had the money, to State x, but not get an abortion, not be able to stay in State y, because that State prohibits abortions.

My concern is what does Judge Souter think about this moral, and it goes beyond being a moral question, it becomes a really heart-wrenching decision that actually goes beyond morality, it goes to the very heart of living, the kind of living that people experience.

Judge SOUTER. I think I have to go back to something that I said to all of the members of the committee when I was speaking at the very beginning, before my testimony this afternoon.

If I have learned one thing, I have learned that whatever we do on any appellate court is not, just as you said it was not, just a case. It affects someone and it changes someone's life, no matter what we do.

One of the consequences undeniably of the situation that you describe would be an inconsistency of legal opportunity throughout this country. Some States would go one way, others would go another. Some would fund abortions, some would not fund abortions. There is no question that that is a consequence that has to be faced.

I do not think that, any more than any other given fact, as tragic as that fact may be, is sufficient to decide a case. We can never decide a case totally that way, and I know you are not suggesting otherwise.

But you remember what I said is the second lesson that I learned as a trial judge, that knowing that any decision we make is going to affect a life and perhaps many lives, we had better use every resource of our minds and our hearts and every strength that we have to get it right. It is the imperative for conscientious judging.

Senator METZENBAUM. Judge, I think you are a very sincere man and I think you are a very moral man. What is bothering me, maybe some others as well, is that you have already expressed concern for the conscientious scruples of physicians in connection with abortion, you have expressed concern for the moral feelings of others in connection with abortions.

The real concern is, would the conscientious scruples of a physician or the moral feelings of others override a woman's decision when and whether or not to have her child.

Judge SOUTER. There is no question that the decision about the future of *Roe* v. *Wade* does not rest upon an assessment of a physician's moral scruples. The issue of *Roe* v. *Wade* is one which, as you know, on the merits I cannot comment on.

But there is one thing that I can say, and I do not know how else to say it, is that whatever its proper resolution may be, it is an issue. It is not simply a label for one view, whether that view be in favor of continuing *Roe* v. *Wade* or in favor of overruling it.

You are asking me at this point have I demonstrated, can I point to something on the record that demonstrates as kind of equality of empathy on either side, and I think the only thing that I can, without self-serving rhetoric, say to you is I have talked and I have counseled with someone on the other side.

I have been the trustee of a hospital which has opened its facilities to people on the other side, people who did not agree with these conscientious doctors, and to the extent that I have a record that goes behind the legal issue in the case, I think you may properly look to that. And you may properly ask, and I hope you will ask yourself, as you and the other members of this committee listen to me over the course of the next few days, you may properly ask whether, on other issues generally, I am open enough to listen.

What you want to avoid is a judge who will not listen, and I will ask you when these hearings are over to make a judgment on me as to whether I will listen or not. I think I have a record as a judge which indicates that I will, and after you and the other members of this committee have finished examining it, I will ask you to judge me on that basis.

Senator METZENBAUM. We will.

In *Griswold* v. *Connecticut,* Justice Douglas articulated the very important privacy concerns that were at stake if Connecticut fully enforced its anticontraceptive statute. He asked, "Would we allow the police to search the sacred precincts of marital bedrooms for telltale signs of the use of contraceptives." This idea is obviously repugnant to everyone.

Surely, the Court has to concern itself with the problems of enforcing statutes regulating reproductive rights. The Court must be willing to reap what it sows, if it overturns *Roe* and permits States to once again criminalize abortion.

I do not have to tell you, until last November, what was occurring in Romania, the draconian regime, the manner in which they enforced their criminal abortion laws, each month police would enter factories to examine women to determine if they were pregnant. No question, that would not happen in this country.

Romanian women who had miscarried were interrogated to make sure they had not had an abortion. We know that will not happen. But if the Supreme Court were to overturn *Roe* and a State passed a statute criminalizing abortion, would it then be constitutional to put a woman in jail for obtaining an abortion?

Judge SOUTER. I think the only answer to that, Senator, is a reference back to the laws that preceded *Roe.* We know that in my own State there were misdemeanor statutes on the book for procuring an abortion. And it was exactly such statutes as that that *Roe* rendered unenforceable.

Senator METZENBAUM. Excuse me, I did not mean to be rude.

Judge SOUTER. I was going to say it was exactly such statutes as that that *Roe* rendered unenforceable.

Senator METZENBAUM. Now, according to news reports at the time you were attorney general, you opposed repealing New Hampshire's criminal abortion statutes which had been passed before *Roe* v. *Wade.*

The legislative archives of the bill that would have repealed the criminal statutes contain a memorandum from the attorney general's office outlining the effects of *Roe* v. *Wade.* Although it is unclear when the memo was written, it was likely written soon after *Roe* was decided in 1973, although I am not certain about that.

At that time, you were deputy attorney general. The memo concluded that "the effect of the Supreme Court decision is to invalidate RSA 585:12, 585:13, and to make RSA 585:14 a nullity."

Are you familiar with that memo?

Judge SOUTER. I do not recall the memo, no.

Senator METZENBAUM. Did you agree then, or do you believe now that the Supreme Court's decision in *Roe* rendered the New Hampshire criminal statutes unconstitutional?

Judge SOUTER. The fact is I cannot give you a categorical answer to that. To begin with, it is an issue that I have not even given thought to for, I guess, 17 years and I do not recall the extent to which I may have been aware of that memorandum at the time.

The further reason for the difficulty and a categorical answer is that you may recall that there are questions about the effect of *Roe* or the *Roe*-type decisions depending on the form of the State statutes in question.

Now, I am going to say something from memory and it may be inaccurate, so I want you to take it with that disclaimer. But my recollection is that the Court's indication of the enforceability of the statute in *Roe* v. *Wade* was different from its indication of the enforceability that came out of *Doe* v. *Bolton.*

Quite frankly, Senator, without a reexamination of precisely what they were saying on whether the statute remained partially enforceable to the extent allowable under *Roe* v. *Wade* as opposed to becoming totally unenforceable, I would have to go back and reread those carefully and parse the New Hampshire statutes, which I have not done.

It is—in one sense I think we are inclined to say, well, that ought to be an easy question, and I do not think it is an easy question.

Judge SOUTER. I see the point that you are making. I am glad to have the opportunity to say that nobody has been subtly or otherwise lobbying me on a particular position.

Senator KOHL. I believe it.

Judge SOUTER. There is no question, a nominee needs help.

Senator KOHL. He also needs independence.

Judge SOUTER. You are absolutely right and, fortunately, these people have given it to me.

Senator KOHL. I understand, yes.

Just a couple of questions on *Roe* v. *Wade*. In 1973, when it was promulgated, you were in the AG's office——

Judge SOUTER. Yes.

Senator KOHL [continuing]. And it is hard to go back to what you did that day or in the days and weeks after, but I am just presuming that there was conversation between you and your colleagues at that time. Do you recall your feelings about *Roe* v. *Wade* back when it was promulgated?

Judge SOUTER. I frankly do not remember the early discussions on it. I mean everybody was arguing it. It was probably fodder for more argument among lawyers than any other case, certainly, of its time. The only thing I specifically remember is I can remember not only I, but others whom I knew, really switching back and forth playing devil's advocate on *Roe* v. *Wade*.

Senator KOHL. You had no opinion about it, other than just to say "wow"?

Judge SOUTER. Oh, I doubtless had an opinion. No, I did not just say "wow."

Senator KOHL. What was your opinion in 1973 on *Roe* v. *Wade*?

Judge SOUTER. Well, with respect, Senator, I am going to ask you to let me draw the line there, because I do not think I could get into opinions of 1973, without there being taken indications of opinions in 1976.

Senator KOHL. OK. With respect, finally, to *Roe* v. *Wade* just once more, is it fair to state, even though you are not prepared to discuss it, understandably, that you do have an opinion on *Roe* v. *Wade*?

Judge SOUTER. I think it would be misleading to say that. I have not got any agenda on what should be done with *Roe* v. *Wade*, if that case were brought before me. I will listen to both sides of that case. I have not made up my mind and I do not go on the Court saying I must go one way or I must go another way.

As you know, the issue that arises when an established and existing precedent is attacked is a very complex issue. It involves not only the correctness or the incorrectness by whatever lights we judge it of a given decision. It can also involve extremely significant issues of precedent.

Senator KOHL. Yes.

Judge SOUTER. And I do not sit here before you, under oath, having any commitment in my mind as to what I would do if I were on that Court and that case were brought before me.

| 101ST CONGRESS | SENATE | EXEC. REPT. |
| 2d Session | | 101-32 |

NOMINATION OF DAVID H. SOUTER TO BE AN ASSOCIATE JUSTICE OF THE UNITED STATES SUPREME COURT

OCTOBER 1, 1990.—Ordered to be printed

Mr. BIDEN, from the Committee on the Judiciary,
submitted the following

REPORT

together with

ADDITIONAL AND MINORITY VIEWS

[To accompany the nomination of David H. Souter to be an Associate Justice of the
United States Supreme Court]

The Committee on the Judiciary, to which was referred the nomination of Judge David H. Souter to be an Associate Justice of the United States Supreme Court, having considering the same, reports favorably thereon, a quorum being present, by a vote of 13 yeas and 1 nay, with the recommendation that the nomination be approved.

CONTENTS

Part Two: Judge Souter's Views on Privacy Reproductive
Freedom and Unenumerated Rights

Prior to the hearings, Judge Souter's record on privacy, reproductive freedom and unenumerated rights was relatively scant.
During the hearings, his testimony on these subjects was mixed.
On some matters, such as unenumerated rights generally, the
Ninth Amendment, the right to marital privacy, and his overall
methodology, Judge Souter's testimony was quite positive and encouraging. On other matters, such as the right of unmarried individuals to use contraception, Judge Souter's testimony was worrisome. On still other matters, such as reproductive freedom, his reticence was troubling.

A. JUDGE SOUTER UNEQUIVOCALLY EMBRACED A GENERAL
UNENUMERATED RIGHT TO PRIVACY

1. Judge Souter supports the concept of unenumerated rights

In clear and unequivocal terms, Judge Souter expressed support
for and appreciation of the concept of unenumerated rights, stating:

> It seems clear to me that the concept of liberty is not
> limited by the specific subjects which the incorporation
> doctrine by bringing, as it were, the entire corpus of the
> stated Bill of Rights into the concept of the Liberty Clause

[of the 14th Amendment]. Liberty is not so limited. (Transcript, Sept. 14, at 9.)

He added in response to questioning by Senator Grassley that it is important to recognize "rights which are implicit in the text of the Constitution itself, * * * which * * * it is the responsibility of the judiciary to find and to state in ways that we can understand." (Transcript, Sept. 14, at 18.)

Elaborating on this view, Judge Souter testified that the Ninth Amendment is "an acknowledgement that the enumeration [of rights in the Bill of Rights] was not intended to be in some sense exhaustive and in derogation of other rights retained." He added that he "do[es] not have a basis for doubting that somewhat obvious and straightforward meaning of the text." (Transcript, Sept. 13, at 108.)

2. Judge Souter supports a right to privacy enforced through the due process clause of the 14th amendment

In response to my questioning, Judge Souter made clear that he also fully supports a general, unenumerated right to privacy. In the nominee's words: "I believe that the Due Process Clause of the 14th Amendment does recognize and does protect an unenumerated right to privacy." (Transcript, Sept. 13, at 103.) Judge Souter left no doubt that his constitutional anchor for such a right is the Due Process Clause, as he testified that "the concept of liberty as enforceable under the Due Process Clause is, in fact, the means by which we enforce those [unenumerated] rights." (Transcript, Sept. 13, at 110.)

Elaborating on this issue in response to questioning by Senator Grassley, Judge Souter said:

> As I indicated to [the Chairman], I think that a fair reading of the Constitution of the United States * * * compels the conclusion that there were values, in the case of our discussion a value of privacy, which were intended to be protected even though they were not spelled out in black-letter detail. (Transcript, Sept. 14, at 8.)

3. Judge Souter supports a right of marital privacy

Judge Souter's testimony included his express support for a marital right to privacy as recognized by the Court in its landmark decision a quarter-century ago, *Griswold* v. *Connecticut*, 381 U.S. 479 (1965). While not specifically commenting per se on the decision in *Griswold*, Judge Souter testified that "on reliable interpretive principles there is certainly * * * a core of privacy which is identified as marital privacy, and I believe it can and should be regarded as fundamental." (Transcript, Sept. 13, at 112–13 (emphasis added).) He added that "my concept of an enforceable right to marital privacy would give it fundamental importance." (Transcript, Sept. 13, at 114.)

In response to my question as to whether Judge Souter considered "procreation * * * a fundamental right," the nominee responded: "I would assume that if we are going to have any core concept of marital privacy, that would certainly have to rank at its fundamental heart." (Transcript, Sept. 13, at 116.)

B. JUDGE SOUTER REJECTED JUSTICE SCALIA'S VIEW THAT THE COURT MUST LOOK TO THE "MOST SPECIFIC TRADITION AVAILABLE" WHEN DETERMINING WHETHER AN ASSERTED LIBERTY INTEREST WARRANTS CONSTITUTIONAL PROTECTION

A critical and emerging debate on the Supreme Court in the area of privacy and unenumerated rights is the methodology—the mode of analysis—that the Court will use when asked to identify and protect an asserted liberty interest. A core question is whether, in examining this nation's history and tradition, the Court will protect only those interests supported by a specific and longlasting tradition, or whether the Court will not so constrict its analysis.

The importance of this issue was highlighted in the Court's recent decision in *Michael H.* v. *Gerald D.*, 109 S. Ct. 2333 (1989). In that case, a majority of the Court concluded that a biological father does not have a constitutionally protected liberty interest in the relationship with a child conceived through an adulterous relationship.

In footnote six in *Michael H.*, Justice Scalia, joined only by Chief Justice Rehnquist, proposed a methodology for identifying liberty interests based on "the most specific level at which a relevant tradition protecting, or denying protection to, the asserted right can be identified." (109 S. Ct. at 2344, n. 6.) In contrast, Justices O'Connor and Kennedy, while joining all other parts of Justice Scalia's opinion, concurred separately in order to note their express rejection of this methodology. In their view, Justice Scalia—

> sketche[d] a mode of historical analysis to be used when identifying liberty interests protected by the Due Process Clause of the Fourteenth Amendment *that may be somewhat inconsistent with our past decisions in this area.* [citing *Griswold and Eisenstadt* v. *Baird*, 405 U.S. 438 (1972)]. On occasion the Court has characterized relevant traditions protecting asserted rights at levels of generality that might not be 'the most specific traditions' available. *I would not foreclose the unanticipated by the prior imposition of a single mode of historical analysis.*" (Id. at 2346–47 (O'Connor, J., concurring) (emphasis added).)

I discussed this methodological issue with Judge Souter on several occasions:

> Chairman BIDEN. [C]ould you tell me which of the two methodologies you would employ?
>
> Judge SOUTER. *I could not accept the view that, as a rule always to be applied, the most specific evidence is the only valid evidence* * * *. [I]t seems to me that the quest for the kind of evidence that we are after should be a quest not for evidence which, as a matter of definition or a matter of absolute necessity has either got to be of narrow compass or of general compass, rather, it has got to be a quest for reliable evidence, *and there may be reliable evi-*

19

dence of great generality." (Transcript, Sept. 14, at 160 (emphasis added).)

*   *   *   *   *

> Chairman BIDEN. [D]o you think we need to determine * * * the narrowest application of the right asserted, or a broader application of the right asserted?
>
> Judge SOUTER. The answer is we cannot, as a matter of definition at the beginning of our inquiry, narrow the acceptable evidence to the most narrow evidence possible * * *. (Transcript, Sept. 14, at 161.)

Furthermore, Judge Souter testified that the relevant tradition need not exist for any set length of time before it will support recognition of the protection for an asserted liberty interest. He said that—

> it is fair to say that you look at the whole continuum for whatever evidence may be worth * * *. I do not thing there is a point at which you can say, well, I draw the line and I will consider no evidence after this point or no evidence before this point. (Transcripts, Sept. 17, at 277–78.) [3]

Justice Scalia's approach is, in my view, unduly narrow, misguided, and fundamentally at odds with the Constitution's majestic and capacious language. If a majority of the Court had adhered to it during the past 25 years, numerous decisions would have been resolved differently. For example, Justice Scalia's approach would have meant that the statute prohibiting interracial marriages struck down in *Loving* v. *Virginia*, 388 U.S. 1 (1967), would have been upheld, since there is no specific tradition recognizing the right of interracial couples to marry.

On the fundamental question presented in *Michael H.* Then, I am encouraged by Judge Souter's express rejection of Justice Scalia's approach, and his willingness to search for "reliable evidence of great generality."

C. CERTAIN ASPECTS OF JUDGE SOUTER'S TESTIMONY ARE TROUBLING AND UNSETTLING

1. Judge Souter did not acknowledge that the due process clause of the 14th amendment supports the right of unmarried individuals to use contraception

A troubling aspect of Judge Souter's testimony on privacy and unenumerated rights is his refusal to acknowledge a rationale for the right of unmarried couples to use contraceptives that is grounded in the Due Process Clause, rather than the Equal Protection Clause, of the Fourteenth Amendment.

---

[3] Along these same lines, Judge Souter parted with a methodology linked to a concept of "ordered liberty," noting that he, like Justice Harlan, would "make a search somewhat further afield than that." (Transcript, Sept. 14, at 9–10.) Elaborating on this view, he added:

I am convinced that Justice Harlan . . . was, in effect, asking for a broader inquiry than we might be engaging in if we limited ourselves to the . . . concept of ordered liberty, because, as was demonstrated in many other cases, there are many limitations upon what we regard as almost garden variety constitutional rights which still could be found in a society which we would not say was fundamentally unjust. (Transcript, Sept. 14, at 22.)

In *Eisenstadt* v. *Baird*, 405 U.S. 438 (1972), the Supreme Court addressed the question of whether unmarried individuals have a constitutional right to use contraception. When I asked Judge Scouter About *Eisenstadt*, the nominee correctly noted that the case had been analyzed on equal protection, and not on due process, grounds, and he indicated his support for the Court's equal protection analysis. (Transcript, Sept. 13, at 111–12.) Despite repeated questioning by Senator Metzenbaum, Senator Leahy, and I, Judge Souter refused to acknowledge support for a rationale grounded in the Due Process Clause of the Fourteenth Amendment. In his view:

> The case has not been decided and the privacy analysis that would be its first step simply has not been done * * *. *That is an open question.* (Transcript, Sept. 17, at 230; emphasis added.)

Judge Souter's approach to this question is worrisome. Indeed, while Judge Souter correctly noted that the specific holding of the Court in *Eisenstadt* was predicated on the Equal Protection Clause of the Fourteenth Amendment, he ignored the Court's oft-repeated statement regarding the privacy rights of individuals:

> It is true that in *Griswold* the right of privacy in question inhered in the marital relationship. Yet the married couple is not an independent entity with a mind and heart of its own, but an association of two individuals each with a separate intellectual and emotional makeup. If the right of privacy means anything, it is the right of the *individual, married or single,* to be free from unwarranted governmental intrusion into matters so fundamentally affecting a person as the decision whether to bear or beget a child. *(Eisenstadt,* 405 U.S. at 453 (emphasis added).)

Thus, I believe that the right of single individuals to use contraception—far from being an "open question"—is indeed quite settled, as the Supreme Court's case law during the past 18 years has illustrated.

Nonetheless, I find some encouragement in Judge Souter's testimony in the context of discussing the *Michael H.* case. There, he testified that the appropriate inquiry in identifying and protecting liberty interests under the Due Process Clause of the Fourteenth Amendment was not to look for the most specific tradition available but to look instead for more general traditions, and that "there may be reliable evidence of great generality." (Transcript, Sept. 14, at 160.) Such an inquiry, were Judge Souter to undertake it, could support a finding by the nominee that unmarried individuals have a fundamental right to use contraceptives.

2. Judge Souter refused to testify in any respect about issues pertaining to reproductive freedom

Judge Souter refused to answer questions pertaining to reproductive freedom that, in my view, he could have answered without compromising his judicial independence or indicating how he would vote on a request to overrule *Roe* v. *Wade*, 410 U.S. 113 (1973)—particularly given his willingness to testify quite specifically about issues that are currently pending before the Court or are at least unresolved.

To understand my belief that Judge Souter could have answered a number of questions pertaining to reproductive freedom, it is necessary to review the Supreme Court's method of analysis in this area. In analyzing unenumerated rights under the Due Process Clause of the Fourteenth Amendment, the Supreme Court examines two operative questions. First, does the claimant have a protected liberty interest with which a governmental body is interfering? Second, assuming there is some interference with a protected liberty interest, does the government has sufficient justification for doing so?

If, in answering the first inquiry, the Court determines that a "fundamental right" is at stake, it will apply "strict scrutiny" to the challenged law or regulation; the Court will ask whether the law or regulation is narrowly tailored to advance a compelling state interest. If, on the other hand, the Court determines that a "ordinary right" is at stake, it will evaluate the challenged law or regulation under the "rational basis" standard—asking whether there is any plausible reason for that law or regulation.

During the hearing, I described this two-part analysis in this way:

> [First] is the value placed upon the liberty interest that is * * * constitutionally protected by the Court * * *. [S]econd is what the Court would conclude to be sufficient evidence to meet the test required under the law, to provide countervailing weight to interpose the State between the woman and that right. (Transcript, Sept. 14, at 142.)

In questioning Judge Souter on reproductive freedom, I focused on the first part of this analysis, asking Judge Souter to weigh the value of a woman's liberty interest not to remain pregnant. Judge Souter repeatedly refused to comment on whether he believes a woman's liberty interest to choose not to remain pregnant is an "ordinary right" or a "fundamental right," even though responding to such questioning in no way indicated, much less suggested, how he would rule on a case challenging the Supreme Court's 1973 decision in *Roe* v. *Wade*.

Illustrative is the following exchange I had with Judge Souter:

> Chairman BIDEN. [L]et us say that a woman and/or her mate uses * * * a birth control device and it fails. Does she still have a constitutional right to choose not to become pregnant?
> Judge SOUTER. Senator, that is the point at which I will have to exercise the prerogative * * * [not to answer]. I think for me to start answering that question, in effect, is for me to start discussing the concept of *Roe* v. *Wade*. (Transcript, Sept. 13, at 117.)

Judge Souter could have answered this question without indicating in any way how he would rule on a challenge to *Roe* v. *Wade*, the specific issue on which, commendably, he did not want to comment. As I explained:

> [I]f you are willing to discuss * * * whether or not this fundamental right of privacy of a married woman regarding pro-

creation * * * ceases at the time she becomes pregnant, or continues for some period of time, you would have not answered in any way how you would rule on *Roe* v. *Wade* because if there is a fundamental right that exists, the State must have an extraordinary reason to interpose itself between the mother's judgment and her state of pregnancy or non-pregnancy. *What you consider to be an overwhelming reason is something I am not asking you.* (Transcript, Sept. 14, at 143–44 (emphasis added).)

Curiously, while Judge Souter stopped short of answering any questions regarding reproductive freedom and the Due Process Clause of the Fourteenth Amendment, he discussed freely several issues that are either pending before the Court or at least have not been resolved definitely. Three such issues on which he commented were the standard of review in gender discrimination cases (Transcript, Sept. 13, at 147, 215–17), the standard of review under the Free Exercise Clause of the First Amendment (Transcript, Sept. 14, at 46, 49, 152), and the constitutionality of capital punishment. (Transcript, Sept. 17, at 61.) I remain unpersuaded that these areas are so much more "settled" than the area of reproductive freedom that Judge Souter could appropriately testify about the former and not the latter.

Nonetheless—and importantly—Judge Souter did testify, in response to Senator Kohl's question, "do [you] have an opinion on *Roe* v. *Wade*?" that:

I have not got any agenda on what should be done with *Roe* v. *Wade*, if that case were brought before me. I will listen to both sides of that case. *I have not made up my mind and I do not go on the Court saying I must go one way or I must go another way.* (Transcript, Sept. 27, at 129 (emphasis added).)

This statement goes a step further than refusing to tell the committee his view on reproductive freedom, and tells us—if Judge Souter is to be believed, and I do believe him—that his mind is an open one.

* * * * * * *

Judge Souter's testimony in this area was mixed at best. While his support for unenumerated rights and marital privacy are quite encouraging—particularly given the nominee's blank record on these issues before the hearings) I remain troubled by his view that whether unmarried individuals have a right to use contraceptives in an "open question." And I remain unpersuaded that his reticence on the issue of reproductive freedom was necessary, as he asserted, to maintain his judicial independence.

Nonetheless, Judge Souter's expansive methodology for interpreting privacy rights generally, and his genuine open-minded view of a woman's privacy right after conception, provide a basis for consenting to his nomination.

ADDITIONAL VIEWS OF SENATOR HATCH

Judge Souter's excellent educational and legal background and his demonstrated knowledge of the law at the hearing all attest to his competence and ability. I believe he will join the Supreme Court with an independent mind, willing to consider different points of view on the cases which will come before him.

I also believe that he will seek to interpret and apply the law according to its original meaning. I do not believe that he will impose his own policy preferences on the American people in the guise of judging. The role of the judicial branch is to enforce the provisions of the Constitution and the laws we enact in Congress as their meaning was originally intended by their framers. That meaning must then be applied to the facts and circumstances before the judge—facts and circumstances perhaps never contemplated by the framers of the legal provision being applied. But the meaning—the underlying principle of the provision—does not change.

In my view, Judge Souter's judicial philosophy is best expressed in his dissenting opinion in the 1986 New Hampshire Supreme Court case of In re Estate of Dionne and his 1990 remarks to a Massachusetts law journal. In the Dionne case, he wrote "that 'the language of the [state] constitution is to be understood in the sense in which it was used at the time of its adoption . . .' The Court's interpretive task is therefore to determine the meaning of the [Constitutional provision] as it was understood when the framers proposed it and the people ratified it as part of the original constitutional text that took effect in June of 1784." In the May 28, 1990, Massachusetts Lawyers Weekly, Judge Souter was quoted as saying: "On constitutional matters, I am of the interpretist school. We're not looking for the original application, we're looking for meaning here. That's a very different thing."

Judge Souter never departed from this view in his testimony.

I note that I don't know whether I will always agree with Judge Souter's conclusion about the original meaning of a particular statute or constitutional provision or with his application of the provision in a given case.

I have read that some people are drawing some rather firm conclusions as to how Judge Souter might have ruled or will rule in the future on some kinds of cases—whether religious liberty cases or cases involving Congressionally mandated racial preferences. The record is clear, however, that Judge Souter did not commit as to how he would rule in those areas or almost any other area. And where he may have been more forthcoming, he is entitled to change his mind after reading the briefs and hearing oral arguments, as he has done in his judicial career thus far.

I mention this to record my view that if, in a case, Judge Souter's opinion seems to be a variance with how one of us anticipated he would rule, no one should claim he misled us. Moreover, I would hope no one would then claim we ought to probe the next nominee even further than the committee probed Judge Souter. While I have often said a senator has the right to ask a nominee any questions he wishes, a nominee is not obligated to answer all questions. I believe in some circumstances he was pressed too far and said more than a nominee should have to say at a confirmation hearing. While some may claim that so long as the nominee is not asked how he will rule in a specific case, he should answer all questions. But asking a nominee whether he endorses a very specific legal or constitutional principle, where respectable arguments can be made both for and against that principle, can in many instances be tantamount to asking how he would rule in particular cases. It clearly asks a nominee, in effect, to prejudge many specific issues. Some questions were even case-specific. As one random example, the nominee was asked whether he believed *Roe* v. *Wade* was settled law. He declined to answer. There is no practical difference between asking that question and asking how he will rule in a specific case, when the issue addressed in *Roe* so clearly remains an issue which can come before the Supreme Court. Judges should feel free to rule as they see fit on the bench and not as others anticipated they would rule.

The trend begun in this committee in the mid-1950s of probing the nominee's views on controversial issues seems to have accelerated in recent years. If the trend continues, that is something I will have to bear in mind if I am here when a member of the other party sends us a Supreme Court nominee.

Finally, I want to address this issue of litmus tests that some groups are seeking to have the Senate impose on nominees, for example, on the issue of abortion.

Some urge us to reject Judge Souter because he did not commit himself to uphold *Roe* v. *Wade*. But what would happen if different senators impose litmus tests on a variety of issues—could any nominee ever be confirmed?

Some people would make a very strong case that religious liberty issues, discrimination issues, federalism issues and other issues are so crucial that we must demand to know in advance how a nominee will rule.

Ben Wattenberg, a Democrat who is a senior fellow at the American Enterprise Institute, says that quotas should be the litmus test. He criticized a 5-4 decision from June permitting racial set-asides in the FCC's award of television and radio licenses. Suppose 20 senators apply that litmus test, and 15 other senators apply a church/state litmus test seeking to reverse the school prayer decisions, and 15 other Senators impose a litmus test on reversing the *Miranda* decision and *Mapp* v. *Ohio* imposing the exclusionary rule on the states.

How can any nominee be confirmed if we viewed our role this way?

A President may one day send us a nominee supported by pro-abortion groups. How would they feel if other senators and I took up Ben Wattenberg's cue on imposing a limus test on reverse discrimination, another group imposed a litmus test on overturning *Miranda* and the exclusionary rule, and a third group of prolife senators, totalling 51 senators, imposed a litmus test on reversing *Roe* v. *Wade?*

MINORITY VIEWS OF SENATOR EDWARD M. KENNEDY IN OPPOSITION TO THE CONFIRMATION OF DAVID H. SOUTER TO BE AN ASSOCIATE JUSTICE OF THE SUPREME COURT

I oppose the confirmation of Judge David H. Souter to the Supreme Court.

The Constitution itself is silent on the standard the Senate should apply in considering a Supreme Court nomination. The role of the Senate in the confirmation of judicial nominees selected by the President was a last-minute compromise reached by the Framers at the Constitutional Convention in 1787. Those who drafted the Constitution had originally proposed that the Senate alone should appoint federal judges. The final compromise, which assigns shared responsibility to the President and the Senate, was adopted as one of the key checks and balances to assure that neither the President nor the Senate would have excessive influence over the Supreme Court and other federal courts.

The genius of the Constitution and Bill of Rights is apparent in the establishment of an independent federal judiciary, sworn to protect the fundamental rights and liberties of individuals against the excesses of government and majority rule. The Supreme Court has the last word on the meaning of the Constitution, and its decisions have a profound impact on all of our lives.

In the past half century, the Supreme Court has played a central role in the effort to make America a better and fairer land. The Court outlawed school segregation in the 1950's, removed barriers to the right to vote in the 1960's, and established a far-reaching right to privacy, including the right to abortion in the 1970's. In other ways as well, the Supreme Court strengthened the basic rights of minorities and took steps to end the second-class status of women in our society. But in the decade of the 1980's, as a result of a strategy of ideological appointments in the Reagan years, the Court has seemed to pause in carrying out this important role, and in many cases has actually turned back the clock. On many of these issues, the current Court seems to be divided 4-4, so that the Senate's decision on this nomination is likely to tip the balance in one direction or the other.

In considering a Supreme Court nomination, the Senate must make two inquiries. The first is the threshold issue: Does the nominee have the intelligence, integrity, and temperament to meet the responsibilities of a Supreme Court Justice?

But that is only the beginning, not the end of the inquiry. The Senate also must determine whether the nominee possesses a clear commitment to the fundamental values at the core of our constitutional democracy.

(83)

299

PRIVACY AND UNENUMERATED RIGHTS

On the issue of whether the Constitution protects a core right to privacy, Judge Souter said he believes that "the Due Process Clause of the Fourteenth Amendment does recognize and does protect an unenumerated right of privacy." He further endorsed the plain meaning of the Ninth Amendment as a source of other rights not enumerated in the Bill of Rights. Finally, Judge Souter categorically stated that "there is certainly, to begin with, a core of privacy which is identified as marital privacy, and I believe it can and should be regarded as fundamental." Procreation, he said, would rank at the "fundamental heart" of marital privacy.

From this promising beginning, however, Judge Souter retreated to a position in which he refused to reveal whether he believed there is any fundamental privacy right outside the marital relationship.

Specifically, in discussing the constitutional status of abortion, Judge Souter would go no further than to say that abortion "would rank as an interest to be asserted under liberty." He refused to suggest how that interest should be evaluated, or whether it would be enforceable against the state, "based upon a valuation that it is fundamental." He gave a vague general statement of what his methodology would be in deciding a case like *Roe* v. *Wade*. His analysis would include "the issue of how the interest is itself valued." It would include "what the countervailing interest may be and how they are to be valued". And, he said, "in a case of re-examining a prior precedent we have to . . . valu[e] that precedent in accordance with the general rules that we have."

In response to a question about whether a state could recognize a fundamental right to abortion in its own constitution in the face of a determination by the U.S. Supreme Court that such a right was not protected under the federal constitution, Souter replied affirmatively, but added "[w]hether there is any basis that could be raised * * * based on the rights of the fetus, rather than on the rights of the mother, that, of course, is a totally undecided issue." In discussing abortion Judge Souter also stated that "whether I do or do not find it moral or immoral, will play absolutely no role in any decision which I make." Under prodding about his "gut reaction" to the dilemma facing women if *Roe* is overruled, he first described it as a federalism problem, then acknowledged that there would be enforcement problems, and finally observed that "whatever the Court does, someone's lives, and indeed thousands of lives, will be affected, and that fact must be appreciated."

Judge Souter's reluctance to discuss specific constitutional issues relating to abortion and the right to privacy contrasted sharply with his willingness to discuss in great detail his views on other constitutional issues likely to come before the Supreme Court, For example, Judge Souter recognized that the case of *Employment Division of Oregon* v. *Smith* is currently subject to a motion for rehearing before the Court. Nevertheless, he said that he personally believed that the government had an obligation to remain neutral in all matters concerning the free exercise of religion. He further commented that while he understood the reasoning of the majority, he also recognized Justice O'Connor's argument that the case could have been evaluated under the strict scrutiny standard. He was also willing to speculate about the possible limiting effect that the *Smith* decision may have on prior case law.

Clearly, Judge Souter's view that the government should remain neutral in matters of religion is a matter of current constitutional debate, as he acknowledged during questioning. And it is likely that the issues in the *Smith* case will come before the Supreme Court again. Yet Judge Souter was still willing to give his definitive personal and constitutional opinion on the matter.

Similarly, Judge Souter had no reluctance to reveal his view that the death penalty is not cruel and unusual punishment. Every year, the Court considers cases raising questions on the death penalty. Every year, defendants argue that the death penalty is cruel and unusual punishment. Yet Judge Souter still felt it appropriate to state his opinion to the committee.

6

JUSTICE CLARENCE THOMAS

In 1991, President George Bush selected Clarence Thomas, a black conservative who had served as chair of the Equal Employment Opportunity Commission under Ronald Reagan, to replace retiring Justice Thurgood Marshall, who as head of the NAACP Legal Defense Fund had argued *Brown* and several other landmark civil rights cases before the Supreme Court. This juxtaposition prompted a confirmation battle heavy with symbolic and practical consequences. Since Justice William Brennan's retirement, Justice Thurgood Marshall had been the rallying point for the liberal position on the Court. By replacing Marshall with an equal and opposite force, the Thomas nomination promised to further tip the balance of the Court.

On the issue of abortion, however, Thomas had made no concrete statements reflecting his views. Indeed, at his confirmation hearings, he consistently stated that he had no views regarding the issue. For those determined to extract from Clarence Thomas's own words his stance on abortion, he had left a trail of marginally related writings and speeches in which he mentioned privacy and *stare decisis*. Yet attempts to extrapolate from these works to anticipate how Thomas would vote on abortion amounted to educated guesswork.

Pro-choice groups responded to this lack of information with immediate suspicion, choosing to presume the worst about a Bush nominee. A coalition of law and other professors, the National Women's Law Center, the Women's Legal Defense Fund, NARAL, NOW, and Planned Parenthood all spoke out against Thomas on the abortion issue. Representative of the views of these groups is the Professors' Report to the Committee which claimed that Thomas's views "endorsed an approach to overruling *Roe* . . . that is so extreme it would create a constitutional requirement that abortion be outlawed in all states. . . ." Nomination of Judge Clarence Thomas to Be Associate Justice of the Supreme Court of the United States: Hearings Before the Senate Comm. on the Judiciary, 102d Cong., 1st Sess. (1991) at 566. Specifically, they focused on his support of a theory of natural law; his approval of an essay by Lewis Lehrman which interpreted natural law as creating an inalienable and superior right to life at the moment of conception; and his "reject[ion of] unenumerated rights as articulated in Griswold, Eisenstadt, and Roe." *Id.* at 572.

With respect to *Griswold* and *Roe*, Thomas's opponents pointed to Thomas's writing "that the judicial decisions that 'make conservatives nervous' are Roe . . . and Griswold . . . ." *Id.* at 572, quoting Thomas, Higher Law Background of the Privileges and Immunities Clause, 12 Harv. J.L. Pub. Pol'y 63, 64. Presumably this comment was interpreted by his opponents as meaning that, because Thomas is a conservative, *Roe* makes *him* nervous, and he would thus vote to overturn the decision. The coalition of professors further pointed to Thomas's 1986 participation "as a member of a White House Working Group on the Family that . . . severely criticized landmark constitutional decisions protecting the right to privacy." *Id.* at 574.

In response to these interpretations of his prior writings, Thomas stated that his "view [was] that there is a right to privacy in the Fourteenth Amendment" and that he "believe[d] the approach . . . reaffirmed in *Griswold* in determining . . . the right of privacy was an appropriate way to go." *Id.* Despite acknowledging the existence of a right to privacy, Thomas would not comment on whether it encompassed the abortion decision.

Thomas surprised many Senators and evoked reactions of utter disbelief when he stated that, although he accepted that *Roe* "has certainly been one of the more important" cases of the last generation, he had never "debated the contents of [*Roe*]." *Id.* Thomas's supporters ultimately praised his response; Senator John Danforth (R-Mo.) characterized Thomas's testimony as expressing an openness "on the Roe versus Wade issue and . . . that he had not expressed even a personal view on the subject." 137 C.R. S13080-81 (daily ed. Sept. 17, 1991).

Danforth, moreover, defended the veracity of Thomas's statement that he had no views on abortion by pointing out that any information related to Thomas's abortion views "certainly would have surfaced during the . . . 2 1/2 months" prior to his Senate confirmation hearings and that opponents of Justice Thomas had even "taken out newspaper ads asking people to come forward if they [had] ever discussed Roe versus Wade with Clarence Thomas." *Id.*; *Id.* at S14423.

Supporters further defended Thomas's silence by noting that commenting on an issue which could come before the Court would compromise the independence of the judiciary. Thomas's opponents, however, were not impressed with this old chestnut culled from the

Souter hearings; rather they attempted to turn Thomas's silence against him. If Thomas was indeed telling the truth, they argued, if he had never developed a view on *Roe*, a case which he "acknowledged . . . [was] among the most important cases decided by the Supreme Court in the last 20 years[,] beg[ged] credulity [and] indicate[d] . . . that he d[id] not have [a] coherent understanding of the Constitution. . . ." 137 Cong. Rec. S13748-49 (daily ed. Sept 26, 1991).

Thomas refused to be baited. Whether he truly had no opinion about *Roe* or whether he was simply unwilling to undermine his confirmation by expressing an unpopular view, he remained tight-lipped on the issue throughout the hearing process. Ultimately, despite the furor and frustration over Thomas's silence, the abortion issue faded out of the spotlight of the Senate's inquiry with the revelation of Anita Hill's sexual harassment charges against Thomas.

Justice Clarence Thomas
Documents

S. Hrg. 102–1084, Pt. 1

NOMINATION OF JUDGE CLARENCE THOMAS TO BE ASSOCIATE JUSTICE OF THE SUPREME COURT OF THE UNITED STATES

HEARINGS

BEFORE THE

COMMITTEE ON THE JUDICIARY
UNITED STATES SENATE

ONE HUNDRED SECOND CONGRESS

FIRST SESSION

ON

THE NOMINATION OF CLARENCE THOMAS TO BE ASSOCIATE JUSTICE OF THE SUPREME COURT OF THE UNITED STATES

SEPTEMBER 10, 11, 12, 13, AND 16, 1991

Part 1 of 4 Parts

J–102–40

Printed for the use of the Committee on the Judiciary

U.S. GOVERNMENT PRINTING OFFICE

56–270   WASHINGTON : 1993

For sale by the U.S. Government Printing Office
Superintendent of Documents, Mail Stop: SSOP, Washington, DC 20402-9328
ISBN 0-16-040835-0

The CHAIRMAN. But let me move, if I may, for a second. As I said earlier, I mentioned that concomitant with those who want to sort of raise up the economic protections and business incorporation to make it harder for government to regulate them without paying them, which is a multibillion-dollar change in the law—not your view—where Mr. Epstein's views take place, the multibillion-dollar expense for the taxpayers if they wanted to continue to regulate the way we now regulate and consider reasonable. As I mentioned earlier, there is a second zone of individual rights, a zone which includes such rights as free speech, religion, and privacy in the family. These rights are also protected as informed by natural law principles.

Now, you say that is not what you mean, informed by natural law principles. But some of the specific protections are very specific. For example, the fourth amendment guarantees personal privacy in a particular context, illegal search and seizures, and other protections are more general, like the 14th amendment that says "nor shall any State deprive any person of life, liberty, or property without due process of law."

Now, Judge, in your view, does the liberty clause of the 14th amendment protect the right of women to decide for themselves in certain instances whether or not to terminate pregnancy?

Judge THOMAS. Senator, first of all, let me look at that in the context other than with natural law principles.

The CHAIRMAN. Let's forget about natural law for a minute.

Judge THOMAS. My view is that there is a right to privacy in the 14th amendment.

The CHAIRMAN. Well, Judge, does that right to privacy in the liberty clause of the 14th amendment protect the right of a woman to decide for herself in certain instances whether or not to terminate a pregnancy?

Judge THOMAS. Senator, I think that the Supreme Court has made clear that the issue of marital privacy is protected, that the State cannot infringe on that without a compelling interest, and the Supreme Court, of course, in the case of *Roe* v. *Wade* has found an interest in the woman's right to—as a fundamental interest a woman's right to terminate a pregnancy. I do not think that at this time that I could maintain my impartiality as a member of the judiciary and comment on that specific case.

The CHAIRMAN. Well, let's try it another way, Judge. I don't want to ask you to comment specifically on *Roe* there. What I am trying to get at, there are two schools of thought out there. There is a gentleman like Professor Michael Moore of the University of Pennsylvania and Mr. Lewis Lehrman of the Heritage Foundation who both think natural law philosophy informs their view, and they conclude one who strongly supports a woman's right and the other one who strongly opposes a woman's right to terminate a pregnancy.

Then there are those who say that, no, this should be left strictly to the legislative bodies, not for the courts to interpret, and they fall into the school of thought represented by John Hart Healy and former Judge Robert Bork, for example, who say the Court has nothing to do with that.

128

Now, let me ask you this: Where does the decision lie? Does it lie with the Court? For example, you quote, with admiration, Mr. Lehrman's article. Mr. Lehrman's article was on natural law and—I forget the exact title here. Let me find it. "Natural Law and the Right to Life." And you say when you are speaking at a gathering that you think that that is a superb application of natural law. You say, "It is a splendid example of applying natural law."

Now, what did you mean by that?

Judge THOMAS. Well, let me go back to, I guess, my first comment to you when we were discussing natural law—I think that is important—and then come back to the question of the due process analysis.

The speech that I was giving there was before the Heritage Foundation. Again, as I indicated earlier, my interest was civil rights and slavery. What I was attempting to do in the beginning of that speech was to make clear to a conservative audience that blacks who were Republicans and the issues that affected blacks were being addressed and being dealt with by conservatives in what I considered a less-than-acceptable manner.

The second point that——

The CHAIRMAN. In what sense? In that they were not——

Judge THOMAS. That they were not.

The CHAIRMAN [continuing]. Invoking natural law.

Judge THOMAS. No, that—no. The second point that I wanted to make to them was that they had, based on what I thought was an appropriate approach, they had an obligation just as conservatives to be more open and more aggressive on civil rights enforcement. What I thought would be the best way to approach that would be using the underlying concept of our Constitution that we were all created equal.

I felt that conservatives would be skeptical about the notion of natural law. I was using that as the underlying approach. I felt that they would be conservative and that they would not—or be skeptical about that concept. I was speaking in the Lew Lehrman Auditorium of the Heritage Foundation. I thought that if I demonstrated that one of their own accepted at least the concept of natural rights, that they would be more apt to accept that concept as an underlying principle for being more aggressive on civil rights. My whole interest was civil rights enforcement.

The CHAIRMAN. Judge, you said in that speech, "The need to reexamine natural law is as current as last month's issue of Time on ethics, yet it is more venerable than St. Thomas Aquinas. It both transcends and underlies time and place, race and custom, and until recently it has been an integral part of the American political tradition. Dr. King was the last prominent American political figure to appeal to it. But Heritage trustee Lewis Lehrman's recent essay in the American Sector on the Declaration of Independence and the meaning of the right to life is a splendid example of applying it. Briefly put, this thesis of natural law is that human nature provides the key to how men ought to live their lives."

And then Mr. Lehrman's article goes on, not you, Mr. Lehrman's article goes on and says, "Because it is a natural right of a fetus, there is no ability of the legislative body to impact in any way on whether or not there can or cannot be an abortion at any time for

309

any reason. And the Court must uphold applying natural law, the principle that abortion is wrong under all circumstances, whether it is the life of the mother, no matter what, all circumstances."

Judge THOMAS. It was not my intention, Mr. Chairman, as I have tried to indicate to you, to adopt—I think I have been explicit when I wanted to adopt someone or say something, adopt a position or say something. I think I have done that.

My interest in the speech I think is fairly clear, or is very clear. My interest was in the aggressive enforcement of civil rights. Remember the context. I am in the Reagan administration. I have been engaged in significant battles throughout my tenure. It is toward the end of the Reagan administration. And I feel that conservatives have taken an approach on civil rights where they have become comfortable with notions that it is okay to simply be against quotas or to be against busing or to be against voting rights and consider that a civil rights agenda.

What I was looking for were unifying themes in a political standpoint, not a constitutional adjudication standpoint, and I used themes that I thought that one of their champions had in a way adopted, not adopting his analysis or adopting his approach, but adopting a theme that he used to serve the purposes that I thought were very important.

The CHAIRMAN. Well, Judge, let me conclude this round by saying that—picking up that context, that you were a part of the Reagan administration. In 1986, as a member of the administration, you were part of what has been referred to here, the administration's Working Group on the Family. This group put out what I think can only be characterized as a controversial report. And you sign that report which recommends more State regulation of the family than is now allowed under the law. That report concludes that the Supreme Court's privacy decisions for the last 20 years are fatally flawed and should be corrected.

Judge, did you read this report before it was released?

Judge THOMAS. Well, let me explain to you how working groups work in the domestic policy context or the way that they worked in the administration. Normally what would happen is that there would be a number of informal meetings. At those meetings, you would express your—there would be some discussion around the table. My interest was in low-income families. I transmitted, after several meetings transmitted to the head of that working group, my views on the low-income family and the need to address the problems of low-income families in the report.

The report, as it normally works in these working groups in domestic policy, the report is not finalized, nor is it a team effort in drafting. You are submitted your document. That document is then, as far as I know, it may be sent around or may not be sent around. But there is no signature required on those.

The CHAIRMAN. Did you ever read the report, Judge?

Judge THOMAS. The section that I read was on the family. I was only interested in whether they included my comments on the low-income family.

The CHAIRMAN. But at any time, even after it was published?

Judge THOMAS. No, I did not.

Senator LEAHY. Thank you very much, Mr. Chairman.

Judge Thomas, welcome back this afternoon. Judge, I would like to just go over a couple of points prompted by some of your earlier testimony.

A couple of thoughts occur to me. I was looking over the notes of your responses to Senator Kennedy's questions yesterday. You recall that when he talked about the Lewis Lehrman article, "the Declaration of Independence and the Right to Life," he referred to your statement, in which you called the Lehrman article a "splendid example of applying natural law."

I understand your answer was that you were speaking in the Lewis Lehrman Auditorium, with Lewis Lehrman sitting there, referring to Lewis Lehrman's article, and that you intended to make your conservative audience more receptive to natural law principles as it applied to civil rights. Is that a fair restatement of your answer?

Judge THOMAS. I think with the possible exception of "Lew Lehrman sitting there."

Senator LEAHY. Oh, that is my misconception. He was not there, then?

Judge THOMAS. Not to my knowledge.

Senator LEAHY. OK. Was the rest a fair restatement?

Judge THOMAS. Yes.

Senator LEAHY. Thank you. So, granting that it was a strategic remark for the reasons that you stated, did you believe the article was "a splendid example of applying natural law"?

Judge THOMAS. As I indicated yesterday, Senator, that I did not and do not think that natural law can be applied to resolve this particular issue, I think it is a constitutional matter and it has to be resolved under constitutional law, as a matter of constitutional law.

Senator LEAHY. But that is not precisely my question. My question was, did you believe the article was a splendid example of applying natural law? Just on that narrow line: Do you believe the article itself was "a splendid example of applying natural law"?

Judge THOMAS. Let me explain what I was trying to say. What I was trying to say——

Senator LEAHY. You cannot answer that specific question?

Judge THOMAS. What I am trying to say, so I am not misunderstood, Senator——

Senator THURMOND. Mr. Chairman, he has a right to explain his position.

Judge THOMAS. What I was trying to say is here is a good example——

Senator LEAHY. If Senator Thurmond wishes to join him at the witness stand—but go ahead, Judge.

Senator THURMOND. I would be glad to do it, but he has a right to explain his answers.

Senator LEAHY. Go ahead, Judge.

Judge THOMAS. Thank you, Senator.

My point was that here is an example of one of yours using natural law. I was not commenting on the substance of its use, so it was an example, it was a splendid example in the sense that it was a compliment to him and it is a compliment to someone they believed in, and I would reaffirm what I said yesterday and I have said consistently, and that is that at no time did I adopt or endorse the substance of the article itself.

My interest in that one sentence, I believe, was to get a conservative audience that was skeptical of a concept to be more receptive to that concept in the area that I wanted to use, in the area of civil rights. That speech is on the treatment of blacks by conservatives, treatment of minority issues in the Reagan administration, and a sort of request and a push or a tug to them to be more receptive in this area and to be aggressive in this area. It was not an endorsement of that article.

Senator LEAHY. Do you feel that your answer today is in any way inconsistent with what you said then?

Judge THOMAS. What I said?

Senator LEAHY. At that time?

Judge THOMAS. Yes.

Senator LEAHY. Thank you. And you understand my confusion in the two answers, but you explain that confusion in that the statement then and your answer today are consistent?

Judge THOMAS. I said that they were consistent.

Senator LEAHY. OK. Then you feel your answer today is consistent with what you said back at the time you spoke in the Lewis Lehrman Auditorium?

Judge THOMAS. Senator, my statement today is consistent with what I intended to do and what I did in the Lew Lehrman Auditorium. My interest, as I indicated to you, and I think I repeated a number of times here, it was in civil rights and finding unifying principles in the area of civil rights.

Senator LEAHY. Well, let me make sure that I understand. Is it your testimony here today and yesterday that you do not endorse the Lewis Lehrman article to the extent that it argues under the natural law principles of the Declaration of Independence that a fetus has an inalienable right to life at the moment of conception? Is that your testimony?

Judge THOMAS. I do not—my testimony is that, with respect to those issues, the issues involved or implicated in the issue of abortion, I do not believe that Mr. Lehrman's application of natural law is appropriate.

Senator LEAHY. Had you read that article before you praised it?

Judge THOMAS. I think I skimmed it, Senator. My interest, again, was in the fact that he used the notion or the concept of natural law, and my idea was to import that notion to something that I was very interested in.

Senator LEAHY. Now, you certainly——

The CHAIRMAN. Excuse me, would the Senator yield? I did not understand one answer.

Did you say that you do not believe that Mr. Lehrman's application of natural law in that article was appropriate?

Judge THOMAS. That's right.

The CHAIRMAN. You do not believe it is appropriate?

Judge THOMAS. That's right.

The CHAIRMAN. Thank you.

Judge THOMAS. I said that my testimony has been that that difficult issue is to be resolved as a matter of constitutional law.

56-270 O—93——8

The CHAIRMAN. Thank you.

Senator LEAHY. Well, the chairman has anticipated my next question. When you gave the speech, which was in 1987, as I recall the testimony, did you understand that the consequences of Mr. Lehrman's position were not just that *Roe* v. *Wade* should be overturned, but that abortion, even in cases of rape and incest, should be banned in every State of the Union? Did you understand that to be the position that he was taking in that article?

Judge THOMAS. Senator, until recently, in reflecting on it, I did not know, I could not recall the entire content of that article until I read recent articles about it. Again, my interest was very, very limited——

Senator LEAHY. I understand——

Judge THOMAS [continuing]. And the——

Senator LEAHY. You have read the article now, though, now that it has been brought up——

Judge THOMAS. I have not re-read it. I have not re-read it.

Senator LEAHY. You have it?

Judge THOMAS. I have not re-read the article.

Senator LEAHY. Do you have the article?

Judge THOMAS. I do not have it with me.

Senator LEAHY. Does somebody want to just—I want to make sure somebody gives it to you, Judge. Let me say that the article, as written, takes a position not just that *Roe* v. *Wade* should be overturned, but that abortion, even in cases of rape and incest, should be banned in every State of the Union. Assuming that is the thrust or one of the main points of the article, do you agree with that?

Judge THOMAS. Again, Senator, it would be, I think, for me to respond to what my views are on those particular issues would really undermine my ability to be impartial in those cases. I have attempted to respond as candidly and openly as I possibly can, without in any way undermining or compromising my ability to rule on these cases.

Senator LEAHY. Well, let's just go, then, to Mr. Lehrman's positions. Under his theory of natural law, every abortion in this country would be criminalized. Do you understand that to be his position? I am not asking whether it is yours, but do you understand that to be his position in that article?

Judge THOMAS. Again, I would have to re-read the article, Senator. I understand the criticisms that you have of the article, but my point to you here today, as well as in other questioning concerning this article, is that I did not adopt or import anything more from this article than the use of this one notion of natural law.

Senator LEAHY. Might I ask you to do this, then, Judge, because we will have another go-round on this. It would only take about 4 or 5 minutes to read that article sometime between now and the next go-round. Could you please find the time to read it? And if you get crammed with too many things between now and then when I get my next turn around, I will just stop and give you time to read it right then.

Judge THOMAS. OK. Thank you.

Senator LEAHY. Now, Mr. Lehrman drew a parallel between the struggle for liberty by slaves with a struggle "for the inalienable right to life of the child-in-the-womb—and thus, the right to life of all future generations." Do you understand the parallel of the struggle for liberty by slaves with the struggle for the inalienable right to life of the child in the womb, and thus, the right to life of all future generations? Do you agree with that comparison?

Judge THOMAS. Again, Senator, I have not re-read this article. I would take you up on your offer to go back and re-read it. My interest was on the issue of slavery, Senator, it was an important issue to me. The concept of liberty and life, et cetera, are very general concepts. I would like to just take the time to go back and re-read it——

Senator LEAHY. Fair enough.

Judge THOMAS [continuing]. And be fair in my response to you.

Senator LEAHY. I absolutely agree.

Judge THOMAS. But let me, if I could say this—my interest in this article was as I have testified before this committee, and I think indicated in some of our prior meetings, it was very important to me to convince conservatives that they should openly support and be aggressive in their support of civil rights.

Senator LEAHY. Judge, does a fetus have the constitutional status of a person?

Judge THOMAS. Senator, I cannot think of any cases that have held that. I would have to go back and rethink that. I cannot think of any cases that have held that.

Senator LEAHY. If somebody were to raise that issue in a court, how would a judge go about making a determination of that? I am not asking you to make a determination, but how would a judge do that? Does he or she go to a medical text, a philosophical text, theological treatises? How does one make such a determination?

Judge THOMAS. Senator, I could only offer this, and I have not made that determination and I have not gone through that kind of analysis, but, of course, one would rely in any case in which one is making a difficult determination, one would rely on the adversarial process to sharpen the issues. One would rely on precedent. One would certainly rely on related areas, such as the area of medicine. In the area of *Roe* v. *Wade,* I think there was considerable reliance on medical evidence. Again, I am doing that in a vacuum, and I was—

Senator LEAHY. I understand that. Of course, even in the adversarial process, a judge can oftentimes shape and direct in a most appropriate way. Any judge I have ever appeared before—if he or she felt that the adversaries did not present enough evidence to help the judge decide—would certainly have the right to ask the adversaries for more information.

In an area like this, do you rely on theology? Do you rely on jurisprudence? Do you rely on medical information? Or do you rely on experience?

Judge THOMAS. Senator, again, I would like to just simply say that, of course, one could see where medical, certainly experience and one could see where precedent would be relevant. I do not see at this point where theology would be relevant.

Again, I would like to refrain from further speculation in this very difficult area. The point that I am making to you, and I think it is an important point, is that when a judge is engaged in any kind of an effort to make difficult decisions in any area, a judge tries to examine the relevant evidence and tries to reach a reasoned conclusion and tries to reach a conclusion, without implicating or without involving his or her personal opinions.

Senator LEAHY. Judge, you were in law school at the time *Roe* v. *Wade* was decided. That was 17 or 18 years ago. You would accept, would you not, that in the last generation, *Roe* v. *Wade* is certainly one of the more important cases to be decided by the U.S. Supreme Court?

Judge THOMAS. I would accept that it has certainly been one of the more important, as well as one that has been one of the more highly publicized and debated cases.

Senator LEAHY. So, it would be safe to assume that when that decision came down—you were in law school, where recent case law is oft discussed—that *Roe* v. *Wade* would have been discussed in the law school while you were there?

Judge THOMAS. The case that I remember being discussed most during my early part of law school was I believe in my small group with Thomas Emerson may have been *Griswold,* since he argued that, and we may have touched on *Roe* v. *Wade* at some point and debated that, but let me add one point to that.

Because I was a married student and I worked, I did not spend a lot of time around the law school doing what the other students enjoyed so much, and that is debating all the current cases and all of the slip opinions. My schedule was such that I went to classes and generally went to work and went home.

Senator LEAHY. Judge Thomas, I was a married law student who also worked, but I also found, at least between classes, that we did discuss some of the law, and I am sure you are not suggesting that there wasn't any discussion at any time of *Roe* v. *Wade?*

Judge THOMAS. Senator, I cannot remember personally engaging in those discussions.

Senator LEAHY. OK.

Judge THOMAS. The groups that I met with at that time during my years in law school were small study groups.

Senator LEAHY. Have you ever had discussion of *Roe* v. *Wade,* other than in this room, in the 17 or 18 years it has been there?

Judge THOMAS. Only, I guess, Senator, in the fact in the most general sense that other individuals express concerns one way or the other, and you listen and you try to be thoughtful. If you are asking me whether or not I have ever debated the contents of it, that answer to that is no, Senator.

Senator LEAHY. Have you ever, in private gatherings or otherwise, stated whether you felt that it was properly decided or not?

Judge THOMAS. Senator, in trying to recall and reflect on that, I don't recollect commenting one way or the other. There were, again, debates about it in various places, but I generally did not participate. I don't remember or recall participating, Senator.

Senator LEAHY. So you don't ever recall stating whether you thought it was properly decided or not?

Judge THOMAS. I can't recall saying one way or the other, Senator.

Senator LEAHY. Well, was it properly decided or not?

Judge THOMAS. Senator, I think that that is where I just have to say what I have said before; that to comment on the holding in that case would compromise my ability to——

Senator LEAHY. Let me ask you this: Have you made any decision in your own mind whether you feel *Roe* v. *Wade* was properly decided or not, without stating what that decision is?

Judge THOMAS. I have not made, Senator, a decision one way or the other with respect to that important decision.

Senator LEAHY. When you came up for confirmation last time for the circuit court of appeals, did you consider your feelings on *Roe* v. *Wade*, in case you would be asked?

Judge THOMAS. I had not—would I have considered, Senator, or did I consider?

Senator LEAHY. Did you consider.

Judge THOMAS. No, Senator.

Senator LEAHY. So you cannot recollect ever taking a position on whether it was properly decided or not properly decided, and you do not have one here that you would share with us today?

Judge THOMAS. I do not have a position to share with you here today on whether or not that case was properly decided. And, Senator, I think that it is appropriate to just simply state that it is—for a judge, that it is late in the day as a judge to begin to decide whether cases are rightly or wrongly decided when one is on the bench. I truly believe that doing that undermines your ability to rule on those cases.

Senator LEAHY. Well, with all due respect, Judge, I have some difficulty with your answer that somehow this case has been so far removed from your discussions or feelings during the years since it was decided while you were in law school. You have participated in a working group that criticized *Roe*. You cited *Roe* in a footnote to your article on the privileges or immunity clause. You have referred to Lewis Lehrman's article on the meaning of the right to life. You specifically referred to abortion in a column in the Chicago Defender. I cannot believe that all of this was done in a vacuum absent some very clear considerations of *Roe* v. *Wade*, and, in fact, twice specifically citing *Roe* v. *Wade*.

Judge THOMAS. Senator, your question to me was did I debate the contents of *Roe* v. *Wade*, the outcome in *Roe* v. *Wade*, do I have this day an opinion, a personal opinion on the outcome in *Roe* v. *Wade*; and my answer to you is that I do not.

Senator LEAHY. Notwithstanding the citing of it in the article on privileges or immunities, notwithstanding the working group that criticized *Roe?*

Judge THOMAS. I would like to have the cite to it. Again, notwithstanding the citation, if there is one, I did not and do not have a position on the outcome.

With respect to the working group, Senator, as I have indicated, the working group did not include the drafting by that working group of the final report. My involvement in that working group was to submit a memorandum, a memorandum that I felt was an important one, on the issue of low-income families. And I thought that that was an important contribution and one that should have been a central part in the report. But with respect to the other comments, I did not participate in those comments.

Senator LEAHY. I will make sure that you have an opportunity to read both the footnote citation and the Lewis Lehrman article before we get another go-round. But am I also correct in characterizing your testimony here today as feeling that as a sitting judge it would be improper even to express an opinion on *Roe* v. *Wade*, if you do have one?

Judge THOMAS. That is right, Senator. I think the important thing for me as a judge, Senator, has been to maintain my impartiality. When one is in the executive branch—and I have been in the executive branch, and I have tried to engage in debate and tried to advance the ball in discussions, tried to be a good advocate for my points of views and listening to other points of views. But when you move to the judiciary, I don't think that you can afford to continue to accumulate opinions in areas that are strongly controverted because those issues will eventually be before the Court in some form or another.

Senator LEAHY. Of course, as Senator Metzenbaum pointed out earlier today, you have spoken about a number of cases, and I understand your differentiation in your answers to his question on that. But I wonder if those cases somehow fit a different category. The expression once was that the Supreme Court reads the newspapers, and I suppose we can update that today to say that Supreme Court nominees read the newspapers and know that this issue is going to be brought up.

But, Judge, other sitting Justices have expressed views on key issues such as—well, take *Roe* v. *Wade*. You know, Justice Scalia has expressed opposition to *Roe*. Does that disqualify him if it comes up? Justice Blackmun not only wrote the decision but has spoken in various forums about why it was a good decision. Is either one of them disqualified from hearing abortion cases as a result?

Judge THOMAS. Senator, I think that each one of them has to determine in his mind at what point do they compromise their impartiality or it is perceived that they have compromised their objectivity or their ability to sit fairly on those cases. And I think for me, shortly after I went on the court of appeals, I remember chatting with a friend just about current events and issues. And I can remember her saying to me, asking me three or four times what my opinion was on a number of issues, and my declining to answer questions that when I was in the executive branch I would have freely answered. And her point was that I was worthless as a conversationalist now because I had no views on these issues. And I told her that I had changed roles and the role that I had was one that did not permit me or did not comport with accumulating points of views.

Senator LEAHY. Well, I might just state parenthetically, I have been both a prosecutor and a defense attorney, and I have been before judges who have expressed very strong views on the idea that when they go on the bench, they do not go into a monastery— they still are part of the populace, able to express views. And I have been there when they have expressed views both for and against a position of a client I might be representing, whether it is the State on the one hand or the defendant on another. But I have also felt secure in knowing that they were fairminded people and would set their own personal opinions aside, as judges are supposed to and as you have testified one should do in such a case.

Let me ask you this: Would you keep an open mind on cases which concern the question of whether the ninth amendment protected a given right? I would assume you would answer yes.

Judge THOMAS. The ninth amendment, I think the only concern I have expressed with respect to the ninth amendment, Senator, has been a generic one and one that I think that we all would have with the more openended provisions in the Constitution, and that is that a judge who is adjudicating under those openended provisions tether his or her ruling to something other than his or her personal point of view.

Now, the ninth amendment has, to my knowledge, not been used to decide a particular case by a majority of the Supreme Court, and there hasn't been as much written on that as some of the other amendments. That does not mean, however, that there——

Senator LEAHY. That is not what I am——

Judge THOMAS. That does not mean, however, that there couldn't be a case that argues or uses the ninth amendment as a basis for an asserted right that could come before the Court that does not—that the Court or myself, if I am fortunate enough to be confirmed, would not be open to hearing and open to deciding.

Senator LEAHY. You are saying that you would have an open mind on ninth amendment cases?

Judge THOMAS. That is right.

Senator LEAHY. I ask that because you have expressed some very strong views, as you know better than all of us, on the ninth amendment. You had an article that was reprinted in a Cato Institute book on the Reagan years. You refer to Justice Goldberg's "invention," of the ninth amendment in his concurring opinion in *Griswold*. And you said—and let me quote from you. You said, "Far from being a protection, the ninth amendment will likely become an additional weapon for the enemies of freedom." A pretty strong statement. But you would say, would you not, Judge, notwithstanding that strong statement, that if a ninth amendment case came before you, you would have an open mind?

Judge THOMAS. Again, Senator, as I noted, my concern was that I didn't believe that—in such an openended provision as the ninth amendment, it was my view that a judge would have to tether his or her view or his or her interpretation to something other than just their feeling that this right is OK or that right is OK. I believe the approach that Justice Harlan took in *Poe* v. *Ullman* and again reaffirmed in *Griswold* in determining the—or assessing the right of privacy was an appropriate way to go.

Senator LEAHY. That is not really my point. The point I am making is that you expressed very strong views—and you have here, too—about the ninth amendment. My question is: Notwithstanding those very strong views you have expressed about the ninth amendment—pretty adverse views about it—would you have an open mind in a case before you where somebody is relying on the ninth amendment?

Judge THOMAS. The answer to that is, Senator, yes.

Senator LEAHY. But if you were to express similar views regarding the principles and reasoning of *Roe* v. *Wade*, you feel that somehow it would preclude you from having that same kind of objectivity as the views you have expressed about the ninth amendment?

Judge THOMAS. I don't believe, Senator, that I have expressed any view on the ninth amendment, beyond what I have said in this hearing, after becoming a member of the judiciary. As I pointed out, I think it is important that when one becomes a member of the judiciary that one ceases to accumulate strong viewpoints, and rather begin to, as I noted earlier, to strip down as a runner and to maintain and secure that level of impartiality and objectivity necessary for judging cases.

Senator LEAHY. Does that mean if you were just a nominee, a private citizen as a nominee to the Supreme Court, you could answer the question, but as a judge you cannot?

Judge THOMAS. I think a judge is even more constrained than a nominee, but I also believe that in this process, that if one does not have a formulated view, I don't see that it improves or enhances impartiality to formulate a view, particularly in some of these difficult areas.

Senator LEAHY. Thank you, Mr. Chairman. My time is up, but I am sure the judge realizes that we will probably have to revisit this subject a tad more. Thank you.

Senator LEAHY. Judge, obviously I have dozens of other questions, but I just realized that the time is running down. I assume by now you have had a chance to read the Lehrman article. I see it sitting there. I did not want you to be disappointed. [Laughter.]

I wanted you to have at least one question that the quarterbacks behind you have been expecting here.

You have read the article?

Judge THOMAS. Yes, I have, Senator.

Senator LEAHY. Thank you. So have I.

In 1987, you called that article "a splendid example of applying natural law." Lewis Lehrman's analysis concludes that because the right to life attaches at conception that abortion of any sort is unconstitutional. Do you agree with that conclusion?

Judge THOMAS. As I indicated, Senator, to you in our last discussion, I have read this article; and as I have noted throughout my testimony and in discussions in reference to this article, my only interest was as stated: To demonstrate to a conservative audience that one of their own used this notion of natural rights——

Senator LEAHY. Judge, I——

Judge THOMAS. And the second point is that, as I have indicated, I do not endorse that conclusion. I do not think—and I have said it—that the declaration or the argument should be made in this fashion. And I have not concluded in any way or reached these conclusions or endorsed this conclusion.

Senator LEAHY. I am not sure just which conclusion we are talking about. I am talking about Lehrman's conclusion that all abortion, under any circumstance—which, of course, would go way beyond any overruling of a Supreme Court decision or anything else—his conclusion that all abortion is unconstitutional. Do you accept that conclusion?

Judge THOMAS. Senator, the——

Senator LEAHY. I am not trying to play word games with you, Judge. I am not sure whether it is the natural law or the conclusion that you disagree with. Do you agree with his—let me ask you this specifically: Do you agree with his conclusion that all abortion is unconstitutional?

Judge THOMAS. And what I am trying to do, Senator, is to respond to your question and at the same time not offer a particular view on this difficult issue of abortion that would undermine my impartiality.

The point that I am making is that I have not, nor have I ever, endorsed this conclusion or supported this conclusion.

Senator LEAHY. Thank you, Mr. Chairman. My time is up. I do not want to intrude on anybody else's time. But I will hold my other questions for the next go-round.

Thank you, Judge. I appreciate it.

JUDGE CLARENCE THOMAS' VIEWS ON
THE FUNDAMENTAL RIGHT TO PRIVACY

A REPORT TO THE UNITED STATES SENATE JUDICIARY COMMITTEE,
SENATOR JOSEPH BIDEN, CHAIRMAN,

September 5, 1991

BARBARA ALLEN BABCOCK, Ernest W. McFarland Professor, Stanford
    Law School
CHRISTOPHER F. EDLEY, JR., Professor, Harvard Law School
THOMAS C. GREY, Nelson Dowman Sweitzer and Marie B. Sweitzer
    Professor, Stanford Law School
SYLVIA A. LAW, Professor, New York University School of Law
FRANK I. MICHELMAN, Professor, Harvard Law School
ROBERT C. POST, Professor, University of California at Berkeley
NORMAN REDLICH, Dean Emeritus, New York University School of Law
JUDITH RESNIK, Orin B. Evans Professor, University of Southern
    California School of Law
STEVEN H. SHIFFRIN, Professor, Cornell Law School

As teachers and scholars of constitutional law committed to the
protection of constitutional liberty, we submit this report to
convey our grave concerns regarding the nomination of Judge
Clarence Thomas to be an Associate Justice of the United States
Supreme Court. Careful examination of Judge Thomas' writings and
speeches strongly suggests that his views of the Constitution,
and in particular his use of natural law to constrict individual
liberty, depart from the mainstream of American constitutional
thought and endanger Americans' most fundamental constitutional
rights, including the right to privacy.

Among the most alarming aspects of his record, and the primary
focus of this report, are the numerous instances in which Judge
Thomas has indicated that he would deny the fundamental right to
privacy, including the right of all Americans, married or single,
to use contraception and the right of a woman to choose to have
an abortion. Judge Thomas has criticized the Supreme Court's
decisions in the landmark privacy cases protecting the
fundamental right to use contraception. He has endorsed an
approach to overruling Roe v. Wade[1] that is so extreme it would
create a constitutional requirement that abortion be outlawed in
all states throughout the Nation, regardless of the will of the
people and their elected representatives. Recent Supreme Court

---

[1] 410 U.S. 113 (1973).

decisions in <u>Webster v. Reproductive Health Services</u>[2] and <u>Rust v. Sullivan</u>[3] have seriously diminished protection for the right to choose. Replacing Justice Thurgood Marshall with Judge Clarence Thomas would likely result in far more devastating encroachments of women's rights, perhaps providing the fifth vote to uphold statutes criminalizing virtually all abortions. Such laws have recently been adopted in Louisiana, Guam and Utah and challenges to them are now pending in the federal courts.

We submit this report prior to Judge Thomas' testimony before the Judiciary Committee in the hope that it will assist the Committee, and the Nation, in formulating questions to discern Judge Thomas' views on fundamental rights to individual privacy and liberty. We urge the Committee to question Judge Thomas on these matters and to decline to confirm his nomination unless he clearly refutes the strong evidence that he is a nominee whose special concept of the Constitution "calls for the reversal of decisions dealing with human rights and individual liberties."[4]

I.   THE SENATE'S ROLE IN THE CONFIRMATION PROCESS

A basic element of our constitutional system of checks and balances is the joint responsibility the Constitution confers upon the President and the Senate for the selection of Supreme Court Justices. In the words of Senator Patrick Leahy:

> When the Framers of the Constitution met in Philadelphia two centuries ago, they decided that the appointment of the leaders of the judicial branch of government was too important to leave to the unchecked discretion of either of the other two branches. They decided that the President and the Senate must be equal partners in this decision, playing roles of equal importance. The 100 members of the United States Senate, like the Chief Executive, are elected by all the people.[5]

The Senate's equal role in selecting Supreme Court Justices is

---

[2] 492 U.S 490 (1989).

[3] 111 S.Ct. 1759 (1991).

[4] Senate Committee on the Judiciary, Nomination of Robert H. Bork to be an Associate Justice of the United States Supreme Court, S. Exec. Rep. No. 100-7, 100th Cong., 1st Sess., Additional Views of Senator Heflin, 210 (1987).

[5] S. Exec. Rep. No. 100-7, 100th Cong., 1st Sess., Additional Views of Senator Leahy, 193-94 (1987).

widely accepted by Senators of both parties. For example,
Senator Arlen Specter has stated that the "Constitutional
separation of powers is at its apex when the President nominates
and the Senate consents or not for Supreme Court appointees who
have the final word. The Constitution mandates that a senator's
judgment be separate and independent."[6]

Although the precise wording has varied, a majority of the
members of the Senate Judiciary Committee have indicated that to
be confirmed a nominee must, at a minimum, demonstrate a
commitment to protect individual rights that have been
established as fundamental under the U.S. Constitution. For
example, Senator Patrick Leahy described the standard as follows:

> The Senate should confirm [a nominee] only if we are
> persuaded that the nominee has both the commitment and
> the capacity to protect freedoms the American people
> have fought hard to win and to preserve over the last
> 200 years. . . . I cannot vote for [a nominee] unless I
> can tell the people of Vermont that I am confident that
> if he were to become [a Justice], he would be an
> effective guardian of their fundamental rights.[7]

Senators have often identified the right to privacy as among the
fundamental rights that a nominee must recognize to meet the
standard for confirmation. As Chairman Joseph Biden stated:

> A nominee who criticizes the notion of unenumerated
> rights, or the right to privacy, would be unacceptable
> in my view. A nominee whose view of the Fourteenth
> Amendment's Equal Protection Clause has led him or her
> to have a cramped vision of the court's role in
> creating a more just society would be unacceptable in
> my view. And a nominee whose vision of the First
> Amendment's guarantees of freedom of speech and
> religion would constrain those provisions' historic
> scope would be unacceptable in my view.[8]

---

[6] S. Exec. Rep. No. 100-7, 100th Cong., 1st Sess. Additional
Views of Senator Specter, 213 (1987).

[7] S. Exec. Rep. No. 100-7, 100th Cong., 1st Sess.,
Additional Views of Senator Leahy, 193-94 (1987).

[8] Statement of Senator Joseph Biden, Chairman, Senate
Judiciary Committee on Nomination of David Souter to be Associate
Justice U.S. Supreme Court (Sept. 27, 1990).

Senator Herbert Kohl similarly stated:

> [A] Supreme Court Justice must, at a minimum, be
> dedicated to equality for all Americans, determined to
> preserve the right to privacy, the right to be left
> alone by the Government, committed to civil rights and
> civil liberties, devoted to ensuring the separation of
> Church and State, willing to defend the Bill of Rights
> and its applications to the States against all efforts
> to weaken it, and able to read the Constitution as a
> living, breathing document.[9]

Although Senator Howell Heflin indicated that he "would favor a
conservative appointment on the Court," for him the question was
"whether this nominee would be a conservative justice who would
safeguard the living Constitution and prevent judicial activism
or whether, on the other hand, he would be an extremist who would
use his position on the Court to advance a far-right, radical,
judicial agenda."[10] As Senator Heflin noted, if a nominee's
"concept of the Constitution calls for the reversal of decisions
dealing with human rights and individual liberties, then people's
rights will be threatened."[11]

Judge Thomas' writings, speeches and professional activities do
not statisfy this standard. They strongly suggest that, if
confirmed, he would interpret the Constitution in a manner that
would dangerously restrict constitutional protection for civil
rights and civil liberties.

The threat Judge Thomas poses to our basic constitutional
freedoms is well exemplified by his views regarding the
fundamental right to privacy and the protection it affords
reproductive rights, including the right to use contraception and
the right to choose to have an abortion. The remainder of this
report focuses on these alarming aspects of Judge Thomas' record.

II. THOMAS ENDORSES A NATURAL LAW "RIGHT TO LIFE" FROM CONCEPTION

At the core of Thomas' claims to constitutional authority and a
dominant theme throughout his writings and speeches is a belief

---

[9] Hearings of the Senate Judiciary Committee on the
Nomination of Judge David Souter (Sept. 13, 1990) (Statement of
Senator Kohl).

[10] S. Exec. Rep. No. 100-7, 100th Cong., 1st Sess.,
Additional Views of Senator Heflin, 211 (1987).

[11] Id. at 210.

that the Constitution should be interpreted in light of "natural law" or "higher law." "[N]atural rights and higher law arguments are the best defense of liberty and of limited government."[12] "Natural law" is a slippery concept. It has been invoked in noble causes, for example, in opposition to slavery, genocide and torture. But it has also been used in invidious ways, for example, to defend slavery and to deny women the right to vote or participate in public life. The key questions that must be posed to a proponent of natural law are: What principles are dictated by natural justice? How do we know that these answers are correct?

Despite the central role natural law plays in his professional writings, Judge Thomas has said surprisingly little about the specific content of his natural law philosophy. His discussions of natural law, though numerous, tend to be abstract and repetitive, often confusing, and sometimes contradictory. Thomas routinely cites the Declaration of Independence as the primary source of the natural law values that should be promoted through constitutional interpretation, and he frequently refers to a religious basis for those values.[13] Beyond these general references, he has been remarkably vague about the content of those values.

One striking exception to Judge Thomas' general failure to provide specific examples of how natural law should be applied is his frequent criticism of the right to privacy. One specific application of Thomas' view of natural law is his enthusiastic endorsement of the assertion that the fetus enjoys a constitutionally protected right to life from the moment of conception. In a 1987 speech to the Heritage Foundation, he stated:

> We must start by articulating principles of government and standards of goodness. I suggest that we begin the search for standards and principles with the self-evident truths of the Declaration of Independence. . .
>   Lewis Lehrman's recent essay in The American Spectator on the Declaration of Independence and the meaning of the right to life is a splendid example of

---

[12] Thomas, The Higher Law Background of the Privileges and Immunities Clause, 12 Harv. J.L. Pub. Pol'y 63, 64 (1989).

[13] See, e.g., Thomas, Why Black Americans Should Look to Conservative Policies, 119 Heritage Lectures (June 18, 1987); Thomas, Toward a "Plain Reading" of the Constitution -- The Declaration of Independence in Constitutional Interpretation, 30 Howard L.J. 983 (1987); Thomas, Civil Rights as a Principle Versus Civil Rights as an Interest in Assessing the Reagan Years (D. Boaz ed.), 391, 398 (1989); Thomas, Notes on Original Intent.

applying natural law.[14]

The Lehrman article that Judge Thomas invokes as exemplary of his approach to natural law argues but one point: interpreting the Constitution, in light of natural law, as derived from the Declaration of Independence, requires that the fetus be protected as a full human being from the moment of conception. Lehrman states that the privacy right protected by the Court in Roe was "a spurious right born exclusively of judicial supremacy with not a single trace of lawful authority," and that even if such a right existed, it would be overridden by the natural, inalienable right-to-life of the fetus from the moment of conception.[15]

This view is far more extreme than that of any current Supreme Court Justice. The Declaration of Independence says nothing about abortion or the fetus. Abortion was then legal. An overturning of Roe premised on the supposed natural right of the fetus not only would strip women of constitutional protection for their reproductive autonomy, it would prohibit individual states or the Congress from allowing legal abortion as an option even in extreme cases. It would require that abortion be defined as murder. It would prohibit states from allowing abortion even where pregnancy resulted from rape or incest or posed grave risk to a woman's health. It would deny to women as responsible individuals the ability to exercise their own religious and moral beliefs concerning abortion.

The Lehrman article does little more than assert that it is a "self-evident" truth that the fetus possesses an "inalienable right to life."[16] We fear that Judge Thomas' strong praise of this application of natural law endorses this radical view on the critical issue of abortion on the basis of an approach to natural law that relies on fixed and unquestionable moral "truth" rather than reasoned debate over the application of American constitutional principles to the circumstances of our times.

Natural law protection of the right to life from the moment of conception has been cited in recent years by opponents of legal abortion, such as members of the group "Operation Rescue," in defense of their actions in violation of laws against trespass, destruction of property and assault and battery while attempting to obstruct women's access to reproductive health care

---

[14] Thomas, Why Black Americans Should Look to Conservative Policies, supra note 13, at 8.

[15] Lehrman, The Declaration of Independence and the Right to Life, The American Spectator 21, 23 (April 1987).

[16] Id. at 22.

facilities.[17] Natural law has further provided a basis for opposition not only to abortion, but to contraception by any means viewed as an interference with "natural" human reproduction.

III. THOMAS REJECTS UNENUMERATED RIGHTS AS ARTICULATED IN GRISWOLD, EISENSTADT AND ROE

The specific content of Judge Thomas' view of natural law can be seen, not only in the applications he praises, such as the "God-given" and "inalienable right to life"[18] of a fetus, but also in the rights and values he rejects. Although Thomas advocates constitutional protection for natural rights not specifically enumerated in the Constitution, he repeatedly attacks the recognition of unenumerated rights under the Ninth Amendment and the Due Process Clause of the Fourteenth Amendment by what he dismisses as "liberal activist"[19] and "run-amok"[20] judges. Most prominent among the judicial opinions that Thomas has thus criticized are those in which the Supreme Court has protected the fundamental right to privacy.

For example, in a law review article he published in 1989, Thomas again selected decisions protecting the right to privacy to illustrate "the willfulness of both run-amok majorities and run-amok judges."[21] Thomas writes that the judicial decisions that "make conservatives nervous" are Roe v. Wade and Griswold v. Connecticut.[22] After describing Roe as "the current case provoking the most protest from conservatives," Thomas affirms

---

[17] See, e.g. Senftle, The Necessity Defense in Abortion Clinic Trespass Cases, 32 St. Louis U.L.J. 523, 546 (1987); City of Kettering v. Berry, 57 Ohio App. 3d 66, 70 (1990) ("The law does not recognize political, religious, moral convictions or some higher law as justification for the commission of a crime"); Brief for Operation Rescue at 7, Roe v. Operation Rescue, No. 88-5157 (E.D. Pa., filed June 29, 1988); Brief for the Catholic Lawyers Guild of the Archdiocese of Boston, Inc., as Amicus Curiae supporting Appellants, Webster v. Reproductive Health Services, 492 U.S. 490 (1989) (arguing that Roe v. Wade should be overruled).

[18] Lehrman, supra note 15, at 23.

[19] Thomas, Notes on Original Intent, supra note 13.

[20] Thomas, Higher Law Background, supra note 12, at 64.

[21] Id.

[22] Id. at 63 n.2.

his "misgivings about activist judicial use of the Ninth Amendment."[23] But, he asserts, his proposed concept of "higher law" would restrain both legislative majorities and judges, and should hence appeal to those he calls "my conservative allies."

Thomas has described the protection afforded the right to privacy under the Ninth Amendment as an "invention" in an opinion in Griswold v. Connecticut, authored by Justice Arthur Goldberg and joined by Chief Justice Earl Warren and Justice William Brennan. Thomas further criticizes Justice Goldberg's opinion and rejects the Ninth Amendment as a source of constitutional protection for rights that are unenumerated in the Constitution, stating:

> A major question remains: Does the Ninth Amendment, as Justice Goldberg contended, give to the Supreme Court certain powers to strike down legislation? That would seem to be a blank check. . . . Unbounded by notions of obligation and justice, the desire to protect rights simply plays into the hands of those who advocate a total state. . . . Far from being a protection, the Ninth Amendment will likely become an additional weapon for the enemies of freedom.[24]

Judge Thomas offers no real explanation in these writings of how protecting the rights of individuals promotes a "total state" or how defining unenumerated rights by reference to "natural law" is either more determinate or less a "blank check" to judges than more traditional means of constitutional interpretation.

Elsewhere, Thomas described the views on the right to privacy of Judge Bork and other proponents of original intent as follows: "restricting birth control devices or information, and allowing, restricting, or (as Senator Kennedy put it) requiring abortions are all matters for a legislature to decide; judges should refrain from 'imposing their values' on public policy."[25] Thomas then criticized this view as leading to an "indifference toward or even contempt of 'values.' Far from being an alternative to leftist activism, it readily complements it, as long as a majority approves."[26]

Although Thomas' discussion of this point is confusing, there is reason to fear it may be another endorsement of the view set out

---

[23] Id.

[24] Thomas, Civil Rights as a Principle, supra note 13, at 398-99.

[25] Thomas, Notes on Original Intent, supra, note 13.

[26] Id.

in the article by Lewis Lehrman in support of a natural right to
life for the fetus. Thomas' discussion of the right to privacy
in the context of arguing that the Constitution must be
interpreted consistent with a particular moral view, and his
expression that this moral view must be employed to constrain
majorities that might otherwise engage in "leftist activism," may
be a further indication that under Thomas' theory of natural law,
the Constitution would not permit states to allow citizens to
have access to abortion or use contraception if these activities
are deemed to violate the natural order of things.

In 1986, Thomas participated as a member of a White House Working
Group on the Family that produced a report on the family that
severely criticized landmark constitutional decisions protecting
the right to privacy. The report went so far as to excoriate a
decision protecting a grandmother's freedom to open her home to
her orphaned grandchildren, without government restriction.[27]
It particularly targeted cases in the area of reproductive
freedom, and called for them to be overruled.[28]

In addition to Roe v. Wade, the working group singled out as
wrongly decided the Supreme Court's decision in Planned
Parenthood v. Danforth, in which the Court struck down a Missouri
law that required a woman to obtain the consent of her husband
before she could obtain an abortion and a minor to obtain the
consent of a parent. The report also criticized the Court's
reasoning in Eisenstadt v. Baird, which protects the right of
unmarried individuals to use contraception, and in particular the
Court's statement that "the marital couple is not an independent
entity with a mind and heart of its own."[29] The working group
described these, and other cases protecting the fundamental right
to privacy, as a "fatally flawed line of court decisions" and
indicated that they "can be corrected, directly or indirectly,
through . . . the appointment of new judges and their
confirmation by the Senate . . . and . . . amendment of the
Constitution itself."[30]

---

[27] Moore v. City of East Cleveland, 431 U.S. 494 (1971).
The Family: Preserving America's Future, A Report to the
President from the White House Working Group on the Family 11
(1986).

[28] Id. at 11.

[29] Id., at 12 quoting, Eisenstadt v. Baird, 405 U.S. 438,
453 (1972).

[30] Id. at 12. The Republican Party platforms for 1980,
1984, and 1988 contained strikingly similar language, pledging to
work for "the appointment of judges at all levels of the
judiciary who respect traditional family values and the sanctity

IV. THOMAS' NATURAL LAW THEORY

As we have noted above, Thomas' approach to constitutional interpretation is highly unusual in its invocation of a body of natural law.[31] Appeals to natural law in constitutional interpretation do not necessarily portend decisions that would restrict the rights of individuals and overturn core constitutional values. Depending on how its methodology and content are specifically understood, natural law might point in various directions. But Thomas' approach to natural law is disturbing, both as a matter of methodology and as a matter of content.

As a matter of constitutional method, natural law is disturbing when invoked to allow supposedly self-evident moral "truth" to substitute for the hard work of developing principles drawn from the American constitutional text and precedent. As we have noted, Judge Thomas has not sought to explain the social and historical reasons supporting the conclusions to which "natural law" leads him. The more traditional common law and constitutional method of open-ended, case-by-case development is a core strength of the American judicial approach to justice for a diverse and ever-evolving country. Natural law norms are not necessarily antithetical to a reasoned, case-by-case approach. But Judge Thomas seems to invoke "higher law" as a substitute for explanation. His concept of natural law appears to mean strict adherence to a perceived set of fixed and undoubtable normative truths. As such, it does not accommodate the principle and precedent exemplified in the work of conservative Justices such as John Harlan and Lewis Powell.

---

of innocent human life." Thomas listed the Republican Party's position on abortion as the first in a list of conservative positions that he believed should attract African Americans to the Republican Party. Thomas, "How Republican can Win Blacks," Chicago Defender, February 21, 1987.

[31] For at least the last fifty years, constitutional interpretation on the basis of natural law has been conspicuously absent from American legal philosophy and judicial opinions. Professor Laurence Tribe commented that Clarence Thomas "is the first Supreme Court nominee in 50 years to maintain that natural law should be readily consulted in constitutional interpretation." Tribe, "Natural Law" and the Nominee, N.Y. Times, July 15, 1991. As Professor John Hart Ely noted, "[t]he concept of [natural law] has . . . all but disappeared in American discourse." J.H. Ely, Democracy and Distrust 52 (1980).

When natural law was last in vogue some eighty years ago, it was employed by the Supreme Court to strike down state laws providing basic health and safety protection to working people. The Court asserted a natural law right of employers to be free of minimum wage laws and health and safety regulations.[32] Natural law has been particularly disabling for women. In 1873, the Court upheld the exclusion of women from the practice of law.[33] Justice Bradley wrote that the "civil law, as well as nature herself, has always recognized a wide difference in the respective spheres and destinies of man and woman . . . . The paramount destiny and mission of woman are to fulfill the noble and benign offices of wife and mother. This is the law of the Creator."[34]

The impact that the application of natural law would have on core constitutional principles thus depends on the particular proponent's personal views of the content and source of the natural law principles to be applied. It is therefore imperative that the Senate Judiciary Committee determine with specificity which fixed principles Judge Thomas has in mind when he advocates the use of natural law in constitutional interpretation and how they will affect the Court's role as guardian of American's fundamental rights. As the preceding analysis indicates, Thomas' record contains compelling evidence that the substantive content of his natural law theory is incompatible with continued protection for the fundamental right of privacy, including the right to choose.[35]

V. CONCLUSION

Particularly given the critical moment in the history of the Supreme Court at which this nomination has occurred, the Senate should reject any nominee who is not committed to protecting fundamental individual liberties. We urge the Senate to shoulder its responsibility to determine whether the nominee "has both the

---

[32] See, e.g., Lochner v. New York, 198 U.S. 45 (1905).

[33] Bradwell v. Illinois, 83 U.S. 130 (1872).

[34] Id. at 141-42 (Bradley, J., concurring).

[35] In addition to Thomas' writings and speeches discussed above, Thomas has disparaged those who have used natural law arguments in support of unenumerated rights, including the fundamental right to privacy. Thomas, "How to Talk About Civil Rights: Keep it Principled and Positive," keynote address celebrating the Formation of the Pacific Research Institute's Civil Rights Task Force, August 4, 1988; Speech of Clarence Thomas at Harvard University Federalist Society Meeting, April 7, 1988. (This speech was prepared but apparently not delivered.)

commitment and the capacity to protect freedoms the American. people have fought hard to win and to preserve over the last 200 years."[36]   Our analysis of Judge Thomas' writings and speeches raises serious questions about whether he meets this standard. We exhort the Committee to probe these questions and to approve the nomination only if satisfied that Judge Thomas has the commitment and ability to contribute to the wise elaboration of our Constitution.

---

[36]   Statement of Senator Patrick Leahy, supra n. 7.

NOMINATION OF CLARENCE THOMAS TO BE AN ASSOCIATE JUSTICE OF THE UNITED STATES SUPREME COURT

OCTOBER 1 (legislative day, SEPTEMBER 19), 1991.—Ordered to be printed

Mr. BIDEN, from the Committee on the Judiciary,
submitted the following

REPORT

together with

ADDITIONAL AND SUPPLEMENTAL VIEWS

[To accompany the nomination of Clarence Thomas to be an Associate Justice of the
U.S. Supreme Court]

The Committee on the Judiciary, to which was referred the nomination of Judge Clarence Thomas to be an Associate Justice of the U.S. Supreme Court, having considered the same, reports the nomination, a quorum being present, without recommendation, by a vote of 13 yeas and 1 nay, having failed to report favorably thereon, by a vote of 7 yeas and 7 nays.

CONTENTS

59–119

ADDITIONAL VIEWS OF CHAIRMAN BIDEN

The decision to oppose the confirmation of a nominee to the U.S. Supreme Court is a solemn one. And with respect to this nominee, Judge Clarence Thomas, I have no doubt about his character, credentials, competence, or credibility. Instead, the basis for my opposition to the confirmation of Judge Thomas concerns his judicial philosophy—the approach he would use in deciding how to interpret the ennobling phrases of our Constitution.

INTRODUCTION

In terms of judicial philosophy, Judge Thomas came to the hearings with a record that was troubling in several respects. Over the course of his professional life, he had expressed views that aligned him with the ultraconservatives seeking to fundamentally alter our society. The constitutional philosophy set forth in Judge Thomas' articles and speeches would result in radical, and in my opinion undesirable, changes in the relationship between government and individuals.

First, Judge Thomas seemed to advocate a change in the degree to which society could protect the environment, the workplace, and the public health and safety. Judge Thomas had approved the notion of an activist Court that would greatly increase the constitutional protection given to economic and property rights, striking down laws that regulated businesses and corporations.

Second, Judge Thomas appeared to seek a change in the degree to which government could interfere in the personal lives of individuals. Judge Thomas had praised or associated himself with arguments for greater government control over matters of family and personal life. In particular, Judge Thomas seemed comfortable with permitting government intrusions into that most private realm of decisions concerning procreation and other intimate matters.

Third, Judge Thomas had endorsed an extreme view of separation of powers which, if taken to the conclusion endorsed by its advocates, would radically redefine the balance of power between the branches of the Federal Government. This view holds that much of the current structure of our government impermissibly infringes on the power of the Executive. Having also expressed a strong hostility to Congress, Judge Thomas seemed to advocate a major shift in power away from the legislative branch and toward the executive branch.

In short, Judge Thomas' writings and speeches sketch a judicial philosophy that, if realized, would reverse the balance this country has struck between the rights of individuals, the obligations of businesses and corporations, and the power of government. The question concerning me as the hearings began was whether this was an accurate picture of Judge Thomas' judicial philosophy.

(7)

During the hearings, Judge Thomas sought to explain his views.
I accept the sincerity of his testimony, and some of his explanations satisfied my concerns. On balance, however, my concerns
remain. First of all, I was troubled by Judge Thomas' repeated resistance to discussing his own views when asked about decisions of
the Supreme Court. Perhaps the best way to gain insight into a
nominee's judicial philosophy is to use the Supreme Court's existing constitutional and statutory decisions to frame the dialog.

Judge Thomas' reluctance even to comment on already decided
cases, apparently for fear of revealing his own views, was pro-
nounced. I discussed this with him in the final hours of his testimony, after hearing yet another of his refusals to discuss a legal principle:

> The CHAIRMAN. * * * Judge, you are going to be * * * a
> judge who is not bound by stare decisis, [who] has nothing
> at all that would bind you other than your conscience, and
> so I am a little * * * edgy when you give an answer and
> you say, "well, that's the policy," as if you are still going
> to be a Circuit Court of Appeals judge * * *
>
> You are going to take a philosophy to that Court with
> you, * * * and you are not limited * * * from reaching a
> conclusion different than that which the Court has
> reached thus far * * *.
>
> Judge THOMAS. Well, I understand that, Mr. Chairman,
> but what I have attempted to do is to not agree or disagree
> with existing cases.
>
> The CHAIRMAN. You are doing very well at that.
>
> Judge THOMAS. The point that I am making or I have
> tried to make is that I do not approach these cases with
> any desire to change them, and I have tried to indicate
> that, to the extent that individuals feel, well, I am fore-
> closed from a——
>
> The CHAIRMAN. If you had a desire to change it, would
> you tell us?
>
> Judge THOMAS. I don't think so * * *. (Transcript, Sept.
> 16, at 172–73.)

Judge Thomas' last comment appears to have been said in jest,
but in the end, he had declined comment or provided only vague
remarks on the many constitutional issues—great and small, con-
tentious and settled—about which he was asked. Perhaps Judge
Thomas was advised that this approach was a sound political strategy designed to ensure confirmation. If that is the case, it is not a
strategy I am prepared to accept.

I had hoped to discuss with Judge Thomas what his views are,
not because I wanted guarantees that he would vote the way I
might like in particular cases—that I would not seek. What I had
hoped to determine was that he believed generally in a framework
of government and of individuals rights that would enable him to
meet the challenges of the next century, whatever they may be.

Thus, the most troubling aspect of Judge Thomas' testimony, for
me, was the number of occasions on which he said he had not appreciated the implications of arguments he previously had made.
This occurred, to some degree, on each of the three subjects I men-

tioned above: Economic and property rights; privacy; and separation of powers.

Caution in embracing an argument because of where it might lead when applied is a critical attribute for a Supreme Court Justice. After all, the Court's interpretation of the Constitution or a statute does not simply decide the particular case before it, it serves as well to set the course of all future interpretations both for itself and for all subordinate courts. Even as he testified at the hearing, Judge Thomas evidenced a lack of appreciation for the implications of the views he had previously endorsed.

With respect to his statements on economic and property rights, he said he was speaking only as a "part-time political theorist." He said his interest derived from concern that individuals, particularly African-Americans, must not encounter barriers in their efforts to earn a living. Yet those who urge the Court to grant stricter protection to economic and property rights—those whose views Judge Thomas finds "attractive"—do not focus their writings on removing barriers keeping minorities from jobs. The implications of the view of these writers could prohibit government from regulating factory owners who pollute the air or water. They could invalidate the workplace safety laws and regulation of facilities like child-care centers. Judge Thomas said he did not mean to advocate these applications of the argument that economic and property rights deserve "more protection." But the arguments he endorsed are likely to lead to these results.

I was also concerned about Judge Thomas' prior statements on the issue of family and personal privacy. None of these statements, in my view, proves that Judge Thomas definitively rejects the idea that the Constitution protects individual and family privacy and unenumerated rights. But every word he uttered prior to his nomination on these issues was hostile to these concepts. Certainly, at the hearing, he distanced himself from his prior statements, saying either his meaning was misunderstood or he had not participated in making the statements. But the implication of his comments was to suggest he would be comfortable with greater government control and less constitutional protection of the right of privacy.

Moreover, Judge Thomas failed during his testimony to explain what he does believe is the proper relationship between the individual and government when intimate personal matters are at issue. In particular, he was persistently evasive on the source, the scope, and the nature of an individual's right of privacy, despite my repeated efforts to elicit his views on the subject. Judge Thomas thus failed to convince me that he has a broad view of personal freedom that will adequately protect individuals as unanticipated conflicts come before the Court in the future.

PART TWO: JUDGE THOMAS' VIEWS ON PRIVACY, REPRODUCTIVE
FREEDOM, AND UNENUMERATED RIGHTS

In supporting the nomination of Justice Souter to the Court last
year, I emphasized that a nominee bears the burden of proving
that he or she falls within the sphere of candidates acceptable to
this committee, and I indicated that a nominee who rejected the
notion that our Constitution protects unenumerated rights, including the right to privacy, would, in my view, be unacceptable. This
is because the rejection of this notion would mean that such a
nominee would put at risk not only those rights the Court has already acknowledged, but also that the nominee lacked an expansive view of our Constitution that would guide us safely into the
future.

Judge Thomas is a nominee who has, in the past, criticized the
notion of unenumerated rights and the right of privacy. Thus, as
we began the hearings, determining what Judge Thomas believed
in this respect was, for me, a critical goal.

Prior to the hearings, Judge Thomas' record on the right of privacy, reproductive freedom, and unenumerated rights generally—
while not definitive—was troubling. To the extent he had expressed
views, they were hostile to these concepts. While Judge Thomas
had addressed the issue of abortion, it was not simply his opinion
on a woman's right to choose that troubled me. My concern was his
apparent much broader criticism of an unenumerated right of privacy—of the very idea that there is a realm of intimate matters
into which the Government may not intrude.

During the hearings, Judge Thomas conceded that the Constitution, and in particular the 14th amendment, protects some sort of
privacy right, at least for married couples. But Judge Thomas declined to provide full answers to most of the questions he was
asked on this subject.

He declined to describe in detail his overall methodology for approaching privacy claims. He did not reveal a decisive view on
whether individuals had a right of privacy protected by the liberty
clause of the 14th amendment. Nor did he say whether, in his view,
the scope of the right of privacy—for married or single people—extended in any circumstances to decisions about procreation. His
reticence to answer these questions, in light of his prior record, is
profoundly troubling. He has failed to convince me that he endorses a broad and expanding conception of the Constitution's protection of the right of privacy.

A. JUDGE THOMAS HAS CRITICIZED JUDICIAL RECOGNITION OF AN UNENUMERATED RIGHT OF PRIVACY

In a series of speeches and articles, Judge Thomas implied his
disagreement with those who believe the Constitution grants broad
protection to the right of each individual to make intimate decisions without government intrusion. He had criticized the constitutional sources identified by the Court as embodying such protection, namely the 14th and the 9th amendments. He had participated in a report that advocated greater government control over personal and family matters.

1. Judge Thomas was critical of the concept of unenumerated rights

In an article on the privileges or immunities clause of the 14th amendment, Thomas stated that "[t]he expression of unenumerated rights today makes conservatives nervous, while at the same time gladdening the hearts of liberals." ("The Higher Law Background of the Privileges or Immunities Clause of the Fourteenth Amendment," 12 Harvard Journal of Law & Policy 63 (Winter 1989) at 63.) In a footnote to this statement, Thomas wrote:

> The current case provoking the most protest from conservatives is *Roe* v. *Wade* [410 U.S. 113 (1973)], in which the Supreme Court found a woman's decision to end her pregnancy to be part of her unenumerated right to privacy established by *Griswold* v. *Connecticut* [381 US. 479 (1965)]. In *Griswold*, Justice Douglas found that "[s]pecific guarantees in the Bill of Rights have penumbras, formed by emanations from those guarantees that help give them life and substance. Various guarantees create zones of privacy." (Id. (citations omitted).)

Thomas then concluded the footnote by referring readers to his comments on *Griswold* he had made in another article, where he "elaborate[d] on [his] misgivings about the judicial use of the Ninth Amendment." (Id. (citation omitted).)

In that other article, Thomas rejected judicial use of the ninth amendment to protect unenumerated rights, complaining that Justice Goldberg "invented" the ninth amendment in *Griswold* v. *Connecticut.*

> A major question remains: Does the Ninth Amendment, as Justice Goldberg contended, give to the Supreme Court to be a blank check. The Court could designate something to be a right and then strike down any law it thought violated that right. * * * Far from being a protection, the Ninth Amendment will likely become an additional weapon for the enemies of freedom. ("Civil Rights As A Principle Versus Civil Rights As An Interest," Assessing the Reagan Years (1988) at 398–99.)

I find this discussion of the right of privacy troubling for two reasons. First, Thomas criticizes judicial use of the ninth amendment to prohibit government interference with a core personal freedom—the decision to use contraceptives and to decide whether and when to bear a child free from governmental interference. Second, the line of Supreme Court privacy cases up through *Griswold* has been accepted even by most conservatives. In recent years, debate has focused not on whether a right to privacy as a component of liberty exists—but how strong, or fundamental, is that right in any particular instance and what type of competing interest can justify government regulation. Anyone who challenges the premise that individuals have a protected privacy right to make intimate decisions without government interference, in my view, advocates an extreme and unacceptable position.

Judge Thomas strongly suggested prior to the hearings that he and I do not share a common vision of unenumerated rights. As he put it, on one of the two occasions on which he spoke of my view:

The conservative failure to appreciate the importance of natural rights * * * culminated in their spectacle of Senator Biden [following Judge Bork's defeat] crowing about his belief that his rights were inalienable * * * We cannot expect our views of civil rights to triumph by conceding the moral high ground to those who confuse rights with willfulness. (Speech at the Pacific Research Institute, August 4, 1988, at 12.)

Again, the issue for me is not whether Judge Thomas accepts my own vision of privacy and unenumerated rights, but whether he believes generally that the Constitution protects individual freedom. His rejection of my views does not definitively tell us whether he has his own theory of privacy and unenumerated rights, but it is a sharp disapproval of at least one approach that embraces an expansive view of these concepts.

Now, at the hearing, Judge Thomas sought to minimize some of his earlier statements. For example, despite his previous characterization of the ninth amendment as a "weapon for the enemies of freedom," when asked at the hearing if he would keep an open mind on whether the ninth amendment might protect a particular right, Judge Thomas responded:

The Ninth Amendment, I think the only concern I have expressed with respect to the Ninth Amendment, Senator, * * * is that a judge who is adjudicating under those open-ended provisions tether his or her ruling to something other than his or her personal point of view.

Now the Ninth Amendment has, to my knowledge, not been used to decide a particular case by a majority of the Supreme Court, and there hasn't been as much written on that as some of the other amendments. That does not mean, however, that there * * * couldn't be a case that argues or uses the Ninth Amendment as a basis for an asserted right that could come before the Court that does not—that the Court or myself, if I am fortunate enough to be confirmed, would not be open to hearing and open to deciding. (Transcript, Sept. 11, at 110.)

And Thomas conceded that the Constitution protects some sort of privacy right: "My view is that there is a right to privacy in the Fourteenth Amendment." (Transcript, Sept. 10, at 149.)

But these statements affirming that Judge Thomas believes in an unenumerated right to privacy reveal not at all what he believes the scope or nature of a fundamental right to privacy to be, nor who in his view enjoys this right. Unfortunately, Judge Thomas refused all invitations to give needed content to his views. I believe that, in light of his prior record, Judge Thomas' admission that some undefined right to privacy exists does not meet his burden of proof on this issue.

2. *Judge Thomas did not dispositively acknowledge that the liberty component of the 14th amendment's due process clause protects the right of individuals, married or single, to make decisions about procreation*

At the hearing, Judge Thomas seemed first to concede that every individual, whether single or married, had a right of privacy with respect to matters of procreation:

> The CHAIRMAN. * * * Now, you said that the privacy right of married couples is fundamental, and as I understand it now, you told me—correct me if I am wrong—that the privacy right of an individual on procreation is fundamental. Is that right?
>
> Judge THOMAS. I think that is consistent with what I said and I think consistent with what the Court held in *Eisenstadt* v. *Baird* [405 U.S. 438 (1972)]. (Transcript, Sept. 12, at 50.)

Shortly thereafter, however, he spoke only of a marital right to privacy in responding to a question asked by Senator Kennedy:

> Judge THOMAS. Senator, * * * I think I have indicated here today and yesterday that there is a privacy interest in the Constitution, in the liberty component of the Due Process Clause, and that marital privacy is a fundamental right, and marital privacy then can only be impinged on or only be regulated if there is a compelling State interest. * * * (Transcript, Sept. 12, at 82.)

As a result, I asked Judge Thomas again about his belief in an individual's right to privacy:

> The CHAIRMAN. Judge, very simply, if you can, yes or no: Do you believe that the Liberty Clause of the Fourteenth Amendment of the Constitution provides a fundamental right to privacy for individuals in the area of procreation, including contraception?
>
> Judge THOMAS. Senator, I think I answered earlier yes, based upon the precedent of *Eisenstadt* v. *Baird.*
>
> The CHAIRMAN. Well, you know, * * * *Eisenstadt* v. *Baird* was an equal protection case. * * * That is not the question I am asking you. Let me make sure and say it one more time. Do you believe the Liberty Clause of the Fourteenth Amendment of the Constitution provides a fundamental right of privacy for individuals in the area of procreation, including contraception?
>
> Judge THOMAS. I think I have answered that, Senator.
>
> The CHAIRMAN. Yes or no?
>
> Judge THOMAS. Yes, and——
>
> * * * * *
>
> I have expressed on what I base that, and I would leave it at that." (Transcript, Sept. 12, at 119-20.)

In an attempt to more clearly understand his views, I submitted to Judge Thomas, after the hearings, a written question on the right of privacy. My letter recited Judge Thomas' testimony on this issue, and asked the following question:

> Do you believe that the due process component of the Fourteenth Amendment's liberty clause—independent of the equal protection clause and the case of *Eisenstadt* v. *Baird*—provides a fundamental right of privacy with respect to procreation and contraception?

Judge Thomas' answer to this question, in its entirely, was as follows:

> As I sought to make clear in my testimony, I believe that *Eisenstadt* was correct on both the privacy and equal protection grounds.

So, despite my explicit request that Judge Thomas express his views on the liberty clause independent of the decsion in *Eisenstadt*, he answered only that he accepts that *Eisenstadt* is right both on privacy and equal protection. Thus, yet again, Judge Thomas failed to answer the question directly or completely.

The result of Judge Thomas' reticence to discuss his views is that, even after the hearings, even after my repeated attempts to engage him in a dialog on this issue, I am left without any clear idea of what Judge Thomas means when he says the 14th amendment protects a right of privacy. What is the scope and nature of that right? Where does it come from? Who enjoys this right? These questions remain unanswered.

3. JUDGE THOMAS DID NOT REJECT THE NOTION THAT GOVERNMENT SHOULD HAVE MORE POWER TO REGULATE PERSONAL AND FAMILY MATTERS THAN IT DOES NOW.

In 1986, Judge Thomas was a member of an administration working group on the family that put out a controversial report recommending greater Government control over family and personal matters. In fact, the report "urge[s] the federal courts to permit the state wide latitude in formulating family policy." It recommends "returning to communities the authority to set norms and affirm values." (Administration Working Group Report at 16–17.)

In addition, the report characterized a number of Supreme Court's privacy decisions of the last 20 years as "fatally flawed." Included in this category, just to name a few, were: *Moore* v. *East Cleveland*, 431 U.S. 494 (1977), protecting a grandmother's right to raise her two grandsons in her own home; *Gomez* v. *Perez*, 409 U.S. 113 (1973), protecting an illegitimate child's right to judicially enforce monetary support from his or her natural father; and a number of the Court's decisions recognizing a fundamental right of privacy with respect to procreation. The group did not think the right of family and personal privacy recognized by these decisions should stand in the way of its recommendations. It said simply:

> [I]n final analysis, * * * A fatally flawed line of court decisions can be corrected, directly or indirectly, through mechanisms * * * [That] include the appointment of new judges and their confirmation by the senate * * *.

The report received extensive press coverage when released, and its conclusions were widely criticized. When asked about the report at the hearing, Judge Thomas acknowledged that there had been controversy over the report when released, but maintained that he had never read it: "To this day, I have not read that report." (Transcript, Sept. 10, at 155.)

I specifically asked Judge Thomas about the report's discussion of the Supreme Court's decision in *Moore* v. *East Cleveland,* where the Court struck down a zoning law that prevented a grandmother from raising her two grandsons in her home, because they were cousins, not brothers. The report objected to this decision because it "forbade any community in America to define 'family' in a traditional way." Simply stated, the working group said that East Cleveland should be permitted to define family in a "traditional way"—even if the result was to force a grandmother to choose between her grandsons or move.

When asked if he agreed with the report's conclusion that this decision was fatally flawed and in need of correction, Judge Thomas replied only that:

> I have heard recently that that was the conclusion, * * *
> If I had known that that section was in the report before it became final, of course I would have expressed my concerns.

> * * * * *

> I provided a significant memo, I believe, on low-income families and families that I felt were at risk in the society and how we should approach resolving those families. (Transcript, Sept. 10, at 157.)
> * * * I indicated that I would have raised concerns, and I believe that those concerns would have been of the same character and the same nature as the concerns that I would raise in this case. I thought that we had a grand opportunity there to focus governmental policy on existing low-income and at-risk families. (Transcript, Sept. 11, at 21.)

I find the recommendations of this working group deeply disturbing. If these views were ever adopted as public policy in this country, it would radically change our current conception of what is private—of what is none of the Government's business. In short, this report is a blueprint for shrinking our rights of marital and family privacy. I accept Judge Thomas' testimony that he did not write nor even read the report. Nonetheless, I cannot accept his failure to repudiate the idea that Government should be given more authority to regulate family and personal matters.

B. JUDGE THOMAS REFUSED TO DISCUSS HIS VIEWS ON REPRODUCTIVE FREEDOM

Certain remarks made by Judge Thomas prior to the hearings raised a concern that he did not believe individuals had a right of privacy in matters of procreation that included the question of whether to terminate a pregnancy. In a speech delivered to the Heritage Foundation in 1988, Thomas argued that conservatives should recognize the "connection between natural law standards and constitutional government." (Heritage Foundation Speech, June 18, 1987, at 20.) He said:

> The need to re-examine the natural law is as current as last month's issue of TIME on ethics. Yet, it is more venerable than St. Thomas Aquinas. It both transcends and underlies time and place, race and custom. And, until recently, it has been an integral part of the American political tradition. Martin Luther King was the last prominent American political figure to appeal to it. But Heritage Trustee Lewis Lehrman's recent essay in "The American Spectator" on the Declaration of Independence and the meaning of the right to life is a splendid example of applying natural law. (Id. at 22.)

At the hearings, when asked whether he agreed with the sole conclusion Mr. Lehrman drew from his application of natural law—that all abortions are unconstitutional—Judge Thomas replied:

> I felt that conservatives would be skeptical about the notion of natural law. I was using that as the underlying approach. * * * I thought that if I demonstrated that one of their own .accepted at least the concept of natural rights, that they would be more apt to accept that concept as an underlying principle for being more aggressive on civil rights. My whole interest was civil rights enforcement. (Transcript, Sept. 10, at 151.)

He also said "I have not, nor have I ever, endorsed [Mr. Lehrman's] conclusion or supported this conclusion." (Transcript, Sept. 13, at 22.) Moreover, Judge Thomas said he had an open mind with regard to whether Roe v. Wade was rightly decided. (Transcript, Sept. 11, at 105.)

I accept Judge Thomas' statement that he has an open mind with respect to a woman's right to choose. And, although I understand that some of his previous comments on this issue had raised a concern going into the hearing, I do not believe these remarks can be viewed as definitive evidence of Judge Thomas' views. I believe that no one can be certain of where Judge Thomas stands on this point.

Nonetheless, I was disappointed by Judge Thomas' reticence to discuss the issue of reproductive freedom even at the most general level. Again, I am not referring to the specific question of whether the result in Roe v. Wade was correct—a question I did not ask Judge Thomas. But Judge Thomas would not even discuss, for example, whether a woman has any protected liberty interest at stake in matters of procreation, or whether the Court should apply strict scrutiny in reviewing such an asserted interest. Answering these questions would not have revealed whether Judge Thomas agreed with Roe, because even if Judge Thomas had acknowledged that women have a fundamental right to choose whether to continue a pregnancy, he could still disagree with the result in Roe.

My concern is that in refusing to discuss the broader question of whether we, as individuals, have a right to make intimate decisions

free from Government intrusion, I can not begin to understand
how Judge Thomas would approach any number of cases in which
the Court that will determine the future relationship of individuals
and Government in our society. Considering his testimony on the
issues of family and personal privacy as a whole, I am not comfortable that Judge Thomas would strike an appropriate balance between the right of individuals and the Government as we move
into the next century.

C. JUDGE THOMAS DID NOT EXPLAIN HOW HE WOULD USE HISTORY AND
   TRADITION TO DETERMINE WHETHER AN ASSERTED LIBERTY INTEREST
   IS CONSTITUTIONALLY PROTECTED

Judge Thomas was similarly reluctant to expound the general
methodology he would use to determine whether an asserted liberty interest is protected by the Constitution. Judge Thomas told the
committee that the meaning of the Constitution's broad phrases—
like "liberty"—are not "self-defining" and must be interpreted
based on the Framers' intent and our history and traditions. (Transcript, Sept. 12, at 27.) Again, this answer does not really say much
about Judge Thomas' approach. All the Justices now on the Court
look to history and tradition in evaluating asserted rights, but they
do so in different ways, with radically different results. The key
question is whether the Court will protect only those interests supported by a specific and longstanding tradition, or whether a less
constricted view of liberty will govern.

ADDITIONAL VIEWS OF SENATORS KENNEDY AND SIMON

The nine Justices of the Supreme Court have the last word on the meaning of the Constitution and the scope of our most basic liberties. For this reason, no Senator should vote to confirm a nominee to the Supreme Court unless that nominee possesses a clear commitment to the fundamental constitutional rights and freedoms at the heart of our democracy.

If a nominee lacking such a commitment is confirmed, our rights as individuals and our future as a nation are jeopardized. Nominees must shoulder the burden of proof that they possess this fundamental commitment, and that they are not outside the mainstream of constitutional interpretation. Judge Thomas has not met that burden, and for that reason, we oppose his nomination.

Throughout his career, Judge Thomas has taken extreme positions on many issues. But during his hearings before the Judiciary Committee, he asked the committee to overlook the inflammatory positions he advocated for years, and to judge him instead on the soothing testimony of one short week when his confirmation was at stake.

Judge Thomas' record and testimony fall far short of demonstrating a commitment to fundamental constitutional values in numerous key respects.

A. NATURAL LAW

Judge Thomas' most obvious retreat during his testimony was his repudiation of natural law. Over and over in his career, he has repeatedly and forcefully advocated the use of natural law in constitutional decisionmaking.[1] He strongly commended Justices who have used natural law to guide their constitutional decisionmaking.[2] But he now says that he does not—and never did—see a role for the use of natural law in constitutional adjudication.[3]

B. PRIVACY AND ABORTION

Judge Thomas' past writings and speeches raise significant concerns about his views on the right to privacy and, in particular, about whether he believes that the right includes the right of a woman to choose abortion.

During his testimony before the committee, Judge Thomas attempted to cloak himself with more moderate views than his

---

[1] See e.g., Thomas, "The Higher Law Background of the Privileges or Immunities Clause of the Fourteenth Amendment," 12 Harv. J. Law & Pub. Pol. 68 (1989) ("The Higher Law Background"); "Notes on Original-Intent," undated speech, at 3–4.

[2] "The Higher Law Background" at 68 (commending Justice Harlan for his use of natural law in *Plessy* v. *Ferguson*); Speech to the Federalist Society, University of Virginia, March 5, 1988 (same); Speech to the Pacific Research Institute, August 4, 1988 (commending Justice Scalia's natural law dissent in *Morrison* v. *Olson*).

[3] See e.g., hearing transcript, Sept. 10, 1991, at 137, 140, 143, 147, 197, 202–03, 207–09.

(57)

record supports. For the first time, he acknowledged the existence of a right to privacy under the 14th amendment. But he refused to answer questions about specific applications of that right.

Judge Thomas' unwillingness to demonstrate how he would determine fundamental privacy rights is particularly troubling with respect to the abortion issue. Judge Thomas' prior record indicates that he may well be prepared to overturn *Roe* v. *Wade*. In a speech to the Heritage Foundation in 1987, Judge Thomas stated:

> Heritage Foundation Trustee Lewis Lehrman's recent essay in "The American Spectator" on the Declaration of Independence and the meaning of the right to life is a splendid example of applying natural law.[4]

The Lehrman article is an extreme anti-abortion polemic. Lehrman argues that a fetus has a constitutionally protected right to life, beginning at the moment of conception. Lehrman describes the right to abortion as a right "born exclusively of judicial supremacy with not a single trace of lawful authority, implicit or explicit, in the actual text or history of the Constitution itself." [5] Lehrman's entire article is devoted to the issue of abortion.

When questioned about his praise for the Lehrman article, Judge Thomas contended that his endorsement was merely rhetorical. In particular, Judge Thomas claimed that he had meant only to encourage conservatives to become more aggressive about enforcement of civil rights, by citing the views of a fellow conservative.[6] Judge Thomas told the committee that his endorsement of the article had been merely a throw-away line. "It was considered, I think by many, as a throw-away line. I saw it as that. * * *"[7]

During questioning about the Lehrman article, Judge Thomas claimed that he had not read the article closely at the time of his speech.[8] Similarly, despite extensive prehearing discussions in the media about the reference to the Lehrman article, Judge Thomas told the committee that he had not re-read the article before the hearing.[9]

> [M]y response to [a] question concerning that article was that I cited or praised it for a very limited purpose or made comments about it for a very limited purpose, and I stated what that purpose was. And that purpose didn't suggest from my standpoint the need to go back and learn everything about that particular article.[10]

Despite claiming to be unfamiliar with the article's conclusions, Judge Thomas repeatedly disassociated himself from those conclusions. Asking the committee to disregard the common-sense interpretation of his language, Judge Thomas explained that his phrase

---

[4] "Why Black Americans Should Look to Conservative Policies," speech to the Heritage Foundation, June 18, 1987, at 8.
[5] Lehrman, "The Declaration of Independence and the Right to Life: One Leads Unmistakably From the Other," The American Spectator 21–23 (April, 1987).
[6] Hearing transcript, Sept. 10, 1991, at 151; Sept. 11, 1991 at 95.
[7] Hearing transcript, Sept. 10, 1991, at 196–197.
[8] Hearing transcript, Sept. 11, 1991, at 97 (Q: "Had you read the article before you praised it?" A: "I think I skimmed it, Senator.")
[9] Hearing, Sept. 11, 1991, at 98. See also hearing transcript, Sept. 11, 1991 at 98.
[10] Hearing transcript, Sept. 13, 1991, at 109.

"splendid example" did not indicate that he agreed with the substance of Lehrman's conclusions.

> [I]t was a splendid example in the sense that it was a compliment to him and it is a compliment to someone [conservatives] believed in, and I would reaffirm what I said yesterday and I have said consistently, and that is that at no time did I adopt or endorse the substance of the article itself.[11]

Finally, after being questioned further by members of the committee on the article, Judge Thomas concluded that he believed Lehrman's application of natural law was inappropriate to resolve the abortion issue—he thought instead that the matter should be resolved using the traditional tools of constitutional adjudication.[12]

Other evidence in his record indicates that Judge Thomas may indeed be hostile to the Court's holding in *Roe* v. *Wade*. In a 1984 article in the Harvard Journal of Law and Public Policy, Judge Thomas wrote that "[t]he expression of unenumerated rights today makes conservatives nervous, while at the same time gladdening the hearts of liberals."[13] In the footnote attached to that statement, Judge Thomas, a self-proclaimed conservative, wrote:

> The current case provoking the most protest from conservatives is *Roe* v. *Wade*, in which the Supreme Court found a woman's decision to end her pregnancy to be part of her unenumerated right to privacy established by *Griswold* v. *Connecticut*.[14]

But when questioned about the citation, Judge Thomas did not remember having made the citation.

> I would like to have the cite to it. Again, notwithstanding the citation, if there is one, I did not and do not have a position on the outcome.[15]

Similarly, in 1987, Judge Thomas argued that blacks and conservatives agree on the abortion issue.[16]

Judge Thomas also claimed to be unfamiliar with a report issued by a White House Working Group on the Family, despite having been a member of the Working Group. The 1986 report sharply criticized the Supreme Court's decision in *Roe*, as well as other abortion and privacy cases.[17] The report stated that this "fatally flawed line of court decisions can be corrected, directly or indirectly, through the appointment of new judges and their confirmation by the Senate.[18]

During his testimony, Judge Thomas said that he had not read any part of the report other than the sections on low-income families, even after the report had generated considerable controver-

---

[11] Hearing transcript, Sept. 11, 1991, at 95.
[12] Hearing transcript, Sept. 11, 1991, at 97. See also hearing transcript, Sept. 10, 1991, at 197.
[13] "The Higher Law Background" at 68.
[14] Id. at n.2.
[15] Hearing transcript, Sept. 11, 1991, at 107.
[16] Thomas, "How Republicans Can Win Blacks," Chicago Defender, Feb. 21, 1987 (Perspective Section), at 22.
[17] "The Family: Preserving America's Future," A Report to the President from the White House Working Group on the Family (1986), at 11–12.
[18] Id. at 12.

sy.[19] He could not recall whether the report itself had been made available for final comment, but remarked that his sole interest in the report had been in the sections on low-income families.[20] Later in the proceedings, Judge Thomas was asked whether he would have objected to the part of the report criticizing the abortion cases had he been aware of it. Ignoring the main thrust of the question, Judge Thomas answered only that he would have expressed concern that the report should be more narrowly focused to concentrate primarily on government policy with respect to low-income and at-risk families.[21]

Judge Thomas repeatedly refused to state his views, either legal or personal, on whether a woman's right to choose abortion is a fundamental right protected under the 14th amendment.[22] Judge Thomas testified that he had neither discussed nor ever formed an opinion on abortion and had never discussed *Roe* v. *Wade* with anyone. In addition, Judge Thomas stated that even if he were to have formed an opinion, it would be inappropriate for him to enunciate his views on a matter that would be coming before the Court next term.[23]

Moreover, other nominees have discussed personal views during their confirmation hearings without compromising their impartiality on the issue. For example, Justice Sandra Day O'Connor during her nomination hearing, felt no compunction about expressing her personal views on abortion.

Moreover, Judge thomas did announce his views on a number of issues which have been recently before the Court and are likely to arise again, including habeas corpus appeals in death penalty cases, victim participation in the criminal process, the uniform sentencing guidelines, and the *Lemon* test for church/state issues.[24]

The Senate should not give its approval to a nominee who refuses to answer fair questions on issues of bedrock importance to the vast majority of Americans. No one is suggesting that a nominees should jeopardize his impartiality by commenting on specific cases. But Judge Thomas readily agreed to answer many questions about various issues before the Court. When we contrast that willingness with his reluctance to discuss issues like abortion, it is transparently clear that he was not demonstrating his impartiality, but defending his prospects for confirmation.

---

[19] Hearing Transcript, Sept. 10, 1991, at 154–55.

[20] Hearing Transcript, Sept. 11, 1991, at 19.

[21] Id. at 22.

[22] Id. at 103–105. Judge Thomas also repeatedly refused to state whether an unmarried individual has a right to privacy protected under the 14th amendment. Hearing transcript, Sept. 12 at 45–50.

[23] Hearing transcript, Sept. 11, 1991, at 103–105.

[24] Moreover, Judge Thomas discussed a case decided by the Supreme Court less than one year ago, notwithstanding the fact that he currently has pending before him a closely related case. See p. 15, infra. Judge Thomas told the committee that he is in favor of some restrictions on the habeas corpus appeals process for death penalty cases, that he is in favor of some form of victim participation in the criminal process, that he believes sentencing guidelines have been effective in reducing disparity and increasing the fairness of the sentencing process, Hearing Transcript, Sept. 10, 1991 at 162–165, and that he has no quarrel with the test used by the Supreme Court in *Lemon* v. *Kurtzman*. Hearing transcript, Sept. 11, 1991, 179–181.

Congressional Record - Senate
Sept. 26, 1991
Pp. 13748-9

THE NOMINATION OF JUDGE CLARENCE THOMAS

Mr. HARKIN. Mr. President, on June 27, I was saddened by the decision of Justice Thurgood Marshall to resign from the Supreme Court. On the Senate floor at that time, I expressed my feelings about Justice Marshall's distinguished career as an attorney and judge. I also expressed my hope that the nominee to replace Justice Marshall be a person who would follow in the path blazed by Justice Marshall.

After the nomination of Clarence Thomas, I openly stated one issue that I particularly wanted the nominee to address, and which would be instrumental in deciding my position on this nomination. That is the question of the fundamental right to privacy in the Constitution.

The right to privacy--the right of each person to decide personal family matters free from government intrusion--is fundamental to our free society. A nominee's view of the right to privacy is a telling indication of his entire approach to constitutional adjudication. A nominee with a broad view of the right to privacy is more likely to vindicate the rights of individuals from governmental excess in other areas. Such a nominee would understand the role of the Supreme Court, in our system of checks and balances, as the last resort for citizens to vindicate their rights. Too often in recent years, the Court has been a rubber stamp to affirm laws and regulations which trample the rights of Americans. Just as I would not vote for a nominee who did not openly support the right to the free exercise of religion or the right to free speech, I cannot support a nominee who does not unequivocally support the fundamental right to privacy.

With this in mind, I have watched the nomination of Clarence Thomas with great interest. I had hoped that a man of his background, who had climbed the ladder of opportunity despite the withering force of racism, a man who benefited from programs and policies intended to redress that discrimination, would grasp the role of the Supreme Court as a bastion of individual freedom. I had hoped that Judge Thomas would understand that the protection of the Court is essential for others to climb that ladder. Unfortunately, it seems likely that Judge Thomas would pull the ladder of opportunity up after him.

Judge Thomas' tenure at the EEOC and his writings on natural law raise serious questions of his commitment to protecting individual rights. I was particularly concerned about his endorsement of Lewis Lehrman's article which would have destroyed the right of privacy with regard to abortion, and would in fact make abortion illegal, even in the case of rape or incest. It would impose a rigid system of Government imposed morality upon women, rather than trusting the wisdom and morality of the women of this country.

He also dismissed Justice Goldburg's analysis of the ninth amendment as a mere invention. That echoes the words of one of the dissenters in the case of Griswald versus Connecticut, which guaranteed the right of married couples to use contraceptives. If Griswald were overturned, the Government could even reach its hand into the bedrooms of married couples. Thomas now says he accepts the right to privacy which was controlling in Griswald. His abrupt change of views at the hearings raises the question in my mind if this is not just a confirmation conversion.

Judge Thomas' testimony before the committee did not dispel my concerns. Thomas apparently repudiated his views of natural law and his endorsement of the Lehrman article, but his wholesale rejection of beliefs which he had repeatedly stated for years is troublesome. Are Thomas's real views the ones he stated in his committee testimony, or are they the ones he stated in years of writing and speaking?

At least as troubling is his refusal to discuss any of the issues which would show how he would approach the critical right of privacy. Despite his willingness to comment on a variety of other issues, including issues which are in controversy before the Court in the next term, he flatly refused to give the Senate any insight into his thought process regarding privacy. He would not even acknowledge that unmarried people have a privacy right to use contraceptives.

Judge Thomas acknowledged that the case of Roe versus Wade is among the most important cases decided by the Supreme Court in the last 20 years. Yet he claims that he has no personal opinion on the decision in Roe versus Wade. He claimed that he has not discussed this issue in private, even with his wife.

This statement begs credulity. It indicates to me that he does not have the coherent understanding of the Constitution that the American people have the right to expect in a person nominated to the Supreme Court.

I take the responsibility to advise and consent on nominees to the Supreme Court very seriously. This body has a coequal role with the Executive in the process of appointing members of the third branch. The Founders gave this power to the Senate as a check on the power of the Executive to appoint Supreme Court Justices. I believe we have the duty to exercise that power to ensure that the Court remains a bulwark against the violation of the rights guaranteed for each and all Americans by the Constitution. Because I do not believe that Judge Clarence Thomas has the necessary qualifications for this important post, and because the views he has expressed on the constitutional right to privacy are contradictory and muddled, I cannot consent to this nomination. Therefore, I will cast my vote against this nomination of Clarence Thomas to be a Justice of the Supreme Court.

Congressional Record - Senate
Sept. 27, 1991
P. 13879

[Mr. WIRTH.] The issue that troubles me most, however--and the primary reason I cannot vote to confirm Clarence Thomas--is his ambiguous stand on the fundamental right to privacy and reproductive freedom. During the hearings, Clarence Thomas was anything but forthcoming in his views about this basic right in our country. It seems incredible that in this decade, after more than a century of progress in defining and protecting individual rights, the Supreme Court may very well turn back the clock by interpreting the Bill of Rights to exclude something so fundamental as a right of privacy. But this is precisely what we are facing, and precisely why it is so important to know how Clarence Thomas interprets this right.

During his hearings, Clarence Thomas responded to a number of questions on several areas of the law that are pending before the Supreme Court. He would not make clear, however, his views on the legal foundation for the fundamental right for a woman to make her own choices about her health care.

I am profoundly disturbed by Clarence Thomas' endorsement of a constitutional protection for the natural right to life--supporting the argument that the fetus has a natural right to life from the moment of conception. Under this interpretation of the Constitution--which would lead to the overruling of Roe--States and Congress would be barred from keeping abortion legal. This is unacceptable, and Clarence Thomas did little to withdraw himself from this position--rather he chose to simply state that he had not reread the statements he had previously made and could not discuss them.

Testimony made it clear to me that Judge Thomas does not believe the ninth amendment protects individuals for unenumerated rights-- including the right to privacy. In fact, he indicated a certain amount of hostility toward the ninth amendment and its protection of individual liberties by describing that right as an invention. The ninth amendment is an invention of our forebearers that warrants celebration --not contempt--because it supports the premise that citizens of this country should have the right to privacy.

Legislatures are democratically elected bodies; by nature and composition the legislative branch necessarily reflects the views of the majority. This branch of Government is often unsuited to the task of protecting the rights of unpopular minorities, including those who are most vulnerable in our society. That is why every individual American has, under our Constitution, the right to look to the Bill of Rights and the Supreme Court for ultimate protection against the intrusions of government--and that is why the debate about the right of privacy and the nomination of Clarence Thomas is so important to every American.

Finally, I think it is important for the Supreme Court--which is, after all, the third coequal branch of Government--to reflect the historically diverse nature of our society. The Supreme Court's deliberations on the great issues of the day should not be dominated by one narrow point of view. This is not to say that the Supreme Court should never speak unanimously. Rather, it is to point out that on a such a broad question of protecting individual rights and the right of privacy, it is disturbing to think that the highest court in the land could be so completely imbalanced and out of step with the views of the society it is charged with protecting.

It is not Clarence Thomas the man, who concerns me--it is Clarence Thomas the Supreme Court Justice. His constitutional and judicial views--not his personality--are what interest me. By refusing to address many of the issues of concern to me and other Members of the Senate, his previous statements and writings must be the record we consider today.

I find it suspicious that Clarence Thomas would be willing to answer many questions about pending cases and issues likely to come before the Court, yet he cannot or will not answer critical questions about his views on the fundamental right of privacy. Even more disturbing is that he did not feel the need to review--after weeks of preparation and days of testimony--articles and reports he had written.

Instead, he put artificial distance between his work on the EEOC and his responses to questions by the Judiciary Committee. Therefore, we are left in the dark as to his judicial philosophy.

In her testimony before the Judiciary Committee, former Gov. Madeleine Kunin of Vermont noted--and I think accurately--that Clarence Thomas would like us to believe that silence equals impartiality--that he is a blank slate and only the facts of the case will determine how he will rule. Even though he was willing in the past to disregard decisions made by the courts based on his own preferences, he would climb up to the most important judicial bench in our country and not bring to it any of the disregard for established law that we have witnessed. Mr. President, I find that impossible to believe.

His record is an indication of the direction Clarence Thomas would like to take the Court. More than 20 years ago, Senator Thurmond raised the red flag on how dangerous that can be to our country by saying:

It is my contention that the Supreme Court has assumed such a powerful role as a policymaker that the Senate must necessarily be concerned with the views of prospective Justices or Chief Justices as it relates to broad issues confronting the American people and the role of the Court in dealing with these issues.

Mr. President, if I had been in the Senate at another time in this Nation's history, I might have been called upon to vote to confirm the nomination of a Justice who would have upheld the constitutionality of slavery as in Dred Scott, or the legality of segregation as in Plessy versus Ferguson. I would hope that given that opportunity, my judgment would have turned on a commitment to civil liberties and fundamental constitutional rights. And just as freedom from slavery and equality in public education and accommodations were hotly debated topics in days past, the constitutional debate today is focused on basic principles such as privacy.

Decisions to be made on the Supreme Court are too important to be left to vague platitudes and philosophical uncertainty. This body should not leave its preference for judicial equanimity, rather than partisan ideology, to chance. Regretfully, I cannot support Clarence Thomas' nomination.

Mr. DANFORTH. Mr. President, David Souter was called the "stealth nominee" for the U.S. Supreme Court. Those were the words used to describe David Souter--the "stealth nominee." Nobody knew what he believed. It was said he would not answer any questions; yet, he was confirmed by a vote of 90 to 9.

Now, it is said the Clarence Thomas is a person we do not know enough about and therefore we cannot vote for Clarence Thomas. What, Mr. President, is the difference between David Souter and Clarence Thomas? As a matter of fact, much of the commentary comparing the Souter nomination with the Thomas nomination is to the effect that David Souter had no track record; that he wrote very little, if anything; that he had not made a lot of speeches; but that Clarence Thomas had quite a paper trail, it was said, quite a paper trail, that people knew what he had said, knew what he had written. That was said to be the difference between David Souter and Clarence Thomas.

So, Mr. President, how can anybody conceivably argue that they will not vote for Clarence Thomas because they do not know Clarence Thomas when 1 year ago yesterday they voted for David Souter? What kind of double standard is that to apply to the Thomas nomination: "Oh, we do not know him"? Well, we knew David Souter enough to vote for him 90 to 9. We do not know Clarence Thomas; therefore, we will not vote for him? No, Mr. President. I do not think that is any kind of argument for voting against the Thomas nomination, that we do not know him. I think that is an excuse rather than a reason.

It is said that Clarence Thomas did not come clean when he was before the committee, that he did not really answer questions that came before him. But, Mr. President, Clarence Thomas took the same position that other Supreme Court nominees have taken. He said that he would not offer an opinion on a matter that could come before the Court, that it would be improper to do so.

He was asked repeatedly about the question of abortion. "What is your position on abortion?" At one point, about halfway through the hearings, Senator Hatch noted that he had counted 70 different times when Clarence Thomas had been asked about abortion one way or another by Members of the Senate Judiciary Committee; 70 times he had been asked about abortion. That was only halfway through the hearings. I have not made a count of how many times he was asked from beginning to end, but it was surely more than 70. Was it 80, 90, 100?

Mr. President, when do we move beyond an honest inquiry into a person's views and badgering somebody? Is it after the first five questions, or 10 or 20, or 50 or 60 or 70?

Repeatedly he was asked the question on abortion as though abortion is the litmus test for serving on the Supreme Court of the United States. "Answer our question on abortion. We insist on knowing what your position is. How would you vote on abortion? What do you think about abortion? Do you have a personal opinion of abortion? Have you ever discussed abortion with anybody?"

I do not know, Mr. President; the nominee said, "Oh, I haven't even discussed it with anybody."

I do not know how to prove a negative. I do not understand how to prove a negative. I know that my administrative assistant, who served as my administrative assistant both when Clarence Thomas was with me in the Attorney General's office and when Clarence Thomas was with me here in Washington, wrote me a letter saying that he has had probably thousands of discussions with Clarence Thomas over the years about everything ranging from English literature to jogging, and he has never discussed abortion with Clarence Thomas.

I know that a lawyer here in town named Chris Brewster, who served with me both in the Attorney General's office and here in Washington, and who worked with me on the brief of my own Supreme Court case on the subject of abortion, said that the whole time he served with Clarence Thomas he never discussed the subject with him.

Most people I suppose are intensely interested in the subject of abortion. It has just never been particularly on Clarence Thomas' screen. People say this is a question of credibility. "Of course he must have talked to somebody." And so the liberal interest groups are now taking out paid advertising in a newspaper to ask people to come forward if they have ever talked about abortion with Clarence Thomas. I ask the Senate: Is that an honest inquiry into a matter that should be discussed by a Supreme Court Justice? Or is it picking on somebody?

I think it is picking on him.

He would not answer the question. He said, "I do not think it is appropriate for somebody to go to the Supreme Court and not be able to decide the case on the basis of the law and the facts in front of him. I think that a judge should be impartial," says Clarence Thomas. And I agree. And so have other people who have been confirmed for the Supreme Court agreed.

A judge should be impartial. And it truly is an interference with the independence of the judiciary to ask a nominee to promise a vote on the Court in exchange for our confirmation in the Senate. It is not right. It interferes with the independence of the judiciary and most Americans know that, no matter what their view is on the subject of abortion.

Have we not had enough judges who were trying to impose some preconceived idea of their own on the American people? And do not really want judges who will decide cases on the basis of the facts and on the basis of the law, without trying to fob off on the American people some personal philosophical point of view?

If a judge has a personal opinion, is not Clarence Thomas exactly right, that personal opinion should be put in the background, that personal opinion should be something that the judge takes off, as Clarence Thomas said, like a runner takes off his extra clothing before running a race.

The issue is the independence of the judiciary. And other nominees have stated that before the Judiciary Committee and their explanation was accepted. And people say, "Oh, we do not know, we do not know what his views are, because he won't prejudge cases for us."

When Justice Marshall, just retired, testified before the Judiciary Committee during his confirmation, a question was put to him by Senator McClellan. Here is the question:

Do you subscribe to the philosophy, as expressed by a majority of the Court in the Miranda case, that no matter how voluntary a confession or incriminating statement by a defendant might be, it must be excluded from evidence unless the prescribed warnings of that opinion were given?

Here is the answer that Thurgood Marshall gave in his confirmation hearings:

Respectfully, I cannot answer your question, because there are many cases pending in the Supreme Court right now on variations of the so-called Miranda rule, and I would suspect that in every State of the

Union there are other cases on different variations of the Miranda rule that are on their way to the Supreme Court, and if I am confirmed, I would have to pass on those cases.

Question:

I will not ask you about any presently pending case here. *** But, I think it has become so critical that we who have this responsibility here of upholding confirmations need to have some idea, at least glimpse, some impression as to the trend of the thinking and the philosophy of the one who is to receive confirmation.

Answer:

My difficulty is that from all of the hearings I have ever read about, it has been considered and recognized as improper for a nominee to a judgeship to comment on cases that he will have to pass on.

7

JUSTICE RUTH BADER GINSBURG

Bill Clinton's June 14, 1993 appointment of former ACLU lawyer and abortion rights supporter Ruth Bader Ginsburg to the Supreme Court buttressed abortion rights and, in so doing, sounded the death knell to the Reagan-Bush campaign to overturn *Roe*. Despite four Justices expressing a willingness to overturn *Roe* in the Court's 1992 *Planned Parenthood v. Casey* decision, Clinton's 1992 election has made it impossible for those four Justices to attract the necessary fifth vote. By claiming that he will make support for abortion rights a litmus test in his Supreme Court appointments, Clinton--unlike his Republican predecessors--will not risk appointing to the Court an individual unwilling to commit herself to the pro-choice position. Indeed, by appointing Ginsburg to succeed Byron White, one of *Roe's* original dissenters and a long-standing opponent of abortion rights, Clinton has ensured that a sixth Justice would join a group of five Justices committed to the preservation of abortion rights.

The Ginsburg appointment, however, is tinged with irony for staunch defenders of the power of the judiciary, through decisions like *Roe*, to settle emotionally divisive issues. Ginsburg has emphasized that judges "play an interdependent part in our democracy. They do not alone shape legal doctrine but . . . they participate in a dialogue with other organs of government, and with the people as well." Ruth Bader Ginsburg, Speaking In a Judicial Voice, 67 N.Y.U. L. Rev. 1185 (1992). Indeed, Ginsburg went so far as to suggest, in December 1992, that Roe "prolonged divisiveness and deferred stable settlement of the [abortion] issue" by short-circuiting early 1970's legislative reform efforts. *Id.* at 1208.

Ginsburg's beef with *Roe* was not with its outcome but with its reasoning. In her writings she suggested that the decision should have focused more on equal protection analysis, "honed in more precisely on the woman's equality dimension of the issue," than the right to privacy. Ginsburg, Some Thoughts on Autonomy and Equality in Relation to *Roe v. Wade*, 63 N.C. L. Rev. 375, 24 (1985). She characterized abortion restrictions as "disadvantageous treatment of a woman because of her pregnancy and reproductive choice [and] a paradigm case of discrimination on the basis of sex." *Id.* at 28. At her confirmation hearing, however, she maintained that the privacy component of the abortion issue should not be ignored completely; she believed the decision should have rested both on privacy and equal protection grounds.

While candidly revealing her disapproval of the *Roe* decision's scope and basis, Ginsburg did not equivocate on the question of her pro-choice beliefs. She told Senator Carol Mosely-Braun (D-Ill.) that the abortion decision "is something central to a woman's life, to her dignity . . . a decision that she must make for herself. And when government controls that decision for her, she is being treated as less than a fully adult human responsible for her own choices." Committee Report at 17.

As Ginsburg seemed to break all the rules outlined by the Bork nomination by openly disclosing both her pro-choice leanings and her criticism of *Roe*, Ginsburg nevertheless assured the Senators that her views would not interfere with her decisionmaking. She valued *stare decisis* as a check on judicial power, and characterized it as "one of the restraints against a judge infusing his or her own values into the interpretation of the Constitution." Committee Report at 12.

Thus it appeared that Ginsburg cut neatly between the two camps on the abortion issue: Ginsburg was openly and adamantly pro-choice in her personal beliefs but she reflected a more moderate, middle-of-the-road jurisprudential position. Nevertheless, some pro-life Senators remained opposed to Ginsburg's confirmation and at least uncomfortable with her abortion views. Senator Jesse Helms (R-N.C.) called her abortion position "outrageously simplistic and callous" and criticized her for using "a great deal of doubletalk." 139 C.R. S10076 (daily ed. August 2, 1993). He criticized her failure to distinguish between abortions at various stages of pregnancy which, according to Helms, could imply a belief that abortions even at nine months should be allowed. Senator Helms also criticized the Senate Judiciary Committee for "its failure to challenge [Ginsburg's] oversimplification." *Id.* Other detractors, including Senator Arlen Specter (R-Pa.), who acknowledged that "she was more forthcoming than recent nominees about her support for the right of a woman to make reproductive choices," were nevertheless unhappy about a perceived reticence on other sensitive issues. 139 C.R. S9925 (daily ed. July 30, 1993).

Despite these grumblings, the Senate overwhelmingly approved Ruth Bader Ginsburg's confirmation. She was certainly not a pro-life nominee; however she was likely the most "sympathetic" pro-choice nominee pro-life forces would see. Her moderate views on most issues, including abortion, helped secure her successful ascension to the Court. Most concerned with the abortion issue were happy: pro-choicers had a woman who believed in the right to choose; pro-lifers had a moderate justice who would respect precedent which chipped away at *Roe*.

Justice Ruth Bader Ginsburg
Documents

ESSAY

SOME THOUGHTS ON AUTONOMY AND EQUALITY IN RELATION TO *ROE V. WADE*†

Ruth Bader Ginsburg‡

The 1973 United States Supreme Court decision in Roe v. Wade *sparked a legal and political controversy that continues to this day. Judge Ginsburg suggests that the* Roe *opinion would have been more acceptable if it had not gone beyond a ruling on the extreme statute involved in the case. She agrees with commentary maintaining that the Court should have adverted specifically to sex equality considerations. Such an approach might have muted the criticism of the* Roe *decision. The breadth and detail of the* Roe *opinion ironically may have stimulated, rather than discouraged, antiabortion measures, particularly with respect to public funding of abortion.*

These remarks contrast two related areas of constitutional adjudication: gender-based classification and reproductive autonomy. In both areas, the Burger Court, in contrast to the Warren Court, has been uncommonly active. The two areas are intimately related in this practical sense: the law's response to questions subsumed under these headings bears pervasively on the situation of women in society. Inevitably, the shape of the law on gender-based classification and reproductive autonomy indicates and influences the opportunity women will have to participate as men's full partners in the nation's social, political, and economic life.[1]

Doctrine in the two areas, however, has evolved in discrete compartments. The High Court has analyzed classification by gender under an equal

---

† This Essay was delivered as the William T. Joyner Lecture on Constitutional Law at the University of North Carolina School of Law on April 6, 1984.

‡ United States Circuit Judge, United States Court of Appeals for the District of Columbia Circuit. The author acknowledges with appreciation the assistance of her 1983-1984 law clerk, Michael Klarman, in the composition of this Essay.

1. *See* Karst, *Foreword: Equal Citizenship Under the Fourteenth Amendment*, 91 HARV. L. REV. 1, 53-59 (1977). In composing this presentation, I have been stimulated, particularly, by the more encompassing and trenchant work of Professor Sylvia Law of New York University Law School, Law, *Rethinking Sex and the Constitution*, 132 U. PA. L. REV. 955 (1984), and Professor Wendy Williams of Georgetown University Law Center, W. Williams, Equality Riddle: Pregnancy and the Equal Treatment/Special Treatment Debate (Mar. 1984) (unpublished manuscript); W. Williams, Pregnancy: Special Treatment vs. Equal Treatment (Mar. 7, 1982) (unpublished manuscript); W. Williams, The Equality Crisis: Some Reflections on Culture, Courts and Feminism (1982) (unpublished manuscript). I owe both of them special appreciation for sharing their draft manuscripts and ideas with me. For the vulnerabilities readers find in this discussion of tense issues, however, I bear sole responsibility.

protection/sex discrimination rubric; it has treated reproductive autonomy under a substantive due process/personal autonomy headline not expressly linked to discrimination against women. The Court's gender classification decisions overturning state and federal legislation, in the main, have not provoked large controversy; the Court's initial 1973 abortion decision, *Roe v. Wade*,[2] on the other hand, became and remains a storm center. *Roe v. Wade* sparked public opposition and academic criticism,[3] in part, I believe, because the Court ventured too far in the change it ordered and presented an incomplete justification for its action. I will attempt to explain these twin perspectives on *Roe* later in this Essay.

Preliminarily, I will relate why an invitation to speak at Chapel Hill on any topic relating to constitutional law led me to think about gender-based classification coupled with *Roe* and its aftermath. In 1971, just before the Supreme Court's turning-point gender-classification decision in *Reed v. Reed*,[4] and over a year before *Roe v. Wade*, I visited a neighboring institution to participate in a conference on women and the law. I spoke then of the utility of litigation attacking official line-drawing by sex. My comments focused on the chance in the 1970s that courts, through constitutional adjudication, would aid in evening out the rights, responsibilities, and opportunities of women and men.[5] I did not mention the abortion cases then on the dockets of several lower courts—I was not at that time or any other time thereafter personally engaged in reproductive-autonomy litigation. Nonetheless, the most heated questions I received concerned abortion.

The questions were pressed by black men. The suggestion, not thinly veiled, was that legislative reform and litigation regarding abortion might have less to do with individual autonomy or discrimination against women than with restricting population growth among oppressed minorities.[6] The

---

2. 410 U.S. 113 (1973).

3. *See, e.g.*, Ely, *The Wages of Crying Wolf: A Comment on* Roe v. Wade, 82 YALE L.J. 920 (1973); Epstein, *Substantive Due Process by Any Other Name: The Abortion Cases*, 1973 SUP. CT. REV. 159.

4. 404 U.S. 71 (1971) (statutory preference for males as estate administrators held unconstitutional).

5. *See* Ginsburg, *Sex and Unequal Protection: Men and Women as Victims*, 11 J. FAM. L. 347 (1971) (presenting text of October 1, 1971 remarks made at the Southern Regional Conference of the National Conference of Law Women, held at Duke University Law School).

6. Law journal commentary around that time discussed population control measures that the government might order. *See, e.g.*, Note, *Legal Analysis and Population Control: The Problem of Coercion*, 84 HARV. L. REV. 1856 (1971). Some commentators explicitly noted links between the abortion and population explosion issues. *See, e.g.*, Leavy & Kummer, *Abortion and the Population Crisis; Therapeutic Abortion and the Law; Some New Approaches*, 27 OHIO ST. L.J. 647, 652 (1966) ("[T]he subject of abortion is riding the wave of the grand dialogue over the population explosion and the need for birth control programs."); Note, *Abortion Reform: History, Status, and Prognosis*, 21 CASE W. RES. L. REV. 521, 523 (1970) ("[T]hose countries that have sanctioned abortion on demand have been rewarded with consequent alleviation of dire overpopulation . . . ."); *see also Survey Finds 50% Back Liberalization of Abortion Policy*, N.Y. Times, Oct. 28, 1971, at A1, col. 1 ("General concern over population growth has become so intense . . . that half the public now favors liberalization of restrictions on abortion."). As the text indicates, blacks—and in particular, black men—also noted the coincidence of rising population with the liberalization of abortion laws, and sometimes were strongly suspicious of the implications. *See, e.g., City Blacks Get Most Abortions*, N.Y. Times, Dec. 6, 1973, at 94, col. 3 (remarking upon "[t]radional

strong word "genocide" was uttered more than once. It is a notable irony that, as constitutional law in this domain has unfolded, women who are not poor have achieved access to abortion with relative ease; for poor women, however, a group in which minorities are disproportionately represented, access to abortion is not markedly different from what it was in pre-*Roe* days.

I will summarize first the Supreme Court's performance in cases challenging explicit gender-based classification—a development that has encountered no significant backlash—and then turn to the far more turbulent reproductive autonomy area.

The Warren Court uncabined the equal protection guarantee in diverse settings,[7] but line drawing by sex was a quarter in which no change occurred in the 1950s and 1960s. From the 1860s until 1971, the record remained unbroken: the Supreme Court rejected virtually every effort to overturn sex-based classification by law. Without offense to the Constitution, for example, women could be kept off juries[8] and could be barred from occupations ranging from lawyer to bartender.[9]

In the 1970s overt sex-based classification fell prey to the Burger Court's intervention. Men could not be preferred to women for estate administration purposes, the Court declared in the pivotal *Reed v. Reed*[10] decision. Married women in the military could not be denied fringe benefits—family housing and health care allowances—accorded married men in military service, the High Court held in *Frontiero v. Richardson*.[11] Social security benefits, welfare assistance, and workers' compensation secured by a male's employment must be secured, to the same extent, by a female's employment, the Supreme Court ruled in a progression of cases: *Weinberger v. Wiesenfeld*,[12] *Califano v. Goldfarb*,[13] *Califano v. Westcott*,[14] and *Wengler v. Druggists Mutual Insurance Co.*[15] Girls are entitled to the same parental support as boys, the Supreme Court stated in *Stanton v. Stanton*.[16] Evidencing its neutrality, the Court declared in

---

. . . black male resistance to abortion" and the view of the "militant [black] movement" that abortion is "genocide").

7. *See* Shapiro v. Thompson, 394 U.S. 618 (1969) (interstate travel); Levy v. Louisiana, 391 U.S. 68 (1968) (discrimination on the basis of out-of-wedlock birth); Harper v. Virginia Bd. of Elections, 383 U.S. 663 (1966) (access to ballot); Reynolds v. Sims, 377 U.S. 533 (1964) (apportionment); Griffin v. Illinois, 351 U.S. 12 (1956) (access to court); Brown v. Board of Educ., 347 U.S. 483 (1954) (race discrimination).

8. *See* Hoyt v. Florida, 368 U.S. 57 (1961) (upholding state statute requiring that, to serve on juries, women, but not men, must volunteer affirmatively for service); Fay v. New York, 332 U.S. 261 (1947) (upholding state's "blue ribbon" jury scheme despite gross disparity between numbers of women and men selected to serve); Strauder v. West Virginia, 100 U.S. 303, 310 (1879) (stating in dictum that states may "confine [juror] selection to males").

9. *See* Goesaert v. Cleary, 335 U.S. 464 (1948) (bartender) (decision "disapproved" in Craig v. Boren, 429 U.S. 190, 210 (1976)); Bradwell v. Illinois, 83 U.S. (16 Wall.) 130 (1872) (lawyer). *See generally* Ginsburg, *Sex Equality and the Constitution*, 52 Tul. L. Rev. 451, 451-57 (1978).

10. 404 U.S. 71 (1971).

11. 411 U.S. 677 (1973).

12. 420 U.S. 636 (1975) (social security).

13. 430 U.S. 199 (1977) (social security).

14. 443 U.S. 76 (1979) (aid to families with dependent children).

15. 446 U.S. 142 (1980) (workers' compensation).

16. 421 U.S. 7 (1975).

Craig v. Boren[17] that boys must be permitted to buy 3.2 percent beer at the same age as girls and, in *Orr v. Orr*,[18] that alimony could not be retained as a one-way street: a state could compel able men to make payments to women in need only if it also held women of means accountable for payments to men unable to fend for themselves. Louisiana's rule, derived from Napoleon's Civil Code, designating husband head and master of the household, was held in *Kirchberg v. Feenstra*[19] to be offensive to the evolving sex equality principle.

However sensible—and noncontroversial—these results, the decisions had a spectacular aspect. The race cases that trooped before the Warren Court could be viewed as moving the federal judiciary onto the course set by the Reconstruction Congress a century earlier in the post-Civil War amendments. No similar foundation, set deliberately by actors in the political arena, can account for the Burger Court sex discrimination decisions.[20] Perhaps for that reason, the Court has proceeded cautiously. It has taken no giant step. In its most recent decision, *Mississippi University for Women v. Hogan*,[21] the High Court recognized the right of men to a nursing school education at an institution maintained by the state for women only. But it earlier had declined to condemn a state property tax advantage reserved for widows,[22] a state statutory rape law penalizing males but not females,[23] and draft registration limited to males.[24] It has formally reserved judgment on the question whether, absent ratification of an equal rights amendment, sex, like race, should rank as a suspect classification.[25]

The Court's gender-based classification precedent impelled acknowledgment of a middle-tier equal protection standard of review, a level of judicial scrutiny demanding more than minimal rationality but less than a near-perfect fit between legislative ends and means. This movement away from the empty-cupboard interpretation of the equal protection principle in relation to sex equality claims largely trailed and mirrored changing patterns in society—most conspicuously, the emergence of the two-career family. The Court's decisions provoked no outraged opposition in legislative chambers. On the contrary, in a key area in which the Court rejected claims of impermissible sex-

---

17. 429 U.S. 190 (1976).

18. 440 U.S. 268 (1979).

19. 450 U.S. 455 (1981). The Louisiana legislation at issue provided specifically that a husband had a unilateral right to dispose of jointly owned property without his wife's consent. *Id.* at 456.

20. The Court once observed that the 19th amendment gave women the vote but only that. *See* Fay v. New York, 332 U.S. 261, 290 (1947).

21. 458 U.S. 718 (1982).

22. Kahn v. Shevin, 416 U.S. 351 (1974).

23. Michael M. v. Superior Court, 450 U.S. 464 (1981).

24. Rostker v. Goldberg, 453 U.S. 57 (1981).

25. *See* Mississippi Univ. for Women v. Hogan, 458 U.S. 718, 724 n.9 (1982); Frontiero v. Richardson, 411 U.S. 677, 691-92 (1973) (Powell, J., concurring).

For a more detailed review of the Burger Court's sex discrimination rulings, *see* Ginsburg, *The Burger Court's Grapplings with Sex Discrimination*, THE BURGER COURT: THE COUNTER-REVOLUTION THAT WASN'T 132 (V. Blasi ed. 1983) [hereinafter cited as THE BURGER COURT].

based classification, Congress indicated a different view, one more sensitive to discrimination against women.

That area, significantly in view of the Court's approach to reproductive choice, was pregnancy. In 1974 the Court decided an issue pressed by pregnant school teachers forced to terminate their employment, or take unpaid maternity leave, months before the anticipated birth date.[26] Policies singling out pregnant women for disadvantageous treatment discriminated invidiously on the basis of sex, the teachers argued. The Court bypassed that argument; instead, the Court rested its decision holding mandatory maternity leaves unconstitutional on due process/conclusive presumption reasoning.[27] Some weeks later, the Court held that a state-operated disability income protection plan could exclude normal pregnancy without offense to the equal protection principle.[28] In a statutory setting as well, under Title VII, the Court later ruled, as it earlier had held in a constitutional context, that women unable to work due to pregnancy or childbirth could be excluded from disability coverage.[29] The classifications in these disability cases, according to the Court, were not gender-based on their face, and were not shown to have any sex-discriminatory effect. All "nonpregnant persons," women along with men, the Court pointed out, were treated alike.[30]

With respect to Title VII, Congress prospectively overruled the Court in 1978. It amended the statute to state explicitly that classification on the basis of sex includes classification on the basis of pregnancy.[31] That congressional definition is not controlling in constitutional adjudication, but it might stimulate the Court one day to revise its position that regulation governing "pregnant persons" is not sex-based.

Roe v. Wade, in contrast to decisions involving explicit male/female classification, has occasioned searing criticism of the Court, over a decade of demonstrations, a stream of vituperative mail addressed to Justice Blackmun (the author of the opinion), annual proposals for overruling *Roe* by constitutional amendment,[32] and a variety of measures in Congress and state legislatures to contain or curtail the decision.[33] In 1973, when *Roe* issued, abortion law was in a state of change across the nation. There was a distinct trend in the states,

---

26. Cleveland Bd. of Educ. v. LaFleur, 414 U.S. 632 (1974).

27. *Id.* at 639-50. The irrebuttable or conclusive presumption mode of analysis has lost favor with the Court in other contexts. *See* Weinberger v. Salfi, 422 U.S. 749, 771-72 (1975).

28. Geduldig v. Aiello, 417 U.S. 484 (1974).

29. General Elec. Co. v. Gilbert, 429 U.S. 125 (1976).

30. *Id.* at 135.

31. Act of Oct. 31, 1978, Pub. L. No. 95-555, 92 Stat. 2076 (amending 42 U.S.C. § 2000e (1976)).

32. *See, e.g.,* Destro, *Abortion and the Constitution: The Need for a Life-Protective Amendment,* 63 CALIF. L. REV. 1250, 1319-25 (1975) (discussing proposed amendments).

33. *See, e.g.,* Hyde, *The Human Life Bill: Some Issues and Answers,* 27 N.Y.L. SCH. L. REV. 1077 (1982) (congressional response); Witherspoon, *The New Pro-Life Legislation: Patterns and Recommendations,* 7 ST. MARY'S L.J. 637 (1976) (state response); Note, *Implications of the Abortion Decisions: Post* Roe *and* Doe *Litigation and Legislation,* 74 COLUM. L. REV. 237 (1974) (state response); *see also infra* notes 50-52 and accompanying text.

noted by the Court, "toward liberalization of abortion statutes."[34] Several states had adopted the American Law Institute's Model Penal Code approach setting out grounds on which abortion could be justified at any stage of pregnancy; most significantly, the Code included as a permissible ground preservation of the woman's physical or mental health.[35] Four states—New York, Washington, Alaska, and Hawaii—permitted physicians to perform first-trimester abortions with virtually no restrictions. This movement in legislative arenas bore some resemblance to the law revision activity that eventually swept through the states establishing no-fault divorce as the national pattern.[36]

The Texas law at issue in *Roe* made it a crime to "procure an abortion" except "by medical advice for the purpose of saving the life of the mother."[37] It was the most extreme prohibition extant. The Court had in close view two pathmarking opinions on reproductive autonomy: first, a 1965 precedent, *Griswold v. Connecticut*,[38] holding inconsistent with personal privacy, somehow sheltered by due process, a state ban on the use of contraceptives even by married couples; second, a 1972 decision, *Eisenstadt v. Baird*,[39] extending *Griswold* to strike down a state prohibition on sales of contraceptives except to married persons by prescription. The Court had already decided *Reed v. Reed*,[40] recognizing the arbitrariness in the 1970s of a once traditional gender-based classification, but it did not further pursue that avenue in *Roe*.

The decision in *Roe* appeared to be a stunning victory for the plaintiffs. The Court declared that a woman, guided by the medical judgment of her physician, had a "fundamental"[41] right to abort a pregnancy, a right the Court

---

34. *Roe*, 410 U.S. at 140; *see also infra* note 81.

35. MODEL PENAL CODE § 230.3 (1980).

36. On the transition from fault to no-fault divorce, see Raphael, Frank & Wilder, *Divorce in America: The Erosion of Fault*, 81 DICK. L. REV. 719, 728 (1976-1977) ("For the past three decades there has been a strong trend away from the traditional notion that one spouse must be guilty of some injury to the other before a divorce may be granted."); Note, *Untying the Knot: The Course and Patterns of Divorce Reform*, 57 CORNELL L. REV. 649 (1972). Long before no-fault divorce legislation became the norm in this country, persons with the financial resources to do so could travel to certain states or outside the country to end their marriages. *See, e.g.*, Friedman & Percival, *Who Sues for Divorce? From Fault Through Fiction to Freedom*, 5 J. LEGAL STUD. 61, 68 (1976) (before the sudden burst of no-fault divorce legislation in early 1970s, "divorce on demand had been available in many states, but at a stiff price"); Wash. Post, Feb. 1, 1972, at A18, col. 1 ("[S]omething is wrong when people who have $400 and a plane ticket can get quickie divorces and those who don't can't."), *quoted in* Zuckman, *Recent Developments in American Divorce Legislation*, 35 JURIST 6, 12 (1975). Similarly, before *Roe*, women of means could end their pregnancies by traveling to states or foreign nations with less restrictive abortion laws. *See* Burt, *The Burger Court and the Family*, THE BURGER COURT, *supra* note 25, at 92, 107-08 (for practical purposes, the availability of abortions in some states undermined the more restrictive regimes); Karst, *supra* note 1, at 59 ("Even before *Roe v. Wade*, wealthy women . . . could obtain abortions by traveling."); *Abortion for Whom*, NEW REPUBLIC, Oct. 25, 1969, at 12 ("The rich have always been able to get abortions by going abroad. The poor cannot travel . . . ."). For example, in 1971, the second year New York's liberalized abortion law was in effect, 60% of the women having abortions in New York were nonresidents. *See Light on Abortion*, N.Y. Times, Sept. 4, 1972, at A14, col. 2.

37. *Roe*, 410 U.S. at 117-18 (citing TEX. PENAL CODE ANN. §§ 1191, 1196 (Vernon 1961)).

38. 381 U.S. 479 (1965). Earlier, in Skinner v. Oklahoma *ex rel.* Williamson, 316 U.S. 535, 541 (1942), the Court had referred to an individual's right to procreate as "a basic liberty."

39. 405 U.S. 438 (1972).

40. 404 U.S. 71 (1971).

41. *See Roe*, 410 U.S. at 152, 155.

anchored to a concept of personal autonomy derived from the due process guarantee. The Court then proceeded to define with precision the state regulation of abortion henceforth permissible. The rulings in *Roe*, and in a companion case decided the same day, *Doe v. Bolton*,[42] were stunning in this sense: they called into question the criminal abortion statutes of every state, even those with the least restrictive provisions.

Roe announced a trimester approach Professor Archibald Cox has described as "read[ing] like a set of hospital rules and regulations."[43] During the first trimester, "the abortion decision and its effectuation must be left to the medical judgment of the pregnant woman's attending physician";[44] in the next, roughly three-month stage, the state may, if it chooses, require other measures protective of the woman's health.[45] During the final months, "the stage subsequent to viability," the state also may concern itself with an emerging interest, the "potentiality of human life"; at that stage, the state "may, if it chooses, regulate, and even proscribe, abortion except where it is necessary, in appropriate medical judgment, for the preservation of the life or health of the mother."[46]

Justice O'Connor, ten years after *Roe*, described the trimester approach as "on a collision course with itself."[47] Advances in medical technology would continue to move *forward* the point at which regulation could be justified as protective of a woman's health, and to move *backward* the point of viability, when the state could proscribe abortions unnecessary to preserve the patient's life or health. The approach, she thought, impelled legislatures to remain *au courant* with changing medical practices and called upon courts to examine legislative judgments, not as jurists applying "neutral principles," but as "science review boards."[48]

I earlier observed that, in my judgment, *Roe* ventured too far in the change it ordered. The sweep and detail of the opinion stimulated the mobilization of a right-to-life movement and an attendant reaction in Congress and state legislatures. In place of the trend "toward liberalization of abortion statutes" noted in *Roe*,[49] legislatures adopted measures aimed at minimizing the impact of the 1973 rulings, including notification and consent requirements,[50]

---

42. 410 U.S. 179 (1973).

43. A. Cox, The Role of the Supreme Court in American Government 113 (1976).

44. *Roe*, 410 U.S. at 164.

45. *Id.*

46. *Id.* at 164-65. The Model Penal Code provision, on which several states had patterned abortion legislation reform, *see Special Project, Survey of Abortion Law*, 1980 Ariz. St. L.J. 67, 109 & nn.229-31, contained no limitation as to the stage of pregnancy at which an abortion could be obtained. *See* Model Penal Code § 230.3(2) (1980).

47. City of Akron v. Akron Center for Reproductive Health, Inc., 103 S. Ct. 2481, 2507 (1983) (O'Connor, J., dissenting).

48. *Id.*

49. *Roe*, 410 U.S. at 140; *see also infra* note 81.

50. *See* City of Akron v. Akron Center for Reproductive Health, Inc., 103 S. Ct. 2481, 2497-99 (1983) (parental and court consent); H.L. v. Matheson, 450 U.S. 398 (1981) (parental notification); Planned Parenthood v. Danforth, 428 U.S. 52, 67-75 (1976) (spousal and parental consent).

prescriptions for the protection of fetal life,[51] and bans on public expenditures for poor women's abortions.[52]

Professor Paul Freund explained where he thought the Court went astray in *Roe*, and I agree with his statement. The Court properly invalidated the Texas proscription, he indicated, because "[a] law that absolutely made criminal all kinds and forms of abortion could not stand up; it is not a reasonable accommodation of interests."[53] If *Roe* had left off at that point and not adopted what Professor Freund called a "medical approach,"[54] physicians might have been less pleased with the decision, but the legislative trend might have continued in the direction in which it was headed in the early 1970s. "[S]ome of the bitter debate on the issue might have been averted," Professor Freund believed; "[t]he animus against the Court might at least have been diverted to the legislative halls."[55] Overall, he thought that the *Roe* distinctions turning on trimesters and viability of the fetus illustrated a troublesome tendency of the modern Supreme Court under Chief Justices Burger and Warren "to specify by a kind of legislative code the one alternative pattern that will satisfy the Constitution."[56]

I commented at the outset that I believe the Court presented an incomplete justification for its action. Academic criticism of *Roe*, charging the Court with reading its own values into the due process clause, might have been less pointed had the Court placed the woman alone, rather than the woman tied to her physician, at the center of its attention. Professor Karst's commentary is indicative of the perspective not developed in the High Court's opinion; he solidly linked abortion prohibitions with discrimination against women.[57] The issue in *Roe*, he wrote, deeply touched and concerned "women's position in society in relation to men."[58]

It is not a sufficient answer to charge it all to women's anatomy—a natural, not man-made, phenomenon. Society, not anatomy, "places a greater stigma on unmarried women who become pregnant than on the men who father their children."[59] Society expects, but nature does not command, that "women take the major responsibility . . . for child care"[60] and that they will

---

51. *See* Planned Parenthood Ass'n v. Ashcroft, 103 S. Ct. 2517, 2521-22 (1983); Planned Parenthood v. Danforth, 428 U.S. 52, 81-84 (1976).

52. *See* Harris v. McRae, 448 U.S. 297 (1980) ("Hyde Amendment" to Title XIX of Social Security Act); Maher v. Roe, 432 U.S. 464 (1977) (state Medicaid regulations).

53. Freund, *Storms over the Supreme Court*, 69 A.B.A. J. 1474, 1480 (1983) (adapted from inaugural Harold Leventhal Lecture at Columbia Law School).

54. *Id.*

55. *Id.*; *cf.* Burt, *supra* note 36, at 107-09 (arguing that *Roe* was "unnecessary" because "majoritarian institutions" were not "unfairly disregard[ing]" interests of "proponents of free abortion"); *infra* note 81.

56. Freund, *supra* note 53, at 1480.

57. Karst, *supra* note 1, at 58; *cf.* M. CAPPELLETTI & W. COHEN, COMPARATIVE CONSTITUTIONAL LAW 614-15 (1979) (observing that Italian Constitutional Court ruling on abortion statutes also avoided treating the matter as a women's rights issue).

58. Karst, *supra* note 1, at 58.

59. *Id.* at 57.

60. *Id.*

stay with their children, bearing nurture and support burdens alone, when fathers deny paternity or otherwise refuse to provide care or financial support for unwanted offspring.

I do not pretend that, if the Court had added a distinct sex discrimination theme to its medically oriented opinion, the storm *Roe* generated would have been less furious. I appreciate the intense divisions of opinion on the moral question and recognize that abortion today cannot fairly be described as nothing more than birth control delayed. The conflict, however, is not simply one between a fetus' interests and a woman's interests, narrowly conceived, nor is the overriding issue state versus private control of a woman's body for a span of nine months.[61] Also in the balance is a woman's autonomous charge of her full life's course—as Professor Karst put it, her ability to stand in relation to man, society, and the state as an independent, self-sustaining, equal citizen.[62]

On several occasions since *Roe* the Court has confronted legislative responses to the decision. With the notable exception of the public funding cases, the Court typically has applied *Roe* to overturn or limit efforts to impede access to abortion. I will not survey in the brief compass of this Essay the Court's series of opinions addressing: regulation of the abortion decisionmaking process; specifications regarding personnel, facilities, and medical procedures; and parental notification and consent requirements in the case of minors.[63] Instead, I will simply highlight the Court's statement last year reaffirming *Roe*'s "basic principle that a woman has a fundamental right to make the highly personal choice whether or not to terminate her pregnancy."[64] In *City of Akron v. Akron Center for Reproductive Health, Inc.*,[65] the Court acknowledged arguments it continues to hear that *Roe* "erred in interpreting the Constitution."[66] Nonetheless, the Court declared it would adhere to *Roe* because "*stare decisis*, while perhaps never entirely persuasive on a constitutional question, is a doctrine that demands respect in a society governed by the rule of law."[67]

I turn, finally, to the plight of the woman who lacks resources to finance privately implementation of her personal choice to terminate her pregnancy. The hostile reaction to *Roe* has trained largely on her.

Some observers speculated that the seven-two judgment in *Roe* was motivated at least in part by pragmatic considerations—population control concerns, the specter of coat hanger abortions, and concerns about unwanted children born to impoverished women. I recalled earlier the view that the

---

61. *But cf.* Regan, *Rewriting* Roe v. Wade, 77 MICH. L. REV. 1569 (1979) (contending that even when the parent-child relationship is involved our law generally does not require a person to submit to a bodily invasion or the imposition of physical pain to save the life of another).

62. Karst, *supra* note 1, at 57-59.

63. The Court's 1975-1981 decisions are listed in City of Akron v. Akron Center for Reproductive Health, Inc., 103 S. Ct. 2481, 2487 n.1 (1983).

64. *Id.*

65. 103 S. Ct. 2481 (1983).

66. *Id.* at 2487.

67. *Id.*

demand for open access to abortions had as its real purpose suppressing minorities.[68] In a set of 1977 decisions, however, the Court upheld state denial of medical expense reimbursement or hospital facilities for abortions sought by indigent women.[69] Moreover, in a 1980 decision, *Harris v. McRae*,[70] the Court found no constitutional infirmity in the Hyde Amendment, which excluded even medically necessary abortions from Medicaid coverage.[71] After these decisions, the Court was accused of sensitivity only to the Justices' own social milieu—"of creating a middle-class right to abortion."[72]

The argument for constitutionally mandated public assistance to effectuate the poor woman's choice ran along these lines. Accepting that our Constitution's Bill of Rights places restraints, not affirmative obligations, on government,[73] counsel for the impoverished women stressed that childbirth was publicly subsidized. As long as the government paid for childbirth, the argument proceeded, public funding could not be denied for abortion, often a safer and always a far less expensive course, short and long run. By paying for childbirth but not abortion, the complainants maintained, government increased spending and intruded upon or steered a choice *Roe* had ranked as a woman's "fundamental" right.[74]

The Court responded that, like other individual rights secured by the Constitution, the right to abortion is indeed a negative right. Government could not intervene by blocking a woman's utilization of her own resources to effectuate her decision. It could not " 'impose its will by force of law.' "[75] But *Roe* did not demand government neutrality, the Court reasoned; it left room for substantive government control to this extent: Action "deemed in the public interest"[76]—in this instance, protection of the potential life of the fetus—could be promoted by encouraging childbirth in preference to abortion.[77]

Financial need alone, under the Court's jurisprudence, does not identify a class of persons whose complaints of disadvantageous treatment attract close scrutiny.[78] Generally, constitutional claims to government benefits on behalf

---

68. *See supra* text accompanying notes 5-6.

69. Poelker v. Doe, 432 U.S. 519 (1977) (per curiam) (equal protection clause does not require public hospitals to perform abortions simply because they provide publicly financed hospital services for childbirth); Maher v. Roe, 432 U.S. 464 (1977) (equal protection clause does not require state participating in Medicaid program to pay expenses incident to nontherapeutic abortions for indigent women simply because it pays expenses incident to childbirth); Beal v. Doe, 432 U.S. 438 (1977) (same ruling under Social Security Act).

70. 448 U.S. 297 (1980).

71. *Id.* at 326-27. *But see* Fischer v. Department of Pub. Welfare, 475 A.2d 873 (Pa. Commw. Ct. 1984) (state denial of Medical Assistance funds to indigent women seeking medically necessary abortions violates equal protection clause of, and equal rights amendment to, state constitution).

72. Shapiro, *Fathers and Sons: The Court, The Commentators, and the Search for Values,* THE BURGER COURT, *supra* note 25, at 218, 229; *see* Karst, *supra* note 1, at 59.

73. *See* Henkin, *Rights: Here and There,* 81 COLUM. L. REV. 1582 (1981); Henkin, *Rights: American and Human,* 79 COLUM. L. REV. 403 (1979).

74. *See Harris,* 448 U.S. at 329 (Brennan, J., dissenting).

75. *Id.* at 315 (quoting Maher v. Roe, 432 U.S. 464, 476 (1977)).

76. *Id.*

77. *Id.*

78. San Antonio Indep. School Dist. v. Rodriguez, 411 U.S. 1 (1973).

of the poor have prevailed only when tied to another bark—a right to travel interstate, discrimination because of out-of-wedlock birth, or gender-based discrimination.[79] If the Court had acknowledged a woman's equality aspect, not simply a patient-physician autonomy constitutional dimension to the abortion issue, a majority perhaps might have seen the public assistance cases as instances in which, borrowing a phrase from Justice Stevens, the sovereign had violated its "duty to govern impartially."[80]

I have tried to discuss some features of constitutional adjudication concerning sex equality, in relation to the autonomy and equal-regard values involved in cases on abortion. I have done so tentatively and with trepidation. *Roe v. Wade* is a decision I approached gingerly in prior comment; until now I have limited my remarks to a brief description of what others have said. While I claim no original contribution, I have endeavored here to state my own reflections and concerns.

Roe, I believe, would have been more acceptable as a judicial decision if it had not gone beyond a ruling on the extreme statute before the Court. The political process was moving in the early 1970s, not swiftly enough for advocates of quick, complete change, but majoritarian institutions were listening and acting.[81] Heavy-handed judicial intervention was difficult to justify and

---

79. See Bennett, *The Burger Court and the Poor*, THE BURGER COURT, *supra* note 25, at 46, 52-53.

80. *Harris*, 448 U.S. at 357 (Stevens, J., dissenting).

81. *See, e.g., Abortion Backers Hopeful of Gains*, N.Y. Times, Oct. 9, 1972, at A9, col. 1 ("Pro-abortion forces believe they are on the verge of major victories that will soon make abortion on request available throughout much of the country."); *Abortion Laws Gaining Favor as New Statutes Spur Debate*, N.Y. Times, Nov. 29, 1970, at A13, col. 2 ("Senator Robert W. Packwood, Republican of Oregon, predicted . . . that most states would abolish laws against abortion within the next 'one to three years.'"). Polls taken prior to the 1970s indicated that substantial majorities of Americans had opposed liberalization of abortion laws. *See Survey Finds 50% Back Liberalization of Abortion Policy, supra* note 6, at A1, col. 1 (1965—91% oppose liberalized abortion policy; 1968—85%; 1969—79%; 1971—50%); *see also Survey Finds Majority, In Shift, Now Favors Liberalized Laws*, N.Y. Times, Aug. 25, 1972, at A1, col. 3 (noting same statistics, and adding to them a 1972 poll revealing that 64% of public believe abortion decision should be left to woman and her doctor).

Testifying to the "superiority of the legislative solution," Second Circuit Judge Henry J. Friendly described what happened in 1970 when New York reformed its law:

I can speak with feeling because I was to have presided over a three-judge court before which the constitutionality of the old law was being challenged. Although we had not yet heard argument, I could perceive not merely how soul wrenching but how politically disturbing—and I use "politically" in the highest sense—decision either way would be. If we upheld the old law, we would be disappointing the expectations of many high-minded citizens, deeply concerned over the human misery it was creating, its discriminatory effects, its consequences for the population explosion, and the hopes of the least privileged elements in the community. These people would never understand that if we held the law constitutional, we would not be finding it good. Indeed, some opponents of reform would have claimed we had done precisely that. If we were to decide the other way, many adherents of a deeply respected religion would consider we had taken unto ourselves a role that belonged to their elected representatives and that we had done what the latter, after full consideration, had refused. If they asked what specific provision of the Constitution was violated by this law of more than a century's standing, we would have had to concede that there was none and that we were drawing on what the Supreme Court has euphemistically termed "penumbras" to construct a new "fundamental" right. How much better that the issue was settled by the legislature! I do not mean that everyone is happy; presumably those who opposed the reform have not changed their views.

appears to have provoked, not resolved, conflict.[82]

The public funding of abortion decisions appear incongruous following so soon after the intrepid 1973 rulings. The Court did not adequately explain why the "fundamental" choice principle and trimester approach embraced in *Roe* did not bar the sovereign, at least at the previability stage of pregnancy, from taking sides.[83]

Overall, the Court's *Roe* position is weakened, I believe, by the opinion's concentration on a medically approved autonomy idea, to the exclusion of a constitutionally based sex-equality perspective. I understand the view that for political reasons the reproductive autonomy controversy should be isolated from the general debate on equal rights, responsibilities, and opportunities for women and men. I expect, however, that organized and determined opposing efforts to inform and persuade the public on the abortion issue will continue through the 1980s. In that process there will be opportunities for elaborating in public forums the equal-regard conception of women's claims to reproductive choice uncoerced and unsteered by government.

But the result is acceptable in the sense that it was reached by the democratic process and thus will be accepted, even though many will not regard it as right.

H. Friendly, Some Equal Protection Problems of the 1970's 14-15 (NYU School of Law 1970) (available at North Carolina Law Review office).

82. *See* Burt, *supra* note 36, at 107-09; *cf.* Blasi, *The Rootless Activism of the Burger Court,* THE BURGER COURT, *supra* note 25, at 198, 212. (*Roe* was "[g]rounded not on principle," but on an "ad hoc comparison of . . . interests"). One pair of commentators observed:

In many respects the abortion controversy of the 1970s is similar to the busing disputes of the late 1960s and early 1970s. Both the pro-life and anti-busing movements began in reaction to decisions of the Supreme Court. Both activated many people who previously had been at the periphery of . . . politics. The two movements each caught on quickly and developed a strong national base.

Uslaner & Weber, *Public Support for Pro-Choice Abortion Policies in the Nation and States: Changes and Stability After the* Roe *and* Doe *Decisions,* 77 MICH. L. REV. 1772, 1787-88 (1979); *see also id.* at 1785.

83. *Cf.* Bennett, *supra* note 79, at 52 (arguing that *Harris* (upholding denial of Medicaid funds for abortion) is inconsistent with Shapiro v. Thompson, 394 U.S. 618 (1969) (declaring inconsistent with equal protection denial of welfare benefits to new residents)).

NEW YORK UNIVERSITY
LAW REVIEW

VOLUME 67   DECEMBER 1992   NUMBER 6

SPEAKING IN A JUDICIAL VOICE

RUTH BADER GINSBURG*

An active participant in the women's movement of the 1970s and, since 1980, a member of the federal judiciary, Ruth Bader Ginsburg has held influential positions as both an advocate and a judge. In this Madison Lecture, then Judge Ginsburg drew upon her experiences to examine the "judicial voice" from two different perspectives. First, she explores the relationship among members of the bench, advocating a greater sense of collegiality among judges. Second, she contrasts the Supreme Court's sweeping opinion in Roe v. Wade with the Court's more restrained approach in contemporaneous cases involving explicitly gender-based discrimination, offering a vision of judicial decisionmaking that recognizes the interdependent role of the judiciary within the American political system.

* Circuit Judge, United States Court of Appeals for the DC Circuit. As this article went to press, the author was appointed Associate Justice, Supreme Court of the United States. This Article originated as the twenty-fourth James Madison Lecture on Constitutional Law at New York University School of Law on March 9, 1993. I acknowledge with appreciation the fine assistance of my 1992-1993 law clerks, David Ellen and Malla Pollack, in the preparation of the Lecture and this Article.

1 See Norman Dorsen, Foreword to The Evolving Constitution, at x (Norman Dorsen ed., 1987).

1185

II

MEASURED MOTIONS IN THIRD BRANCH DECISIONMAKING

Moving from the style to the substance of third branch decision-making, I will stress in the remainder of these remarks that judges play an interdependent part in our democracy. They do not alone shape legal doctrine but, as I suggested at the outset, they participate in a dialogue with other organs of government, and with the people as well.[76] "[J]udges do and must legislate," Justice Holmes "recognize[d] without hesitation," but "they can do so," he cautioned, "only interstitially; they are confined from molar to molecular motions."[77] Measured motions seem to me right, in the main, for constitutional as well as common law adjudication. Doctrinal limbs too swiftly shaped, experience teaches, may prove unstable.[78] The most prominent example in recent decades is *Roe v. Wade*.[79] To illustrate my point, I have contrasted that breathtaking 1973 decision with the Court's more cautious dispositions, contemporaneous with *Roe*, in cases involving explicitly sex-based classifications,[80] and will further develop that comparison here.

---

[76] See generally Louis Fisher, Constitutional Dialogues: Interpretation as Political Process (1988). Recent commentary on court-legislature communication includes Shirley S. Abrahamson & Robert L. Hughes, Shall We Dance? Steps for Legislators and Judges in Statutory Interpretation, 75 Minn. L. Rev. 1045 (1991); Robert A. Katzmann, Bridging the Statutory Gulf Between Courts and Congress: A Challenge for Positive Political Theory, 80 Geo. L.J. 653 (1992); Deanell Reece Tacha, Judges and Legislators: Renewing the Relationship, 52 Ohio St. L.J. 279 (1991).

[77] Southern Pac. Co. v. Jensen, 244 U.S. 205, 221 (1917) (Holmes, J., dissenting).

[78] The Supreme Court's post-1970 decisions on alienage as a "suspect" category are illustrative. Compare Graham v. Richardson, 403 U.S. 365, 372 (1971) (invalidating state legislation denying public assistance benefits to resident aliens, Court declared that "classifications based on alienage, like those based on nationality or race, are inherently suspect [under equal protection principles] and subject to close judicial scrutiny") (footnotes omitted) with Cabell v. Chavez-Salido, 454 U.S. 432, 436 (1982) (upholding citizenship requirement for a state's probation officers, Court commented that alienage cases "illustrate a not unusual characteristic of legal development: broad principles are articulated, narrowed when applied to new contexts, and finally replaced when the distinctions they rely upon are no longer tenable").

[79] 410 U.S. 113 (1973).

[80] Ruth Bader Ginsburg, Some Thoughts on Autonomy and Equality in Relation to *Roe v.*

The seven to two judgment in *Roe v. Wade*[81] declared "violative of the Due Process Clause of the Fourteenth Amendment" a Texas criminal abortion statute that intolerably shackled a woman's autonomy; the Texas law "except[ed] from criminality only a *life-saving* procedure on behalf of the [pregnant woman]."[82] Suppose the Court had stopped there, rightly declaring unconstitutional the most extreme brand of law in the nation, and had not gone on, as the Court did in *Roe*, to fashion a regime blanketing the subject, a set of rules that displaced virtually every state law then in force.[83] Would there have been the twenty-year controversy we have witnessed, reflected most recently in the Supreme Court's splintered decision in *Planned Parenthood v. Casey?*[84] A less encompassing *Roe*, one that merely struck down the extreme Texas law and went no further on that day, I believe and will summarize why, might have served to reduce rather than to fuel controversy.

In the 1992 *Planned Parenthood* decision, the three controlling Justices accepted as constitutional several restrictions on access to abortion that could not have survived strict adherence to *Roe*.[85] While those Justices did not closely consider the plight of women without means to overcome the restrictions, they added an important strand to the Court's opinions on abortion—they acknowledged the intimate connection between a woman's "ability to control [her] reproductive li[fe]" and her "ability . . . to participate equally in the economic and social life of the Nation."[86] The idea of the woman in control of her destiny and her place in society[87] was less prominent in the *Roe* decision itself, which coupled with the rights of the pregnant woman the free exercise of her

---

Wade, 63 N.C. L. Rev. 375 (1985).

[81] Justices White and Rehnquist dissented.

[82] *Roe*, 410 U.S. at 164 (emphasis in original).

[83] In a companion case, Doe v. Bolton, 410 U.S. 179 (1973), the Court, again 7-2, held unconstitutional several provisions of Georgia's abortion law. The Georgia statute, enacted in 1968, had moved a considerable distance from the Texas extreme. It was based on the American Law Institute's Model Penal Code formulation, and resembled reformed laws then in force in about one-fourth of the states. The Court might have deferred consideration of Doe v. Bolton pending its disposition of *Roe*; indeed, the Court might have awaited the Fifth Circuit's resolution of an appeal taken by Georgia to the intermediate appellate court instead of ruling immediately on plaintiffs' direct appeal from a three-judge district court decision holding in substantial part for plaintiffs. See *Doe*, 410 U.S. at 187 & n.8.

[84] 112 S. Ct. 2791 (1992).

[85] See id. at 2841-43 (Stevens, J., concurring in part and dissenting in part) (maintaining that 24-hour delay requirement and counseling provisions conflicted with Court precedent); id. at 2846, 2850-52 (Blackmun, J., concurring in part, concurring in the judgment in part, and dissenting in part) (maintaining that counseling, 24-hour delay, and parental consent provisions conflicted with Court precedent).

[86] Id. at 2809. On this point, the controlling Justices—Justices O'Connor, Kennedy, and Souter—spoke for the Court.

[87] See generally Rachel N. Pine & Sylvia A. Law, Envisioning a Future for Reproductive Liberty: Strategies for Making the Rights Real, 27 Harv. C.R.-C.L. L. Rev. 407 (1992).

physician's medical judgment.[88] The *Roe* decision might have been less of a storm center[89] had it both homed in more precisely on the women's equality dimension of the issue and, correspondingly, attempted nothing more bold at that time than the mode of decisionmaking the Court employed in the 1970s gender classification cases.

In fact, the very Term *Roe* was decided, the Supreme Court had on its calendar a case that could have served as a bridge, linking reproductive choice to disadvantageous treatment of women on the basis of their sex. The case was *Struck v. Secretary of Defense*;[90] it involved a Captain the Air Force sought to discharge in Vietnam War days. Perhaps it is indulgence in wishful thinking, but the *Struck* case, I believe, would have proved extraordinarily educational for the Court and had large potential for advancing public understanding. Captain Susan Struck was a career officer. According to her commanding officer, her performance as a manager and nurse was exemplary.[91] Captain Struck had avoided the drugs and the alcohol that hooked many service members in the late 1960s and early 1970s,[92] but she did become pregnant while stationed in Vietnam. She undertook to use, and in fact used, only her accumulated leave time for childbirth. She declared her intention to place, and in fact placed, her child for adoption immediately after birth. Her religious faith precluded recourse to abortion.[93]

Two features of Captain Struck's case are particularly noteworthy. First, the rule she challenged was unequivocal and typical of the time. It provided: "A woman officer will be discharged from the service with the least practicable delay when a determination is made by a medical officer that she is pregnant."[94] To cover any oversight, the Air Force had a back-up rule: "The commission of any woman officer will be terminated with the least practicable delay when it is established that she . . . [h]as given birth to a living child while in a commissioned officer status."[95]

A second striking element of Captain Struck's case was the escape

---

[88] See Roe v. Wade, 410 U.S. 113, 164-65 (1973) ("abortion decision . . . must be left to the medical judgment of the pregnant woman's attending physician"; "decision [in *Roe*] vindicates the right of the physician to administer medical treatment according to his professional judgment").

[89] See Paul A. Freund, Storms over the Supreme Court, 69 A.B.A. J. 1474, 1480 (1983).

[90] 409 U.S. 947 (granting certiorari in 460 F.2d 1372 (9th Cir. 1971)), remanded for consideration of mootness, 409 U.S. 1071 (1972); see also Note, Pregnancy Discharges in the Military: The Air Force Experience, 86 Harv. L. Rev. 568 (1973).

[91] See Appendix to Brief for Petitioner at 34a, *Struck* (No. 72-178) (Memorandum of Colonel Max B. Bralliar, May 14, 1971, recommending waiver of discharge for Captain Struck).

[92] See Brief for Petitioner at 67-69 & n.70, *Struck* (No. 72-178).

[93] See id. at 3-5, 56.

[94] Air Force Regulation 36-12(40), set out in relevant part in Brief for Petitioner at 2-3, *Struck* (No. 72-178); see also *Struck*, 460 F.2d at 1374.

[95] *Struck*, 460 F.2d at 1374.

route available to her, which she chose not to take. Air Force regulations current at the start of the 1970s provided: "The Air Force Medical Service is not subject to State laws in the performance of its functions. When medically indicated or for reasons involving medical health, pregnancies may be terminated in Air Force hospitals . . . ideally before 20 weeks gestation."[96]

Captain Struck argued that the unwanted discharge she faced unjustifiably restricted her personal autonomy and dignity; principally, however, she maintained that the regulation mandating her discharge violated the equal protection of the laws guarantee implicit in the fifth amendment's due process clause.[97] She urged that the Air Force regime differentiated invidiously by allowing males who became fathers, but not females who became mothers, to remain in service and by allowing women who had undergone abortions, but not women who delivered infants, to continue their military careers.[98] Her pleas were unsuccessful in the lower courts, but on October 24, 1972, less than three months before the *Roe* decision, the Supreme Court granted her petition for certiorari.[99]

At that point the Air Force decided it would rather switch than fight. At the end of November 1972, it granted Captain Struck a waiver of the once unwaivable regulation and permitted her to continue her service as an Air Force officer. The Solicitor General promptly and successfully suggested that the case had become moot.[100]

---

[96] Appendix to Brief for Petitioner at 22a, *Struck* (No. 72-178) (quoting Air Force policy on therapeutic abortion, contained in Air Force Regulation 169-12(C2) (Sept. 23, 1970)). On his second full day in office, President Clinton ended a total ban on abortions at U.S. military facilities, imposed during the 1980s, and ordered that abortions be permitted at such facilities if paid for with non-Department of Defense funds. See Memorandum on Abortions in Military Hospitals, Jan. 22, 1993, 29 Weekly Comp. Pres. Doc. 88 (Jan. 25, 1993).

[97] As earlier observed, see text accompanying note 14 supra, the original Constitution and the Bill of Rights contain no equality guarantee. Since 1954, however, the Supreme Court has attributed to the fifth amendment's due process clause an equal protection principle regarding federal action corresponding to the fourteenth amendment's equal protection clause controlling state action. See Bolling v. Sharpe, 347 U.S. 497, 499 (1954) (initial recognition); cf. Weinberger v. Wiesenfeld, 420 U.S. 636, 638 n.2 (1975) ("Court's approach to Fifth Amendment equal protection claims has always been precisely the same as to equal protection claims under the Fourteenth Amendment").

[98] See *Struck*, 460 F.2d at 1380 (Duniway, J., dissenting); Brief for Petitioner at 8, 54-55 *Struck* (No. 72-178). The Air Force had asserted that the purpose of its pregnancy discharge regulation was to "encourage" birth control. Brief for Respondents in Opposition to Certiorari at 11, *Struck* (No. 72-178). In response, Captain Struck observed, inter alia, that the " 'encouragement' [was] directed at females only": "A man serves in the Air Force with no unwarranted governmental intrusion into the matter of his sexual privacy or his decision whether to beget a child. The woman serves subject to 'regulation'; her pursuit of an Air Force career requires that she decide not to bear a child." Brief for Petitioner at 54, 55, *Struck* (No. 72-178).

[99] *Struck*, 409 U.S. 947, 947 (1972).

[100] See Memorandum for the Respondents Suggesting Mootness (Dec. 1972), *Struck* (No. 72-178); *Struck*, 409 U.S. at 1071 (remanding for consideration of mootness).

Given the parade of cases on the Court's full calendar, it is doubtful that the Justices trained further attention on the *Struck* scenario. With more time and space for reflection, however, and perhaps a female presence on the Court, might the Justices have gained at least these two insights? First, if even the military, an institution not known for avantgarde policy, had taken to providing facilities for abortion, then was not a decision of *Roe*'s muscularity unnecessary? Second, confronted with Captain Struck's unwanted discharge, might the Court have comprehended an argument, or at least glimpsed a reality, it later resisted—that disadvantageous treatment of a woman because of her pregnancy and reproductive choice is a paradigm case of discrimination on the basis of sex?[101] What was the assumption underlying the differential treatment to which Captain Struck was exposed? The regulations that mandated her discharge were not even thinly disguised. They declared, effectively, that responsibility for children disabled female parents, but not male parents, for other work—not for biological reasons, but because society had ordered things that way.[102]

Captain Struck had asked the Court first to apply the highest level of scrutiny to her case, to hold that the sex-based classification she encountered was a "suspect" category for legislative or administrative action.[103] As a fallback, she suggested to the Court an intermediate standard of review, one under which prescriptions that worked to women's disadvantage would gain review of at least heightened, if not the very highest, intensity.[104] In the course of the 1970s, the Supreme Court explicitly acknowledged that it was indeed applying an elevated, labeled "intermediate," level of review to classifications it recognized as sex-based.[105]

Justice O'Connor carefully traced that development in last year's Madison Lecture,[106] and I will recall it only summarily. Until 1971, women did not prevail before the Supreme Court in any case charging

---

[101] See Reva Siegel, Reasoning from the Body: A Historical Perspective on Abortion Regulation and Questions of Equal Protection, 44 Stan. L. Rev. 261 (1992).

[102] Cf. Weinberger v. Wiesenfeld, 420 U.S. 636, 653 (1975) (holding unconstitutional, as a violation of the equal protection principle, the denial to a widowed father of child-in-care social security benefits Congress had provided solely for widowed mothers).

[103] See Brief for Petitioner at 26, *Struck* (No. 72-178) ("[T]he regulation applied to petitioner establishes a suspect classification for which no compelling justification can be shown.").

[104] Id. (citing Bullock v. Carter, 405 U.S. 134, 144 (1972), as precedent for "an intermediate standard" under which the challenged classification would be " 'closely scrutinized' ").

[105] See Craig v. Boren, 429 U.S. 190, 197 (1976) (sex-based classification would not be sustained if merely rationally related to a permissible government objective; defender of classification would be required to show a substantial relationship to an important objective); see also Mississippi Univ. for Women v. Hogan, 458 U.S. 718, 724 (1982).

[106] Sandra Day O'Connor, Portia's Progress, 66 N.Y.U. L. Rev. 1546 (1991).

unconstitutional sex discrimination.[107] In the years from 1971 to 1982, however, the Court held unconstitutional, as violative of due process or equal protection constraints, a series of state and federal laws that differentiated explicitly on the basis of sex.[108]

The Court ruled in 1973, for example, that married women in the military were entitled to the housing allowance and family medical care benefits that Congress had provided solely for married men in the military.[109] Two years later, the Court held it unconstitutional for a state to allow a parent to stop supporting a daughter once she reached the age of 18, while requiring parental support for a son until he turned 21.[110] In 1975, and again in 1979, the Court declared that state jury-selection systems could not exclude or exempt women as a class.[111] In decisions running from 1975 to 1980, the Court deleted the principal explicitly sex-based classifications in social insurance[112] and workers' compensation schemes.[113] In 1981, the Court said nevermore to a state law designating the husband "head and master" of the household.[114] And in 1982, in an opinion by Justice O'Connor, the Court held that a state could not limit admission to a state nursing college to women only.[115]

The backdrop for these rulings was a phenomenal expansion, in the years from 1961 to 1971, of women's employment outside the home,[116]

---

[107] The turning-point case was Reed v. Reed, 404 U.S. 71 (1971). *Reed* involved a youth from Idaho who had committed suicide while in his father's custody, the "mother's preference" regarding custody having endured only while the boy was "of tender years." The boy's mother and father, long separated, had each applied to be the administrator of their son's property. The Idaho court appointed the father under a state statute that provided: as between persons "equally entitled to administer, males must be preferred to females." Id. at 73 (quoting Idaho Code § 15-314 (1948)). The Court unanimously ruled that the statute denied to the mother the equal protection of the laws guaranteed by the fourteenth amendment.

[108] See Wendy W. Williams, Sex Discrimination: Closing the Law's Gender Gap, in The Burger Years: Rights and Wrongs in the Supreme Court 1969-1986, at 109 (Herman Schwartz ed., 1987); see also Ruth Bader Ginsburg, The Burger Court's Grapplings with Sex Discrimination, in The Burger Court: The Counter-Revolution that Wasn't 132 (Vincent Blasi ed., 1983).

[109] Frontiero v. Richardson, 411 U.S. 677, 688 (1973).

[110] Stanton v. Stanton, 421 U.S. 7, 17 (1975).

[111] Taylor v. Louisiana, 419 U.S. 522, 525 (1975) (invalidating law restricting service by women to volunteers); Duren v. Missouri, 439 U.S. 357, 360 (1979) (invalidating law allowing "any woman" to opt out of jury duty).

[112] Weinberger v. Wiesenfeld, 420 U.S. 636, 639 (1975) (extending to widowers social security benefits Congress had provided for widows); Califano v. Goldfarb, 430 U.S. 199, 201-02 (1977) (same); Califano v. Westcott, 443 U.S. 76, 85 (1979) (extending to unemployed mothers public assistance benefits Congress had provided solely for unemployed fathers).

[113] Wengler v. Druggists Mut. Ins. Co., 446 U.S. 142, 147 (1980).

[114] Kirchberg v. Feenstra, 450 U.S. 455, 461 (1981).

[115] Mississippi Univ. for Women v. Hogan, 458 U.S. 718, 723 (1982).

[116] This expansion reflected a new reality: in the 1970s, for the first time in the nation's history, the "average" woman in the United States was experiencing most of her adult years in a household not dominated by childcare requirements. That development, Columbia Univer-

the civil rights movement of the 1960s and the precedents set in that struggle,[117] and a revived feminist movement, fueled abroad and in the United States by Simone de Beauvoir's remarkable 1949 publication, *The Second Sex*.[118] In the main, the Court invalidated laws that had become obsolete, retained into the 1970s by only a few of the states.[119] In a core set of cases, however, those dealing with social insurance benefits for a worker's spouse or family,[120] the decisions did not utterly condemn the legislature's product. Instead, the Court, in effect, opened a dialogue with the political branches of government. In essence, the Court instructed Congress and state legislatures: rethink ancient positions on these questions. Should you determine that special treatment for women is warranted, i.e., compensatory legislation because of the sunken-in social and economic bias or disadvantage women encounter, we have left you a corridor in which to move.[121] But your classifications must be refined, adopted for remedial reasons, and not rooted in prejudice about "the way women (or men) are."[122] In the meantime, the Court's decrees removed no benefits; instead, they extended to a woman worker's husband, widower, or family benefits Congress had authorized only for members of a male worker's family.[123]

The ball, one might say, was tossed by the Justices back into the legislators' court, where the political forces of the day could operate. The Supreme Court wrote modestly, it put forward no grand philosophy;[124] but by requiring legislative reexamination of once customary sex-

sity professor of economics Eli Ginzberg observed, may be "the single most outstanding phenomenon of our century." Jean A. Briggs, How You Going to Get 'Em Back in the Kitchen? (You Aren't.), Forbes, Nov. 15, 1977, at 177 (quoting comment by Eli Ginzberg).

[117] See, e.g., Brief for Appellant at 12-13, Reed v. Reed, 404 U.S. 71 (1971) (No. 70-4) (urging Court not to repeat "the mistake" of Plessy v. Ferguson, 163 U.S. 537 (1896)—which had upheld a state statute requiring railway companies to provide, inter alia, separate, but equal, accommodations for blacks and whites—and to rank sex-based classifications with the recognized suspect classifications).

[118] Simone de Beauvoir, The Second Sex (1949).

[119] For example, the male preference at issue in Reed v. Reed, described at note 107 supra, had been repealed, but not retroactively, before the Supreme Court heard the case; the categorical exemption of women from jury service had been largely abandoned in state systems by the time the Court heard Duren v. Missouri, described at note 111 supra.

[120] See the *Wiesenfeld* and *Goldfarb* cases cited in note 112 supra.

[121] See Califano v. Webster, 430 U.S. 313 (1977) (upholding classification, effective from 1956 to 1972, establishing more favorable social security benefit calculation for retired female workers than for retired male workers).

[122] Ruth Bader Ginsburg, Some Thoughts on Benign Classification in the Context of Sex, 10 Conn. L. Rev. 813, 823 (1978).

[123] See Ruth Bader Ginsburg, Some Thoughts on Judicial Authority to Repair Unconstitutional Legislation, 28 Clev. St. L. Rev. 301, 310-12 (1979).

[124] Notably too, the equal rights or sex equality advocates of the 1970s urged no elaborate theory. They did argue that by enshrining and promoting the woman's "natural" role as selfless homemaker, and correspondingly emphasizing the man's role as provider, the state im-

based classifications, the Court helped to ensure that laws and regulations would "catch up with a changed world."[125]

Roe v. Wade,[126] in contrast, invited no dialogue with legislators. Instead, it seemed entirely to remove the ball from the legislators' court. In 1973, when *Roe* issued, abortion law was in a state of change across the nation. As the Supreme Court itself noted, there was a marked trend in state legislatures "toward liberalization of abortion statutes."[127] That movement for legislative change ran parallel to another law revision effort then underway—the change from fault to no-fault divorce regimes, a reform that swept through the state legislatures and captured all of them by the mid-1980s.[128]

No measured motion, the *Roe* decision left virtually no state with laws fully conforming to the Court's delineation of abortion regulation still permissible.[129] Around that extraordinary decision, a well-organized and vocal right-to-life movement rallied and succeeded, for a considerable time, in turning the legislative tide in the opposite direction.

Constitutional review by courts is an institution that has been for some two centuries our nation's hallmark and pride.[130] Two extreme modes of court intervention in social change processes, however, have

---

peded both men and women from pursuit of the opportunities and styles of life that could enable them to break away from familiar stereotypes. The objective, however, was not "assimilationist" in the sense of accepting "man's world" and asking only that self-regarding, economically advantaged women be allowed to enter that world and play by men's rules. The endeavor was, instead, to remove artificial barriers to women's aspiration and achievement; if women became political actors in numbers, it was thought, they could then exercise their will and their judgment to help make the world and the rules fit for all humankind. See Ruth Bader Ginsburg & Barbara Flagg, Some Reflections on the Feminist Legal Thought of the 1970s, 1989 U. Chi. Legal F. 9, 17-18; cf. Herma Hill Kay, The Future of Women Law Professors, 77 Iowa L. Rev. 5, 18 (1991) ("The future of women law professors is not to adapt to legal education by being 'one of the boys,' but to transform the enterprise so that all of its participants are equal members of the same team.").

125 Williams, supra note 108, at 123. This brand of review has been aptly called "judicial enforcement of constitutional accountability." Guido Calabresi, The Supreme Court, 1990 Term—Foreword: Antidiscrimination and Constitutional Accountability (What the Bork-Brennan Debate Ignores), 105 Harv. L. Rev. 80, 103-08 (1991).

126 410 U.S. 113 (1973).

127 Id. at 140; see also Ginsburg, supra note 80, at 385 & n.81.

128 See Herma Hill Kay, Equality and Difference: A Perspective on No-Fault Divorce and its Aftermath, 56 U. Cin. L. Rev. 1, 4-14, 26-55 (1987); see also Ginsburg, supra note 80, at 380 & n.36.

129 See Vincent Blasi, The Rootless Activism of the Burger Court, in The Burger Court: The Counter Revolution that Wasn't 198, 212 (Vincent Blasi ed., 1983) (*Roe* "burst upon the constitutional scene with very little in the way of foreshadowing or preparation."); Geoffrey C. Hazard, Jr., Rising Above Principle, 135 U. Pa. L. Rev. 153, 166 (1986) ("By making such an extensive change, the Court [in *Roe*] foreclosed the usual opportunities for assimilation [and] feedback . . . that are afforded in a decisional process involving shorter and more cautious doctrinal steps.").

130 See generally Louis Henkin, The Age of Rights 141-80 (1990).

placed stress on the institution. At one extreme, the Supreme Court steps boldly in front of the political process, as some believe it did in *Roe*.[131] At the opposite extreme, the Court in the early part of the twentieth century found—or thrust—itself into the rearguard opposing change, striking down, as unconstitutional, laws embodying a new philosophy of economic regulation at odds with the nineteenth century's laissez-faire approach.[132] Decisions at both of these poles yielded outcries against the judiciary in certain quarters. The Supreme Court, particularly, was labeled "activist" or "imperial," and its precarious position as final arbiter of constitutional questions was exposed.[133]

I do not suggest that the Court should never step ahead of the political branches in pursuit of a constitutional precept. *Brown v. Board of Education*,[134] the 1954 decision declaring racial segregation in public schools offensive to the equal protection principle, is the case that best fits the bill. Past the midpoint of the twentieth century, apartheid remained the law-enforced system in several states, shielded by a constitutional interpretation the Court itself advanced at the turn of the century—the "separate but equal" doctrine.[135]

In contrast to the legislative reform movement in the states, contemporaneous with *Roe*, widening access to abortion, prospects in 1954 for state legislation dismantling racially segregated schools were bleak. That was so, I believe, for a reason that distances race discrimination from discrimination based on sex. Most women are life partners of men; women bear and raise both sons and daughters. Once women's own consciousness was awakened to the unfairness of allocating opportunity and responsibility on the basis of sex, education of others—of fathers, husbands, sons as well as daughters—could begin, or be reinforced, at home.[136] When blacks were confined by law to a separate sector, there was no similar prospect for educating the white majority.[137]

---

[131] Cf. Archibald Cox, Direct Action, Civil Disobedience, and the Constitution, in Civil Rights, the Constitution, and the Court 2, 22-23 (1967) ("[S]harp changes in the law depend partly upon the stimulus of protest.").

[132] See, e.g., Lochner v. New York, 198 U.S. 45 (1905) (state maximum hours regulation for bakery employees, covering men and women alike, held unconstitutional). But cf. Muller v. Oregon, 208 U.S. 412 (1908) (upholding maximum hours legislation for women only).

[133] Cf. Calabresi, supra note 125, at 86 (typing bold court intervention as the "judicial supremacy" model of constitutional review).

[134] 347 U.S. 483 (1954).

[135] See Plessy v. Ferguson, 163 U.S. 537, 540 (1896).

[136] See Ginsburg & Flagg, supra note 124, at 18.

[137] See United States v. Carolene Products Co., 304 U.S. 144, 152 n.4 (1938) (suggesting heightened judicial scrutiny of legislation disadvantageous to "discrete and insular minorities," i.e., classifications tending "seriously to curtail the operation of those political processes ordinarily to be relied upon to protect minorities"); cf. Owen M. Fiss, Groups and the Equal Protection Clause, 5 Phil. & Pub. Aff. 107, 152 (1976) (stressing situation of blacks as "a numerical minority" and "their economic status, their position as the perpetual underclass").

It bears emphasis, however, that *Brown* was not an altogether bold decision. First, Thurgood Marshall and those who worked with him in the campaign against racial injustice, carefully set the stepping stones leading up to the landmark ruling.[138] Pathmarkers of the same kind had not been installed prior to the Court's decision in *Roe*.[139] Second, *Brown* launched no broadside attack on the Jim Crow system in all its institutional manifestations. Instead, the Court concentrated on segregated schools;[140] it left the follow-up for other days and future cases. A burgeoning civil rights movement—which *Brown* helped to propel—culminating in the Civil Rights Act of 1964,[141] set the stage for the Court's ultimate total rejection of Jim Crow legislation.

Significantly, in relation to the point I just made about women and men living together, the end of the Jim Crow era came in 1967, thirteen years after *Brown*: the case was *Loving v. Virginia*,[142] the law under attack, a state prohibition on interracial marriage. In holding that law unconstitutional, the Court effectively ruled that, with regard to racial classifications, the doctrine of "separate but equal" was dead—everywhere and anywhere within the governance of the United States.[143]

---

[138] See Richard Kluger, Simple Justice 256-84 (1976) (chronicling the efforts of Marshall and others in connection with Sipuel v. Board of Regents of the Univ. of Oklahoma, 332 U.S. 631 (1948); Shelley v. Kraemer, 334 U.S. 1 (1948); Sweatt v. Painter, 339 U.S. 629 (1950); and McLaurin v. Oklahoma St. Regents for Higher Educ., 339 U.S. 637 (1950)); Jack Greenberg, Litigation for Social Change: Methods, Limits and Role in Democracy, 29 The Record of the Ass'n of the Bar of the City of New York 320, 327-34 (1974) (discussing the "litigation campaign" preceding *Brown*).

[139] Compare The Orison S. Marden Lecture in Honor of Justice Thurgood Marshall, 47 The Record of the Ass'n of the Bar of the City of New York 227, 254 (1992) (comments of Constance Baker Motley) ("[N]o civil action was ever initiated under [Marshall's] leadership unless it was part of an overall strategy .... No major legal thrust was made without months if not years of careful legal research and planning such as occurred in the early voting cases, teacher salary cases, restrictive covenant cases, interstate travel cases as well as the school desegregation cases.") with Blasi, supra note 129, at 212 (*Roe* "could not plausibly [be] justif[ied] ... as the working out of a theme implicit in several previous decisions.").

[140] The Court relied on the psychological harm, empirically documented, that segregated schools caused black children. See 347 U.S. at 493-94 & 494 n.11.

[141] Pub. L. No. 88-352, 78 Stat. 241 (codified as amended at 28 U.S.C. § 1447, 42 U.S.C. §§ 1971, 2000a-2000h-6 (1988 & Supp. II 1990)).

[142] 388 U.S. 1 (1967).

[143] The legislative reapportionment cases of the early 1960s present a second notable instance of the Court confronting blocked political processes. Before the 1960s, many state legislatures arranged their districts in ways that diluted the voting power of urban voters. Under precedent then in place, legal objections to these malapportioned schemes were not justiciable in federal court. See Colegrove v. Green, 328 U.S. 549 (1946). In Baker v. Carr, 369 U.S. 186 (1962), this changed: the Supreme Court declared challenges to malapportioned schemes justiciable and thereby opened the way for their invalidation by federal court decree. As one leading commentator on the reapportionment cases observed:

> The ultimate rationale to be given for Baker v. Carr and its numerous progeny is that when political avenues for redressing political problems become dead-end streets, some judicial intervention in the politics of the people may be essential in order to *have* any

The framers of the Constitution allowed to rest in the Court's hands large authority to rule on the Constitution's meaning; but the framers, as I noted at the outset, armed the Court with no swords to carry out its pronouncements. President Andrew Jackson in 1832, according to an often-told legend, said of a Supreme Court decision he did not like: "The Chief Justice has made his decision, now let him enforce it."[144] With prestige to persuade, but not physical power to enforce, with a will for self-preservation and the knowledge that they are not "a bevy of Platonic Guardians,"[145] the Justices generally follow, they do not lead, changes taking place elsewhere in society.[146] But without taking giant strides and thereby risking a backlash too forceful to contain, the Court, through constitutional adjudication, can reinforce or signal a green light for a social change. In most of the post-1970 gender-classification cases, unlike *Roe*, the Court functioned in just that way. It approved the direction of change through a temperate brand of decisionmaking, one that was not extravagant or divisive. *Roe*, on the other hand, halted a political process that was moving in a reform direction and thereby, I believe, prolonged divisiveness and deferred stable settlement of the issue. The most recent *Planned Parenthood* decision[147] notably retreats from *Roe*[148] and further excludes from the High Court's protection women lacking the means or the sophistication to surmount burdensome legislation.[149] The latest decision may have had the sanguine effect, however, of contributing to the ongoing revitalization in the 1980s and 1990s of the political movement in progress in the early 1970s, a movement that addressed not simply or dominantly the courts but primarily the people's representatives and the people themselves. That renewed force, one may hope, will—within a relatively short span—yield an enduring resolution of this

---

effective politics. In Tennessee, [for example,] at the time its legislative composition was challenged in Baker, there was a history of several years of unsuccessful state court litigation and unsuccessful efforts for corrective legislation.

Robert G. Dixon, Jr., Democratic Representation: Reapportionment in Law and Politics 8 (1968) (emphasis in original).

[144] The decision in the legend is Worcester v. Georgia, 31 U.S. (6 Pet.) 515 (1832).

[145] Learned Hand, The Bill of Rights 73 (1958).

[146] Cf. Archibald Cox, The Role of the Supreme Court: Judicial Activism or Self-Restraint?, 47 Md. L. Rev. 118, 124-25 (1987) (though the "style of interpretation" of Chief Justice Marshall's Court "was active and creative," that Court, "[i]n expanding national power[,] . . . was moving in step with the dominant trend in the political branches").

[147] Planned Parenthood v. Casey, 112 S. Ct. 2791 (1992).

[148] Three years before its *Planned Parenthood* decision, the Court had come close to overruling *Roe*. See Webster v. Reproductive Health Servs., 492 U.S. 490 (1989), discussed in Sylvia A. Law, Abortion Compromise—Inevitable and Impossible, 1992 U. Ill. L. Rev. 921, 923-26.

[149] The hostile reaction to *Roe* has hit most heavily women who are most vulnerable—"the poor, the unsophisticated, the young, and women who live in rural areas." Law, supra note 148, at 931; see also Ginsburg, supra note 80, at 383-85.

vital matter in a way that affirms the dignity and equality of women.[150]

CONCLUSION

To sum up what I have tried to convey in this lecture, I will recall the counsel my teacher and friend, Professor Gerald Gunther, offered when I was installed as a judge. Professor Gunther had in mind a great jurist, Judge Learned Hand, whose biography Professor Gunther is just now completing. The good judge, Professor Gunther said, is "open-minded and detached, . . . heedful of limitations stemming from the judge's own competence and, above all, from the presuppositions of our constitutional scheme; th[at] judge . . . recognizes that a felt need to act only interstitially does not mean relegation of judges to a trivial or mechanical role, but rather affords the most responsible room for creative, important judicial contributions."[151]

---

[150] Indicative of the changed political climate, President Clinton, on his second full day in office, January 22, 1993, signed five Memoranda terminating abortion-related restraints imposed in the 1980s. See 29 Weekly Comp. Pres. Doc. 87-89 (Jan. 25, 1993) (Memorandum for the Secretary of Health and Human Services, on Federal Funding of Fetal Tissue Transplantation Research; Memorandum for the Secretary of Health and Human Services, on the Title X [of the Public Health Services Act] "Gag Rule"; Memorandum for the Acting Administrator of the Agency for International Development, on AID Family Planning Grants/Mexico City Policy; Memorandum for the Secretary of Defense, on Privately Funded Abortions at Military Hospitals; Memorandum for the Secretary of Health and Human Services, on Importation of RU-486). Cf. Law, supra note 148, at 931-32 (setting out opposing assessments and commenting that "[o]nly time will tell").

[151] Professor Gerald Gunther Speaks at Investiture of Judge Ruth Ginsburg in Washington, D.C., The Colum. Law Alumni Observer, Dec. 31, 1980, at 8.

29 Weekly Comp. Pres. Doc. 1078
June 15, 1993

The President's News Conference

. . .

Supreme Court Nominee

Q. Mr. President, getting back to Judge Ginsburg for a moment, I know that you're familiar with her Madison lecture and her rather provocative statements about the judicial reach of Roe versus Wade. Can you tell me how comfortable you are with her challenge to the whole theoretical construct to that landmark ruling and whether you feel confident that she will, once on the Court, meet what you had said during the campaign was your concerns about continuing --

The President. I think if you read the lecture, she is clearly pro-choice in the sense that she believes the Government should not make that decision for the women of America. She disagrees with the rationale of the decision. I'm not sure I agree with her, as a matter of fact, on that issue, but I thought it was a very provocative and impressive argument. As a matter of fact, I have always thought that Roe v. Wade was the most difficult case decided in the last 25 years because it was such a difficult issue and that the Court did the best it could under the circumstances. She made a very interesting alternative suggestion, but there is no suggestion in any of her writings that she's not pro-choice. And that was to me the important thing.

Q. Can I follow? How much did you actually discuss legal theory with her? Can you give us some sense of --

The President. I didn't discuss that with her. I'd read the writings, and they'd been widely discussed. When we talked for about an hour and a half, I talked to her a little bit and asked her about a couple of cases that she had been associated with in the business law area and a couple of the cases she fought for women's rights on, just to sort of talk about them, to get a feel for it. And we talked a little bit about one of the religious liberty cases she dealt with involving the right of a soldier to wear a yarmulke. Again, I just wanted to hear her talk about that. That whole issue of religious freedom is a very big issue in my judgment, and I wanted to hear her discuss it.

Q. Did you discuss homosexual rights with her?

The President. Not at all. It never came up.

Q. And are you at all concerned about some of her rulings in that area?

The President. No.

S. Hrg. 103–482

NOMINATION OF RUTH BADER GINSBURG, TO BE ASSOCIATE JUSTICE OF THE SUPREME COURT OF THE UNITED STATES

HEARINGS

BEFORE THE

COMMITTEE ON THE JUDICIARY
UNITED STATES SENATE

ONE HUNDRED THIRD CONGRESS

FIRST SESSION

ON

THE NOMINATION OF RUTH BADER GINSBURG, TO BE ASSOCIATE JUSTICE OF THE SUPREME COURT OF THE UNITED STATES

JULY 20, 21, 22, AND 23, 1993

Serial No. J–103–21

Printed for the use of the Committee on the Judiciary

U.S. GOVERNMENT PRINTING OFFICE

75–974   WASHINGTON : 1994

For sale by the U.S. Government Printing Office
Superintendent of Documents, Congressional Sales Office, Washington, DC 20402
ISBN 0-16-044114-5

Senator METZENBAUM. Thank you very much, Mr. Chairman.

I am happy to see you here, Judge Ginsburg.

Before I begin my questions, I thought that it might be appropriate to make a brief response to Senator Thurmond's remarks about the need for finality in death penalty cases. This committee held a hearing on the death penalty with two witnesses who were sentenced to death, but later freed because they were innocent, totally innocent. They were close to losing their lives.

One was an Alabama black man who had been in the penitentiary for 6 years. Another was a Texas white man who was in the penitentiary for 10 years. Just this month, a Maryland man was released after 9 years in the penitentiary.

I understand Senator Thurmond's point of view, but, frankly, we have to be careful, because the finality of judgments in death sentences can mean death for innocent persons. That really does not relate specifically, Judge Ginsburg, but I did not want to leave the record open with the implication that everybody who has been found guilty and hasn't finished their rights of appeal should have been executed.

Judge Ginsburg, I have always believed it is important that the men and women who serve on the Court have a good sense of the reality that litigants face and the practical implications of their decisions. I expect that your broad range of professional and personal experiences would give you an understanding of the world faced by the individuals who are before the Court.

Having said that, I am frank to say that I am puzzled by your often repeated criticisms of the decision in *Roe* v. *Wade*, that the Court went too far and too fast. You stated the decision need only have invalidated the Texas abortion law in question. You have also stated that *Roe* curtailed a trend toward liberalization of State abortion statutes.

I am frank to say that some, including this Senator, would question whether women really were making real progress towards obtaining reproductive freedom, when *Roe* was decided in 1973. Would you be willing to explain your basis for making those statements about *Roe* and the state of abortion law at the time of the *Roe* decision?

Judge GINSBURG. Yes, Senator Metzenbaum, I will try. The statement you made about the law moving in a reform direction is taken directly from Justice Blackmun's decision in *Roe* (1973) itself. He explained that, until recently, the law in the States had been overwhelmingly like the Texas law, but that there had been a trend in the direction of reform. The trend had proceded to the extent that some one-third of the States, in a span of a very few years, had reformed their abortion laws from the point where only the life of the woman was protected. In relatively few years, one-third of the

States had moved from that position to a variety of positions. Most of the States followed the American Law Institute model, allowing abortion on grounds of rape, incest, and some other grounds. Four States had by then moved to permit abortion on the woman's request as advised by her doctor.

So I took that statement not from any source other than the very opinion, which I surely do not criticize for making that point. I accept it just as it was made in *Roe* v. *Wade*.

Senator METZENBAUM. Would you not have had some concern, or do you not have some concern that had the gradualism been the reality, that many more women would have been denied an abortion or would have been forced into an illegal abortion and possibly an unsafe abortion?

Judge GINSBURG. Senator, we can't see what the past might have been like. I wrote an article that was engaging in "what if" speculation. I expressed the view that if the Court had simply done what courts usually do, stuck to the very case before it and gone no further, then there might have been a change, gradual changes.

We have seen it happen in this country so many times. We saw it with the law of marriage and divorce. In a span of some dozen years, we witnessed a shift from adultery as the sole ground for divorce to no-fault divorce in almost every State in the Union. Once the States begin to change, then it takes a while, but eventually most of them move in the direction of change.

One can say this with certainty: There was a massive attack on *Roe* v. *Wade*; the Court's opinion became a clear target at which to aim. Two things happened. One side had a rallying cry, the other—a movement that had been very vigorous—relaxed to some extent. Pro-choice advocates didn't go home, but they were less vigorous than they might have been had it not appeared that the Court had taken care of the problem.

So while one side seemed to relax its energy, the other side had a single target around which to rally. My view is that if *Roe* had been less sweeping, people would have accepted it more readily, would have expressed themselves in the political arena in an enduring way on this question. I recognize that this is a matter of speculation. It is my view of "what if". Other people hold a different view.

Senator METZENBAUM. In the *Roe* case, the Supreme Court held that a woman's right to terminate her pregnancy was protected by the Constitution. The Court said that constitutional right was fundamental and deserved the highest standard of protection from government laws and regulations that interfere with the exercise of the right. States had to have a compelling State interest to regulate the right to choose.

In *Planned Parenthood of Southeastern Pennsylvania* v. *Casey*, the Court did not overrule *Roe* v. *Wade*. However, the case in *Casey* lowered the standard for protecting a woman's right to choose. The Court held that States may regulate the right to choose, as long as they do not create an undue burden on women.

After the *Casey* decision, some have questioned whether the right to choose is still a fundamental constitutional right. In your view, does the *Casey* decision stand for the proposition that the right to choose is a fundamental constitutional right?

Judge GINSBURG. The Court itself has said after *Casey* (1992)—
I don't want to misrepresent the Supreme Court, so I will read its
own words. This is the statement of a majority of the Supreme
Court, including the dissenters in *Casey*: "The right to abortion is
one element of a more general right of privacy * * * or of Fourteenth Amendment liberty." That is the Court's most recent statement. It includes a citation to *Roe* v. *Wade*. The Court has once
again said that abortion is part of the concept of privacy or liberty
under the 14th amendment.

What regulations will be permitted is certainly a matter likely to
be before the Court. Answers depend, in part, Senator, on the kind
of record presented to the Court. It would not be appropriate for
me to go beyond the Court's recent reaffirmation that abortion is
a woman's right guaranteed by the 14th amendment; it is part of
the liberty guaranteed by the 14th amendment.

Perhaps I can say one thing more. It concerns an adjustment we
have seen moving from *Roe* to *Casey*. The *Roe* decision is a highly
medically oriented decision, not just in the three-trimester division.
Roe features, along with the right of the woman, the right of the
doctor to freely exercise his profession. The woman appears together with her consulting physician, and that pairing comes up
two or three times in the opinion, the woman, together with her
consulting physician.

The *Casey* decision, at least the opinion of three of the Justices
in that case, makes it very clear that the woman is central to this.
She is now standing alone. This is her right. It is not her right in
combination with her consulting physician. The cases essentially
pose the question: Who decides; is it the State or the individual?
In *Roe*, the answer comes out: the individual, in consultation with
her physician. We see in the physician something of a big brother
figure next to the woman. The most recent decision, whatever else
might be said about it, acknowledges that the woman decides.

Senator BROWN. I always suspected that those who came in number one in their class at Harvard or Columbia did things like that, but I didn't know. [Laughter.]

You have attracted some attention by observing with regard to *Roe* v. *Wade* that perhaps a different portion of the Constitution may well deserve attention with regard to that question; specifically, if I understand your articles correctly, the equal protection clause of the Constitution rather than the right to privacy evolving from the due process right contained in the 14th amendment.

Would you share with us a description of how your writings draw a relationship between the right to choose and the equal protection clause?

Judge GINSBURG. I will be glad to try, Senator. May I say first that it has never in my mind been an either/or choice, never one rather than the other; it has been both. I will try to explain how my own thinking developed on this issue. It relates to a case involving a woman's choice for birth rather than the termination of her pregnancy. It is one of the briefs that you have. It is the case of *Captain Susan Struck* v. *Secretary of Defense* (1972). This was Capt. Susan Struck's story.

She became pregnant while she was serving in the Air Force in Vietnam. That was in the early 1970's. She was offered a choice. She was told she could have an abortion at the base hospital—and let us remember that in the early 1970's, before *Roe* v. *Wade* (1973), abortion was available on service bases in this country to members of the service or, more often, dependents of members of the service.

Capt. Susan Struck said: I do not want an abortion. I want to bear this child. It is part of my religious faith that I do so. However, I will use only my accumulated leave time for the childbirth. I will surrender the child for adoption at birth. I want to remain in the Air Force. That is my career choice.

She was told that that was not an option open to her if she wished to remain in the Air Force. In Captain Struck's case, we argued three things:

First, that the applicable Air Force regulations—if you are pregnant you are out unless you have an abortion—violated the equal protection principle, for no man was ordered out of service because he had been the partner in a conception, no man was ordered out of service because he was about to become a father.

Next, then we said that the Government is impeding, without cause, a woman's choice whether to bear or not to bear a child. Birth was Captain Struck's personal choice, and the interference with it was a violation of her liberty, her freedom to choose, guaranteed by the due process clause.

Finally, we said the Air Force was involved in an unnecessary interference with Captain Struck's religious belief.

So all three strands were involved in Captain Struck's case. The main emphasis was on her equality as a woman vis-a-vis a man who was equally responsible for the conception, and on her personal choice, which the Government said she could not have unless she gave up her career in the service.

In that case, all three strands were involved: her equality right, her right to decide for herself whether she was going to bear the child, and her religious belief. So it was never an either/or matter, one rather than the other. It was always recognition that one thing that conspicuously distinguishes women from men is that only women become pregnant; and if you subject a woman to disadvantageous treatment on the basis of her pregnant status, which was what was happening to Captain Struck, you would be denying her equal treatment under the law.

Now, that argument—that discrimination, disadvantageous treatment because of pregnancy is indeed sex discrimination—was something the Supreme Court might have heard in the *Struck* case, but the Air Force decided to waive her discharge. Although the Air Force had won in the trial court and won in the court of appeals, the Supreme Court had granted certiorari on Captain Struck's petition. At that point, perhaps with the advice of the Solicitor General, the Air Force decided it would rather switch than fight, and Captain Struck's discharge was waived. So she remained in the service, and the Court never heard her case.

In the case the Court eventually got, one less sympathetic on the facts, the majority held that discrimination on the basis of pregnancy was not discrimination on the basis of sex. Then this body, the Congress, in the Pregnancy Discrimination Act, indicated that it thought otherwise.

The *Struck* brief, which involved a woman's choice for birth, marks the time when I first thought long and hard about this question. At no time did I regard it as an either/or, one pocket or the other, issue. But I did think about it, first and foremost, as differential treatment of the woman, based on her sex.

Senator BROWN. I can see how the equal protection argument would apply to a policy that interfered with her plan to bear the child. Could that argument be applied for someone who wished to have the option of an abortion as well? Does it apply both to the decision to not have an abortion, as well as the decision to have an abortion, to terminate the pregnancy?

Judge GINSBURG. The argument was, it was her right to decide either way, her right to decide whether or not to bear a child.

Senator BROWN. In this case, am I correct in assuming that any restrictions from her employer to that option, or to that right, would be constrained by the equal protection clause?

Judge GINSBURG. Yes. In the *Struck* case, it was a woman's choice for childbirth, and the Government was inhibiting that choice. It came at the price of an unwanted discharge from service to her country. But you asked me about my thinking on equal protection versus individual autonomy. My answer is that both are implicated. The decision whether or not to bear a child is central to a woman's life, to her well-being and dignity. It is a decision she must make for herself. When Government controls that decision for her, she is being treated as less than a fully adult human responsible for her own choices.

Senator BROWN. I also appreciate that you simply presented this not as the only approach, but as an option that was looked at.

With regard to the equal protection argument, though, since this may well confer a right to choose on the woman, or could, would it also follow that the father would be entitled to a right to choose in this regard or some rights in this regard?

Judge GINSBURG. That was an issue left open in *Roe* v. *Wade* (1973). But if I recall correctly, it was put to rest in *Casey* (1992). In that recent decision, the Court dealt with a series of regulations. It upheld most of them, but it struck down one requiring notice to the husband. The ruling on that point relates to a matter the chairman raised earlier.

The *Casey* majority understood that marriage and family life is not always all we might wish them to be. There are women whose physical safety, even their lives, would be endangered, if the law required them to notify their partner. And *Casey,* which in other respects has been greeted in some quarters with great distress, answered a significant question, one left open in *Roe; Casey* held a State could not require notification to the husband.

Senator BROWN. I was concerned that if the equal protection argument were relied on to ensure a right to choose, that looking for a sex-blind standard in this regard might also then convey rights in the father to this decision. Do you see that as following logically from the rights that can be conferred on the mother?

Judge GINSBURG. I will rest my answer on the *Casey* decision, which recognizes that it is her body, her life, and men, to that extent, are not similarly situated. They don't bear the child.

Senator BROWN. So the rights are not equal in this regard, because the interests are not equal?

Judge GINSBURG. It is essential to woman's equality with man that she be the decisionmaker, that her choice be controlling. If you impose restraints that impede her choice, you are disadvantaging her because of her sex.

Consider in this connection the line of cases about procreation. The importance to an individual of the choice whether to beget or bear a child has been recognized at least since *Skinner* v. *Oklahoma* (1992). That case involved a State law commanding sterilization for certain recidivists. Sterilization of a man was at issue in *Skinner,* but the importance of procreation to an individual's autonomy and dignity was appreciated, and that concern applies to men as well as women.

Abortion prohibition by the State, however, controls women and denies them full autonomy and full equality with men. That was the idea I tried to express in the lecture to which you referred. The two strands—equality and autonomy—both figure in the full portrayal.

Recall that *Roe* was decided in early days. *Roe* was not preceded by a string of women's rights cases. Only *Reed* v. *Reed* (1971) had been decided at the time of *Roe.* Understanding increased over the years. What seemed initially, as much a doctor's right to freely exercise his profession as a woman's right, has come to be understood more as a matter in which the woman is central.

Senator BROWN. I was just concerned that the use of the equal protection argument may well lead us to some unexpected conclusions or unexpected rights in the husband.

You had mentioned earlier, I thought, a very sage observation, that provisions that, if I remember your words correctly, provisions that limited opportunities have been sometimes cast benignly as favors, that we ought to take a new look at these things that are thought as favors in the past. I think that is a fair comment and a very keen observation.

I guess my question is: If you look at these provisions of law that treat women differently than men and decide that they genuinely are favorable, not unfavorable, or practices that are favorable, not unfavorable, does this then mean that they are not barred?

Judge GINSBURG. Senator, that sounds like a question Justice Stevens once asked me at an argument. I said I had not yet seen a pure favor. Remember, I come from an era during which all the favors in the end seem to work in reverse. I often quoted the lines of Sarah Grimke, one of two wonderful sisters from South Carolina, and they said to legislators in the mid-1900's, I ask no favor for my sex, all I ask of my brethren is that they take their feet from off our necks. That is the era in which I grew up. I had not seen a protection that didn't work in reverse.

Many of today's young women think the day has come for genuinely protective laws and regulations. Were the legislature filled with women, I might have more faith in that proposition. But, yes, you can see the difference, you can distinguish the true favor from the one that is going to have a boomerang effect, maybe so. I reserve judgment on that question.

Senator BROWN. My time is out, but I look forward to chatting with you again. Thank you.

The CHAIRMAN. He's going to see if he can think of a favor for you, Judge.

Senator Simon.

Senator SIMON. Thank you, Mr. Chairman.

PANEL CONSISTING OF PAIGE COMSTOCK CUNNINGHAM, PRESIDENT, AMERICANS UNITED FOR LIFE, CHICAGO, IL; ROSA CUMARE, HAMILTON & CUMARE, PASADENA, CA; NELLIE J. GRAY, PRESIDENT, MARCH FOR LIFE EDUCATION AND DEFENSE FUND, WASHINGTON, DC; SUSAN HIRSCHMANN, EXECUTIVE DIRECTOR, EAGLE FORUM, WASHINGTON, DC; KAY COLES JAMES, VICE PRESIDENT, FAMILY RESEARCH COUNCIL, WASHINGTON, DC; AND HOWARD PHILLIPS, CHAIRMAN, THE CONSERVATIVE CAUCUS, VIENNA, VA

STATEMENT OF PAIGE COMSTOCK CUNNINGHAM

Ms. CUNNINGHAM. Thank you, Mr. Chairman.

Mr. Chairman and members of the Judiciary Committee, I thank you for this opportunity to testify on the nomination of Ruth Bader Ginsburg to the U.S. Supreme Court.

I am an attorney, a graduate of Northwestern University School of Law. I am a wife and I am a proud mother of three children. I think all those things bear on the testimony that I am giving today, because it is likely that I have reaped in my own career from the seeds that were sown by Judge Ginsburg in her efforts to abolish sex discrimination.

As you mentioned, I am also the president of Americans United for Life, which is the legal arm for the pro-life movement, and we are the oldest national pro-life organization in this country. We are nonpartisan and we are secular, and we are committed to the protection of the vulnerable and the innocent human life from conception to natural death.

Although Judge Ginsburg may possess the credentials to sit on the Supreme Court, we are concerned about the process by which she was nominated and her views on abortion, and appreciate this opportunity to fully educate the Nation, and that is what I appreciate about this process of a thorough look and an opportunity to speak.

I am troubled because, in the first time in our history, a Supreme Court nominee has been required to pass a test, an abortion litmus test. President Clinton made this very clear before he nominated Judge Ginsburg to the High Court. This is a litmus test which prior nominees were wrongly accused of passing, and why one of them was defeated.

I think it is a tragedy that supporting an act which ends the life of one being and scars the future of another should be considered the supreme test for the Supreme Court. And just as disturbing as this unprecedented litmus test is Judge Ginsburg's attempt to justify the decision in *Roe* v. *Wade* on the ground that abortion is somehow necessary for women' sequality, that women cannot be equal in the law or in society, without abortion, through all 9 months of pregnancy for any reason.

Outside of abortion, *Roe* v. *Wade* has done absolutely nothing to advance women's rights. State and Federal courts have handed down dozens of decisions striking down various forms of sex discrimination, and few, if any, of these courts, including the Supreme Court, have relied on or even mentioned *Roe*.

The real advances in women's rights have come not through the court cases, but through laws enacted by Congress and by State legislatures. These are the laws that have banned sex discrimination in public and private employment, in the sale and rental of housing, in education, laws that mandate equal pay for equal work, to name just a few. Do you know what? Not one of those laws depends on abortion.

Judge Ginsburg has repeatedly stated that abortion is protected by the equal protection clause of the Constitution or that that ought to have been the basis, rather than the due process clause. But she has gone farther than the Court and suggested in her writings that there ought to be a public policy supporting taxpayer funded abortions.

Her writings also reveal that she would oppose laws protecting women in crisis pregnancies, laws upheld by the Supreme Court just a few months ago, last year, laws such as a woman's right to know, a 24-hour reflection period to think about information about a decision that she cannot change and that she will live with for the rest of her life, laws involving parents. These laws received overwhelming public support. After all, they are reasonable laws.

Judge Ginsburg has testified before you that abortion is central to a woman's dignity. But what is this legacy of *Roe*? Has a generation of abortion on demand solved any of the problems for which it was offered? Has abortion reduced the rates of child abuse or illegitimacy or teen pregnancy or the feminization of poverty? Has it enhanced respect for women? After 20 years of abortion on demand, abortion has flunked the test as the miracle cure for the social problems it promised to solve.

The only obvious benefit of legalized abortion is the economic one. A $300 abortion is much cheaper than a $3,000 delivery of a baby. But what about the cost to women's bodies and women's lives? Thousands of women now bear the scars of perforated uteruses, lost fertility and higher breast cancer risks. Close to 70 percent of all relationships end in the first year after an abortion. Many women are abandoned by the baby's father as soon as the crisis of pregnancy is solved by abortion.

Some women say they can't even pass a playground or turn on a vacuum cleaner, because it sounds like a suction machine. All too often, they fall into a pattern of self-abuse, that abuse which mirrors their abuse by others. The destruction and tragedy caused by 28 million abortions is a gaping national wound, a wound whose ugliness is covered up by polite tolerance and rhetoric about a woman's right to choose and keeping government out of private choices.

And make no mistake about it, coercion to have abortions is real. The coercion may be possible precisely because abortion is legal. That is the unspoken price for progress in our careers. Female medical residents, in an article in the New England Journal of Medicine, reported that tragedy. We attorneys have discovered that same price. And why not? Because if a woman demands that complete autonomy in her abortion decision, it only seems fair that she bear complete responsibility for the consequences of that, and women once again are left alone to pay the price.

Our radical abortion policy, which Judge Ginsburg apparently supports wholeheartedly, would not expand or advance women's issues. I believe it has actually set the clock back on women's dignity, including the dignity of motherhood. Children should be a shared responsibility. Our educational goals and professional dreams should not depend on an elective surgery that creates second-class citizens out of the voiceless.

Abortion goes against the core values of feminism, equality, care, nurturing, compassion and nonviolence. If we women, who have so recently gained electoral and political voice, do not stand up for the voiceless and the politically powerless, who will? Those who promote abortion rights do not represent the women of America. The 1.8 million members of the National Women's Coalition for Life prove that you can be pro-woman and pro-life. Our feminist pioneers, including Susan B. Anthony and Elizabeth Cady Stanton, cited with approval by Judge Ginsburg, were strongly against abortion and recognized it as child murder and a crying evil.

Judge Ginsburg wrote that the greatest judges "have been independent thinking individuals, with open, but not empty minds, individuals willing to listen and to learn." Unless there is convincing evidence that Judge Ginsburg is willing to reexamine her premises about abortion, which she has so recently stated, then we cannot withdraw our objection to her confirmation.

We ask the committee to seriously consider this statement and our more extensive written testimony. The future of women, men and generations of many yet unborn depend on it.

Thank you.

[The prepared statement of Ms. Cunningham follows:]

___

JUDICIAL SELECTION MONITORING PROJECT

A project of the Free Congress Foundation's Center for Law & Democracy

• 717 SECOND STREET, N.E. • WASHINGTON D.C. 20002 • PHONE: (202) 546-3000 • FAX (202) 543-8425

Thomas L. Jipping, M.A., J.D.
Director

Marianne E. Lombardi
Deputy Director

A STEP IN THE LEFT DIRECTION

An analysis of
President Bill Clinton's nomination of

RUTH BADER GINSBURG

to be an Associate Justice of the U.S. Supreme Court

by
Thomas L. Jipping, M.A., J.D.

June 24, 1993

IV. ABORTION AND *ROE v. WADE*

Judge Ginsburg founded the ACLU's Women's Rights Project and served as the ACLU's general counsel from 1974 to 1980. Anyone who thinks she does not support constitutional protection for the right to choose abortion does not know what those four letters represent. Noting her criticism of *Roe v. Wade*,[83] the Supreme Court's decision creating the right to abortion, one analyst concluded that her objection did not extend to "the ultimate goal of a right to abortion fully anchored in the Constitution and secure against political undermining."[84]

President Clinton, however, promised during the presidential campaign to choose someone as his first Supreme Court appointee who is a "strong supporter of *Roe* [*v. Wade*]." At least since the late 1970s, Judge Ginsburg has criticized the constitutional basis and practical political impact of that decision. This slight departure from the politically correct text immediately raised questions about whether Bill Clinton correctly applied his abortion litmus test. Indeed, even he has backed off, insisting now only that Judge Ginsburg "is clearly pro-choice" on abortion.[85] Kathleen Quinn brands Judge Ginsburg's views "alarming" and "stunning."[86]

A. Constitutional Foundation

1. The Supreme Court's decision

Judge Ginsburg has devoted nearly all of her professional life to crafting and implementing a unified approach to issues of concern to women based on the Constitution's requirement of "equal protection of the laws." During the 1970s, she argued and won

---

[83]   410 U.S. 113 (1973).

[84]   Greenhouse, "On Privacy and Equality," *New York Times*, June 16, 1993, at A1.

[85]   Murray, *supra* note 4.

[86]   Quinn, "Treat Judge Ginsburg Like a Man," *New York Times*, June 20, 1993, at 17.

landmark cases in the Supreme Court requiring courts to constitutionally scrutinize laws that treat men and women differently. The nature of her criticism of *Roe*'s constitutional foundation, then, may not seem surprising.

On January 22, 1973, by a 7-2 vote, the Supreme Court handed down its decision in *Roe v. Wade* striking down a century-old Texas statute that prohibited all abortions except those necessary to save the life of the mother. The Court decided, for the first time, that the Fourteenth Amendment's due process clause[87] protects a woman's decision whether to terminate her pregnancy by abortion. The Court went past striking down that law--the most restrictive in the nation--and crafted a scheme of rules for balancing the woman's right and the state's interests in maternal health and fetal life during different stages of pregnancy.

2. Judge Ginsburg's views

Judge Ginsburg has criticized the decision for basing the right to choose abortion on the due process clause rather than the equal protection clause.[88] For example, while still a law professor, she wrote in a review of the Supreme Court's 1976-77 Term:

> Significantly, the opinions in *Roe v. Wade* and *Doe v. Bolton* barely mention "women's rights." They are not tied to any equal protection or equal rights theory. Rather, the Court anchored stringent review of abortion prohibitions to concepts of bodily integrity, personal privacy or autonomy, derived from the due process guarantee.[89]

When Professor Ginsburg became Judge Ginsburg, she continued raising the same question. Delivering the Joyner Lecture on Constitutional Law at the University of North

---

[87] The Fourteenth Amendment's due process clause reads: "nor shall any State deprive any person of life, liberty, or property, without due process of law."

[88] The Fourteenth Amendment's equal protection clause reads: "[nor shall any State...] deny to any person within its jurisdiction the equal protection of the laws." While the Fifth Amendment, which applies to the federal government, does not contain a similar clause, the Supreme Court has decided that its due process clause has an equal protection component and has thereby imposed the same restrictions on the federal government that the Fourteenth Amendment imposes on state governments. See *Weinberger v. Wiesenfeld*, 420 U.S. 636,638 n.2 (1975); *Bolling v. Sharpe*, 347 U.S. 497 (1954). Ruth Bader Ginsburg successfully *Weinberger* before the Supreme Court.

[89] Ginsburg, "Gender in the Supreme Court: The 1976 Term," in B. Justice & R. Pore (eds.), *Constitutional Government in America* (1980), at 223.

Carolina School of Law in April 1984, she observed: "The High Court has analyzed classification by gender under an equal protection/sex discrimination rubric; it has treated reproductive autonomy under a substantive due process/personal autonomy headline not expressly linked to discrimination against women."[90]

Judge Ginsburg repeated the same observation in a 1992 article: "But the Supreme Court did not rest its *Roe v. Wade* decision on an equal stature for women or sex discrimination rationale. Instead, the Court ruled on a personal privacy or autonomy analysis that had few precedents."[91]

Unfortunately, Judge Ginsburg has never described just how, based on the equal protection clause, an opinion striking down the restrictive Texas statute might have been written. In fact, she has never explicitly stated that *Roe v. Wade* was itself wrongly decided or that it should be overruled. She has simply observed that the Court based its opinion on the due process clause rather than on the equal protection clause. Most of her writings on this subject are descriptive rather than analytical.

3. Analysis

Judge Ginsburg is not alone in asserting that laws prohibiting or restricting abortion constitute sex discrimination in violation of the equal protection clause. In *Webster v. Reproductive Health Services*,[92] for example, the parties challenging abortion restrictions asked that, should the Court abandon *Roe*'s due process theory for abortion rights, the Court "remand th[e] case for consideration of what other Constitutional principles can support the right recognized in *Roe*." They offered an equal protection theory as an alternative.

Harvard law professor Laurence Tribe has observed that "[t]he plaintiffs in *Roe v. Wade* and *Doe v. Bolton* did not challenge the abortion restrictions as a form of sex discrimination....The national ACLU's Reproductive Freedom Project has long pursued a policy of discouraging sex discrimination claims in abortion cases."[93] This may be the result of fundamental conceptual problems with the theory itself.

---

[90] Ginsburg, "Some Thoughts on Autonomy and Equality in Relation to *Roe v. Wade*," 63 *North Carolina Law Review* 373, 373-74 (1985).

[91] Ginsburg, "A Moderate View on Roe," *Constitution*, Spring-Summer 1992, at 17.

[92] 492 U.S. 490 (1989).

[93] L. Tribe, *American Constitutional Law* (2nd ed. 1988), at 1353 n.109.

Judge Ginsburg refers to an "equal protection or equal rights theory"[94] or an "equal protection/sex discrimination rubric"[95] as a better way of approaching cases challenging abortion restrictions. The equal protection clause ensures that similarly situated individuals are treated similarly.[96] Applying this concept to the question of abortion rights creates some difficulty. If women and men could both become pregnant, a law prohibiting only women from obtaining abortions would violated the equal protection clause. This law would treat women differently **because of their sex.**

Men, of course, cannot become pregnant and, therefore, women and men cannot be similarly situated with respect to either pregnancy or its termination. Denying to women a course of action that only they can take--in this case, a particular method of pregnancy termination--cannot be said to discriminate against them because of their gender; all persons able to take that course of action are of the same gender.

Perhaps the best way to make this point is to use examples from the very sex discrimination cases that Ruth Bader Ginsburg participated in litigating on behalf of the American Civil Liberties Union's Women's Rights Project. Each of these cases involved women being treated differently than similarly situated men because of their gender.

- *Reed v. Reed*[97] challenged an Idaho law requiring that men be preferred over equally qualified women to be estate administrators.

- *Frontiero v. Richardson*[98] challenged two statutes providing military servicemen with automatic dependency benefits for housing or medical care for their spouses but providing such benefits for military servicewomen only if her spouse depended on her for more than half his support.

- *Kahn v. Shevin*[99] challenged a tax break for widows that was unavailable for widowers.

---

[94] Ginsburg, *supra* note 89, at 223.

[95] Ginsburg, *supra* note 90, at 373.

[96] See *City of Cleburne v. Cleburne Living Center*, 473 U.S. 432,439-40 (1985).

[97] 404 U.S. 71 (1971).

[98] 411 U.S. 677 (1973).

[99] 416 U.S. 351 (1974).

- *Weinberger v. Wiesenfeld*[100] and *Califano v. Goldfarb*[101] challenged Social Security benefits available to women but not to men.

- *Craig v. Boren*[102] challenged an Oklahoma law setting the age for purchasing beer at 18 for women and 21 for men.

One of her former clerks summarized Judge Ginsburg's views on this point: "The disadvantageous treatment of a woman because of pregnancy or reproductive choice, Judge Ginsburg has written, is a paradigm case of discrimination on the basis of sex."[103] Roger Pilon counters:

> Disadvantageous treatment of a woman because of her pregnancy is treatment based, as the proposition states, on her pregnancy, not her sex. Otherwise every woman would be so treated, which not even Judge Ginsburg asserts. It is true, of course, that only women become pregnant. But from that fact it no more follows that pregnancy discrimination is sex discrimination than that punishment for having committed a crime is punishment for being a person--it being a fact also that only people commit crimes.[104]

Exclusive focus on women, therefore, necessarily negates the equal protection argument because individuals in the resulting class share the same gender. Yet an exclusive focus on women is exactly what Judge Ginsburg advocates. *Roe*, she writes, would be less subject to criticism "had the Court placed the woman alone...at the center of its attention."[105] Doing so, however, cannot be accomplished through the equal protection clause since determining whether a woman has been treated "equally" with respect to her gender requires reference to the treatment of similarly situated individuals of a different gender, namely, men.

Remember how her former clerk put it: "The disadvantageous treatment of a woman because of her pregnancy or reproductive choice...is a paradigm case of discrimination on

---

[100] 420 U.S. 636 (1975).

[101] 430 U.S. 199 (1977).

[102] 429 U.S. 190 (1976).

[103] Huber & Taranto, *supra* note 25.

[104] Pilon, *supra* note 33.

[105] Ginsburg, *supra* note 90, at 382.

the basis of sex." Only women can become pregnant and, therefore, only women can obtain abortions. Therefore, any abortion restriction is a "disadvantageous treatment of a woman because of her pregnancy or reproductive choice" because no abortion restriction, no matter how slight, can be applied against a man. To apply an equal protection theory to abortion rights, then, requires arguing that any abortion restriction violates the equal protection clause by definition.

The Supreme Court has already rejected this idea. In *Geduldig v. Aiello*,[106] the Court upheld against an equal protection challenge a state program that excluded from insurance coverage disabilities accompanying pregnancy. The Court held:

> The California insurance program does not exclude anyone from benefit eligibility because of gender but merely removes one physical condition--pregnancy--from the list of compensable disabilities. While it is true that only women can become pregnant it does not follow that every legislative classification concerning pregnancy is a sex-based classification.[107]

Judge Ginsburg believes that "[t]he disadvantageous treatment of a woman because of pregnancy...is a paradigm case of discrimination on the basis os sex." The Supreme Court has rejected the notion that "every legislative classification concerning pregnancy is a sex-based classification." No wonder the ACLU's Reproductive Freedom Project counsels against making sex discrimination claims in abortion cases.

B. Practical Political Impact

1. The Supreme Court's decision

During the 19th century, every state passed laws prohibiting all abortions except those necessary to save the life of the mother.[108] Between 1965 and 1972, every state considered

---

[106] 417 U.S. 484 (1974).

[107] *Id.* at 496 n.29.

[108] See Quay, "Justifiable Abortion--Medical and Legal Foundations," 49 *Georgetown Law Journal* 395,447-520 (1961).

proposals to liberalize these statutes and many chose to do so.[109] A study by the Planned Parenthood Federation found that approximately half the states adopted proposals to reform or repeal their abortion statutes.[110]

In 1973, when the Supreme Court decided *Roe*, three types of statutes existed. Thirty-one states retained the traditional restrictive statute.[111] Another 15 states had adopted statutes permitting abortions in specific circumstances.[112] The final four states allowed abortions for any reason but only during early pregnancy.[113]

The Texas statute reviewed in *Roe* was of the first type and *Roe* obviously rendered it unconstitutional. In a case decided the same day as *Roe*, the Court made clear that its decision also rendered the second, more liberal, type of statute invalid.[114] There is almost universal agreement among scholars, analysts, and commentators that *Roe* effectively struck down all existing abortion laws.[115] None was liberal enough to survive the new scheme of rules constructed by the Court in *Roe*. Its rigid framework has been applied since 1973 to invalidate nearly every abortion restriction including, for example, parental and spousal consent,[116] standard of care in post-viability abortions,[117] second physician requirement

---

[109] See Comment, "A Survey of the Present Statutory and Case Law on Abortion: The Contradictions and the Problems," 1972 *University of Illinois Law Forum* 177.

[110] "Abortion in the U.S.: Two Centuries of Experience," in *Constitutional Amendments Relating to Abortion: Hearings Before the Subcommittee on the Constitution of the Senate Committee on the Judiciary*, 97th Cong., 1st Sess. 357 (1981).

[111] See *Roe*, 410 U.S. at 118 n.2.

[112] *Id.* at 140 n.37. These circumstances typically included a threat to the mother's life or health, likely fetal deformity, rape, or incest. This type of statute was modeled on the American Law Institute's Model Penal Code section on abortion.

[113] *Id.*

[114] *Doe v. Bolton*, 410 U.S. 179 (1973).

[115] See, e.g., Sarvis & Rodman, *The Abortion Controversy* (New York: Columbia University Press, 1973), at 57 (Court's decision in *Roe* "renders all original and reform laws unconstitutional").

[116] See, e.g., *Planned Parenthood v. Danforth*, 428 U.S. 52 (1976).

[117] See, e.g., *Colautti v. Franklin*, 439 U.S. 379 (1979).

for post-viability abortions,[118] informed consent requirements,[119] or two-parent notification.[120]

2. Judge Ginsburg's views

Judge Ginsburg clearly views this sudden and universal trumping of the legislative process, and the wiping out of all existing abortion laws--restrictive and lenient--in a negative light.

On March 9, 1993, Judge Ginsburg delivered the Madison Lecture at New York University School of Law and observed that *Roe v. Wade* "halted a political process that was moving in a reform direction and thereby, I believe, prolonged divisiveness and deferred stable settlement of the issue."[121] She noted that the Court "seemed entirely to remove the ball from the legislators' court."[122]

Judge Ginsburg had previously observed in 1992 that "[t]he *Roe* decision, by stopping a political process that was moving in a reform direction, may have prolonged divisiveness and deferred stable settlement of the abortion controversy."[123]

Judge Ginsburg wrote in a 1990 article: "There was at the time [of *Roe*], as Justice Blackmun noted in his opinion, a distinct trend in the states 'toward liberalization of abortion statutes.' Had the Court written smaller and shorter, the legislative trend might have continued in the direction in which is was clearly headed in the early 1970s."[124]

She wrote in 1985 that, in *Roe*, the Court "called into question the criminal abortion statutes of every state, even those with the least restrictive provisions."[125] In doing so, the

---

[118] See, e.g., *Thornburgh v. American College of Obstetricians and Gynecologists*, 476 U.S. 747 (1986).

[119] See, e.g., *Akron v. Akron Center for Reproductive Health*, 462 U.S. 416 (1983).

[120] See, e.g., *Hodgson v. Minnesota*, 497 U.S. 417 (1990).

[121] Verbatim, *supra* note 31, at 11.

[122] *Id.*

[123] Ginsburg, *supra* note 91.

[124] Ginsburg, "On Muteness, Confidence, and Collegiality: A Response to Professor Nagel," 61 *University of Colorado Law Review* 715,718-19 (1990).

[125] Ginsburg, *supra* note 90, at 381.

decision "ventured too far in the change it ordered."[126] Judge Ginsburg agreed with the assessment of Professor Paul Freund, namely, that the Court "properly invalidated the Texas proscription" but should have "left off at that point" so that "the legislative trend might have continued in the direction in which it was headed in the early 1970s."[127] Professor Freund had written in 1983 that the detailed trimester framework in *Roe* "illustrated a troublesome tendency of the modern Supreme Court...'to specify by a kind of legislative code the one alternative pattern that will satisfy the Constitution'."[128]

3. Analysis

Not everyone agrees with Judge Ginsburg's reading of history. The *New York Times* editorialized that she "was too hard on Roe and probably misread history."[129] Author David Garrow writes that her criticisms of *Roe* "manifest a surprising ignorance of abortion law developments in the five years preceding the January 1973 decision."[130]

When Judge Ginsburg, on the one hand, argues that the Court in *Roe* "ventured too far"[131] and should have "written smaller and shorter"[132] and, on the other hand, challenges *Roe*'s doctrinal foundation, she suggests that her preferred equal protection theory would be less expansive than the due process theory the Court adopted. In fact, however, her recommended alternative has no limitation whatsoever.

Judge Ginsburg has offered no reason, and none is apparent, why a law prohibiting abortion for a particular reason--even sex selection--or during a particular stage of pregnancy--even the ninth month--would not amount to sex discrimination just as readily as would a law prohibiting all abortions. If restricting a course of action that only women can take is prohibited sex discrimination, then it is so throughout pregnancy. Restriction on sex selection abortions or on late-term abortions only affect women.

---

[126] *Id.*

[127] *Id.* at 382.

[128] *Id.*, quoting Freund, "Storms Over the Supreme Court" 69 *A.B.A. Journal* 1474, 1480 (1980)

[129] Editorial, *New York Times*, June 15, 1993, at A26.

[130] Garrow, "History Lesson for the Judge," *Washington Post*, June 20, 1993, at C3.

[131] *Id.* at 381.

[132] Ginsburg, *supra* note 124, at 719.

Judge Ginsburg has, on the one hand, criticized the Supreme Court's *Roe v. Wade* decision for going too far in striking down an abortion restriction while, on the other hand, criticizing the Supreme Court for going too far in upholding restrictions on public funding of abortions. The Court has consistently held that the Constitution does not require the state to pay for abortions under any circumstances. Judge Ginsburg has criticized these decisions as "incongruous"[133] and the "[m]ost unsettling of the losses" for women's rights.[134] She wrote in 1985: "If the Court had acknowledged a woman's equality aspect, not simply a patient-physician autonomy constitutional dimension to the abortion issue, a majority perhaps might have" ruled differently.[135]

One would think from Judge Ginsburg's criticism of both the due process theory of abortion rights and the Court's abortion funding cases that the Court had decided the funding cases on a due process rationale. Not so. It applied the equal protection clause.

* In *Maher v. Roe*,[136] the Court held that the equal protection clause does not require a state to pay expenses for elective abortions when it chooses to pay expenses for childbirth.

* In *Poelker v. Doe*,[137] the Court held that the equal protection clause does not require a city to provide publicly financed hospital facilities for abortions when it provides such facilities for childbirth.

* In *Harris v. McRae*,[138] the Court held that the so-called Hyde Amendment, which restricts the use of funds in the federal Medicaid program to pay for abortions, does not violate the equal protection clause.

* In *Williams v. Zbaraz*,[139] the Court held that a funding restriction similar to the Hyde Amendment in a state statute does not violate the equal protection component of the Fifth Amendment.

---

[133] Ginsburg, *supra* note 90, at 386.

[134] Ginsburg, *supra* note 89, at 224.

[135] Ginsburg, *supra* note 90, at 385.

[136] 432 U.S. 464 (1977).

[137] 432 U.S. 519 (1977).

[138] 448 U.S. 297 (1980).

[139] 448 U.S. 358 (1980).

• In *Webster v. Reproductive Health Services*,[140] the Court held that a statutory restriction on the use of public employees or facilities for abortions does not violate the equal protection clause.

One can only conclude that Judge Ginsburg simply thinks that the government is obligated to pay for abortions, regardless of how the equal protection clause applies. It appears, at least in this area, that Judge Ginsburg is willing to have "the Supreme Court step boldly in front of the political process,"[141]exactly what she criticized the Court for doing in *Roe*.

On the one hand, Judge Ginsburg writes that "the legislative trend"[142] of the 1960s and early 1970s should have been allowed to continue "in the reform direction."[143] On the other hand, she writes: "Nor can the political process be relied upon to respond to the plight of the indigent woman."[144] It appears she only opts for allowing the legislative process to operate in the abortion area as long as it is heading in a "reform direction" toward results she approves.

Is Judge Ginsburg's preferred theory--equal protection--more modest or more expansive than the Supreme Court's preferred theory--due process--has been? Does Judge Ginsburg think that the legislative process should be allowed to move toward a "stable settlement of the abortion controversy"[145] or doesn't she? She apparently equates "stable settlement" with widely available legal abortion.

Judge Ginsburg writes that "the *Roe v. Wade* decision is not fairly described as 'moderate'"[146] and elsewhere described that decision as "no measured motion."[147] Yet it is not at all clear that her preferred theory makes any more sense or is any more moderate. Judge Ginsburg has made it clear that her theory could be used to require public financing of abortions and a cursory look suggests that her theory could be used to eliminate restrictions that *Roe v. Wade* would allow.

---

[140] 492 U.S. 490 (1989).

[141] Ginsburg, *supra* note 31, at 11.

[142] Ginsburg, *supra* note 124, at 719.

[143] Ginsburg, *supra* note 91.

[144] Ginsburg, *supra* note 89, at 224.

[145] Ginsburg, *supra* note 91.

[146] *Id.*

[147] Ginsburg, *supra* note 31, at 11.

V. CONCLUSION

Judicial philosophy and judicial style are two very different facets of a judicial nominee. Judicial philosophy encompasses a nominee's fundamental views about the role of courts and the difference between law and politics, between judges and policy makers. Judge Ginsburg has an activist judicial philosophy.

* She believes that the Supreme Court can, and sometimes should, change its interpretation of the Constitution because of social changes.[148]

* She believes that the Supreme Court can, and sometimes should, creatively interpret constitutional provisions in order to accommodate a modern vision of society.[149]

* She believes in the need for "interventionist" judicial decisions when legislatures do not or will not act.[150]

* She believes that "boldly dynamic interpretation" that departs "radically from the original understanding" is sometimes necessary to reach certain results.[151]

* She believes the Constitution can survive only if supported by judicial interpretations that are neither too "mushy" or too "rigid."[152] She believes that a jurisprudence of original understanding is too rigid.[153]

Judicial style is a combination of practical factors that describe the functioning, rather than the role, of a judge. Judge Ginsburg has a moderate judicial style. It is only in this sense that she can be called a "moderate," the label that so many are so quick to place on her.

* She opposes frequently writing separate opinions.[154]

---

[148] See *supra* notes 39-41 and accompanying text.

[149] See *supra* notes 42-44 and accompanying text.

[150] See *supra* notes 45-46 and accompanying text.

[151] See *supra* note 59 and accompanying text.

[152] See *supra* note 60 and accompanying text.

[153] See *supra* note 58 and accompanying text.

[154] See *supra* note 74 and accompanying text.

32

* She believes that judges should write no more than necessary to decide a particular case and should "take the low ground, and resist personal commentary" when writing for the court.[155]

Judge Ginsburg's views on abortion and *Roe v. Wade* are driven by her politics. Consistent with her activist judicial philosophy, she believes the Supreme Court quite properly involved itself in the abortion controversy, and should have done so by striking down the restrictive law at issue in *Roe* on equal protection, rather than on due process, grounds. This way, the Court could have encouraged a liberalizing political trend that, in Judge Ginsburg's view, recognizes the independence of women in our society.

Consistent with her moderate judicial style, Judge Ginsburg has criticized the Supreme Court for going beyond invalidating the Texas law and announcing a set of complicated rules that effectively struck down all other abortion restrictions--tough as well as lenient--existing in 1973, and most of those enacted since.

Judge Ginsburg's preferred equal protection theory, however, has serious conceptual problems. Most important, men and women cannot be similarly situated with respect to either pregnancy or its termination and, as such, it is impossible to discuss whether women are being treated "equally" because of their gender. Since women are the sole focus of this view, applying an equal protection theory to abortion rights necessarily means defining any restriction on abortion--a course of action that only women can take--as impermissible sex discrimination. As such, this theory would go beyond the policy established by *Roe v. Wade*. Judge Ginsburg objects to the Supreme Court's decisions that the state is not constitutionally required to pay for abortions, even though the Court applied her preferred equal protection theory in those cases.

---

[155] See *supra* note 65 and accompanying text.

NOMINATION OF RUTH BADER GINSBURG TO BE AN ASSOCIATE JUSTICE OF THE UNITED STATES SUPREME COURT

AUGUST 5, 1993 (legislative day, JUNE 30), 1993.—Ordered to be printed

Mr. BIDEN, from the Committee on the Judiciary,
submitted the following

REPORT

together with

ADDITIONAL VIEWS

[To accompany the nomination of Ruth Bader Ginsburg to be an Associate Justice of the U.S. Supreme Court]

The Committee on the Judiciary, to which was referred the nomination of Judge Ruth Bader Ginsburg to be an Associate Justice of the U.S. Supreme Court, having considered the same, reports favorably thereon, a quorum being present, by a vote of 18 yeas and 0 nays, with the recommendation that the nomination be approved.

CONTENTS

79–119

★(Star print)

IV. JUDGE GINSBURG'S THEORY OF *STARE DECISIS*

The committee is satisfied that Judge Ginsburg holds an appropriate respect for the principle of *stare decisis* and abiding understanding of the value of precedent. At the same time, she recognizes the importance of achieving the correct result in matters of constitutional interpretation, where the Court is the final arbiter. She distinguishes the somewhat diminished importance of *stare decisis* in the constitutional context from statutory interpretation, when stability becomes more important and errors by courts can be corrected by legislatures. In response to a question from Senator Heflin, the nominee associated herself with the views of Justice Brandeis, as expressed in *Burnet* v. *Coronado Oil & Gas,* 285 U.S. 393, 405 (1935) (Brandeis, J., dissenting). She testified:

> Justice Brandeis said some things are better settled, and especially when the legislature sits. So if we are talking

about a precedent that has to do with the construction of a statute, *stare decisis* is more than just the soundness of the reasoning. Reliance interests are important; the stability, certainty, predictability of the law, people know what the law is, they can make their decisions, set their course in accordance with that law. So that the importance of letting the matter stay decided has to do with more than just if the Court decides next year, well, maybe it would have been better to have decided the other way. That is not enough.

If it is a decision that has to do with the Constitution, * * * then the Court's view is the legislature can't come to the rescue if we got it wrong, if we are saying this is what the Constitution requires. So that is for us to correct. But even there, *stare decisis* is one of the restraints against a judge infusing his or her own values into the interpretation of the Constitution. (Transcript, July 21, at 82–83; see also Transcript, July 22, at 131–32, Questioning by Senator Leahy.)

Judge Ginsburg rejects the view of some theorists that the doctrine of *stare decisis* is of less importance in areas such as criminal law. These theorists believe *stare decisis* applies with the most force with respect to contract or property rights, where, according to the theory, stability is more important because of the public's reliance on settled law. She stated:

I don't think that reliance is absent from the criminal law field either in the way courts—one thing is that the precedent is set for the way the courts will behave, the way the police will behave, the way prosecutors will behave. And so I don't think that one can say in that area reliance doesn't count. (Transcript, July 21, at 85.)

Judge Ginsburg's testimony in other contexts exemplified her respect for precedent and inclination to adhere to the principle of *stare decisis*. She agreed with Senator Hatch's assertion that the abortion funding cases of *Maher* v. *Roe,* 432 U.S. 464 (1997), and *Harris* v. *McRae,* 448 U.S. 297 (1980), were the Supreme Court's precedent. She stated that she had no "agenda to displace them." (Transcript, July 22, at 28.) Likewise, in response to Senator Grassley, she expressed the view that the Supreme Court's decision in *Planned Parenthood* v. *Casey,* 112 S. Ct. 2791 (1992), reflected the importance of precedent. She said the case, which reaffirmed the basic right of a woman to choose whether or not to terminate her pregnancy, "stresses the reliance interest that has been built up around a precedent about the generation of women who have grown up thinking that *Roe* v. *Wade,* [410 U.S. 113 (1973)], was the law of the land." (Transcript, July 22, at 112.)

V. CONCLUSION

The sum of her testimony, as well as written record, demonstrates that Judge Ginsburg enjoys an appropriate respect for the principle of judicial restraint. She understands the role and place of the judicial branch within our constitutional system, a system that envisions that activism should arise primarily in the political branches. At the same time, she understands that there are circumstances in which the political branches and popular majorities fail to protect fully the great ideals of our Constitution. In those circumstances, the Court must step forward to fill the void.

The committee is satisfied that Judge Ginsburg's understanding of constitutional principles such as liberty and equality, as well as her historical perspective, informs her approach to constitutional decisionmaking and results in a method of judging that is not unduly restrictive. Her record suggests that she will be a voice on the Court for deliberate and reasoned constitutional evolution.

PART 3: JUDGE GINSBURG'S VIEWS ON UNENUMERATED RIGHTS, PRIVACY, AND REPRODUCTIVE FREEDOM

Judge Ginsburg's testimony and writings on unenumerated rights, the right of privacy, and reproductive freedom set her apart from all other recent nominees to the Supreme Count. Judge Ginsburg enthusiastically embraced the concept of unenumerated rights and the right of privacy. She also forthrightly supported a woman's right to reproductive freedom, under either a privacy or an equal protection analysis.

I. JUDGE GINSBURG EMBRACED THE CONCEPT OF UNENUMERATED RIGHTS, INCLUDING A RIGHT OF PRIVACY

A. Judge Ginsburg supports the concept of unenumerated rights

In clear and unequivocal terms, Judge Ginsburg expressed support for and appreciation of the concept of unenumerated rights—the view that each American citizen has rights independent of and apart from those specifically listed in the Constitution. She stated, in response to the very first question of the hearings, by Chairman Biden:

> I think the Framers are shortchanged if we view them as having a limited view of rights, because they wrote, Thomas Jefferson wrote, "We hold these truths to be self-evident, that all men are created equal, that they are endowed by their Creator with certain inalienable rights, that among these"—among these—"are life, liberty, and the pursuit of happiness," and that Government is formed to protect and secure those rights.
> Now when the Constitution was written, as you know, there was much concern over a Bill of Rights. There were some who thought a Bill of Rights dangerous because one couldn't enumerate all the rights of the people; one couldn't compose a complete catalogue. * * *
> But there was a sufficient call for a Bill of Rights, and so the Framers put down what was in the front of their minds in the Bill of Rights.
> * * * And then * * * the Framers were fearful that this limited catalogue might be understood, even though it is written as a restriction on Government rather than a conferring of rights of people, that it might be understood as skimpy, as not stating everything that is. And so we do have the Ninth Amendment stating that the Constitution shall not be construed to deny or disparage other rights.

So the Constitution * * * the whole thrust of it is people
have rights, and Government must be kept from trampling
on them. (Transcript, July 20, at 110–11.)

Judge Ginsburg here compared the American Constitution to the
French Declaration of the Rights of Man, which confers rights,
rather than restricting government, and thus (unlike the Constitution) presupposes a world in which citizens have no rights other
than those specifically given. (Transcript, July 20, at 111.)

Elaborating further on this view, Judge Ginsburg testified that
"the Ninth Amendment is part of the ideal that people have rights,
the Bill of Rights keeps the government from intruding on those
rights. We don't necessarily have a complete enumeration here."
(Transcript, July 21, at 112.)

B. *Judge Ginsburg subscribes to the views of Justice Harlan and
Justice Powell with respect to when the Court should recognize
an unenumerated right*

Judge Ginsburg testified that in determining whether an asserted unenumerated right is protected by the Constitution—in
particular, by the broadly worded Due Process Clause of the 14th
amendment—she would follow the approach articulated by Justice
Harlan in *Poe* v. *Ullman*, 367 U.S. 497 (1961), and by Justice Powell in *Moore* v. *City of East Cleveland*, 431 U.S. 494 (1977).

Justice Harlan wrote in *Poe*, in arguing for a flexible conception
of due process, not limited by the specific rights granted elsewhere
in the Constitution:

> Due process has not been reduced to any formula; its
> content cannot be determined by reference to any code.
> The best that can be said is that through the course of this
> Court's decisions it has represented the balance which our
> Nation, built upon the postulates of respect for the liberty
> of the individual, has struck between that liberty and the
> demands of organized society. If the supplying of content
> to this Constitutional concept has of necessity been a ra-
> tional process, it has certainly not been one where judges
> have felt free to roam where unguided speculation might
> take them. The balance of which I speak is the balance
> struck by this country, having regard to what history
> teaches are the traditions from which it developed as well
> as the traditions from which it broke. That tradition is a
> living thing. A decision of this Court which radically de-
> parts from it could not long survive, while a decision which
> builds on what has survived is likely to be sound. No for-
> mula could serve as a substitute, in this area, for judg-
> ment and restraint. (367 U.S. at 542 (Harlan, J., dissent-
> ing).)

Judge Ginsburg testified that "I associate myself with *Poe* v. *Ullman* and the method that is revealed most completely by Justice
Harlan in that opinion." (Transcript, July 22, at 62.)

Similarly, Judge Ginsburg read from Justice Powell's opinion in
Moore in response to Senator Hatch's characterization of the dan-
gers of substantive process. In *Moore*, Powell wrote:

There *are* risks when the judicial branch gives enhanced
protection to certain substantive liberties without the guidance of the more specific provisions of the Bill of Rights.
As the history of the *Lochner* era demonstrates, there is
reason for concern lest the only limits to such judicial
intervention become the predilections of those who happen
at the time to be Members of this Court. That history
counsels caution and restraint. But it does not counsel
abandonment.

* * * * * * *

Appropriate limits on due process come not from drawing
arbitrary lines but rather from careful "respect for the
teachings of history [and] solid recognition of the basic values that underlie our society." (431 U.S. at 502–03.)

Judge Ginsburg described this passage as the "most eloquent statement" of her own position after *Poe*. (Transcript, July 22, at 33.)

Significantly, Judge Ginsburg rejected the method adopted by
Justice Scalia to identify interests protected by the Due Process
Clause. In what Judge Ginsburg termed in her testimony "the famous Footnote Six" of *Michael H.* v. *Gerald D.*, 491 U.S. 110, 127,
n.6 (1989), Justice Scalia proposed limiting the scope of the due
process clause to those interests which, most specifically defined,
received the historic protection of the Government. Justices O'Connor and Kennedy, who joined most of Justice Scalia's opinion, declined to join this footnote, explaining that under the proposed
method "many a decision would have reached a different result."
Id. at 132. In response to a question from Chairman Biden, Judge
Ginsburg associated herself with the views of Justice O'Connor and
Kennedy on this subject, as opposed to those of Justice Scalia:

I have stated in response to Senator Hatch that I associate myself with *Poe* v. *Ullman*. * * * My understanding of
the O'Connor/Kennedy position in the *Michael H.* case is
that they, too, associate themselves with that position.
Justice O'Connor cited *Poe* v. *Ullman* as her methodology.
(Transcript, July 22, at 62–63.)

In adopting Justice Harlan's approach, and rejecting Justice
Scalia's, Judge Ginsburg has selected a method for identifying
unenumerated rights in keeping with the Constitution's majestic
and capacious language. As Justices O'Connor and Justice Kennedy
recognized in *Michael H.*, "requiring specific approval from history
before protecting anything in the name of liberty" effectively
"squashes * * * freedom." 491 U.S. at 132. It is Justice Harlan's
approach—an approach of measured change and rooted evolution—
that comports with both the intent and the draftsmanship of the
Constitution. Judge Ginsburg's embrace of this approach provides
excellent reason to support her.

C. Judge Ginsburg recognizes a right to privacy

Judge Ginsburg's testimony left no dobut that she supports the
Supreme Court's recognition of a general, unenumerated right to
privacy. Her views were evident in an exchange with Senator
Leahy:

Senator LEAHY. Is there a constitutional right to privacy?

Judge GINSBURG. There is a constitutional right to privacy which consists I think of at least two distinguishable parts. One is the privacy expressed most vividly in the Fourth Amendment, that is the government shall not break into my home or my office, without a warrant, based on probable cause, the government shall leave me alone.

The other is the notion of personal autonomy, the government shall not make my decisions for me, I shall make, as an individual, uninhibited, uncontrolled by my government, the decisions that affect my life's course. Yes, I think that whether it has been lumped under the label, privacy is a constitutional right, and it has those two elements, the right to be let alone and the right to make basic decisions about one's life course. (Transcript, July 21, at 54–55.)

In a subsequent colloquy with Senator Hatch, Judge Ginsburg elaborated on her view of the right to privacy as protecting personal autonomy, including personal control over matters of marriage and family. Judge Ginsburg said:

It starts in the 19th century. The right of the individual, the Court then said no right is held more sacred or is more carefully guarded by the common law. It grows from our tradition, and the right of every individual to the possession and control of his person. It goes on through *Skinner* v. *Oklahoma* [316 U.S. 535 (1942)], which was the right to have offspring recognized as a basic human right.

I have said to this committee that the finest expression of that idea of individual autonomy and personhood and the State leaving people alone to make basic decisions about their personal life is *Poe* v. *Ullman,* Justice Harlan's position in that. (Transcript, July 22, at 32–33.)

Judge Ginsburg added that in this line of cases, the Court was "affirming the right of the individual to be free." (Transcript, July 22, at 34.)

Although Judge Ginsburg never explicitly referred to the right to privacy as a "fundamental right"—a term the Court commonly has used—she made clear that the Government must meet a very high burden before interfering with the right. In response to a question of the chairman, Judge Ginsburg stated:

The line of cases that you just outlined, the right to marry, the right to procreate or not, the right to raise one's children, the degree of justification that the State has to have to interfere with that is very considerable. (Transcript, July 22, at 53.)

Judge Ginsburg thus indicated that the right to privacy protected by the Constitution is a right of real meaning and consequence.

Judge Ginsburg's willing acknowledgment of the right to privacy, her characterization of the strength of that right, and most of all, her understanding of the values underlying that right—all of these set Judge Ginsburg apart from most recent nominees to the Supreme Court. Her testimony shows that she appreciates the importance of preventing government from controlling or burdening an individual's most central and personal decisions. Her testimony shows that she believes this restraint on government to be a central aspect of freedom.

II. JUDGE GINSBURG SUPPORTS THE RIGHT OF WOMEN TO REPRODUCTIVE FREEDOM

Prior to her nomination, Judge Ginsburg discussed her views on reproductive rights in two speeches, reprinted as articles; the most recent of these, presented in March 1993, is generally known as the Madison Lecture. (Madison Lecture; *see also* Ginsburg, William T. Joyner Lecture on Constitutional Law, Some Thoughts on Autonomy and Equality in Relation to *Roe* v. *Wade,* Address before the University of North Carolina School of Law (April 6, 1984) *in* 63 N.C. L. Rev. 375 (1985).) During her hearings, Judge Ginsburg clarified and expanded on her thoughts on this subject.

The premise of the Madison Lecture is that the Constitution protects in some measure the right of women to choose for themselves whether or not to terminate a pregnancy. Judge Ginsburg thus wrote that the Court should have struck down the extreme anti-abortion law under review in *Roe* v. *Wade*—a law she characterized as "intolerably shackl[ing] a woman's autonomy." (Madison Lecture at 23.)

Similarly, in her testimony, Judge Ginsburg left no doubt of her conviction that the Constitution protects the right to choose. In her most strikingly articulated of many statements on the issue, judge Ginsburg told Senator Brown:

> This is something central to a woman's life, to her dignity. It is a decision that she must make for herself. And when government controls that decision for her, she is being treated as less than a fully adult human responsible for her own choices. (Transcript, July 21, at 106.)

In response to another question of Senator Brown, exploring whether fathers may have rights relating to the decision to terminate a pregnancy, Judge Ginsburg added that "in the end it's [a woman's] body, her life. * * * [I]t is essential * * * that she be the decisionmaker, that her choice be controlling." (Transcript, July 21, at 108.)

In the Madison Lecture, Judge Ginsburg seemed to argue that the right to terminate a pregnancy arose from the equal protection guarantee, rather than from the right to privacy. There, Judge Ginsburg stated that the *Roe* Court should have "homed in more precisely on the women's equality dimension of the issue," arguing that "disadvantageous treatment of a woman because of her pregnancy and reproductive choice is a paradigm case of discrimination on the basis of sex." (Madison Lecture at 24, 28.) Similarly, in an earlier speech and article, Ginsburg contended that abortion regulations affect "a woman's autonomous charge of her full life's course—* * * her ability to stand in relation to man, society, and the state as an independent, self-sustaining equal citizen." (Ginsburg, William T. Joyner Lecture on Constitutional Law, Some Thoughts on Autonomy and Equality in Relation to *Roe* v. *Wade,* Address before the University of North Carolina School of Law

(April 6, 1984) *in* 63 N.C. L. Rev. 375, 383 (1985) (footnote omitted).)

In her testimony, Judge Ginsburg repeatedly stated that her emphasis on the equality aspect of reproductive freedoms was meant to supplement, rather than supplant, the traditional privacy rationale for the right to terminate a pregnancy. This point emerges clearly in the following exchange between Judge Ginsburg and Senator Feinstein:

> Senator FEINSTEIN. If I understand what you are saying—correct me if I am wrong—you are saying that *Roe* could have been decided on equal protection grounds rather than the fundamental right to privacy. * * *
>
> Judge GINSBURG. Yes, Senator, except in one respect. I never made it either/or. * * * I have always said both, that the equal protection strand should join together with the autonomy of decisionmaking strand; so that it wasn't a question of equal protection or personal autonomy, it was a question of both.
>
> *   *   *   *   *   *   *
>
> So I would have added another underpinning, one that I thought was at least as strong, perhaps stronger. But it was never equal protection rather than personal autonomy. It was both. (Transcript, July 21, at 193–94.)

Similarly, Judge Ginsburg replied to a question by Senator Brown by noting that "the State controlling the woman is *both* denying her full autonomy and full equality with men * * *" (Transcript, July 21, at 108.)

Judge Ginsburg's effort to highlight the equality dimension of reproductive freedoms thus serves to enhance, rather than diminish, these important rights. Judge Ginsburg's analysis focuses on an aspect of reproductive rights the Court recently hinted at in *Casey* v. *Planned Parenthood,* 112 S. Ct. 2791 (1992)—the effect of these rights on the status of women in our society. In Judge Ginsburg's view, this analysis need not result in a weaker level of constitutional scrutiny than that demanded by the Court in *Roe*. It is true that gender discrimination currently receives only intermediate scrutiny, whereas the recognition of a fundamental right of privacy, as occurred in *Roe,* provokes strict scrutiny. But Judge Ginsburg made clear that equality is but one aspect of reproductive freedom; and she further noted on several occasions that the Court may yet hold sex distinctions to demand strict scrutiny.

In another aspect of her Madison Lecture, as well as in an earlier article, Judge Ginsburg suggested that the Court in *Roe* went too far too fast—that it should have struck down only the extreme anti-abortion law before it, leaving for another day the question of the constitutionality of other, more moderate abortion restrictions. Such an approach, Judge Ginsburg posited in the Madison Lecture, "might have served to reduce, rather than to fuel controversy." (Madison Lecture at 23.) According to Ginsburg, quoting *Roe* itself, "there was a marked trend in state legislatures 'toward liberalization of abortion statutes.'" (*Id.* at 32 (footnote omitted).) If *Roe* had limited its ruling—if it had, in Judge Ginsburg's words, "invited * * * dialogue with legislators"—that trend might well have continued. (Id.) By issuing its decision in *Roe*, Ginsburg argued, the Court halted this process, provoked popular backlash, and "prolonged divisiveness." (Id. at 37.)

Senator Metzenbaum and Judge Ginsburg engaged in an exchange on this subject:

> Senator METZENBAUM. Would you not have had some concern, or do you not have some concern, that had the gradualism been the reality, that many more women would have been denied an abortion or would have been forced into an illegal abortion and possibly an unsafe abortion?
>
> Judge GINSBURG. Senator, we can't see what the past might have been like. I wrote an article that was engaging in what if. I expressed the view that if the Court had simply done what courts usually do, stuck to the very case before it and gone no further, then there might have been a change, gradual changes.
>
>   *   *   *   *   *   *   *
>
> There was the one thing that one can say for sure: There was a massive attack on *Roe* v. *Wade*. It was a single target to hit at. I think two things happened. One is that a movement that had been very vigorous became relaxed, * * *.
>
> So one side seemed to relax its energy, while the other side had a single target around which to rally, but that is my "what if," and I could be wrong about that. My view was that the people would have accepted, would have expressed themselves in an enduring way on this question. And as I said this is a matter of speculation, this is my view of what if. Other people can have a different view. (Transcript, July 20, at 183–84.)

Judge Ginsburg's testimony on this matter—as well as the two articles it is based on—reflect her broad judicial philosophy: most notably, her commitment to gradual change and her respect for the political process. But Judge Ginsburg's testimony and articles do not call into question her fundamental commitment to reproductive rights. The committee understands her articles as presenting a view of how such rights can best be achieved and maintained—of how *any* rights can best be achieved and maintained—in a democratic society, rather than as expressing doubts about the rightful place of these rights in the constitutional order.

Questions remain open as to the approach Judge Ginsburg would follow, if confirmed, in cases soon to come before the Court involving abortion regulations. Judge Ginsburg, in responding to questions posed by Senator Metzenbaum, would not comment on whether the right to choose remains a fundamental right after *Casey;* neither would she comment on the level of scrutiny that should be applied to abortion regulations or on the permissibility of any particular regulations. (Transcript, July 20, at 184–85; July 21 at 196.) These questions are of obvious importance with respect to the future scope of reproductive freedoms.

But the committee knows far more about Judge Ginsburg's views on reproductive rights than it has known about any previous nominee's. Judge Ginsburg's record and testimony suggest both a broad commitment to reproductive freedoms and a deep appreciation of the equality and autonomy values underlying them.

Congressional Record - Senate
Aug. 2, 1993
Pp. 10076-78

NOMINATION OF RUTH BADER GINSBURG

Mr. HELMS. Mr. President, it had been my tentative inclination prior to this past weekend to vote to confirm Ruth Bader Ginsburg to serve on the U.S. Supreme Court despite disagreement with some of her declarations about constitutional matters and other matters. I have a small habit which I have not been able to break, I am not inclined to break, and I have not tried to break, that is, on each major nomination to come before the Senate I assemble all available information about the nominee including testimony before the committee hearing of his or her nomination.

I did that this past weekend. I spent a part of the weekend reviewing various documents regarding Mrs. Ginsburg, and never have I been more disappointed in a nominee. This lady, whom I have regarded as a pleasant, intellectual liberal is, in fact, a woman whose beliefs are 180 degrees in opposition to some fundamental principles that are important not only to me but, I believe, to the majority of other Americans as well.

Therefore, it would be hypocritical of me to keep silent about Mrs. Ginsburg's beliefs, let alone her nomination to be quietly confirmed by the Senate, like a ship passing in the night.

I confess great disappointment that the Senate Judiciary Committee in conducting the hearing on Mrs. Ginsburg's nomination did not press her on a number of matters -- for example, her outrageously simplistic and callous position on abortion. The lady used a great deal of doubletalk and, sad to say, the Judiciary Committee let her get by with it. For example, she declared that a woman has a constitutional right to abortion, no qualification whatsoever, presumably through and including -- she was not clear one way or another -- the ninth month of pregnancy. She murmured that this is, as she put it, "the notion of personal autonomy." And then she defined autonomy as "the right to be let alone and to make basic decisions about one's life's course."

Mr. President, I did not find one syllable of challenge by any member of the Judiciary Committee to this outrageous oversimplification by a nominee whose demeanor appeared to be one of amused tolerance of Senators too timid to ask questions that needed to be asked. Why, Mr. President, in the name of God did someone not ask, "But, Mrs. Ginsburg, what about that unborn innocent and helpless child's right to be left alone, that child who is about to be destroyed because of specious reasoning by people like Ruth Bader Ginsburg?"

Mrs. Ginsburg also made such unchallenged declarations as that the Hyde amendment is unconstitutional; that the implication -- that went unchallenged -- was that, as a member of the Supreme Court, she is likely to uphold the homosexual agenda; and, three, the States should be required to pay for abortions.

There were other such remarkable assertions. But the able Senator from Pennsylvania, Mr. Specter, did put it aptly when he said:

I'm not suggesting that Judge Ginsburg will be defeated, or that she should be, but I am suggesting that her coronation in advance is irresponsible.

And that is putting it mildly, Mr. President.

Let me emphasize, in conclusion, Mr. President, that I hold no personal animus for Mrs. Ginsburg. But based on what she has said, and what she clearly meant, I cannot support her nomination. She will be confirmed, yes. And I may be the only Senator opposing her. But I pray that as a sitting Justice of the Supreme Court, she will rethink some of her positions.

. . .

[From the Family Research Council, Washington, DC]
JUDGE RUTH BADER GINSBURG: GROUNDS FOR QUES-
TIONS
(By David M. Wagner, Director of Legal Policy)

In choosing Appeals Court Judge Ruth Bader Ginsburg for the U.S. Supreme Court, President Clinton has achieved a triple goal: An easy confirmation process; political credit for selecting a "moderate"; and a probably reliable liberal vote on key social issues, with the legal acumen to make her opinions influential.

In deciding whether to oppose Judge Ginsburg's confirmation, conservative and pro-family groups have to weigh how much worse Clinton's selection could have been, against how much damage can be

427

done by a careful liberal jurist with a non-negotiable commitment to far-reaching, if slow-paced, social change.

This paper will set forth some areas of Judge Ginsburg's record that should provide material for questioning when she appears before the Senate Judiciary Committee, or for the casting of an informed vote by members of the Senate.

GINSBURG ON ABORTION

It is being said that Judge Ginsburg has "criticized Roe v. Wade." Technically this is true; in fact, her most recent "criticism" of Roe came in a speech delivered just last March, shortly before Justice Byron White announced his intention to resign. That speech may well account for the absence of Judge Ginsburg's name from most observers' lists of possible nominees throughout April and May.

However, in these "critiques" of Roe there is actually less than meets the eye. Judge Ginsburg's criticisms of Roe are basically two:

1. By laying down a framework for all subsequent abortion law, the Court in Roe forced a more rapid reform than most state legislatures were willing to allow, thereby strengthening the right-to-life movement. Had the Court been content merely to strike down the Texas statute that was at issue in Roe, without announcing the rigid "trimester" system, the pro-abortion drift of the state legislatures would have continued without interruption. In other words, Judge Ginsburg criticizes Roe for being a less effective vehicle for abortion rights than it could have been.

In her recent speech she noted that Roe "halted a political process that was moving in a reform direction and thereby, I believe, prolonged divisiveness and deferred stable settlement of the issue." n1 And she wrote in a 1990 article: "There was at the time [of Roe], as Justice Blackmun noted in his opinion, a trend 'toward liberalization of the abortion statutes.' Had the Court written smaller and shorter, the legislative trend might have continued in the direction in which it was clearly headed in the early 1970s." n2

Furthermore, as she noted in a 1985 article based on a 1984 speech: "The sweep and detail of the opinion stimulated the mobilization of a right-to-life movement and an attendant reaction in Congress and state legislatures." n3

2. Roe grounded the abortion right on personal privacy and autonomy, rather than on sex discrimination. In contrast, Judge Ginsburg

believes the Court should have grounded the abortion right on the theory that, since only women become pregnant, all restrictions on abortion discriminate on the basis of sex, and therefore violate the Equal Protection Clause of the Fourteenth Amendment. Closely allied to this legal argument is the overtly political argument that abortion is necessary to the civic and professional equality of women. n4

Displaying her penchant for announcing her own views by quoting approvingly from others', Judge Ginsburg wrote in 1985:

"Professor Paul Freund explained where he thought the Court went astray in Roe, and I agree with his statement. The Court properly invalidated the Texas proscription, he indicated, because '[a] law that absolutely made criminal all kinds and forms of abortion could not stand up; it is not a reasonable accommodation of interests.' ***

"I commented at the outset that I believe the Court presented an incomplete justification for its action. Academic criticism of Roe, charging the Court with reading its own values into the due process clause, might have been less pointed had the Court placed the woman alone, rather than the woman tied to her physician, at the center of its attention. Professor Karst's commentary is indicative of the perspective not developed in the High Court's opinion: he solidly linked abortion prohibitions with discrimination against women. The issue in Roe, he wrote, deeply touched and concerned 'women's position in society in relation to men.' n5 "

It should be particularly noted that, while some abortion regulations survive scrutiny under the Roe test as modified by Planned Parenthood v. Casey, n6, Judge Ginsburg's equal protection analysis would strike down any and all abortion regulations (though a ban on sex-selection abortion might present an arguable question for her), on the theory that any and all abortion regulations create unequal burdens on women and men.

Judge Ginsburg also points out that her theory would even require striking down the Hyde Amendment -- i.e., it would require the federal government to fund abortions. She wrote: "If the Court had acknowledged a woman's equality aspect, not simply a patient-physician autonomy dimension to the abortion issue, a majority might perhaps have seen the public assistance cases as instances in which, borrowing a phrase from Justice Stevens, the sovereign had violated its 'duty to govern impartially.'" n7

Thus, just at the time the Clinton administration is fine-tuning its health care plan and proposing to include abortion coverage in it, the court is getting a new Justice who believes the Constitution requires the federal government to fund abortion.

. . .

CONCLUSION

Let us return to the passage by Justice Frankfurter, quoted by Judge Ginsburg in her Georgia Law Review article. It reads (without Judge Ginsburg's edits):

"There is a good deal of shallow talk that the judicial robe does not change the man within it. It does. The fact is that on the whole judges do lay aside private views in discharging their judicial functions. This is achieved through training, professional habits, self-discipline and that fortunate alchemy by which men are loyal to the obligation with which they are entrusted." n28

To the extent that Judge Ginsburg is here engaging in her well-tested practice of stating her own views through quotation of others, we take heart. Even the most activist of attorneys is capable of making the transition to the very different mindset of the judge, and Judge Ginsburg's own career is an example of the transition.

Nonetheless, it would be an abdication of a grave responsibility if Senators, especially those of the opposition party, fail to ask her questions about, inter alia:

What regulations of abortion, if any, would survive a consistent application of the test she outlined in her North Carolina Law Review article (note: she could answer this without committing herself to using that test as a Supreme Court Justice);

What the original intent behind the Fourteenth Amendment was, and how, if at all, this intent should influence constitutional judging today;

What the principles that undergird judicial restraint are, and how she has or has not lived up to those principles.

Far from a fire-breathing ideologue of the left, but a committed liberal nonetheless -- that is our impression of Judge Ginsburg, based on her writings, and that is how we expect she will appear after questioning by the Judiciary Committee. The President who appointed her, and the Senators who will probably vote to confirm her, should receive both full credit and full blame for what they are presently rushing to do.

Congressional Record - Senate
Aug. 3, 1993
Pp. 10161-62

Mr. DURENBERGER. Mr. President, I rise today in support of the nomination of Judge Ruth Bader Ginsburg to be Associate Justice of the U.S. Supreme Court.

DISTINGUISHED BACKGROUND

Judge Ginsburg has had a remarkable career, not only as a lawyer, judge, and teacher, but also -- as she pointed out during her confirmation hearings 2 weeks ago -- as a proud and devoted wife, mother, and grandmother.

Judge Ginsburg has demonstrated during her 13 years on the U.S. Court of Appeals for the District of Columbia Circuit that she is, as my friend and colleague from Ohio, Senator Metzenbaum, has said: "a judge's judge."

Her judicial record demonstrates that she understands and respects the proper role of the judiciary in our tripartite system of Government. As Judge Ginsburg said during her confirmation hearings before the Senate Judiciary Committee: "Judges must be mindful of what their place is in society." She went on to emphasize that a judge is not an advocate, and reminded the committee that, "a judge is not a politician." I should also point out that Judge Ginsburg received the highest possible rating from the American Bar Association.

In addition to her long and important career on the Federal bench, Judge Ginsburg has distinguished herself as an advocate on behalf of women's rights, arguing -- and winning -- landmark cases during the 1970's that were instrumental in extending the constitutional guarantee of equal protection of the law to women.

Judge Ginsburg is a woman of impeccable character, intelligence, and temperament. Moreover, she is a first generation American who has risen on the strength of her own determination and ability to one of the highest offices in America. If confirmed, she will be only the second woman in the history of our country to serve on the Supreme Court.

PRESIDENT CLINTON'S SELECTION OF JUDGE GINSBURG

When Justice Byron White announced that he was retiring after 31 years on the High Court, I did not expect that President Clinton and I would agree on the perfect Associate Judge candidate to succeed him. This is the first time a Democratic President has had the opportunity to make an appointment to the Supreme Court in over a quarter of a century.

The President of the United States is entitled to some deference in his choice of a Supreme Court Justice. I truly believe that Ruth Bader Ginsburg is the best choice we can expect to see from this President. Let me note in this regard, Mr. President, that I am not in absolute philosophical sympathy with this nominee -- but I want the Senate to continue in its tradition of being open to nominees who are distinguished and highly qualified. My friends on the other side of the aisle have often voted for conservative nominees to the Supreme Court -- resisting the temptation to ideologize this very important decision. I want to encourage this kind of openmindedness and bipartisanship.

JUDGE GINSBURG'S JUDICIAL CAREER SHOULD LAY TO REST ANY FEARS OF JUDICIAL ACTIVISM

Judge Ginsburg's long career on the court of appeals here shows a clear demarcation between Ruth Bader Ginsburg the advocate, and Judge Ruth Bader Ginsburg the jurist committed to rule of law. I have studied Judge Ginsburg's complete record, and I am convinced that, despite her earlier career as an advocate on behalf of the American Civil Liberties Union and some of her academic writings, Judge Ginsburg has not used her position as a Federal judge to advance any personal agenda.

In fact, she has been the model of judicial moderation and restraint. As a rule, she has limited her decisions to the confines of prior precedent, even where those decisions may conflict with her personal, more liberal views. As she explained to the Judiciary Committee, "No judge is appointed to apply his or her personal values." Instead:

Judges must be mindful of what their place is in this system and must always remember that we live in a democracy that can be destroyed if judges take it upon themselves to rule as platonic guardians.

The New York Times noted that:

According to a computerized study of the appeals court's 1987 voting patterns published in Legal Times, Judge Ginsburg voted more consistently with her Republican-appointed colleagues than with her fellow Democratic-appointed colleagues. For example, in 1987 cases that produced division on the court, she voted with Judge Bork 85 percent of the time and with Judge Patricia M. Wald 38 percent of the time. [New York Times, 6/27/93, at 20]

According to another study of the D.C. Circuit, in 1983-84 year, Judge Ginsburg voted with Judge Bork 100% of the time, and with then-Judge Scalia 95% of the time. [Edwards, Public Misperceptions Concerning The "Politics" Of Judging, 56 Colo. L. Rev. 619, 644 (1985)]

CONCLUSION

Having said this, there is -- of course -- no way to predict with certainty what a nominee will do, or how a nominee will vote, once she becomes a member of the Supreme Court. The best we can do is to judge a nominee's character, intelligence, professional background, academic record, judicial experience, and temperament. On all these scores, Judge Ginsburg has acquitted herself well.

So while I do not agree with Judge Ginsburg's personal view that a right to abortion can be based on the equal protection clause, Judge Ginsburg's record on the Federal bench should, in my view, disabuse concerned conservatives of any notion whatsoever that she would allow her personal views to affect her duties and decisions as a judge.

Judge Ginsburg has never allowed her experience as an advocate or her academic speculations to manifest themselves as judicial activism. In fact, her distinguished judicial record demonstrates that she is a restrained, moderate jurist who subjugates her personal views to the rule of law.

As I said earlier, I would never expect to agree with 100 percent of the views of any Supreme Court nominee. That is especially true when that nominee is chosen by a President from the Democratic Party. After studying Judge Ginsburg's record, however, I am satisfied that she is one of the best choices for the High Court that this President could make.

Therefore, I intend to cast my vote in support of Judge Ginsburg, and I urge my colleagues to do the same.